CHRISTOPHE HONORÉ

A Critical Introduction

David A. Gerstner *and* Julien Nahmias

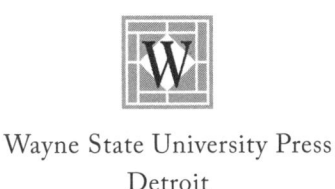

Wayne State University Press
Detroit

© 2015 by Wayne State University Press, Detroit, Michigan 48201.

All rights reserved. No part of this book may be reproduced

without formal permission.

Manufactured in the United States of America.

19 18 17 16 15   5 4 3 2 1

Library of Congress Control Number: 2015938163

ISBN 978-0-8143-3863-6 (paperback)

ISBN 978-0-8143-3864-3 (ebook)

Designed and typeset by Bryce Schimanski

Composed in Adobe Caslon Pro

CHRISTOPHE HONORÉ

CONTEMPORARY APPROACHES TO FILM AND MEDIA SERIES

General Editor
Barry Keith Grant, Brock University

Advisory Editors
Robert J. Burgoyne, University of St. Andrews

Caren J. Deming, University of Arizona

Patricia B. Erens, School of the Art Institute of Chicago

Peter X. Feng, University of Delaware

Lucy Fischer, University of Pittsburgh

Frances Gateward, California State University, Northridge

Tom Gunning, University of Chicago

Thomas Leitch, University of Delaware

Walter Metz, Southern Illinois University

A complete listing of the books in this series can be found online at wsupress.wayne.edu

For our friend Charles Silver

CONTENTS

Preface ix
Acknowledgments xiii

Introduction 1

THE TRILOGY

Part I: *Dans Paris* (2006) 49

Part II: *Les chansons d'amour* (2007) 85

Part III: *La belle personne* (2008) 127

Interview with Christophe Honoré 171

Appendix A. Filmography 203
Appendix B. Authored Books 211
Appendix C. Other Media Productions 213
Notes 215
Bibliography 237
Index 245

PREFACE

Christophe Honoré: A Critical Introduction brings the French filmmaker Christophe Honoré into focus for an English-speaking audience. Although he has wide exposure in Europe—the United Kingdom is the largest English-speaking nation to encounter his films—distribution of and reception to his work in the United States has been uneven. Nonetheless, when Honoré's films open in the United States, a significant number of film critics in larger cities review them. But Honoré's name has yet to take firm hold in American consciousness—scholarly or otherwise—in relationship to contemporary French filmmaking. This is particularly true in relationship to queer film studies. The limited release of Honoré's films beyond France (and Europe more generally) has much to do with this relationship and has shortchanged a larger public's access to a prolific and rewarding filmmaker who has made nearly a dozen films since 2000. And while films such as *Ma mère* (2004) and *Homme au bain* (2010) found a discrete cinephile audience in the United States, Honoré's "trilogy"—*Dans Paris* (2006), *Les chansons d'amour* (2007), and *La belle personne* (2008)—has received the most critical attention from media and a handful of scholars.

Like most Honoré films, the trilogy garnered mixed reviews in the popular press (some highly spirited in their critiques). To be sure, and at first glance, it is tempting to view the films in the trilogy as works created by a skilled filmmaker—a *metteur-en-scène*—who, when viewed positively, offers smart and delightful films with French élan. When pitched negatively, the films are seen as banal homage to Jean-Luc Godard and Jacques Demy. Such assessments, however, neglect Honoré's sustained place as an important auteur and, specifically, as an important queer auteur.

This volume seeks to correct hasty criticism, whether positive or negative. However, to revise these assessments, it is necessary to raise some thorny methodological questions and concerns. Honoré's films are complex works, extremely detailed in concept and meticulous in execution; they deserve thoughtful and considered criticism. What, then, is the most suitable way to "critically introduce" a lesser-known yet highly productive French filmmaker? Is it best, for instance, to introduce him through a broad overview of all his films? Or, given that our intention is to write for an audience that has limited access to Honoré's cinema, should a scholarly introduction focus primarily on the films readily available on DVD or through Internet streaming services? In making our decision, it was important that our project provide a portrait of the filmmaker while rigorously demonstrating Honoré's carefully crafted, demanding, and assertive cinematic signature. We have chosen, therefore, to concentrate on the trilogy precisely because it comprises his most recognized and the most accessible films outside France. Crucially, the films that make up the trilogy present key cinematic and cultural themes that shape Honoré's oeuvre: family relations, Eros and Thanatos, and cinema as a discrete art form. Hence, a study of the trilogy opens critical discourse onto and further study into the director's body of work (as we will see, this includes other media such as literature).

As such, the themes that Honoré explores in the trilogy spotlight the reasons we identify him as a "queer auteur." We are aware that to mark a subject in this way risks the pitfalls of cliché. To avoid the slippery prospects that an overused term invites, we take care to clarify the specific cinematic turns on which Honoré pivots and to concentrate on the ways his films queerly pollinate the ever-shifting terrain of queer French culture. Our project offers a theoretical definition of "queer auteur" that, on the one hand, serves a sui generis study of Honoré while, on the other hand, suggests theoretical models for expanding, more generally, inquiries about the vexed figure called the "queer auteur."

Hence, we meet a filmmaker whose name in France courts controversy as much as it is bestowed with critical acclaim. Honoré's recent film *Métamorphoses* divided critics in France when it opened in September 2014 and earlier that summer at the Venice Film Festival.[1] Indeed, the discussions around his work and his critical declarations in such venues as *Cahiers du Cinéma* have raised the ante on French filmmaking. The implications for his work are only just beginning to be digested as symposiums, edited collections, and dissertations tackle Honoré's suggestive cinema. For instance, *Christophe Honoré: Le cinéma nous inachève*, edited by

Jean Cléder and Timothée Picard, collects writings by several of Honoré's collaborators and those who participated in a colloquium in 2011 at the Université de Rennes. In February 2015, another day-long symposium dedicated to Honoré's interdisciplinary cinematic style was held at the Université François-Rabelais de Tours ("Journée d'études doctorale: Christophe Honoré ou l'invention d'une écriture").[2] *A Companion to Contemporary French Cinema* includes several short discussions about Honoré's cinema in relationship to current modes of film production in France.[3] As part of the Centre national de la littérature pour la jeunesse, the Bibliothèque nationale de France sponsored an event in which the journalist Philippe-Jean Catinchi interviewed Honoré about his children's books and films. In the United States in 2014, doctoral students turned their attention to Honoré's films in their dissertation projects.[4] The director's name, not unlike those of Pier Paolo Pasolini in Italy and Rainer Werner Fassbinder in Germany (as we point out in the book), has made its way into French public discourse and reenergized discussions about film, art, politics, family, and sexuality. Honoré's filmmaking and auteur status will resonate for some time to come.

Honoré is thus a contemporary French queer filmmaker who is not only at the center of cultural debates in France; he is, moreover, a catalyst for the ongoing yet vibrant debates that revolve around the film auteur. The auteur debate in twenty-first-century France is alive and well. Put simply, the terms for the debate often straddle a "pro–" or "anti–" New Wave stance (Honoré aligns himself with the "pro–New Wave"). And not unlike the long-standing tradition that characterizes the auteurist heydays of Godard and Truffaut, wrangling over cinematic form crosses with a director's cultural and/or political position.

The current auteur debate is made more complicated when "queer" is brought into the mix, particularly since France is battling over the very ideals that are reshaping gender and sexuality studies in Western democracies. Where does Honoré as a "*Nouvelle* Nouvelle Vague" filmmaker fit within these heated and passionate cultural scenes? Is Honoré "queer" enough to dislodge hetero-masculinist traditions associated with auteur practice and theory? Is he "queer" enough to pass the queer litmus test set by queer cultural custodians? In short, does his claim as "homosexual narrator" prove to be integral to the way his art and social practice is shaped? We argue, yes. We contend that Honoré's filmmaking resists *proper* queer representation as such and thereby challenges—in order to rethink—the very premises associated with "queer" culture in, but certainly not exclusively, France.

In this light, the trilogy holds a vital place. The cinematic triptych signals Honoré's auteurist principles while placing him squarely in the crosshairs of popular and scholarly criticism. Some critics wonder, for example, whether his cinematic strategies for addressing AIDS are simply a ruse to elaborate an aesthetic metaphor. Some suggest that his LGBTQ politics are flimsy and align with a conservative and hetero-bourgeois agenda. Are his films and his politics derivative? Is Honoré, in other words, merely a filmmaker who spins a queer twist on the New Wave? As with most things "Honoré," a response to these issues is no simple matter. The trilogy offers the ground from which we can firmly and rigorously address the criticisms.

Our method, then, to argue for Honoré as a French queer auteur is linked to cinematic aesthetics, queer subjects, and auteurist concepts. Because the trilogy nestles cinematic properties with queer culture, our analysis considers the cultural implications of cinematic form. In other words, our study puts into service close film analysis with queer theory. To these ends, along with a comprehensive interview with the director and a comparative analysis of Honoré's work with that of François Ozon, we turn to the likes of the film theorists and critics Rudolf Arnheim, Raymond Durgnat, and Jean Mitry, as well as the queer theorists Eve Kosofsky Sedgwick, Rey Chow, and Leo Bersani. By fusing their writing with Honoré's cinematic *écriture*, we interrogate forms of methodology so as to yield a fresh interface between film and queer studies.

In our interview with Honoré, he states, "I've always thought that making films involved thinking about others' films and about defining a particular idea about cinema."[5] In joining him in his enthusiasm and love for expanding the "*idea about cinema,*" we offer this book as a dialogue with the director, film scholars, queer theorists, filmmakers, and cinéastes. Honoré is a critical filmmaker—*a critical queer auteur*—whose work requires a multidisciplinary study that does not, nay, *cannot*, neglect cinematic practice as the privileged tool through which the director queries the ideology of culture.

ACKNOWLEDGMENTS

This book benefits from the good graces and critical eyes of many friends and colleagues in the United States, France, and New Zealand. Institutionally, generous support from a PSC-CUNY grant provided critical funding toward the completion of our book. As on many other occasions, the College of Staten Island and the Graduate Center at the City University of New York have set the stage for rewarding engagement with faculty, students, and administrators, albeit in quite different ways.

We are especially grateful for our colleagues at Wayne State University Press who have supported a book dedicated to Christophe Honoré's work. From the moment in which a casual conversation with Annie Martin took place at the Society for Cinema and Media Studies, the press remained committed to our project. Annie's steadfast encouragement will not be soon forgotten. Barry Keith Grant, while maintaining his insight and attention to detail in film studies, allowed us creative and scholarly space to develop a theoretical intersection between film and queer studies. We are very pleased to have the opportunity to contribute to Barry's invaluable film studies series. The staff at the press—Kristin Harpster, Jamie Jones, Sarah Murphy, Emily Nowak, Bryce Schimanski, Kristina Stonehill—ensured that all the I's were dotted and T's crossed. Andrew Katz's copyediting skills are at once thoughtful, detailed, and gifted with a light touch. Finally, the anonymous reviewers assigned to review our manuscript offered a keenly critical and sensitive eye. They are generous scholars who approached our theoretical experiments thoughtfully and with deep consideration. The peer-review process is incredibly stressful. Participating with readers who delight in the active work of scholarship defines academic publishing at its best.

Christophe Honoré, on whom this book concentrates, has been more than gracious with his time. His enthusiasm for this project has sustained us through its writing. His films challenge the viewer and, without doubt, challenge the critic who takes on his cinema. In freely giving his time for the interview included in this book, Honoré provides the reader with an incisive look at his aesthetic concepts, cinematic technique, and the historical contexts in which his filmmaking developed. We are grateful to David Powell for translating the interview and bringing Honoré's conceptual thinking to an English-speaking audience.

We are fortunate to work with colleagues and students who love cinema and all its imaginative possibilities. The following inspire our commitment to the intellectual pleasures of cinema studies: Anne-Laure Barbarit, Matt Bell, William Boddy, Cécile Boulaire, Stéphane Bouquet, Iris Brey, Tara Burk, V. J. Carbone, Cynthia Chris, Dennis Cooper, Ludovic Cortade, Marc and Sandra Décimo, Camille Domain, Catherine Douzo, Anne Duggan, Éric Fassin, William Fritz, Margaret Galvan, Racquel Gates, Dave and Geneviève Gerstner, Ellen Grasso, Alison Griffiths, Amy Herzog, Daniel Humphrey, Sarah Keller, Rémi Lecompte, Sébastien Lévy, Ivone Marguiles, Stephen Mamber, Rebecca Martin, Edward D. Miller, Adeline Monzier, Martine Pelletier, Bruno Perreau, Patrice Petro, Matthew Solomon, Janet Staiger, Matthew Tinkcom, Christophe Wall-Romana, Samuel Weber, and Carol Wilder. Paula J. Massood and Joe McElhaney deserve singular recognition for their abiding friendship and support.

We are indebted to Sally Milner, who provided countless hours reading the manuscript and offering prompt and incisive commentary. David would like to once again thank Michael for his endless support and love during the book-writing process. It is good fortune to have another writer in the house.

In 1970, the year that Christophe Honoré was born, Charles Silver began his career as a supervisor for the Film Studies Center at the Museum of Modern Art in New York. Along with his duties in overseeing the museum's film collection and archival documents, Charles served as a film curator. In this capacity as guardian of film and bringing its riches to the public at MoMA, he has programmed a breathtaking number of film programs, written books and museum literature on the cinema, encouraged and supported queer film, and remained committed to the study and significance of film as a major art form. For these reasons, we dedicate this book to him.

INTRODUCTION

To write about the French filmmaker Christophe Honoré is to engage in a discussion that draws together a number of established concepts in film theory, film aesthetics, and French cinema. Honoré elegantly and rigorously navigates the complex relationship that exists between French culture and French cinema from short films such as *Hôtel Kuntz* (2008) to highly polished features such as *Les bien-aimés* (2011; translations listed in filmography). He is a published novelist, a theatrical producer, and an author of a prolific stream of children's books. As such, a study of his filmmaking involves a consideration of formal dimensions associated with the other arts. On the one hand, Honoré's filmmaking sits squarely within the New Wave (*Nouvelle Vague*) cinematic style now firmly associated with French cinema (especially the films of Jean-Luc Godard, Jacques Demy, François Truffaut, Jacques Rivette, Éric Rohmer, and Jean Eustache); on the other hand, Honoré interjects New Wave aesthetics into contemporary issues that touch on national identity, particularly in relationship to desire, queer sexuality, pleasure, urban friendships, family relations, death, and not insignificantly, AIDS.[1] In short, his films hinge on the long-standing thematic tension in the arts, Eros and Thanatos—that is, erotic desire and death. It is the often controversial and disturbing intermingling of these aesthetics and conceptual impulses in films such as *Tout contre Léo* (2002), *Ma mère* (2004), and *Les chansons d'amour*

(2007) that bring to light a filmmaker who—although he distances himself from such terminology—queerly penetrates French cinematic traditions and family relations. Yet, if Honoré is identified as a "queer" auteurist, as we argue here, it may be said that he is so to the extent that he reimagines heterocentricities and the place they occupy in French cinema and culture. Honoré's filmmaking touches an aesthetic and ideological nerve because he engages the queerly erotic negotiations that operate within the family.

To study the filmmaker and his intricate rehearsal of cinematic form, we concentrate our efforts on Honoré's "trilogy." In these films—*Dans Paris* (2006), *Les chansons,* and *La belle personne* (2008)—Honoré's narratives pivot on Eros and Thanatos. As a whole, the trilogy is Honoré's best-known work beyond France.[2] *Dans Paris*'s brooding storyline played well to art-house audiences, while *Les chansons* gained success with its "charming" songs. And while not quite as successful as the first two films, *La belle personne* was nonetheless noted for including song, "a leftover from [Honoré's] previous film, 'Love Songs.'"[3]

With a rich body of filmmaking, as well as a provocative oeuvre of children's books, theatrical productions, and, most recently, opera, Honoré's cinematic dynamics offer some of the most compelling filmmaking in the twenty-first century.[4] Because Honoré is prolific across several art forms, our study revolves around his sharp attention to creative multimedia platforms. Determinedly applied to the cinema, Honoré's formal concerns, theoretical impulses, and relationship to French culture penetrate his cinematic canvas. "I know that post-modern perspective on the arts is frowned upon," Honoré suggests in an interview, "but one of the things I like about it is the idea that cinema, paintings, and literature contain the memory of other art that has preceded it."[5] Such mixing of artistic remains, when parlayed through Honoré's cinema, resiliently renders history, art, and—as the director puts it—"memory." It is a key concern of our work, then, to piece together the director's formal processes that filter the art historical through the cinema. And since Honoré forthrightly asserts that New Wave filmmakers play a decisive role in his approach to cinematic form, the historical and aesthetic connections across the arts are all the more critical to any thorough recounting of his films. This is especially true since the New Wave filmmakers to whom he is unapologetically indebted consistently integrated their voracious appetite for multiple art forms into their films. Following their trademark, Honoré links his cinema to art history (in its broadest definition). In this way, cinema is memory, aestheticized and mobile.

Our book introduces Honoré as an active agent who *cinematizes* French cultural memory. This volume does not seek to provide the director's biography as such. Instead, while we highlight his films, arguing for their significance to and within film history, Honoré's biographical details invariably emerge through interviews and through our discussion of the films themselves. The central aim for our work is to theoretically locate Honoré as a queer auteur. Through this critical lens, we argue that Honoré's oeuvre is significant because it resists easy aesthetic and ideological categorization and it invites a study of his cinematic form as a foil to glib or facile meaning. In attending to the films this way, we do not discount their ideological complexities. Indeed, Honoré insists on a cinematic aesthetic that troubles simplistic interpretation. Hence, while his neat—if not overt—alignment with the French New Wave cinematics of Godard and Truffaut is fitting when discussing Honoré's films, it is more provocative to bring him into focus with the likes of the directors Pier Paolo Pasolini (1922–1975) and Rainer Werner Fassbinder (1945–1982) as well as the (like Honoré) Brittany-born and less heterocentric New Wave filmmaker Jacques Demy (1931–1990). But we also consider Honoré in relationship to twenty-first-century queer French filmmaking. To do this, Honoré's queer counterpart, François Ozon, is instrumental to our argument because Ozon allows us to identify the distinguishing marks of Honoré's French queer cinema. By placing Honoré and Ozon side by side, however, it is not our intention to foreclose "French queer cinema" as any one thing. Instead, we propose these cinematic relationships with other queer filmmakers because Honoré's filmmaking lends itself to what Thomas Elsaesser, in his study of Fassbinder, refers to as the "double bind." This is to say that the queer, or unsettling, filmmaker "complicates the nature of the bond that exists between the screen, the characters, and the spectator."[6] Pairing Ozon with Honoré illuminates Honoré's provocative queer cinema in such a way that it places it more readily with Fassbinder's and Pasolini's filmmaking. Like his queer German and Italian counterparts for whom cinematic form took prominence, Honoré is interested in a cinema in which "there is no subject in a film; the subject is the production" (JNCH, 180). Because of this aesthetic emphasis, in connection with his identity as a homosexual filmmaker, Honoré, we argue, confronts the ideological conundrums and critical controversies that Pasolini and Fassbinder experienced in tandem with their film aesthetics.

TOWARD A QUEER *NOUVELLE VAGUE* . . .

By our positioning Honoré in relationship to the New Wave, the aesthetic impulses that drove more queer-identified directors (Demy, Pasolini, and Fassbinder), and his queer contemporary (Ozon), he is not only readily seen as a provocative auteur; he is positioned as a significant French queer auteur. The "double bind" that Elsaesser proffers in relating Fassbinder's complicated cultural history and filmmaking to the critical reception of his films is valuable in tracing queer auteurism; or, more precisely, it is valuable in that it identifies a mode of queer auteurism in which spectatorial response is torn. The "double bind" response prompted by queer auteur cinema thus depends on a critical tension. Its queer sensibility leaves the spectator and critic in the lurch about whether their political and aesthetic expectations have been confirmed. In other words, queer auteur cinema resists any obligation to deliver a totalized political "message" that purportedly falls in line with the director's public identity. The "double bind," for instance, in which Fassbinder and Pasolini continually found themselves, participates in the knowledge that they were homosexual and, politically, to the left. As such, and as we discuss in detail later, when their films were perceived by the left to be less than pro-gay (Fassbinder's *Faustrecht der Freiheit* [*Fox and His Friends*], 1975) or less than pro-Marxist (Pasolini's *Teorema*, 1968), their ideological credentials were called into question. Much in the same way, Honoré, as a twenty-first-century gay man, provokes criticism by cultural theorists in regard to his treatment of homosexuality and women. We will return to Elsaesser's argument on the "double bind" since it is critical to furthering our definition of French queer cinema and the queer auteur.

Because Honoré marshals film aesthetics in order to disturb—*while eroticizing*—French heterocentricities, he introduces a cinema riddled by an unsettlingly queer seduction. While queer and *non*queer reviewers may feel more at ease with, say, Olivier Ducastel and Jacques Martineau's gay-romance films (consider *Jeanne et le garçon formidable* [*Jeanne and the Perfect Guy*, 1998] and *Drôle de Félix* [*The Adventures of Félix*, 2000]), Honoré finds these films "a bit boring" or too much "in harmony [about] sexuality."[7] Whether tapping into Jacques Demy–style cinematic airiness in *Drôle de Félix* or reflecting on French post-'68 culture in *Nés en 68* (*Born in 68*, 2008), Ducastel and Martineau neatly and linearly organize sexual and political identity through fait accompli cause-and-effect narrative structure. Often, their films are framed by an AIDS narrative that revolves around the search for a father or father figure (*Félix* and *Nés en 68*, for example). Honoré's investment in Demy, on the other hand, is not guided by pastiche in which a romantic narrative is dutifully sealed. Honoré's boredom with harmonious sexuality in films such as those made by Ducastel and Olivier is boredom with a cinema that presents sexual desire, love, and erotics as narratologically comprehensible.

To be clear, Honoré does not reject narrative as such. For instance, his cinema is not experimental in the way that the gay French filmmaker Lionel Soukaz approaches French queer subject matter. Honoré's cinematic narratives are more akin to the likes of Demy, Fassbinder, and Pasolini in that his characters *move through time and space* within the shell of a narrative *driven by erotic love and death*. Honoré's cinematic narratives set the stage for but do not regulate action. Instead, his cinema—the cinematography, editing, soundtrack, lighting, and so forth—steals away the authority of the narrative and thus broadens the implications for mise-en-scène and character gesture.

Honoré's filmmaking reminds us that cinema is, as André Gaudreault puts it, "the merging of the two basic modes of narrative communication: narration and monstration."[8] The "two basic modes," however, are weighted and applied to different effect by different filmmakers. If mise-en-scène and character movement are vital aspects of Honoré's cinema, to what extent does his filmmaking prioritize monstration (*showing*) over narration (*telling*)? What are the implications in weighting cinema this way? By following Gaudreault's line of thinking, we can trace the way Honoré adheres to New Wave practices and their embrace of cinema's formal properties. Truffaut is particularly relevant for Honoré on this count. As Honoré points out, "Reading Truffaut—especially his articles in *Cahiers*—is like reading a manual for how to become a film director" (JNCH, 181). Indeed, Truffaut makes clear that *showing* must take precedence over talking in the art of cinema. His assertion on this matter formidably appears in his introduction to his interview with Alfred Hitchcock. Here, Truffaut stresses the Hollywood auteur's uncanny ability to do away with dialogue as the vehicle for making meaning in the narrative. "Since," Truffaut asserts, "Hitchcock chooses to express everything by purely visual means," the use of straightforward dialogue in his films would only leave the spectator "bewildered" or, "worse, indifferent to the proceedings on the screen." As Truffaut sees it, "Whatever is *said* instead of being *shown* is lost upon the viewer."[9] Following Truffaut's filmmaking "manual," Honoré places "monstration" as the foremost concern in his "idea of cinema."

But in what way do we extend the critical engagement of monstration and narration in relationship to auteur practices when defining *queer* auteur cinema? If we are to get at what is "queer" about Honoré's cinema, it is necessary to consider the way Honoré *makes*, indeed *shows*, cinema as queer. It is necessary, then, to study the way his films evoke what the director refers to as a "queer spirit" rather than confirm a queer narrative and aesthetic (JNCH, 181). Finally, it is necessary to distinguish Honoré's queer cinema of monstration from that of his contemporaries who emphasize a queer cinema of narration. For this reason, we pair Honoré's filmmaking practices with that of François Ozon. Honoré's cinema of *showing* (as learned from Truffaut and Hitchcock before him) not only challenges the contemporary cinematic form and a reliance on a cinema of narration (such as Ozon's); Honoré's cinema troubles the very definitions of "queer" in French culture. Hence, before we address the "double bind" in which Honoré often finds himself as a "queer" auteur, we explore the cinematic and cultural groundwork he inherited from the New Wave and the ways he queerly translates this gift from those whom he alternatively calls his *"grandpères"* or "godfathers."

INHERITANCE

The place to unpack Honoré's relationship to the "double bind" begins, of course, with the French New Wave, its auteurs, and the aesthetic split that continues to occupy a new generation of filmmakers in France.[10] On whatever side contemporary French filmmakers fall, their position de facto wrestles with the New Wave's legacy. Not insignificantly, the aesthetic divide may be provocatively explored through the lens of France's two most prolific and recognized contemporary queer filmmakers: Honoré (1970–) and François Ozon (1967–). André Téchiné (1943–), Patrice Chéreau (1944–2013), and Jacques Nolot (1943–) are firmly identified with a gay/bisexual auteur cinema that immediately succeeded the classic New Wave. This group is thus more rightly recognized as Honoré's and Ozon's cinematic fathers, whereas Jean-Luc Godard (1930–), François Truffaut (1932–1984), and Jacques Demy (1931–1990) are more aptly positioned, Honoré suggests, as his and his contemporaries' grandfathers (JNCH, 184).[11] Aesthetically, the twenty-first-century queer filmmakers—to which Honoré belongs—leapfrog this in-between generation by addressing (if not *re*dressing) their grandfathers' heterocentric cinema.

"The New Wave's appearance in France at the end of the 1950s," Michel Marie writes, "marked a rejuvenation, bringing a new generation into the film industry at a time of creative sclerosis."[12] Marie argues that the core filmmakers of the New Wave—Truffaut, Godard, and Claude Chabrol—constituted a school that existed in fact, not just in mere mythology and legend (28, 47). Their films form an "artistic trend . . . closely tied to a collection of critical concepts held by a fairly coherent group" (26). As a newer-generation critic for *Cahiers du Cinéma* (1995–2000), Honoré would agree with Marie's assessment that the New Wave was a "school," grounded by tightly held "critical concepts," and that it resuscitated French cinema during the postwar period. Moreover, Honoré's indebtedness to the school comes about since, as a committed acolyte, he follows in their creative footsteps as film critic and (then) filmmaker.

And because the New Wave took shape through critical engagement with filmmaking, the "school" traded on a range of film practices and, therefore, cannot be seen as aesthetically monolithic. "Critical concepts," in Marie's terms, yield wide-ranging cinematic possibilities and experimentation. Hence, Godard's films are obviously distinct from Chabrol's, as are Alain Resnais's from Jacques Demy's. Indeed, the idea of filmmaking as "critical concept" with its attendant possibilities remains at the heart of France's signature filmmakers. Following suit, Honoré's adherence to New Wave concepts requires rigorous scholarly analysis that pays sharp attention to its inter- and intracinematic distinctions. Close critical analysis of his films is essential since his rewriting of New Wave concepts involves queer interference. Honoré's films are indebted to New Wave critique and aesthetics, but at the same time, they produce their own distinctive—*distinctively queer*—set of "critical concepts."

The hypercharged creative energy that the New Wave left in its wake is unequivocal. Honoré absorbs this energy when he repays his gratitude to his cinematic *grandpères* through overt homage. To identify the New Wave's emphatic resonance for queer filmmakers, it is valuable to investigate the ongoing debate that takes place within Honoré's immediate cinematic family. Since Honoré's generation continues to refer to their professional activities in relationship to "cinematic fathers and/or grandfathers," the critical and cinematic dialogue that occurs between Honoré and Ozon is strikingly akin to a family squabble between cinematic *frères*.

Like Honoré, Ozon takes his aesthetic cues from his response to the New Wave. While both queer filmmakers deal with similar themes—family, death, AIDS, the role of women, youth, queer sexuality—their films offer an approach to cinematic "narrative and monstration" that rehearses variations on New Wave aesthetic discourses. To be sure, Ozon's rejoinder to the New Wave follows a different historical and aesthetic trajectory than Honoré's. Ozon's turn to Maurice Pialat (1925–2003), the filmmaker who angrily and publicly dismissed the New Wave, provocatively suggests distinct aesthetic registers for his and Honoré's approaches to French queer cinema. The aesthetic debate between the two queer cinematic brothers—Ozon being the older of the two filmmakers—underscores their grandfathers' aesthetic sins while highlighting the intricate forms of public relations that both generations have employed to mark their cinematic territory. The critical debate for French queer cinema that plays out in this instance draws on Pialat's public stance against the New Wave, especially the New Wave associated with Godard. Pialat's aesthetic split remains salient and serves Ozon's filmmaking practices in a specific and historical way. Honoré admires Pialat and holds him in esteem, at arm's length. To whatever degree Pialat is seen—and we will return to his place in relationship to Ozon's and Honoré's cinematic concepts—to get at a queer *Nouvelle Vague*, he must be drawn into the picture.

INTRODUCTION

CINEMATIC *HOMOPARENTALITÉ*

In 2007, Max Cavitch laments in *Screen*, "It is remarkable, given Ozon's prolific output and success in making films that revel in impropriety and trouble notions of stable sexual identities, that no major critics and theorists of the New Queer Cinema discuss any of the seventeen shorts and eleven features he has directed since 1988."[13] In the same journal in 2012, Fiona Handyside claims, "The assertion that François Ozon's films are part of 'a new queer cinema' has become a commonplace of academic writing about the director."[14] In a short time, Ozon's "prolific output" and stature made him the go-to French queer auteur for critics and scholars. Born in 1967 and raised in Paris, Ozon grew up in "the heart of the French capital."[15] Encouraged by his family, Thibaut Schilt tells us, Ozon developed into "a precocious film enthusiast" (9) with an "ardent, if not obsessive, cinephilia" (10). The oldest of five children in a home where they were "allowed to read and watch anything [they] wanted," François Ozon "quickly became attracted to films that were not meant for children" (Ozon, quoted in Schilt, 9–10). Ozon was drawn at an early age to (and borrowing the director's term) "pretentious" cinema (10). Resnais's *Providence* (1977) and Roberto Rossellini's *Germania anno zero* (*Germany Year Zero*, 1948) were more to his liking. "I remember the state of shock *Germania anno zero* put me in," Ozon recounts, "the story of a kid my age who commits suicide in Berlin's ruins" (quoted in Schilt, 10).

Ozon's remarks about the child projected on the screen highlight an ongoing and critical perspective that plays out in his films. By drawing out Ozon's consideration of the child, we are more able turn to Honoré's cinematic concept of the child, core to his creative energies, as he explores the erotic tensions it engenders in the French family. Indeed, homosexuality, family, and the child are hotly contested matters in France. In regard to French cinema, Kate Ince argues in "Queering the Family?" that the family functions "as a metaphor for the state of the French nation" and "parallels" the universalist principles that support "French national identity." Ince points to Ducastel and Martineau's *Drôle de Félix*, in which the film's discrete sections draw the gay protagonist into a range of familial arrangements that nonetheless reaffirm "universalist principles." In other words, where "differences" occur within the family setting, they are "tolerated as long as they fit in; the French family, like the French nation is governed by a restrictive type of universalism that accepts difference only as the individual difference of personhood."[16] It is a matter that Joan Wallach Scott elegantly describes in her book *Parité* when she posits that, since homosexuals are not seen to reproduce biologically, the nation's offspring and, hence, its future are undermined. The heterosexually determined family structure (one man, one woman) is deemed the "cultural imperative,... the guarantee of the species." "Homoparentalité," or the raising of children with persons of the same sex, is anathema to national tradition. "Sexual difference," Scott writes, "embodied by the heterosexual couple, was taken to be the symbolic mastercode of humankind—immutable, 'primordial,' not natural but 'cultural,' a reality 'objective' and 'universal.'"[17]

If Honoré, as queer auteur, seeks to imbricate himself into the child's perspective within the hetero-family dynamic and its place in culture more generally, Ozon assumes the role of the gifted auteur (i.e., Rossellini); he is an *observer* with mature eyes. When Honoré identifies himself as "the homosexual narrator," as we will see, his look to the child is less that of observer. Rather, Honoré intimately connects himself and his work *with* the experience of the child. As is often the case in Ozon's films, a child's role is consequential only to the extent that he or she is witnessed through the point of view of older observers, including that of the filmmaker. As Schilt tells us, Ozon's "personal experiences" are noted for the way they inform his cinematic point of view (157). *Le temps qui reste* (*Time to Leave,* 2005) is instructive in this regard.

Le temps qui reste focuses on a young gay character, Romain (Melvil Poupaud), who is dying from cancer (it is possible to read Romain's illness as AIDS related; see Schilt, 105). Romain's impending death prompts him to reflect on the *idea* of the child. Specifically, he reimagines an ideal past self. As an embodied figure, the child holds little interest for Romain, but his look back at the "idea" of the child gives succor to the emotional and psychological state in which he finds himself as a dying adult. We see the "idea" of the child explored through Romain's/Ozon's gaze onto other children who pass through his remaining days. While flashbacks are used to recall Romain's own childhood—flashbacks in which, in fact, he sees himself as a child in a playground or on the beach—the images of his past self morph with his present. In other words, Romain's imagined child / past self is presented as a daydream. However, the image of the child, seen as his past self, is found to be one of mistaken identity when Romain realizes he has projected his desire onto an anonymous child in the playground. As death appears imminent, the haunting image of "the child"/past self increasingly shares the scene with Romain's lived present.

The young adult's understanding of self, prior to death, is thus organized around an idealized memory of "the child" since he is not at all interested in the actual presence of a child. When he agrees to father a child for a woman he accidently encounters, he promptly heads to a lawyer to prepare his inheritance for his never-to-be-seen heir. Here, the child-as-ideal future measures equally with the child-as-ideal past. Positioned in this way, the adult's view of the child is one that sentimentalizes past and future for the purposes of the adult's existential present; the child-ideal thus gives sustenance to adulthood, gay or straight.

This idea of the child as a vehicle for coming to grips with queer adulthood in *Le temps* is reinforced across Ozon's filmmaking. Ozon's short film *La petite mort* (1995) follows a young twenty-something gay photographer, Paul (François Delaive), who seeks to root out from his life his fraught relationship with his now-dying father. In one sequence, Paul pastes onto one of his baby photos a recent photograph of his facial expression during orgasm, a photograph shot by his boyfriend. The laying on of this older version of self suggests Paul's assertion of his identity as a gay man. His baby picture, now hidden by his current life, conjures a past image of self, which his father had referred to as "ugly." Later, after photographing his unwitting father, who is dying in a hospital bed, Paul, in a dramatically Oedipal gesture, cuts the eyes from his father's image. With the eyes removed, Paul then places his father's image over his face so that he now sees, as it were, through his father's eyes. Paul's fresh perspective reconfirms the experience of the child as best understood by an adult viewpoint.

Cavitch concludes that Ozon's engagement with the figure of the child is significant for queer cinema. According to him, it portrays a world where the gay couple in *La petite mort*, for instance, "pursue their bodies' pleasures in a way that is distinctly contraceptive" (323). In other words, if recent gay culture puts a premium on having children of their own—"a conscious repopulation project in response to the AIDS-related decimation of communities" (323)—it has done so at the expense of an eroticized and sexualized queer culture that does *not* take reproduction as its aim.[18] Cavitch further contends that since the hetero-fantasy of reproducibility refuses the "proposition that mourning *is* an erotic narrative, [and] that sexual desire does not evaporate in the face of loss" (324; emphasis in original), Paul's process of mourning in *La petite mort* indeed involves acting on sexual desire.

But another and final photograph appears at the end of the film. Once Paul's father dies, Paul sits on a bench and searches through a box of his father's memorabilia. In it, he finds what will be the final photograph we see in the film of father and son. It is a photo that overrides the radical gestures that Paul performed earlier when he photographed his dying father, fragmenting the images and then overlaying a portion of them on his own body. The final snapshot in the film shows his father lovingly holding Paul as a baby. The image rekindles paternal memories. The deus ex machina discovery of the photo delivers a rethinking of Paul's relationship to his father, a rethinking already anticipated by the laying on of faces. Rather than invigorating his homosexual desire or suggesting incestuous desire between father and son, the indexical image in which his father embraces Paul evokes paternal sentimentality. Hence, the earlier photograph that Paul ocularly castrated and placed over his own face suggests that Paul's "seeing through his father's eyes" is more a sentimental than a queer radical refusal of the father. While Paul apparently does not lose his gay sexual desire, Ozon's "queer" narrative returns an idealized, sentimentalized, and desexualized image of the family experience.

This view of the child as a corrective to the adult-child relationship continues in *Ricky* (2009), a film about a fantastical child. In this case, the child is positioned in relationship to the mother's perspective. In this highly polished fantasy film, a single mother meets a new boyfriend at work. They establish a relationship and give birth to a son. The baby suddenly appears to have unexplained bruises along his shoulder blades. The marks lead the mother, Katie (Alexandra Lamy), to accuse her boyfriend/father-of-Ricky, Paco (Sergi López), of child abuse. After Paco leaves, the film follows Katie and her daughter, Lisa (Mélusine Mayance), raising Katie's different (read: queer) son, who has transformed into an angel who flies.

The media soon discover Ricky. The queer baby quickly becomes a sensational news item. Paco returns, and a press conference is arranged outside the family's suburban apartment complex. Katie and Lisa are hesitant about turning Ricky into a spectacle, but Paco—not in any way maliciously—realizes that the flying baby will generate necessary cash for its unique medical care. At the press conference, Katie "accidently" sets Ricky free into the open air, and we see him fly off into the distance.

In this, as with Ozon's other films, the process of mourning directs the narrative's outcome in terms of how the child is situated in relationship to adult desire. During the period in which Katie mourns her lost baby, Paco and Lisa patiently support her. One day, Katie decides to return to the lake where Ricky was last seen. As she deliberately enters the water, presumably to commit suicide, Ricky reappears, perhaps as a haunting. Schilt describes the climactic scene: "After a monologue, [Katie] shares her maternal pride and love with the toddler" (149). Her guilt is absolved by the vision and her "monologue" confession that enable Katie to move forward and rejoin her male partner and their child. The mother's desire is thus framed as desire for the family. Ricky—the child-ideal—is the adult vision that secures ideal adulthood. Katie, once again pregnant, and her regenerated family survive precisely because their memories of Ricky (or, in the case of Katie, her imaginative projections of the child) hold *their* world together.

Ricky "talks," Ozon explains, "about the *relationship to* a child, but also the tendency that a mother can have to merge with her child; this type of bond doesn't leave space for the man, for the husband, for the father, and creates jealousy from her other child" (quoted in Schilt, 158; emphasis added).[19] "To merge" with the child in Ozon's universe is to reject adult needs, desires, and obligations. To satisfy adult desire and obligation—"to leave space for the man" in the case of women—the child must necessarily remain unattached and separate. For Ozon, one has a "relationship *to*" the child, not *with* the child.[20] In this way, the adults of his films establish their sense of self because of the image of the child.[21]

If Ozon's queer cinema is revealed as one in which the moments of Eros and Thanatos are "talked about" and "the child" is perceived from the distance of adulthood, or as seen through the eyes of the auteur, Honoré's queer cinema more intimately and erotically imagines the child as corporeally and transgenerationally intermingled within the family dynamic. For Honoré, the child is not idealized or sentimentalized through indexically mounted memories; instead, the child is shown to be integrally embodied within and critical for adult sexual desire. The family dynamic in Honoré's cinema involves erotic encounters among its members.

Honoré makes a direct link between writing for children and his method for writing a screenplay: "I wrote many children's books, which kept me from writing bad screenplays or at least writing screenplays that I would never get to produce. Rather than writing screenplays that I would shove into a drawer or making shorts, I siphoned my desire to tell stores through kids' books. That was my way of testing my stories; it was an artistic experiment. It still is" (JNCH, 174). For Honoré, film finds its most rewarding aspect when it is conceived *as if through and for* the eyes of a child. It is rewarding because Honoré's queer adult memory emerges as a cinematic experience in which the child and adult are emotionally and malleably intertwined.

A QUEER TRINITY: HOMOSEXUALITÉ, BRETAGNE ET ADOLESCENCE

Honoré's 2005 book *Le livre pour enfants* is an invaluable example of the "artistic experiment" of telling tales of queer erotics. *Le livre pour enfants* is a roman à clef about the director's experiences as a young boy growing up gay in Rostrenen, Brittany, and his move to Paris "to be gay" and to make film. In multiple folds of time and place, then, *Le livre* recounts Honoré's relationship to his family, his father's death when he was fifteen years old, his young-adult affairs with both men and women, his making of the film *Ma mère*, and, mutatis mutandis, his life as a queer cinephile. Rossellini, Carl Dreyer, and Pialat play across the text as their films ground the author's coming-of-age as a queer French boy growing up in Brittany.

The book's narrator—Honoré—is not dissimilar to the narrator we encounter later in his film *Dans Paris*. In both works, the narrators deliver their tale through an apostrophe, an address to the dead or absent (directly announced as such in *Dans Paris*). The literary device turned cinematic by Honoré in *Dans Paris* as well as *Le livre pour enfants* situates the text's narrator as the autobiographical guide for the spectator/reader. Honoré's narrator thus embodies the narrative's past, present, and future. In this way, the novel and the film are infused with passages by the narrator, who yearns to describe the weight of his past as it disseminates—and, so, makes available—the present while it anticipates the future.

In *Le livre pour enfants*, the linking of time and space is critical for Honoré's impulses as a queer filmmaker. The book's narrator, Honoré, tells of his "sudden" and "immediate" decision that "film was a priority."[22] His enthusiasm recalls the "Eureka!" moment in Truffaut's *Les quatre cents coups* (*The 400 Blows*, 1959) when Antoine Doinel discovers Balzac. But time and its immediacy is not the only element that serves Honoré's cinematically rendered memory. The place in which he lived as a child and teenager is as crucial as the time spent there. "Ni ville ni village," Rostrenen, La Bretagne, "est mon décor" (37). It is, as such, an inestimable site for Honoré's queer existence: "Je suis Homosexualité, Bretagne et Adolescence," he declares (32; see, further, JNCH, 175). The trinity that is his existence, established as a young Breton, fills each and every crevice of past, present, and future. Experienced this way, the spatial and temporal trinity—"Homosexualité, Bretagne et Adolescence"—is always already present for the queer auteur. The trinity is critical to Honoré's cinematic signature.

Because this "book for children" involves family, queer sexual desire, and the cinema, it is a treatise on his vexed aesthetic emplacement as, to use Honoré's terms, "le narrateur homosexuel." Indeed, Honoré folds the trinity into this single figure. In the following passage from *Le livre pour enfants,* Honoré reckons with this self-identified position following a rendezvous at the cinema with his friends. He waxes philosophically about his relationship to writing and his cultural identity:

> Because I am a homosexual narrator. This will not have escaped my close reader. Because I have the idea that my reader—if I admit to being read, and that this book, and the novels and films that have preceded are read as discreetly addressed letters—is convinced of my sexual preference. I fought against this idea, and also against writing for someone in this way; I extended myself without fear of ridicule about my stubbornness not to write for any particular person, just write, by discipline, as one goes to church, to a gym for my damaged soul, as if in so tiny a trance, a fragile experience. But no. I write for both, and because I write

for both, I am a homosexual narrator. I thought only for me, I doubted the reader, but that's over. The proof: I am not afraid to invite you into this text. Courage returns. I write for both. The evidence: I have written books for children. And again, I was a homosexual narrator.[23]

Like his cinema, Honoré's books—and this passage is indicative—wrestle with the aesthetic that shapes queer content and form as it, in fact, wrestles with France's "cultural imperative" that views homosexuals as not bona fide citizens for the reproduction of its future or for the care and upbringing of children. Hence, Honoré's navigation of form and content folds his complex relationship as homosexual narrator into the larger and more abstract dynamic of the relationship between the homosexual and the child.[24]

Honoré's "Because I am a homosexual narrator" passage reveals an unanswerable conundrum that he continually faces as the writer of children's books: how is it possible that the "homosexual narrator" can so intimately know his subject and readers, especially children? As the father of a young daughter in France, he faces the question, more pertinently, "why is this a question?" His homosexuality has never been a secret, and his love for his child is not conditional because of it. At the same time, he is aware of the emotional and erotic tensions that underscore familial relations between parent and child. It is precisely because of the hetero-manufactured conundrum in which he finds himself that Honoré critically and queerly conceptualizes its overdetermined heterocentricities. It is, in other words, within heterocentric cultural presumptions—*French universalism*—that Honoré foregrounds familial intimacy and its attending erotics. This is Honoré's project: to trouble what Joan Wallach Scott describes as France's "cultural imperative" about family. If, as Scott reminds us, "sexual difference became figured exclusively as a heterosexual couple, ... the key to life itself," then Honoré messes with the hetero-driven imperative by presenting "*homoparentalité*" as precisely the "key to life."[25] *Homoparentalité*'s life-giving force—one torn between Eros and Thanatos—involves, for Honoré, his homosexuality as it is bundled with his fatherhood as well as his life as an artist. Honoré thus queerly reproduces the life of France.

In terms of aesthetic form, *Le livre pour enfants* illuminates Honoré's detailed attention to *écriture*—that is, *cinematic écriture*. All his multimedia work is cinematic: indeed, "film is a priority." By theorizing his position as "homosexual narrator" in relationship to *and* within his texts—novels, films, and children's books—he grapples with the inside and outside position he ultimately occupies in French culture and cinema. To be sure, to assert oneself as the "homosexual narrator" is to choose a voice that is both in and out. It is an aesthetic choice in which the responsibility to act on his homosexuality, *to write as,* opens the auteur "out" toward his unique aesthetic investment in the world: "Homosexualité, Bretagne et Adolescence." At the same time, it encloses him. He is marked, typecast, and his "close reader" expects the "homosexual narrator" to deliver that which "convinces" them that yes, he is indeed "the homosexual narrator" and more. The invariable tensions, against which the "homosexual narrator" struggles, haunt Honoré's cinematic place. The queer auteur's presence is inexorable as it saturates the cinematic scene of *Le livre pour enfants* and the films made in its wake. The "homosexual narrator" is a presence that does not just observe "the child" from a distance or recollect the idea of the child from an adult's past perspective; instead, the homosexual narrator penetrates the idea of the child at all times and through each character's perspective. In this way, the "homosexual narrator," through cinematic *écriture,* unsettles and queers the French family. Honoré's assertions are the terms for the double bind in which he and his films are continually ensnared.

As a queer cinephile, Honoré takes seriously his responsibility for his inheritance. In other words, he recognizes the debt to his family (in all senses of the term), to the lived experiences that derive from his Bretagne "décor," and to the films that write his life. The cinematic path drawn for us in Honoré's *Le livre pour enfants* reveals a distinct aesthetic engagement with the child, one that is quite different from the child placed at arm's length in Ozon's films. As such, the queer auteur's relationship to the child sets the stage for the aesthetic groundwork that we discover in the versions of French queer cinema that Honoré and Ozon offer.

QUEER CINEMATIC AUTEURS—HONORÉ AND OZON

How were Honoré's and Ozon's critical designs on cinema developed? Through what cultural and theoretical lenses did they operate? And in what way did their critical approaches enable French queer cinema? While Honoré and Ozon intersect at key points of film history and aesthetics, their career paths have made for very different concepts in their filmmaking. In this and the following section, we trace the overlapping yet distinct trajectories of the two young filmmakers as they involved themselves in the cinema.

With "film as a priority," Honoré channeled his "desire to tell stories" through his writing of children's books and, soon after, film criticism. From his youth in Brittany to his move to Paris, Honoré's cinematic imagination drove his creative impulses. Before Paris, he attended the University of Rennes 2 (less than a two-hour drive from Rostrenen), where he took classes in literature and film. He is listed as an alumnus of the university (1992), but his filmmaking practices were not formally structured (unlike Ozon's instruction in filmmaking).[26] In 1995, Honoré arrived in Paris. "I didn't know anybody," he recounts in an interview. "I was lucky because I sent a letter with an article to *Cahiers du cinéma*, and they offered me a writing position very quickly."[27] As a critic, he, on occasion, assumed the nom de plume Roland Cassard as a nod to Demy's suave protagonist in *Lola* (1961) and *Les parapluies de Cherbourg* (1964).

Honoré notes that his arrival to the capital was the moment he recognized a significant loss. He tells the *Huffington Post* that by the time he arrived in Paris, the generation of queer filmmakers and cinephiles to whom he looked for guidance and inspiration—his "godfathers"—were "wiped out by AIDS." He continues, "It's true—all the people I admired as an adolescent from an artistic standpoint and in the way they lived their homosexuality—whether it was writers like Hervé Guibert, or filmmakers like Jacques Demy, or Serge Daney, the cinema critic—I got to Paris and they were already dead."[28]

Nevertheless, his name was soon on the lips of French cinephiles, critics, and filmmakers when, in 1998, he dramatically repeated François Truffaut's *cinema-maudit* gesture. Following his idol's scathing report on the state of French cinema in 1954 in *Cahiers du Cinéma*, "Une certaine tendance du cinéma français," Honoré penned his own polemic, also for *Cahiers du Cinéma*, "Triste moralité du cinéma français." Like Truffaut, Honoré challenged French filmmakers and French cinema culture to rethink their complacent international position as well as the way they conceived the idea of cinema. His short and smartly crafted essay resuscitates the very same frustration Truffaut felt during the 1950s over France's aesthetically dull cinema, or the "tradition of quality."

In "Triste moralité du cinéma français," Honoré lambastes the banal—yet nonetheless award-winning—French cinema offered in 1997. Films such as Robert Guédiguan's *Marius et Jeannette* (1997)—a film that screened at Cannes as a selection of "Un certain regard" and received the 1997 Prix Louis-Delluc—"bored the hell out of [him]."[29] And while French critics cheered Anne Fontaine's *Nettoyage à sec* (1997) for being subversive, Honoré asked, "Cinéaste subversive, Anne Fontaine? Cinéaste super-bourgeoisie, oui!" (4). At the time, international films such as Wong Kar Wai's *Happy Together* (1997), Tsai Ming-liang's *The River* (*He liu*, 1997), David Lynch's *Lost Highway* (1997), and Wes Craven's *Scream* (1996) were "thirty-thousand times more interesting than the best of the best French films of the year."[30] His view on French cinema has changed little since writing this article.

INTRODUCTION

Retracing Truffaut's path to filmmaking via film criticism is important for understanding Honoré's approach to French cinema. By following his elder's cinephile footsteps, we are in a position to see how and why Honoré developed the critical concepts that he did. Soon after making his first films and garnering a reputation as either controversial or a true critic-auteur, Honoré went on to give lectures at La Fémis (École Nationale Supérieure des Métiers de l'Image et du Son), the Parisian-based film school. La Fémis, as we discuss later, is where Ozon studied filmmaking. Here, Honoré took the opportunity to assume the role that his queer "godfathers" were unable to provide for him. At La Fémis, for instance, Honoré instructed Mikael Buch in one of his classes. Buch went on to direct *Let My People Go* (2011) with Honoré coauthoring the film's screenplay. When the *Huffington Post* asked how he became involved with the project, he answered, "I was the godfather for Mikael Buch, who was the filmmaker. When he was going to graduate, he let me read a screenplay he was going to do after graduation, and I said, 'You're not in school anymore, you have to stop doing shorts. You have to do a full-length feature.' He was pretty nervous, but I encouraged him and helped him find a producer."[31] In invoking himself as Buch's "godfather"—the absent figure for him—Honoré puts in place a queer cinematic family, a milieu he firmly believes nurtures young queer filmmakers.

Ozon's career in cinema, however, was approached less polemically and was established within institutional film studies. He attended the Université de Paris I, where he developed and honed his craft. Here, he obtained a master's degree in the late 1980s. Between the completion of this degree and 1990, Ozon directed three short Super 8mm films that, as Schilt notes, "contain many of the elements that would become Ozon's cinematic signatures: candid, unfiltered portrayals of human behavior; a taste for (preferably patricidal) murder; a fascination for the gruesome, a postmodern tendency to toy with generic conventions; and, in the case of *Les doigts dans le ventre* (1988), an ephemeral yet clearly queer intrusion" (16). Ozon's concentration on familial relations in which "queer intrusions" occur remains steadfast and ongoing.

In Ozon's work on the family, "patricidal murder" or, more accurately, the loss of the father occupies a central force (as seen in our earlier descriptions of his films). Honoré invokes the patriarch as well as the matriarch but draws them in as eroticized objects of desire within the family. Just as in Ozon's films, the erotic, loss, and mourning are critical to Honoré's narratives about family. For Honoré, however, we are less likely to encounter loss through violence or sentimentality. Nonetheless, the familial tensions in both filmmakers' work arise through the lens of Eros and Thanatos. As such, the similarity and differences that mark the queer *frères*' cinema draw us nearer to the aesthetic tensions that the New Wave

INTRODUCTION

left as an inheritance for young French filmmakers. Moreover, the New Wave's critical—and very heterocentric—narrative models make way for Honoré's and Ozon's critically queer conceptualization of the cinematic family in relationship to Eros and Thanatos. "An inheritance," Derrida tells us, "is always the reaffirmation of a debt, but a critical, selective, and filtering reaffirmation."[32] It is, importantly, "a responsibility," a "debt" to one's history. Rereading Marx's *The Eighteenth Brumaire of Louis Bonaparte,* Derrida reminds us that a "revolution repeats, and it even repeats the revolution against the revolution" (108). If repeating the revolution is "a responsibility" in which "critical, selective, and filtering reaffirmation" is required, then Michel Marie's emphasis on "critical concepts" as a centerpiece to New Wave filmmaking is crucial for how we envisage the legacy of queer auteurism. The New Wave's "revolution," stoked by its critical concepts, carried significant responsibility, a responsibility that looks back in time (just as Truffaut et al. did to Renoir and others) as much as it necessarily looks forward (insofar as a younger generation looks back *at* them). As queer auteurs, Honoré and Ozon are thus responsible for the "filtering reaffirmation" of their inheritance from the New Wave. They are indebted to the New Wave as much as they are responsible to those up-and-coming queer filmmakers (Mikael Buch, for instance) to whom they bequeath their ancestors' revolutionary remains.

For Ozon, debt and responsibility to the cinema began with academic training in film school; for Honoré, debt and responsibility to the cinema began with film criticism and cinephilic culture. Hence, the queer auteurs' roads to filmmaking in France are strikingly different. Class, birthplace (Honoré growing up in Rostrenen, Ozon in Paris), and familial environment play critical roles as they developed their worldviews (Honoré's father passed away when he was young, while Ozon's father financially and emotionally supported his schooling in the arts and cinema). With Honoré born into a petit-bourgeois household (his father was a prosthodontist), the City of Light's gay culture provided him with an energized and creative atmosphere for his cinematic objectives. Ozon, born in Paris within a bourgeois upbringing and encouraged by a family who loved cinema and participated in the arts, developed his love for cinema under very different circumstances.

In 1990, Ozon studied at La Fémis, where he attended classes led by the New Wave filmmakers Éric Rohmer and Jacques Rivette. In a comprehensive account of the school, Tim Palmer describes the Paris-based institution as the most significant—if not the most critically "neglected"—film school in which scholars might best understand today's French cinema culture.[33] La Fémis promotes itself as "a complete technical, artistic, and cultural education in the field of cinema and the audio-visual" (quoted in Palmer, 203). It is home to staunch cinephilia that demands students view filmmaking not only through technological practice; more comprehensively, La Fémis insists that students understand filmmaking as a "systematic process of 'intensive artistic *research*'" (quoted in Palmer, 203; emphasis in original). With its highly selective admission, La Fémis draws a student cohort whose dedication to the craft and heritage of cinema is emboldened by the institution's "instantiation of cineliteracy, and, ultimately, cinephilia" (206). Institutionalized as such, Palmer argues, La Fémis is a "fixture of [Paris's] film culture" (204). It proved to be an ideal and familiar location for Ozon. At La Fémis, his cinematic skills were rigorously refined in the areas of direction, screenwriting, cinematography, sound, editing, production design, and set design.

According to Schilt, Ozon never felt comfortable caught within the highly charged and firmly entrenched debates at La Fémis in which "France's well-known and persistent attachment to the notion of 'auteur cinema'" remains in place (16). Ozon, Schilt contends, wished to maintain a neutral position on the matter: "he strongly believed there was nothing antithetical about liking all [filmmaking] equally" (17). Yet, elsewhere and paradoxically, Schilt points out that while Truffaut, Chabrol, and Rohmer "taught [Ozon] the trade of filmmaking" and that Ozon cites Godard as "an influence and model," the director "does not feel the weight [*lourdeur*] of a cinephilic heritage" (31–32). Neutrality to his "cinephilic heritage" notwithstanding, when Ozon selected Pialat for his thesis topic at La Fémis, he made a telling choice. To choose the renegade filmmaker associated, contentiously, with the New Wave era bespeaks an aesthetic and intellectual curiosity on Ozon's part that reaches toward a brand of French cinema that at once drives a wedge between New Wave proponents and opponents while nevertheless winking and nodding to New Wave influence. Ozon's "neutral" position that (at times) augurs a "neither/nor" or (at other times) an "embrace/refuse" binary leads Honoré to succinctly identify Ozon's relationship to the New Wave: "I don't think he likes the New Wave. In fact, I think he hates it" (JNCH, 184).

From Honoré's perspective, and although he grants that Ozon's cinematic talents are formidable, he argues that his queer *frère*'s cinematic skills are best suited for genre-driven narratives, such as comedy.[34] Following Ozon's uneven remarks on the New Wave, Honoré challenges his purported neutrality. Importantly, Honoré establishes a link between Ozon's sights in securing his place as *the* French gay filmmaker and his disdain for the New Wave. "Ozon, who must be about my age," Honoré posits, "started long before me. He was already an established director when I started making films. For that matter, I think he was somewhat irritated when several gay directors showed up as competition for the top spot. We don't really make the same kind of films" (JNCH, 184).

If Honoré's assertion is correct and Ozon's distaste for the New Wave is in fact connected to claims that serve to distinguish his place as France's gay filmmaker, it is worth revisiting Schilt's contention about Ozon's neutral position on French auteur cinema. To address this—and at the risk of oversimplification—we propose a preliminary line of division between the New Wave and our French queer auteurs. For the moment, we posit the following set of binaries: Ozon/Pialat and Honoré/Godard. The preliminary divide, although not entirely random, allows room to sort through some of the creative tensions at play in contemporary French queer cinema. The artificial split we devise is only useful to the extent that it serves as aesthetic working points. Once the dust settles, less rigid applications of New Wave aesthetics appear in Honoré's and Ozon's filmmaking. Nevertheless, with our authorial divide in mind, we take up France's "attachment to the notion of auteur cinema" and its critical and historical association with the New Wave as a key premise on which French queer filmmaking emerges.

In 1998, when *Cahiers du Cinéma* hosted a roundtable of filmmakers to discuss the impact of the New Wave on their work, a discussion about Pialat's work surfaced.[35] Two relevant comments emerge from this discussion. First, Cédric Kahn expresses his frustration over Pialat's marginalization from New Wave renown: "Pialat's films are the ones that have particularly impressed me. I must not be the only one because he has an enormous influence on young filmmakers.... Why isn't he considered part of the New Wave, why did he always feel he was excluded from it?"[36] Marja Warehime, in her book *French Film Directors: Maurice Pialat,* adds to Kahn's remarks by referring to an earlier interview with the filmmaker Arnaud Desplechin, who insists, the "director who has the strongest and most consistent influence on young French filmmakers is not Jean-Luc Godard, but Maurice Pialat" (3).

In the second apposite comment, the director Noémie Lvovsky admits her admiration for Pialat's ability "to touch emotions you feel in real life" (3). At the same time, she is quick to point out (as summarized by Warehime), "one reason why Pialat never achieved the recognition given to New Wave directors [is due to] the playfulness of New Wave films" (3). Although Pialat "touched" Lvovsky at a gut level, she nonetheless took pleasure in the "light-hearted moments in Truffaut films [that] made her love the experience of seeing movies, going to the theatre, waiting for the lights to go down; seeing the images flickering on the screen" (3). Pialat's film, in Lvovsky's view, successfully reached more deeply and viscerally than Truffaut's "light-hearted" fare.

What is the aesthetic chord that strikes and resonates differently for filmmakers such as Kahn and Desplechin, Claire Denis, Catherine Breillat, Ozon, and Honoré? How does Pialat evoke a visceral and emotional response for

Lvovsky while not yielding quite the excited anticipation of a Truffaut film? What bearing does the adamant defense of Pialat's influence on young filmmakers over that of Godard shape the way we approach French queer auteurism? To follow this line of questioning, it is productive to look at Pialat's position within *and* without the New Wave movement. It is, furthermore, useful to identify the way the auteur strategically manages the discursive practices that secure his or her privileged station.

On the one hand, Warehime notes, Pialat saw himself as an auteur who—acknowledged or not—participated in methods associated with New Wave modes of production (9, 27). This is to say that he worked with inexperienced actors while relishing improvisational performance, he worked from "highly fragmented" narratives and often entered production with no detailed script or scenario, and he involved himself as a hands-on director throughout the entire filmmaking process.

On the other hand, "Pialat remained attached to a certain idea of professionalism grounded in studio filmmaking where ample budgets would allow for doing period films or undertaking ambitious projects" (26). Indeed, the "tension between Pialat's belief in the value of large-budget studio productions and his own cinematic practice, far closer to that of the New Wave, explains the contradictions of his assessment of two important predecessors: Jean Renoir and Marcel Carné" (26).[37]

What is it about Pialat's straddling of Renoir's auteurist budget-smart sensibilities and Carné's delight in studio artifice and budgets that enabled cinematic techniques that appeals to a younger generation of cinephiles and auteurs, including the young Ozon and—albeit briefly—Honoré?[38] To be sure, Pialat vociferously set the terms for the debate that continues to play out at La Fémis and elsewhere. Pialat's tantrum against the New Wave is well known: "You know, *I'm angry* (I mean it: I'm angry).... The New Wave was all about a group of friends and when you weren't part of it, you had trouble making films."[39] For all the bluster to vocally declare his outsiderness to the New Wave, he is considered by many filmmakers (as Kahn's and Desplechin's remarks confirm) as one of the tribe. What becomes clear is that Ozon's "neutrality" shares a similar effect to Pialat's outburst. Both Ozon's and Pialat's gestures announce a "(n)either/(n)or" relationship to the New Wave. Kahn's and Desplechin's commitment to Pialat's cinema, however, plays out differently than Ozon's because, like Pialat, his standing outside film history (the debates and so forth) purportedly identifies a singular and unequaled auteur. Not insignificantly, Honoré refuses to position himself "outside" the New Wave (or film history *tout court*) because to his mind such a view is untenable.

In this way, Honoré's Pialat "kick" is part and parcel of a film history in which he is deeply seeped. This is why he is candid that his New Wave affiliation, like the work of those members of the New Wave to whom he is attached, draws widely from multiple cinematic roots; it is not possible for an auteur to be divorced from his historical past. "As I see it," Honoré insists on the significance of a personal film history, "for filmmakers working in the film industry, it is nothing more than thinking about the films they saw when they were teenagers. Film is nothing but recollection" (JNCH, 183). By situating himself squarely within New Wave film history—the films he viewed as a teenager (including those of Godard *and* Pialat)—he strongly delineates his aesthetic impulses from Ozon's more ambiguous, if not strategic, self-placement outside, if not beyond, the effects of this history. To be inside film history is to admit, as Honoré does, that its aesthetic traces indelibly wash across one's work.

Of course, both Ozon's and Pialat's public posturing about creative positions must be viewed as part of a long-standing tradition in film history. It is commonplace for industry folks and other artists to manage their legacies. The role of the critic and scholar is to sift through the discursive pileup in order to identify where a kernel of accurate agency may be identified. As Sarah Projansky and Kent A. Ono argue, "the filmmaker's role as subject ... includes an examination [by critics] of the author-function, or the production of the auteur in various public discourses about a particular filmmaker and her or his film, including discourses produced by the filmmaker herself or himself."[40] Hence, Honoré's discursive formation of self is one that acknowledges and recognizes an aesthetic lineage from which French filmmakers in particular cannot escape: "That's why I get so annoyed when other directors contend they've invented something and claim they've never seen any films" (JNCH, 183). For him, the French film industry, cultural critics, and Ozon are deeply implicated by their cinematic past, their cinematic "recollection." With Honoré and Ozon, then, we are faced with two discursive versions of queer auteurism in France. Like the New Wave before them, their critical concepts and how these are written into their films bespeak distinct ways in which they envisage French queer thought, culture, and identity.

SHOW AND TELL

Our purpose with the preceding discussion is not to prove that Honoré is a "better" queer auteur than Ozon is.[41] Nor is it our intention to suggest that because Ozon looks askance at his historical relationship to the New Wave that Honoré is a more sincere queer auteur than Ozon is. Arguments of these kinds are limited and explain little about how we come to the very question about what queer cinema is in its French context. Certainly, both filmmakers' generic range is wide and far-reaching. We need only look at Ozon's aesthetic breadth as exemplified by *8 femmes* (*8 Women*, 2002), *Gouttes d'eau sur pierres brûlantes* (*Water Drops on Burning Rocks*, 2000), *Swimming Pool* (2003), *Ricky* (2009), *Potiche* (2010), and his spate of short films. Our own study demonstrates Honoré's extensive cinematic mastery.

Yet Honoré's remarks about Ozon's strength in making certain generic films and the distrust he holds for filmmakers who have no memory of their cinematic past (or declare as much) are key to understanding the terms for Honoré's cinema. *8 femmes* and *Potiche*, for example, strengthen Honoré's case since these two films stand out in Ozon's oeuvre. They are sharp, clever, and tightly directed films with an acute eye on gay sensibilities. They unabashedly nod to camp classics such as George Cukor's *The Women* (1939), Douglas Sirk's *All That Heaven Allows* (1955) and *Imitation of Life* (1959), and Demy's French musicals. By convening France's most beloved female actresses and employing heightened mise-en-scène and dialogue in his internationally successful films such as *8 femmes*, Ozon has secured a prominent place as France's gay auteur. Through this cinematic framework, the director's opaque position on the New Wave, which is mixed with his knowledge of Pialat's "radical realism," may be viewed as a cinema that seeks a more surely shaped and well-defined narrative structure. Read this way, Ozon's queer cinema returns us to the implications of "narration" and "monstration" as they are revealed in his and Honoré's films. Thus, in making this return, we are more able to specifically identify these two cinematic modes in which both directors fervently engage and debate. We discover provocative possibilities for queer cinema when we closely analyze on which cinematic mode the French queer auteur comes down. To do this, let us return to our selected binaries: Ozon/Pialat and Honoré/Godard.

A good deal of the anger that Pialat directed at the New Wave was due, in part, to the delay in making *L'enfance nue* (*Naked Childhood*, 1968), his first major film, and the financial hurdles he and the film encountered. It was Pialat's intent to complete and distribute his film around the time of the New Wave's explosive entrance in 1959. Ironically, given Pialat's rejection of the New Wave, it was Truffaut who came to the film's rescue and served as its coproducer. Importantly, Pialat's *L'enfance nue* was, Warehime informs us, "conceived as a documentary." It is a film grounded in one year of immersive research so that Pialat shaped the film's narrative "out of documentary material rather than conceiving his film in terms of a story about his characters" (32). In this way, Pialat's research methodology in preparing his film "reverses the relationship between documentary and fiction operative in Truffaut's *Les Quatre cents coups* (*The 400 Blows*, 1959)" (32). As Warehime points out, Pialat provocatively integrates the documentary approach with fictional narrative. Adam Bingham further notes that Pialat's style reveals "a director whose fierce independence, unflinchingly personal conception of cinema, and abiding emphasis on ragged, imploding families ... [elucidate] the intimate, often documentary (indeed almost home-movie) tone and mode of address in his cinema."[42]

If, as Ozon states in his interview with Schilt, his "films come from personal experiences" (157), and his "intensive" and required thesis "*research*" at La Fémis brought him directly into contact with Pialat's aesthetic drives, it is worth a brief look at how narrative and "personal experience" inform Ozon's work. The structure of Pialat's *L'enfance nue* and Truffaut's *Les quatre cents coups* is helpful when considering Honoré's and Ozon's different approaches to narration and monstration. Pialat's and Truffaut's films are informed by autobiographical details and address French youth culture from their generation, yet Honoré's and Ozon's debt to these filmmakers is to their aesthetic as much as it is to the way their storytelling draws on personal biography. By looking at Truffaut's and Pialat's first two major films, we are in a better position to identify Honoré's and Ozon's rendering of the "personal" through the cinematic, or what Bingham refers to as an "unflinchingly personal conception of cinema." The comparison, moreover, gives us access to the way that Honoré and Ozon queer their relationship to the New Wave.

Both *L'enfance nue* and *Les quatre cents coups* tell the story of a young boy who experiences abandonment—physically and emotionally—at the hands of his mother. Antoine Doinel (Jean-Pierre Léaud) in *Les quatre* and François (Michel Terrazon) in *L'enfance* are ultimately sent away from their homes and left in uncertain circumstances in the narratives' conclusions. Both films are inflected by documentary and fictional-narrative styles. The films successfully trade on the spectator's sympathies—albeit through different cinematic strokes—with the stories about rejected young boys.

Even as Ozon disregards his "cinephilic heritage," it is clear that Pialat's cinematic concepts are just as important as Truffaut's narrative fictions. *Sous le sable* (*Under the Sand*, 2000) and *Swimming Pool* evoke Pialat's documentary-ness that we see not only in *L'enfance nue* but also in *Nous ne vieillirons pas ensemble* (*We Won't Grow Old Together*, 1972), and *À nos amours* (1983); at the same time, Truffaut's male-centered bildungsromans hover over many of Ozon's films.[43] Romanticized boys searching for inner truth through art can be found with Antoine Doinel and his adoration of Balzac as well as, for instance, Ozon's Claude and his turn to Montaigne in *Dans la maison*. The same can also be said for Honoré's searching boys in *Dans Paris*, *Les chansons d'amour*, and *La belle personne* (it is a young woman who is the central character in *La belle personne*, but the boys that surround her are endlessly looking to art to provide meaning in life). All four filmmakers place us in the realm of French youth abandoned to varying degrees by immediate family members. In short, we are in the realm of unsettled queer youth and the search to satisfy desire. At the same time, a vital distinction can be made between Ozon's and Honoré's generic fusion of Truffaut's and Pialat's aestheticized narratives. As our book proceeds, the specific contours of Honoré's engagement with his cinematic grandfathers will become clear. For now, and to establish the comparison, we highlight Ozon's queer cinema as it makes use of New Wave tradition. If Pialat's "character-engaged" situations do not "[conceive] of his films in terms of a story" and instead focus on moments of unpredictability, elliptical narrative events, circumstantial entrances and exits, and unresolved terms for character relations, Ozon's Pialat-esque films (as those noted earlier) are structured with narratives that deliver transparent and clear trajectories and narrative closure. His "neutral" stake in the New Wave notwithstanding, Ozon is truer to Truffaut's New Wave cinematic principles than he may be willing to admit. To paraphrase and invert Warehime's description of Pialat's documentary-first/fiction-second method, we can offer the inverse when describing Ozon's style: Ozon's films are conceived out of story first and then treated with documentary-style overtures.

To demonstrate this, we spotlight Ozon's film *Dans la maison* in order to set a stage that allows us to distinguish and analyze the weight given to cinematic showing when queer auteurs tell stories about queer youth. The film directs us back to the intermingled "relationship between documentary and fiction" as we see it unfold in *Les quatre cents coups* and *L'enfance nue*. While *Sous le sable* and *Swimming Pool* recall Pialat's aesthetic turns—contemplative and mannered long takes, synchronous dialogue, comprehensible emotional arcs, simple but elegant cinematography, lack of jump cuts or disruptive editing—a film such as *Dans la maison* highlights a key difference: Ozon's cinema is narrative driven, with conclusive endings. Pialat's films end with far more open-ended possibilities. In this regard, Honoré aligns himself with Pialat's complex narrative ambiguities.

Dans la maison is thus particularly useful when comparing Honoré's and Ozon's queer cinema because, on the one hand, it works through matters of youth and desire. On the other hand, it is a film that investigates cinematic form itself as a mode to express the terms for desire. It is a relevant film for our discussion about Honoré because it highlights the inter(con)textual dynamic that occurs between questions of (cinematic) art and young people's desire *to indeed desire*. The thematic intersection is a centerpiece for both Honoré and Ozon. The direction the filmmakers take to make the point, however, varies widely.

Dans la maison follows the journey of a young high-school boy, Claude (Ernst Umhauer), from unfortunate lower-middle-class home circumstances (disabled father, mother who abandons them) who seeks an understanding of self through his creative writing. Tutored by his French literature teacher, M. Germain (Fabrice Luchini), Claude develops the skills to write a work of literature. The project on which Claude embarks is based on a calculated relationship to his high-school chum Rapha Artole (Bastien Ughetto) and his family. Claude, in his bid to research a "normal" French middle-class family, finagles himself a role as Rapha's math tutor. He becomes intimately involved in the family's everyday lives, eventually developing an erotic relationship with Rapha's mother. The film follows Claude's engagement with the family and his subsequent penning of it into literary form. For M. Germain, Claude's sociological experiment with the family is perfect fodder for writing since M. Germain insists that good literature involves "peeping through the keyhole." Recalling Pialat's "research" prior to making *L'enfance*, M. Germain believes that observing the everyday lives of ordinary people ideally serves in the crafting of great literature. The job of a good writer, however, is to capitalize on the banal conflicts of the everyday by aestheticizing those conflicts through dramatic "problem solving." In other words, documenting people's lives (through the keyhole) only becomes literature when it is turned into art.

Bundling the creative process within the film's diegesis, Ozon's narrative moves among the "real time" of M. Germain's tutoring of Claude, M. Germain's relationship with his wife, Jeanne (Kristin Scott Thomas), and Claude's developing relationship with Rapha and his family. As the story proceeds, the idea of the "real" is ambiguously marked since the oral telling folds events into one another as part of Claude and M. Germain's creative process in which the "real" is turned into fiction. By the film's end, M. Germain is forced to leave teaching because, in order to help Claude expend his energies on writing and not tutoring Rapha, he had stolen a colleague's math test so that Claude's mentee passed the exam. Jeanne leaves him after she and Claude have a sexual affair (or so it is implied). Finally, M. Germain is left sitting alone on a park bench, where he looks out onto an apartment complex. Claude soon arrives on the scene, and they direct their attention to the apartments. As they gaze onto the dwellings, they conjure possible narratives about the lives of the characters behind the windows. Their narratives differ, yet both are plausible given the multiple actions we see before us. As the camera pulls back, we see that what lie before Claude and M. Germain are a series of stages, or *Rear Window*–like projections, in which numerous scenarios are displayed. For Ozon, every window tells a story, but the telling of the story demands precision on the part of the artist.

Dans la maison foregrounds two central differences in Ozon's and Honoré's queer filmmaking: cinematic address and cinematic "narration" (in the Gaudreaultean sense). As regards combined and applied elements to their filmmaking, both Honoré and Ozon are committed to the active participation of their viewer.

"The idea," as Honoré sees it, "is to push the viewer to stop deluding him- or herself about the story or the language and to get back to the role of the spectator who is faced with forms and that *it's the form that creates interest and reflection*" (JNCH, 181; emphasis added). Ozon is arguably more inviting and less challenging in the way he perceives his audience: "Fortunately there is no such thing as a 'typical' spectator. Some of them understand everything that I wanted to say, and in talking to others I may realize that they didn't see the same things at all. And the film gets away from you, so you could say that there are as many different versions of a film as there are spectators" (quoted in Schilt, 167).

Ozon's claims about his audience are clearly announced in *Dans la maison*, in which Jeanne serves as the spectator's surrogate. Throughout the film, she listens intently to Claude's tale as her husband relays new drafts of his student's writing. She thus gives pause to *Dans la maison*'s narrative events by adding and suggesting possible areas for character and story development. Jeanne and M. Germain banter about the relevance of plot lines, the ethics of what is told, and the best outcomes for Claude's tale. Jeanne is an ideal representative of Ozon's concept of the spectator insofar as she serves as the spectator's internal "voice" that poses questions while watching film ("what if?" "why is this happening?" and so on). Moreover, her discussion with her husband informs the pedagogical and aesthetic terms under which M. Germain addresses Claude. As the manager for a local art gallery, Jeanne struggles with the question of art. Is it a commodity to be packaged for middle-class patrons? Or should art remain pure in essence and form?

The aesthetic tension in the art gallery boils over at one point about what Jeanne should exhibit. How abstract or representational should the art be in a provincial art gallery in France? M. Germain—the aesthetic pedagogue—finds her concerns boring. At one point, when reiterating the importance of narrative conflict and problem solving in writing, he scolds Claude for turning his sociological experiment into a Pasolini film (*Teorema*, one presumes). In another context, Jeanne reaffirms her husband's claim as she confronts submissions to her gallery by artists who, as she sees it, have the inability to distinguish between "presence and representation." In short, as M. Germain (Ozon?) sees it, distinct form must follow strategically aestheticized content. Pasolini is too much about "presence" and not enough about "representation." *Dans la maison* is thus instructive for sharpening the contrasting aesthetics between Honoré's and Ozon's queer auteur practices. *Dans la maison* is not Pasolini's queer cinema. And it is not Honoré's. Seen this way, we can say that Ozon's cinema is weighted toward a narrational mode of cinema, while, we argue, Honoré's cinema strongly emphasizes a cinema of monstration. Simply put, Ozon relies a good deal on *talk*.

Exceptions exist (the short film *X2000* [1998] is the most obvious), but *Dans la maison* is representative of Ozon's dialogue-driven cinema—even when song is involved—which is critical for his narrational impulses. The short films *Scènes de lit, Un lever de rideau* (*A Curtain Raiser,* 2006), and *Regarde la mer,* as well as the features *Swimming Pool* and *Potiche* are exemplary in this regard. In fact, *Dans la maison*'s tale depends on and expressly relays a narrative in which communicating ideas aesthetically requires *talking through* those very ideas. Earlier, Ozon described his film *Ricky* as one that "*talks* about the relationship to a child." His declaration that his films "talk about" something succinctly locates an aesthetic break between his and Honoré's filmmaking. Honoré prefers to show, rather than to tell.

QUEER ENOUGH?

Ozon's comments on French auteurship notwithstanding, his filmmaking is indebted to a cinephilic heritage that derives, in part, from the "intensive research" of Pialat that he developed while a student at La Fémis. Undoubtedly—and precisely because of his interactions at La Fémis—Ozon found himself engaged with New Wave concepts associated with Truffaut, Godard, Chabrol, Rivette, and Rohmer. Like many strong French filmmakers, Ozon's generic and aesthetic practices mark his auteurist signature. We have suggested that the stature Ozon occupies in film scholarship, as a French queer auteur, depends on a cinematic mode of "narration." While his films are not the trite or oversimplified narratives encountered in Martineau and Ducastel's films, the "queer intrusions" identified by Schilt in Ozon's films *represent* queer *as such* through digestible narrative form. Therefore, we are interested in the way Honoré's films are less easily digested, how they are more concerned with "presence" and less with "representation."

Throughout this work, then, we emphasize the implications for Honoré's queer cinema and its turn to *or* troubling of fait accompli cinematic narrative. Honoré's queer auteurist cinema emphasizes, instead, "monstration" as its formal centerpiece and, in this way, calls to mind Peter Wollen's notes on Godard's concept of "film as a process of writing in images, rather than a representation of the world."[44] If film is a "process of writing"—and Derrida not unimportantly considers "cinematography" as a significant form of *écriture*—how might this process be filtered as critical to queer filmmaking?[45]

Following Derrida's cue, Lee Edelman offers "homographesis" as a dynamic queer concept of writing that we, in turn, extend to cinematic writing. If, explains Edelman, "homosexuality is constituted as a category . . . that *must be represented as determinate, as legibly identifiable,*" it is constituted as such through writing.[46] "Writing," however, "though it marks or describes those differences upon which the specification of identity depends, works simultaneously ... to 'de-scribe,' efface, or undo identity by framing difference as the misrecognition of a 'différance' whose negativity, whose purely relational articulation, calls into question the possibility of any positive presence or discrete unity" (10). Homographesis posed as *cinematic écriture*, therefore, suggests a queer cinema that serves a "double operation," one that "[codifies] identities in its labor of disciplinary inscription" while, at the same time, is "resistant to that categorization, intent on *de*-scribing the identities that order has so oppressively *in*scribed" (10). Homographesis, Edelman posits, "conserves what it contests" (14).

Honoré's cinema, it may be said then, is *cinematic homographesis* to the extent that, while it "conserves" its cinephilic heritage to the New Wave and elsewhere, it simultaneously and queerly "contests" its very terms. In this light, Honoré's emphasis on film *as showing* is crucial to his queer filmmaking because it *de*-scribes rather than *in*scribes once and for all. Honoré's filmmaking queers "disciplinary inscription." It uses cinematic technique—*cinema-graphesis*—not so much to offer a "representation of the world"; instead, Honoré's cinema reveals an imaginative process of writing in queer cinematic images.

The New Wave's historical imprimatur, as it is for international filmmaking, cannot be underestimated for Honoré's critical assessment of and aesthetic interests in cinema. But as the "grandchild" within the genealogy of the movement's founders and the "son" of the gay French filmmakers André Téchiné and Patrice Chéreau (as Honoré identifies himself) and the gay brother of François Ozon, Honoré's "familial" response can be seen as both an embrace of and resistance to his cinematic heritage (conserving what it contests). To simultaneously embrace and resist one's family is, in fact, a central theme that runs throughout his films. And by assuming the status of queer offspring to his cinematic forebears, he promptly puts himself at odds with contemporary French filmmakers, critics, and spectators. Our discussion heretofore amply indicates the conflicted position that Honoré holds. To Honoré's mind, much "contemporary French cinema that is prized at home and abroad does not correspond to [his] taste."[47] Since he holds the New Wave in high regard while strongly criticizing contemporary French cinema "prized at home and abroad," Honoré (as critic and artist) is viewed as derivative, indeed, "at home and abroad."[48]

And yet Honoré relishes the barbs made by his critics who chastise his cinematic tastes. To bear the brunt of such criticism is, in many ways of course, a rite of passage when carrying the mantle of the New Wave and the French auteur. As his predecessors had done before him, Honoré prods his critics with his aesthetic choices, formal techniques, and controversial subject matter. His eroticizing of the family unit, his representation of women, and his heavy use of cinematic quotation are not always regarded favorably. On counts of both form and content, his films trigger robust and, to put it gently, varied responses.

On the release of *Les chansons,* the critics weighed in with what is now representative for the reception of an Honoré film. While Peter Bradshaw at the *Guardian* declares, "[Honoré's] New-Wave-ish mannerisms make me break out in a rash," Thomas Dawson at the BBC finds *Les chansons* "an emotionally affecting work."[49] Although *Les chansons* sometimes "exceeds [the director's] grasp," Lee Hill in *Vertigo* also applauds Honoré's "unapologetic embrace" of the New Wave; with *Les chansons,* he—like Truffaut, Rivette, Demy, and Eustache before him—gains "prominence as an auteur sharing the preoccupations of art, love, and death."[50]

"Still, for all [*Le chansons'*] imperfections," A. O. Scott writes in the *New York Times,* the film "is a worthy and intriguing experiment," while Kevin Thomas in the *Los Angeles Times* calls the film "beguiling and bittersweet"; it "strikes a strongly contemporary note in its calm acceptance of the fluidity of desire and emotion."[51] In the *Village Voice,* Honoré is recognized for his "talent," but "*Love Songs* adds up to considerably less than the sum of its [New Wave] references." Ultimately, "we're left with little more than a pile of celluloid naval lint" and a film that "stays as icy to the touch as Julie's premature corpse."[52]

In France, the criticism ranges widely. The reviewer for avoir-alire.com refers to Honoré as an "uneven but endearing filmmaker" who, although he "revives the spirit of the New Wave" in *Les chansons,* manages to create a "funny but sad love story that never ends." The film, the reviewer concludes, is "as exciting as a dour, politically correct sitcom."[53] Elsewhere, the *Chronic'art* critic finds the film's references to Eustache and Demy "predictable," while a "Godardian superego" permeates the production's "inert" story line.[54] *Le Monde*'s Thomas Sontinel offers a friendlier perspective: "Like all musicals, *Les Chansons d'amour* demands a lot from the viewer and the actors. It is necessary to overcome that uncertain moment when the characters stop talking and start singing, especially since listening to the lyrics ... by Alex Beaupain is essential to understanding the characters. Beyond all this, we enter a movie where love songs mingle with love itself."[55]

Although scholars recognize Honoré's nod to the New Wave, their critical attention more generally focuses on his films' representation of gender and sexuality.[56] Ginette Vincendeau charges in her review of *Dans Paris,* for instance, that the film is "a game of spot the reference."[57] The review targets what she sees as Honoré's aesthetic playfulness and its unbroken link to New Wave masculinism. As such, to "spot the reference" in *Dans Paris* coincides with negative representations of women that shore up "sensitive male subjectivity in which women are inadequate mothers, neurotic girlfriends or easygoing playmates."[58] Following Vincendeau's critique of *Dans Paris*, Nick Rees-Roberts argues that Honoré "reproduces the troubling sexual politics of the New Wave through much male soul-searching and fraternal bonding."[59] He further suggests that the sexual relations between women in *Les chansons* are "reduced to the status of 'sister love' and whimsical experimentation," while lesbianism is "disparagingly" rendered in the film (111). Rees-Roberts concludes that *Les chansons* merely "borrows more of the normative politics of heterosexual experimentation outlined in *Ma mère* in which [Isabelle] Huppert and [Joana] Preiss's 'lesbian' sex scene was for male eyes only" (111). On this count, in particular, we challenge Rees-Roberts's contention in our discussion of Honoré's film.

From these perspectives, we see that Honoré poses not only aesthetic unease; he is politically a moving target. Hence, David Calhoun in *Time Out* calls *Les chansons* a "simple failure" in which the film's "implausible" story line with "dreadful" songs and its "portrayal of both death and romance" reaffirms French characters as caricatures. They are "conceited, lazy, depraved, and representative of all that is wrong with France." When Honoré inserts a poster of then-president Nicholas Sarkozy, he "plays right into his hands."[60] In other words, although Honoré publicly stated his distaste for Sarkozy's "crudeness and stupidity," his French tales are perceived as milquetoast cinema that, because they are not overtly political one way or another, actually embrace banal national ideals about romance and French identity.[61] Later, we consider Honoré's political stakes in French culture and how he acts on "the political."

And while we highlight reviews dedicated to *Les chansons* and *Dans Paris*, a similar pattern of critique recurs for most Honoré films.[62] Our analysis addresses these criticisms and reconsiders the implications for what have been critiqued as Honoré's "sensitive male subjectivity," "male soul-searching," "[reduction] to sister love," and "normative politics." On the one hand, we argue that Honoré's cinematic aesthetics—in particular, on the count of homage or "spot the reference"—are a formal device that requires complicated responses when considering his portrayal of women, family, and "romance." On the other hand, Honoré's relationship to the "political" is of a piece with the double bind that Fassbinder and Pasolini faced.

Since Honoré relishes his *cineaste maudit* status and takes pleasure in rebuking criticisms levied against his filmmaking, it is worth querying why disparate accounts of and responses to his films take place. Honoré, nevertheless, persists: "When I saw the attacks levied against *Les chansons d'amour* or *Dans Paris*, I decided, 'Okay, let's go on sticking their noses in it!' And *La belle personne* came specifically from that" (JNCH, 180). Honoré's "sticking" it to his critics does not involve simply mirroring Godardian technique. His queer narratives, tightly navigated through precise cinematic form, challenge those who find fault with his representation of women or those who break into a "rash" for any other reason when watching his films. A second critical line of inquiry is necessary, therefore, one that raises the stakes on Honoré's homage to a particular cinematic heritage and, at the same time, its relationship to the history of certain queer auteurs.

Homage—a commonplace gesture in auteurist cinema—requires rethinking when studying Honoré. For him, homage is a critical tool as much as it is an erotic encounter, to the extent that it is an incestuous cinephilic encounter. Here, cinematic quotation is something more than an echo. In what way is homage a particularly queer practice? And if it is commonplace in auteur cinema to enact this gesture, what are the implications for Honoré's turn to homage? First, it is necessary to identify those to whom Honoré offers cinematic gratitude. Jean-Luc Godard's radical shifts in cinematic form and Jacques Demy's musicalized-incest narratives are central to Honoré's queer homage, as are the "double operations" at work in Pasolini's and Fassbinder's films. And while Godard's import registers throughout this book, Honoré's queer French "godfather," Demy, requires detailed attention. Through Demy, Godard's significance for Honoré is seen more critically. Additionally, by attending to Demy, we are in a position to consider the aesthetic and political "double bind" in which Fassbinder and Pasolini found themselves and which Honoré now confronts.

... AND THE DOUBLE BIND

If Michel Marie's invaluable study rigorously recounts the ideologies and practices that gave rise to the New Wave, his analysis only briefly and hastily refers to Demy and his politicized marginalization (75). Rodney Hill addresses this oft-made omission and argues for Demy's vital place in the New Wave "school."[63] Yet Hill's canonizing ignores the queer place that Demy occupies in French New Wave aesthetics and culture. Ann Duggan's *Queer Enchantments* goes some way in correcting the de-queered position that critics usually assign to Demy. Concentrating on his "fairy-tale films," Duggan suggests, "Demy takes what initially may appear to be utopian heterosexual fantasies and brings out their internal tensions, at times turning them into dystopian tales."[64] And though the critics noted earlier who write for the popular press acknowledge Demy's influence on Honoré's work, the silence maintained by scholars about Demy's queerness—from his choice of aesthetics to his death by AIDS—dilutes his significant contribution to cinema.

INTRODUCTION

What is it about Demy's filmmaking that is so queer yet, for many critics so *un*remarkable as such?[65] Indeed, Honoré does not miss the queer connection to the director with whom he "became quickly fond ... definitely because of the gay angle" and the "queer spirit" that Demy's films invoke. For Honoré, the "queer spirit" pivots on the director's cinematic aesthetics, his death from AIDS, and a filmmaking that concentrates on familial erotics (JNCH, 181).

In short, Demy's queer spirit can be found in several elements that tantalize the queer filmmaker and spectator. Honoré is undoubtedly seduced by his elder's participation with glamorous French film stars (especially Catherine Deneuve, who later contributed to her own cinematic genealogy with her daughter, Chiara Mastroianni—both of whom appear in Honoré's films). Demy's uniquely queer stylization of the musical genre infuses an incestuous sensuality that is critical to films such as *Peau d'âne* (*The Donkey's Skin*, 1970) and *Trois places pour le 26* (1988). To be sure, the gay kiss included in the snazzy musical *Parking* (1985) seals the deal for a queer filmmaker. Honoré draws himself into Demy's oeuvre by exploring his films in such a way that is as critically involved as it is erotically gratifying. In this regard, Honoré's cinematic contribution to film history—*through film*— provides a critical lens onto Demy's filmmaking and Demy's queerness.

Honoré, identifying with his queer elder who he lost at the moment his film career began, experiences—in "queer spirit"—an aesthetically and erotically formed familial connection with Demy. Demy's aesthetic interests established a creative distance and, certainly, a distinctiveness from his more androcentric-inclined colleagues in the New Wave circle.[66] In fact, Demy's identification with the so-called Left Bank auteurs from the period (Agnès Varda, Alain Resnais) kept him at a remove from the auteur boys' club associated with the "Right Bank" (Godard, Truffaut, Chabrol).[67] Like Honoré's twenty-first-century historical relationship to New Wave luminaries and his aesthetic distance from his contemporaries, Demy's apartness was due in no small part to his queer sensibilities, sensibilities that did not always go down well—politically—with many in his immediate creative circles and with film critics more generally. His queer sensibility clashed head-on with left-wing critics following the events of May 1968. When *Une chambre en ville* was released in 1982, Demy's queer filmmaking style was considered a disservice to what Alain Badiou noted at the time was a "crisis of Marxism."[68] Filtering the workers' movement through opera, according to Badiou, Demy reduced labor and laborers to "a nostalgia for the 1950s" through "spiffy" formalism (64, 65). Queer aesthetics such as Demy's were not viewed as politically viable. Although not accused of failed or faulty Marxism, Honoré (as seen earlier in the comments about *Les chansons d'amour* on gender and sexuality) finds himself in similar ideological and aesthetic kerfuffles in feminist and queer criticism.

Yet such controversy about aesthetic form and "the political" is precisely where we usefully return to Elsaesser's concept of the "double bind" and from where the queer auteur emerges. In the book *Fassbinder's Germany: History, Identity, Subject*, Elsaesser argues that Fassbinder's films "complicate the nature of the bond that exists between the screen, the characters, and the spectator."[69] This is the case, Elsaesser posits, because Fassbinder not only "[reappraised] the ideals, but also the failures of 'May 68.'" By doing so, Fassbinder demolished "the idea of false consciousness, at least insofar as it implies as its opposite the possibility of true consciousness" (54). In refusing to assert "political slogans of the day" (54), which prompted criticism that he "abandoned his heroes to their hopelessness" (34), Fassbinder presented films that "cohere in their formal and narrative structure around the tighter and tighter knots of mutual exploitation" (34). Through this cinematic model, Fassbinder demonstrated the way militant voices from the "left" and from the "right" only reinforced the "knot" of culture-industry ideological sameness. Fassbinder rejected simple dialectic form.

Pasolini confronted criticism along the same lines during the height of 1960s political activism. "Ignoring ideology and dialectics," Naomi Greene writes, "Pasolini had 'escaped,' [the critics] charged, into an ahistorical, aestheticized world of Absolutes—a world where Death, Sacredness, and Myth ruled supreme."[70] Just as Fassbinder was to do soon after him, Pasolini defended his "apolitical stance" and "denounced the very concept of 'committed' art." For Pasolini, Greene points out, art containing a political message "was nothing more than a new form of 'socialist realism' promulgated by 'left-wing fascists.' . . . He argued polemically against an overtly political cinema that 'vulgarizes and simplifies problems.' . . . [A demand for such films exists only within] neocapitalism that exalts action and usefulness above all else, by destroying culture and demanding militant art [and] only furthers neocapitalist or bourgeois values" (168–69).

And like Fassbinder, Pasolini's cinematic form confounded critics who insisted on clear and concise characters and narrative structure. In his refusal to be easily "digested" by the consuming public in a "false democracy," Pasolini preferred "formal invention (not formalist)" (quoted in Greene, 171). Pasolini, through cinematic aesthetics and theoretical writings, clearly expresses the "hope that the 'myth and technical awareness of form' might enable artists to effect a 'possible' revolution in bourgeois culture" (171). If a "message" is to be located in Pasolini's work, it takes shape as a *cinematic message* that is "unconsumable" as such. Supplying "the" message is duplicitous. From Pasolini's point of view, "young militants ... think they are breaking the [ideological] circle, [when] they are only reinforcing it" (quoted in Greene, 169).

Perhaps not surprisingly, those who chastised both Pasolini and Fassbinder for their problematic political stances also accused them of paying too much attention to Freud and not enough to Marx.[71] To the critics' minds, the filmmakers eschewed their political allegiance to class issues and embraced, instead, a perverse engagement with middle-class individualism and familial erotics. The critical move to marshal Pasolini, Fassbinder, and Demy as perverse formalist Freudians rather than didactic Marxists served the purpose of marking their filmmaking—narrative *and* formal structure—as less than committed or, to use the term leveled against Pasolini and Fassbinder, decadent. Honoré occupies a homologous critical reception. The "double bind" he faces, however, unwinds in relationship to feminist and queer politics, or what might be termed, more generally, identity politics. If Demy, Fassbinder, and Pasolini were explicitly assaulted for their un-Marxist cinema and implicitly for their disturbing accounting of bourgeois heteronormativity, Honoré is accused of backward-looking representations of women and "heteronormative" displays of sexuality that are said to merely recapitulate "the heterocentric imperative of Eustache's *La maman et la putain* (1973)" (Rees-Roberts, 111).

If the double bind is predicated on a containment of aesthetics and politics within ideological repetition—a *fort/da* effect—then the four queer auteurs here fully recognized the inevitable limitations associated with political slogans in film. For them, queer cinema rubs against cultural and political assumptions that are framed as "correct" or "wrong." Queer cinematic form challenges such assertions and their rationale at every turn. Honoré addresses his critics:

> I try to find more poetic answers. I'm not someone who lives in a bubble, but I wouldn't ever at any moment want my films to deliver a message. I'd feel like I was dealing in propaganda. I really think that what makes me sick the most in film is when a director takes over. I try to make films in which I delegate my power as much as possible. I really have a hard time with directors, especially French directors, with whom—from my perspective—I only see them taking over, either the actors or the spectators or the self-righteous approach.... I think that to send a self-righteous message by putting a white person, a black person, and a yellow person together to show your antiracist politics and open-mindedness is an aesthetic vision of absolute stupidity and absolute ugliness. (JNCH, 199)

Honoré's response to his critics echoes Pasolini's: "[They] think they are breaking the [ideological] circle, [when] they are only reinforcing it."

MAKING A CINEMATIC BED

A terrific comforting nostalgia / Unreels in us; celluloid memory invades us; / Our flesh is unraveled by inches.

Parker Tyler, "Ode to Hollywood"

Honoré's critical reception, the "double bind," resides in the shadows of a controversial and deeply resonant issue that haunted the filmmaking of Demy, Fassbinder, and Pasolini.[72] It is an issue that Honoré stresses as *the* "family issue": "There is a type of sensuality within the family that interests me. I have this idea that sexuality is a family issue. It's something that is taken care of without questioning" (JNCH, 178). Again, and moreover, "the family is a privileged locus for talking about one's sexuality rather than a place where one defines one's sexuality. Obviously this is exactly the opposite of what most people think" (JNCH, 190). While Honoré is not overtly accused of being a Freudian, as his predecessors once were, his concentration on the "incest taboo" moves him into proximity with his fellow queers.

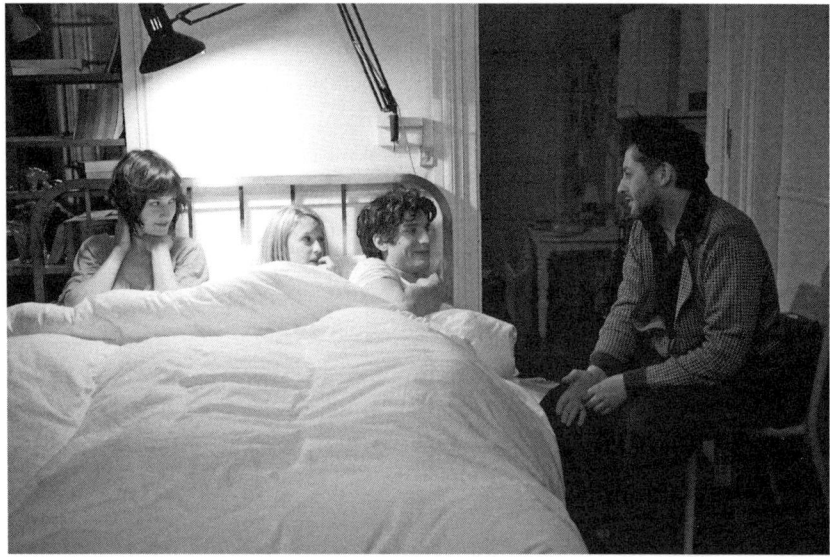

1. Christophe Honoré shares *Les chansons d'amour*'s all-important bed with his cast: Clotilde Hesme (Alice), Ludivine Sagnier (Julie), and Garrel (Ismaël).

INTRODUCTION

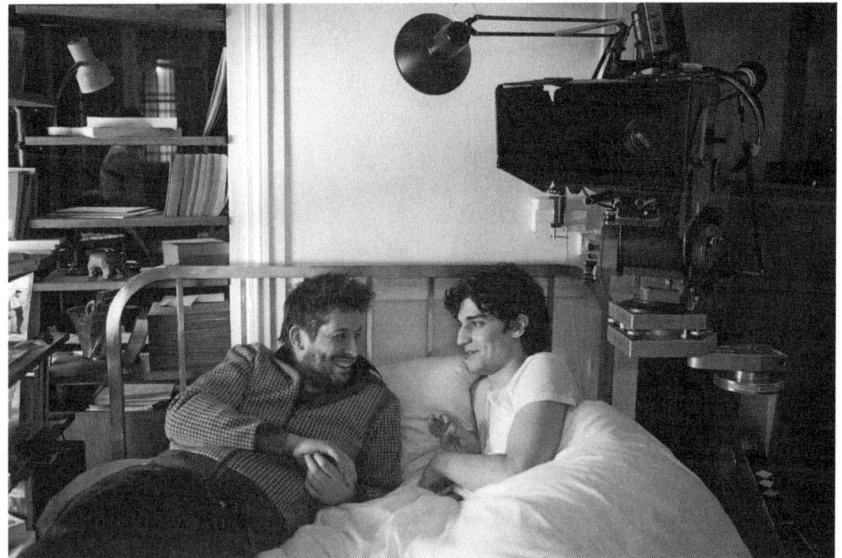

2. Christophe Honoré on the set of *Les chansons d'amour* with Louis Garrel.

When Alexander Kluge remarked that Fassbinder's *Beware of a Holy Whore* (1971) was about incest, Fassbinder replied, "All my movies are about incest."[73] Given that not every film by Fassbinder is a tale about incest per se, what does Fassbinder's response to Kluge suggest? Elsewhere, when interviewed about *Oedipus Rex* (1967, a film in which Oedipus has sex with his mother, Jocasta, even *after* being made aware of their familial relationship), Pasolini declares, "I have felt my love for my mother very, very deeply, and all my work is influenced by this, but it is an influence whose origin is very deep down inside me and, as I said, rather outside history."[74] Closer to home, Demy has been noted for his "fascination with incest." Scholars and reviewers alike frequently comment on this topic when reviewing Demy's films.[75] Demy gets something of a pass, however, when dealing with incest in his fairy-tale films. Without hesitation, incest is mentioned without much bother when *Peau d'âne* (1970) is described. The topic is buoyantly pointed to, then collapsed into the film's aesthetics, in which "a delightfully and deliciously colourful fairy tale" is told.[76]

It is difficult to know to what extent Pasolini's Greek mythological tale or Demy's fairy-tale cinema provide cover for the filmmakers' profound interest in incest. If Fassbinder is right that all his films deal with incest, we may give purchase to his claim by reading Pasolini's "very, very deeply" felt love for his mother as an articulation of the unconscious. What is at hand is how we see the way

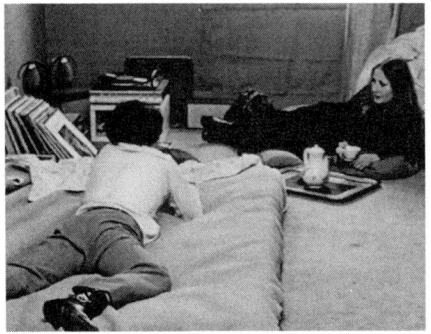 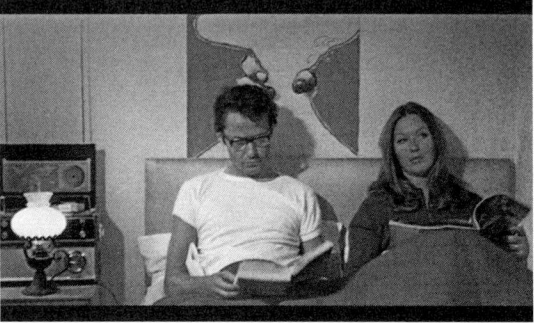

3. "Films teach you how to live, how to make a bed." *La maman et la putain* (Jean Eustache, 1973).

4. *2 ou 3 choses que je sais d'elle* (Jean-Luc Godard, 1967).

queer auteurs reckon with incest, with the unconscious, in all their films. How do we see it? How is incest, the memory of familial sensuality, aestheticized and made cinematic? To reckon with the issue, Honoré makes a cinematic bed, a family bed that returns a cinematic homage.

Much of the activity that occurs in Jean Eustache's *La maman et la putain*—a much favored work by Honoré—takes place in a bed. While Alexandre (Jean-Pierre Léaud) lies across the bed of his lover, Marie (Bernadette Lafont), he tells his newfound lover, Veronika (Françoise Lebrun), "Film teaches you how to live, how to make a bed." The bed as presented in Eustache's film is also a well-rehearsed cinematic trope for filmmakers such as Truffaut and Godard. For the scenes in which we see performers in bed, the camera setup used by these New Wave filmmakers often echoes spectator positions, seated side by side at a movie theater. As such, the bed is as much a cinematic experience as the movie theater is equal to the comforts of a bed. In French cinematic beds, then, bodies intimately connect—intellectually, politically, pleasurably, and erotically. "Films" do indeed "teach you how to live, how to make a bed."

Honoré notes, expressing what he has learned from cinematic beds of the past, "From a cinematic standpoint, I seem to deal with beds as if they were dining room tables" (JNCH, 191). People talk, think, watch/read, smoke cigarettes, and make love in Honoré's bed-tables. The bed is the place where visceral encounters are consumed, digested (or not), and expressed. Action in Honoré's beds involves an unusual amount of discussion, sometimes through song, about bodily functions. Moreover, the activity in Honoré's bed-space often hinges on an anticipated, if uncertain, future that, at the same time, uneasily swings on memory and unexpected loss. We will see such spatial/temporal intimacies

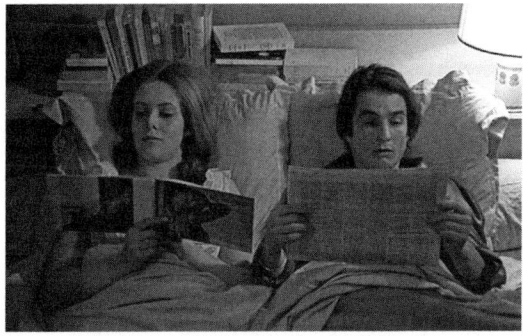 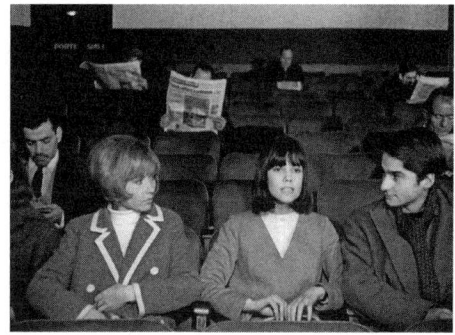

5. *Domicile conjugal* (François Truffaut, 1970).   6. *Masculin féminin* (Jean-Luc Godard, 1966).

between brothers in *Dans Paris*, the nuclear family in *Les chansons*, and the lovers in *La belle personne*. The cinematic imbrication of space *and* time is essential to Honoré's aesthetic concept and the queer incest we encounter in his films.

How might Honoré's cinema demonstrate time saturating space and/or space saturating time? The question is not new for filmmakers and film theoreticians. It remains a driving force when considering cinematic aesthetics. But it is also a pressing matter for queer theorists. With cinema, Jean Mitry observes, "as in real life, only the *present* exists: a present, however, which is forever looking forward to the *future*. What we *actually* perceive in this recording of the future as it *develops*, of the present as it occurs, is nothing more than space, space in motion. And we are unable to perceive its duration because it is the same as our perception, developing and changing with it—with us."[77] Just as Mitry insists on the cinema's spatial/temporal flow as the crucible through which the spectator's "real life" transforms with the events on the screen, Eve Kosofsky Sedgwick calls on queer readers/spectators not to neglect the "ecological field" of the "rich dimensions of space."[78] For her, the emphasis on time in queer theory has short-changed a vibrant aspect to queer experience. "When [Judith] Butler draws on [Esther] Newton's work [*Mother Camp*] at the end of *Gender Trouble*," Sedgwick recounts, "the ecological attention to space collapses in favor of a temporal emphasis on gender as 'stylized repetition' and 'social temporality'":

> With the loss of its spatiality, however, the internally complex field of drag performance suffers a seemingly unavoidable simplification and reification. In fact, I think this loss of dimension may explain why so many readers, wrongly, interpreted Butler's discussion as prescribing

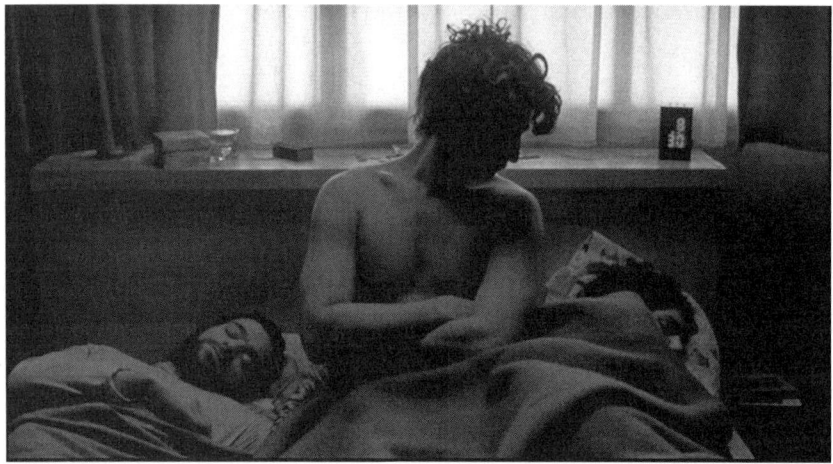

7. *Dans Paris.*

> a simplistic voluntarity. Although temporal and spatial thinking are never really alternative to each other, I've consistently tried in *Touching Feeling* to push back against an occupational tendency to underattend to the rich dimension of space. (9)

Sedgwick's reading of Newton's work on drag performance within specific venues foregrounds "the strengths of [its] spatially precise analysis" because it illuminates "an extra alertness to the multisided interactions among people 'beside' each other in a room" (9). A cinematic bed is thus made by bringing Sedgwick and Mitry together, by putting them "beside" each other (like spectators at a movie theater). To paraphrase Sedgwick, a queer cinematic ecological field emerges in which bodies intermingle and navigate the contours of space and time.

When, as we noted earlier, Honoré states that the idea behind his cinema is to "push the viewer to stop deluding him- or herself about the story or the language and to get back to the role of the spectator who is faced with forms and that it's the form that creates interest and reflection" (JNCH, 181), he invites the spectators who, in their role as spectators, sit side by side in the cinema and sit *as well* "beside" the performers on the screen. Honoré's cinematic bed gives way to "presentification" (to borrow Mitry's term), in which a queer time *and* space enfolds; it is sort of *a queer se dérouler* that only the cinema enables. In the epigraph that opened this section, Parker Tyler aptly describes this cinematic sensation: "A terrific comforting nostalgia / Unreels in us; celluloid memory invades us; / Our flesh is unraveled by inches."[79] While cinema places us in the time of

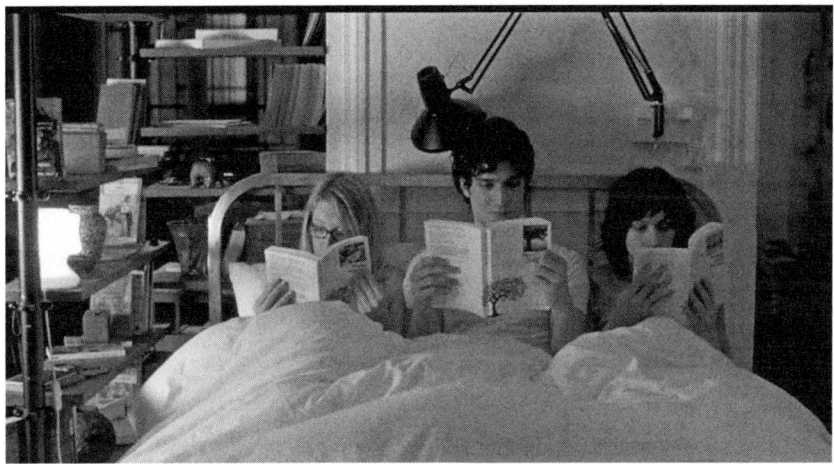

8. *Les chansons d'amour.*

the film's fiction, it does so to the extent that its "objective duration," Mitry continues, "exists only within the permanence of my relationship with the world.... We can perceive duration—or *feel its effects*—only when it has been *experienced*, i.e., when we consider a past reality from the mobility of an action in which we are involved."[80] Honoré's intermingled cinematic *involves* us through form and content that, in turn, unrolls temporal *and* spatial queer mobility so that, as Tyler tells it, our "flesh is unraveled by inches."

As we move toward our analyses of Honoré's films, and the queer spatial/temporal mobility facilitated by cinematic form and content, we note three themes that Honoré foregrounds in his cinematic beds: (1) Eros and Thanatos, (2) knowledge and choice, and (3) cinematic technique and its relationship to the body. First, Eros and Thanatos, erotic desire and death, are inseparable components for all Honoré's films. Although we concentrate here on the trilogy, *Ma mère, Homme au bain,* and *Les bien-aimés* also draw their energy from the Eros/Thanatos tension in which the bed serves as the fulcrum where emotional struggle is confronted, particularly when dealing with familial relations. Incest, as Honoré tells us, is a centerpiece to his films and revolves around sharp navigation of form and content. He claims (as noted) "that sexuality is a family issue. It is something that is taken care of without questioning" (JNCH, 178). Through cinema, Honoré takes care of this neglected family tenderness through a complex dance between Eros and Thanatos.

Second, beds are revelatory. Here, knowledge is queried and wrestled with, and choices are enacted. In bed, performers challenge and are challenged by

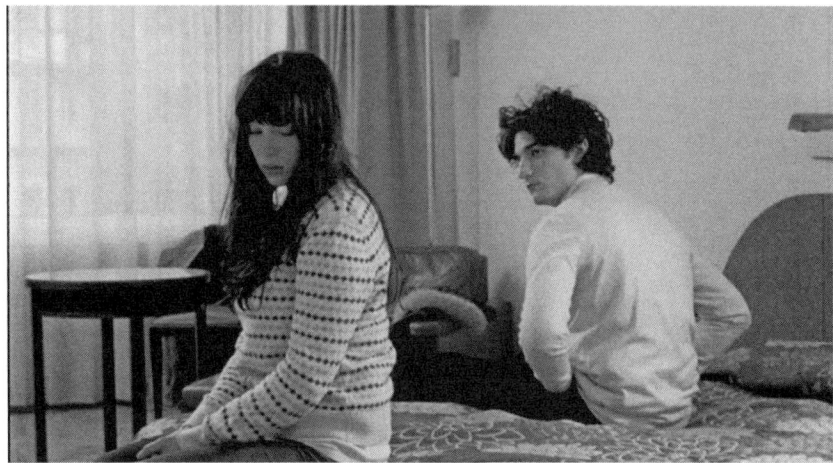

9. *La belle personne.*

preconceived ideas about the world they occupy. They query shifting levels of affection and the tenuous cultural boundaries established for relationships. Constrained by the mise-en-scène, the delimited space of the bed, characters reconsider their longing for another, if not the cost involved in longing, *tout court.* They—especially women in Honoré's world—strategically confront and stretch restrictive hetero-masculinist culture expectations. Junie's (Léa Seydoux) final decision in *La belle personne*—a decision made from a bed—is representative of constraints women face in light of men's romanticized views of themselves in the world. Nevertheless, for "right" or for "wrong," Junie chooses and moves on.

The final theme derived from Honoré's cinematic beds is that of cinema itself. Because each scene in bed is precisely prepared and its cinematic technique is composed with an acute eye for the implications that the film's formal dimensions bring to the bodies that move within the frame, Honoré ably tests cinema's own confined aesthetic boundaries. His cinematic beds are tightly choreographed sequences in which camera and body perform a pas de deux. In this way, he embraces the possibilities that film technique, along with its history and theories, have supplied filmmakers. The intimacy of the cinematic bed is thus significant for both its place in French cinema and its relevance to cinematic aesthetics as an affective device. Honoré's cinematic bed announces queer incest across time and space. At the point at which Honoré's narrative gives way to cinematic expression and film history's memory—that is, *homage*—spectators not only play a reflective "role"; through Honoré's cinema of monstration, they are, moreover, queerly touched within a newly formed queer ecological field.

INTRODUCTION

HOMAGE: WRITING THE QUEER AUTEUR

Homage is quintessentially a queer gesture. Historically, homage operates as an important aesthetic for gay culture. Susan Sontag famously notes this when she asserts, "Camp sees everything in quotation marks."[81] Sontag's canonical definition of camp succinctly locates camp as a mode of parodic yet honorific repetition. In short, to camp is *to make homage,* exponentially. For Sontag, camp—to recall Edelman's turn on *homo-écriture*—is a form of "*de*-scribing" the ostensibly heterosexual text that is rerendered through queer performance and queer gestures. From Oscar Wilde to Jack Smith (Sontag's representative queer aestheticians), camp can *only always* be a form of homage.

Queer cinematic homage in Honoré's queer French films is thus a form of particularized camp. The classic definitions of camp in relationship to homage are instructive when making this point; these definitions, however, are in need of revision when considering Honoré and his "quotation" of Godard, Demy, and the New Wave "school" more generally. Jack Babuscio, for instance, claims, "*Camp* describes those elements in a person, situation, or activity that express, or are created by, a gay sensibility. Camp is never a thing or person per se, but, rather a relationship between activities, individuals, situations, and gayness."[82] The vagueness of "gay sensibility" notwithstanding, Babuscio importantly notes that camp is a *dynamic relationship involving multipronged activities.* It is, in other words, a relationally performed gesture that intermingles bodies and (con)texts. Richard Dyer, filtering his discussion directly through film scholarship, further draws links to the workings of camp as a form of homage: "Basically, [camp] is a way of prizing the form of something away from its content, of reveling in the style while dismissing the content as trivial."[83] Dyer's emphasis on "form" is crucial here because, again, *to camp* involves a "prizing away" from something and playfully—queerly—*re*representing it.

Yet, while Dyer's definition holds true, and Honoré certainly "prizes the form . . . away from its content," he "camps" toward different ends. His French camp is not a trivialization of content per se. Far from it. It is, however, a "decoding," insofar as it is "homographesis." It "conserves" while it transforms a particular cinematic form that is recognized for its hetero-masculinist sensibilities and the history that gives shape to this form. In the twenty-first century, Honoré's *homographetic* homage revisits and revises how we might discuss camp in French queer cinema. This is to say that Honoré reimagines the way cinematic bodies intermingle on the screen and, often, in bed. With the trilogy, he writes into film history a queerness that had not existed before.

With this said, and given that film form is critical to French queer auteur practices, homage is no simple matter to study. In what way might we turn to film and queer theory, such as that offered by Mitry and Sedgwick, Dyer and Babuscio, Sontag, and Edelman, that allows us to rethink Honoré's queer auteur homage (or what Chris Darke refers to as cinematic "genuflecting")?[84] Put another way, what are the implications for Honoré's cinematic mode of monstration as it bears on the bodies that move across the cinematic frame and the spectators who participate with it? To what extent does Honoré's trinity—"Homosexualité, Bretagne et Adolescence"—inform such an analysis? When Raymond Durgnat composed his exhaustive analysis of the oeuvre of Jean Renoir—an important director for Honoré—he precisely queried the parameters of auteur studies as it intersects with "secondary sources" *and* textual analysis, while resisting "naïve biographism."[85] "We say," Durgnat begins,

> that a close study of a poet's rough drafts, or certain autobiographical details, or other works by the same artist, or psychoanalytical or other interpretations, "throw additional light" on the final text. In other words we begin to find meanings which aren't quite in the text (since we had to resort to secondary resources). Nonetheless we transfer to the final text the credit for somehow "possessing" these meanings. Perhaps what we mean is that we are grateful to it for stimulating us to go deeper or further and begin to understand undercurrents and overtones between the lines.... The fact seems to be that an artwork can absorb prodigious quantities of accident, of extraneous matter, of non-*auteur* content, yet be recognisable as one *auteur*'s work, so long as certain conspicuous traits of his style subsist.[86]

To unearth Honoré's complex dimensions of cinematic form and "the prodigious quantities of accident, of extraneous matter" it "absorb[s]," we offer a version of film criticism that is guided by studies in film aesthetics as much as it is by feminist and queer theory. By intersecting the potent concepts that feminist and queer theorists introduce to critical thinking, and with the rigor associated with the writings by film critics and theorists, Honoré is viewed as a complex queer auteur.

Our writing about Honoré, then, is indebted, in the first instance, to "classical" film criticism (c. 1920–1970).[87] This period of film criticism is not chosen blithely since it informs much of Honoré's thinking on the cinema, as it does the authors of this book. Hence, Jean Epstein, André Bazin, François Truffaut, Jean-Luc Godard, Jean Mitry, Raymond Durgnat, and Peter Wollen resonate throughout these pages, as does their critical jousting over the implications of auteur and film theory. Whether in their criticism or their filmmaking—and, in some cases, both—matters about the auteur, film form, film theory, and aesthetics were key themes in their rigorous debates. Their ideas reenergized new modes of critical film theory beyond Manichaean concerns over "good/bad" or "positive/negative."

A new generation of scholars and their work has also proved invaluable for the way we intend to approach Honoré. Heeding the critical work noted earlier, this group returns to and revives the specificities attending film theory. Sarah Keller and Christophe Wall-Romana as well as Daniel Morgan take it upon themselves to spotlight theorists such as Jean Epstein and André Bazin (respectively) so as to make available film theories that may have lost luster in some corners of film studies.[88] Wall-Romana's writing provides a useful bridge between Epstein's queer modernist-cinematic impulses and Honoré.[89] In his essay "Epstein's *Photogénie* as Corporeal Vision: Inner Sensation, Queer Embodiment, and Ethics," Wall-Romana draws a powerful line between film form and Epstein's homosexuality. Here, Epstein's queer "embodiment" intersects with film theory and filmmaking to the extent that *photogénie*—cinema's unique ability to precipitate a phenomenologically rich experience for the spectator precisely because of cinematic technique—"[reamplifies] the inner sensory state of the spectator" (58). Through this rich modernist concept, Wall-Romana reminds us about the significance of cinematic form in relationship to queer auteurist practices. He cites Epstein: "Beyond the scenario's drama, the screen violently resonates with an immense trove of wild desires and continual worries, the spirit, *photogénie*'s sweet smell like that of sainthood, poetic persona" (58). Our reading of the queer Breton Honoré fits snuggly with Epstein's queer modernism since many of the latter's films shot between 1928 and 1948 were made in Brittany (several of which are homoerotically charged). Honoré's homosexuality, like Epstein's before him, is pliant, interpellated, and transformative. It is a form of desire through which the queer auteur turns to render experience through cinematic techniques to match the "trove of wild desires and continual worries."

Our writing, moreover and importantly, connects with feminist and queer critical theory. The inroads made by the best of these theoretical interventions, especially for French cinema, are vital for any contemporary study of film. Hence, and although we critically engage Vincendeau's reading of *Dans Paris*, her work cannot be underestimated for the invaluable unveiling of—among other things—the New Wave's hetero-androcentrism. Along with Laura Mulvey, Kelley Conway, Geneviève Sellier, James S. Williams, and Wall-Romana,

Vincendeau has provided us with an ideal critical position for evaluating Honoré's contributions to French cinema from a feminist and queer perspective.[90]

If homage, then, as queer *écriture* is unequivocal in Honoré's work and, as we have seen, involves eroticizing family relations through cinematic beds in a perverse reamplification of memory, we contend that his films offer a challenging perspective on French culture and cinema. To put Honoré in this light, our turn to classical film theory—itself a form of homage—pinpoints homage as a particular act of cinematic homographesis. In part a camp aesthetic, in part honorific "genuflection," cinematic homage announces pleasure by acknowledging and dramatically announcing it. Each auteur offers unique articulations of this pleasure. For Honoré, filling beds with actors who embody French film history (Marie France Pisier, Catherine Deneuve, Chiara Mastroianni, Isabelle Huppert, and Louis Garrel) and aesthetically ghosting his favored film directors (Godard, Truffaut, Eustache, et al.), his cinematic bed is nothing less than a queer boy's wet dream.

When homage in Honoré's films is reduced to what Rees-Roberts refers to as New Wave "vintage memorabilia" or Demy-esque pastiche (an assignation we consider more aptly applied to Ducastel and Martineau), a very queer pleasure is removed from Honoré's cinematic experience (111). His queer homage is a cinematic aesthetic that eroticizes by manipulating time and space—that is, Honoré eroticizes historical memory. This manipulation, in turn, revises the spectator's world as it becomes intimately involved with the event on the movie screen. The spectator is thus folded into, along with the bodies on the screen, queer time and space. Honoré masterfully negotiates the boundaries of cinematic time and space, history and memory, and their aesthetic convergence through cinematic monstration.

In a scene we discuss later from *Les chansons d'amour*, Christophe Honoré's friend the queer filmmaker Gaël Morel appears in the film. In this scene, he passes ticket holders at a movie theater and remarks to each spectator, "I was after him." At once a wink from Honoré to his friend, who is also a contemporary queer French director, Honoré playfully blurs the temporal lineage/line we encounter with film homage. Homage as we posit it—and as we believe Honoré puts it to use—necessarily involves not only *how* but *why*. And because he approaches cinema in a way that "involved thinking about others' films, and about defining a particular idea about cinema," and, moreover, because he scoffs at the notion that "other directors contend they've invented something and claim they've never seen any films," Morel's "I was after him" declaration augurs something more provocative. To be "I was after him" raises the stakes for homage *as* film history, *as* queer film history. To make film (*the how*) necessarily draws on the queer world, the "trove of wild desires and continual worries," to which the queer filmmaker awakens each day (*the why*).

INTRODUCTION

Honoré's films are the memory of the past as much as they are the memory of what is to come. Cinema is the future anterior.

TO PARIS

In *An Attempt at Exhausting a Place in Paris*, Georges Perec writes,

> There are many things in Place Saint-Sulpice; for instance: a district council building, a financial building, a police station, three cafés, one of which sells tobacco and stamps, a movie theater, a church on which Le Vau, Gittard, Oppenord, Servandoni, and Chalgrin have all worked, and which is dedicated to a chaplain of Clotaire II, who was bishop of Bourges from 624 to 544 and whom we celebrate on 17 January, a publisher, a funeral parlor, a travel agency, a bus stop, a tailor, a hotel, a fountain decorated with statues of four great Christian orators (Bossuet, Fénelon, Fléchier, and Massillon), a newsstand, a seller of pious objects, a parking lot, a beauty parlor, and many other things as well.
>
> A great number, if not majority, of these things have been described, inventoried, photographed, talked about, or registered. My intention in the pages that follow was to describe the rest instead: that which is generally not taken note of, that which is not noticed, that which has no importance: what happens when nothing happens other than the weather, people, cars, and clouds.[91]

We quote at length Perec's elegant but failed/impossible description of a singular place in Paris because not only *must* one quote Perec at length for obvious practical reasons (his descriptions of the ostensibly simple are never so simple) but to quote Perec's passage at length helps to visualize the way Honoré's films might be seen to coincide with the artist's *pleasure in failing* to describe the city. By concentrating on the trilogy, we find Honoré wandering the city searching for a way, like Perec, to describe Paris. Perec's detailed, yet inevitably inaccurate, description of Paris anticipates filmmakers such as Honoré who take pleasure in this failure. Perec and Honoré—through their different media but both image conjurers nonetheless—put to use multiple aesthetic tricks as they make an "attempt at exhausting a place in Paris."

For a queer boy from the provinces, such exhaustive gestures indeed manifest endless pleasure. Growing up in Rostrenen, Honoré early on developed a queer perspective toward cinema and France's traditional cultures. "Brittany," he tells us, "offers the advantage of being a region steeped in Catholicism with a peculiar relationship to death. I am just as fond of Brittany as I am repulsed by it" (JNCH, 171). Yet, and like so many queer boys before him who hail from the country, Honoré set his sights on the big city.⁹² His Parisian characters, like him, are internal outsiders who uneasily move through the city landscape. He gives shape to his and their uneasily queer positions in the city precisely through cinema's formal means of expression. In short, he *shows* a queer Paris.

The trilogy is an ideal place to start a study of Honoré since at its heart is Paris. For a queer auteur, there is no better cinematic bed in which to exhaust a place. The city's at once myriad yet strategically conceived street patterns provide the ideal mise-en-scène for Honoré's exploration of cinematic emotion. Paris, unfolding as it does from the center as multiple streets perpendicularly intersect, steers the trilogy's efforts to render the body's suppleness when sudden and surprising events interject. Sensitive to this sensation, Honoré capitalizes on cinema's historical and formal dimensions in such a way that our "inner sensory state" is (re)amplified.

I

Dans Paris

The analysis ["an exploration of the *dream-work*"] will deal with the *beginning*—the credits and opening sequence—considered as endowed with a certain structural autonomy (the sequence) and as a privileged link in the chain that constitutes the film: a segment where the entire film may be read, *differently*.

Thierry Kuntzel

What then is truth? A mobile army of metaphors, metonyms, and anthropomorphisms—in short, a sum of human relations which have been enhanced, transposed, and embellished poetically and rhetorically, and which after long use seem firm, canonical, and obligatory to a people: truths are illusions about which one has forgotten that this is what they are; metaphors which are worn out and without sensuous power; coins which have lost their pictures and now matter only as metal, no longer as coins.

Friedrich Nietzsche

NARRATIVE ARC

Dans Paris tells the story of two brothers, Jonathan and Paul, who live with their father in Paris. Their mother, after divorcing their father, has moved out and remarried. When the film opens, Paul has recently returned to Paris after leaving the family home in the city to live with his girlfriend in the countryside. They break up, and on his return to the city, Paul suffers from romantic heartache. The depression that follows his breakup is debilitating. Paul's sorrow, however, is older and deeper than his recent romantic failure. The family history, including the death of a sister, bears as heavily on his sadness as his lost lover does. The intimacy shared between the two brothers becomes crucial for the way Paul survives loss. Memory and loss drive both the film's narrative and its formal structure.

The epigraphs from Kuntzel and Nietzsche set in motion the critical tools for our analysis of Christophe Honoré's trilogy. They are vital to our discussion because they illuminate the critical and often-difficult work involved in studying the cinematic language that Honoré puts to use in the service of his films. The filmmaker's decidedly rich background in historical French intellectual and popular culture, in fact, places heavy critical demands on the spectator. For us, then, a turn to Nietzsche, Kuntzel, and (as we do throughout) Roland Barthes, Jean-Luc Godard, and other philosophers is by no means an intellectual stretch when discussing Honoré's filmmaking. His films insist on such theoretical approaches. Our analysis begins with the first, and arguably most complex, film in the trilogy. As our study shows, this film has an elaborate formal structure, and it is precisely because of this intricate form that it has to be understood as more than simply the trilogy's beginning. *Dans Paris* shoulders much of the spatial and temporal heavy lifting that fills out the trilogy's cinematic narratives.

Dans Paris's title sequence juxtaposes credit inserts with images from nighttime Paris in such a way as to deliver on Kuntzel's rewarding methodology while ushering us into Honoré's cinematic world, in which the erosion of language—as Nietzsche suggests—reveals "truths as illusions." Taken together, Kuntzel and Nietzsche (along with Godard in this regard) provide fertile ground on which to study Honoré's cinematic "truth." As the first film that launches Honoré's Parisian trilogy, *Dans Paris*'s title sequence yields a good deal of information about the director's cinematic relationship to New Wave cinema, his intimate dynamic with actors, and his connections to the urban milieu in which he lives and makes his films. The trilogy is also rich with the larger themes that our book describes—family, sexuality, and death. As Kuntzel argues, the film's "beginning" is "endowed . . . as a privileged link in the [narrative-cinema] chain that allows us to read a film *differently*." In this spirit, we turn to Honoré's filmmaking—beginning with *Dans Paris*—to work through the director's vibrant yet complex thematic structures that are introduced in the film's title sequence and draw us into the two subsequent films in the trilogy.

To open, *Dans Paris*'s credits introduce us to the film's production companies and financial backers (see figures 10.1–10.15). From the very first, the film situates its historical cinematic place with the New Wave. Specifically, the typographical font used in the title cards is well recognized as Godard's favored Antique Olive.[1] The second card introduces Paulo Branco's contribution (producer).[2] Initially, Branco's name appears set in sharp profile of white type on black; his name remains, but the card then dissolves into a nondescript shot of predawn Paris (typical apartment and office buildings). From this image of the city, we cut to two title inserts that separately present the actors, "Roman Duris" and "Louis Garrel." Like Branco, their names are placed against the bold black-and-white striping—colors that evoke Paris's architectural palette against the blackness of night. However, unlike the Branco transition, no image separates the titles on which the two actors' names are presented.

The linked but separate cards for Duris and Garrel anticipate the intimate relationship, yet distinctive personalities, that these two men portray in the film. Underscoring this linked-yet-separate title-card sequence, a key shot follows. Honoré cuts to an image in which we unevenly zoom in to see Garrel and Duris in repose, side by side, on a mattress (figures 10.6 and 10.7 form a single shot). The cinematic portrait establishes a rapport between the men, giving us a peek into the complex circumstances we are soon to encounter. The reframing and sudden refocusing strike a rehearsal mode for the camera; it further anticipates a "behind-the-scenes" look into *Dans Paris*. But as Honoré reminds us in his interview included in this volume, his films are always already "behind the scenes": "In my films, the 'making-of' is already included. . . . I rather like the idea that my films are the documentaries of the moments when we were filming" (JNCH, 189).[3] The particular title portrait in *Dans Paris* reminds us that the production of an Honoré film is a contained "ecological field" (to recall Sedgwick's terms) from start to finish, from outtakes to final print.

Because we see Duris and Garrel in bed together, their close bond is suggestively ambiguous. Lovers? Brothers? Friends? To what extent does the relationship they share take place on and off camera? The brief portrait, characterized by the rehearsal camera, toys with Honoré's interest in expressing the blurred line between actor and character, actor and director, and on-screen/off-screen space. As such, Honoré's closeness—the familial cinematic structuring

PART I

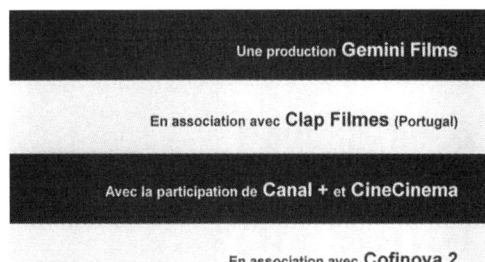

10.1

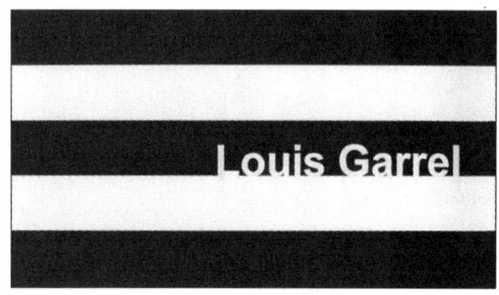

10.5

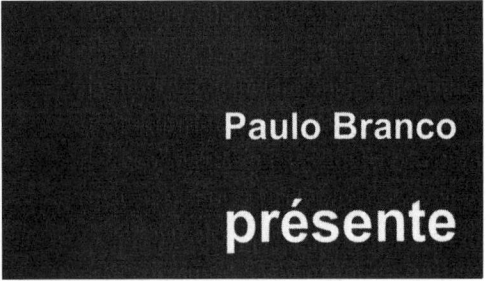

10.2

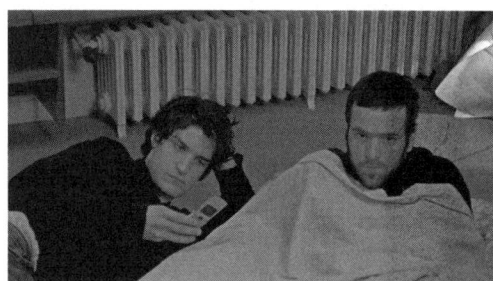

10.6

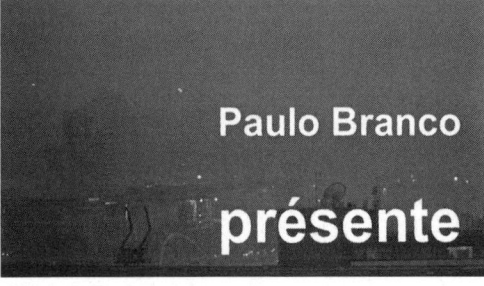

10.3

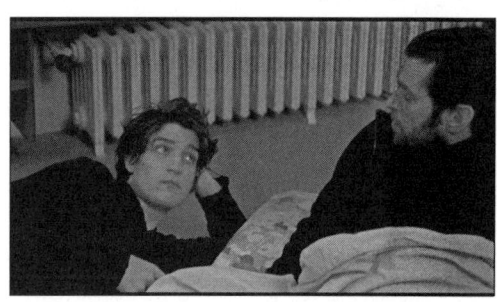

10.7

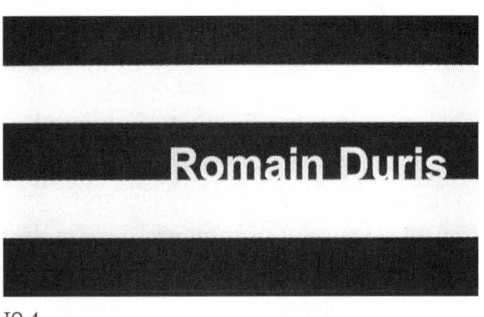

10.4

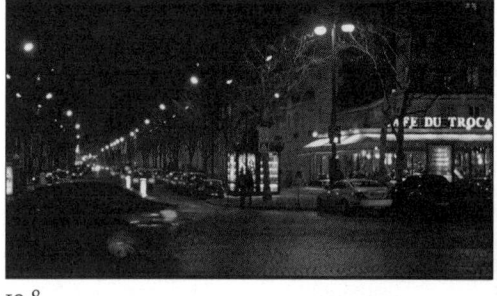

10.8

10.1–10.15. Credit sequence, *Dans Paris*.

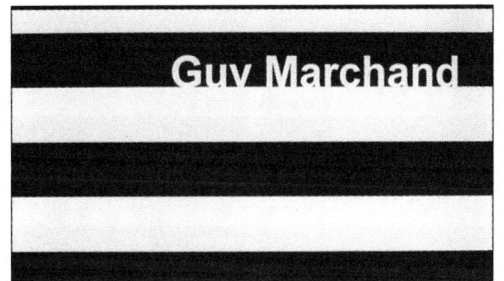
10.9

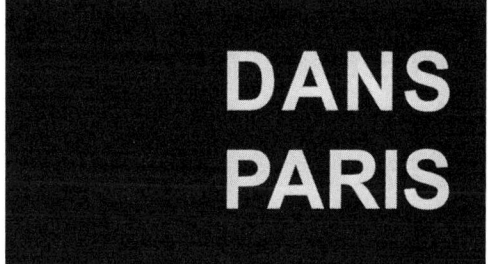
10.13

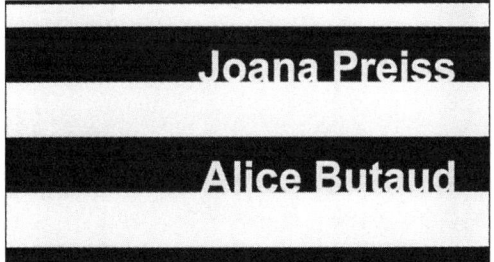
10.10

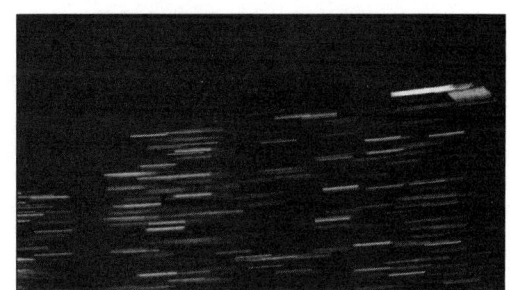
10.14

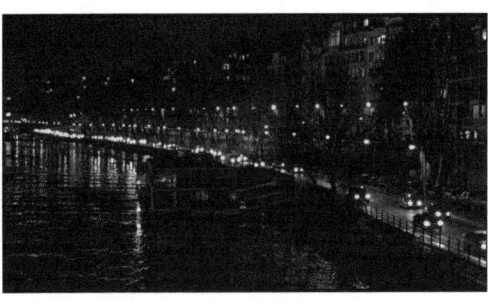
10.11

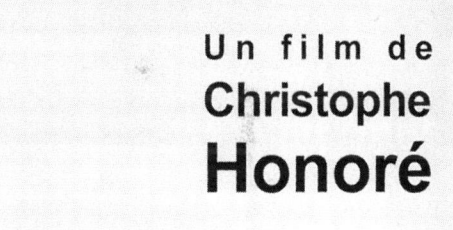
10.15

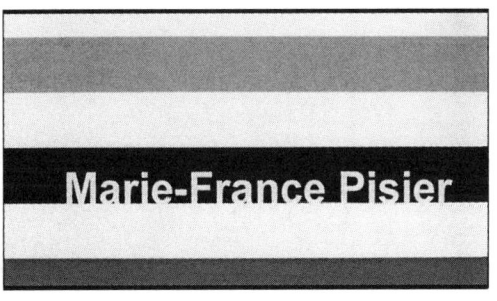
10.12

of his relationship with his actors—is also something of a queer-erotic turn on Godard's laying-bare-the-cinematic device.[4] The boys' look at each other is erotic and intimate, while it simultaneously cements what we soon discover to be a tight sibling relationship between them. Their shared look is deliciously coy, sensual, and familiar. For example, the shot opens with Garrel nonchalantly playing with his mobile phone and Duris gazing directly at the camera; they then glance at each other. Duris looks to Garrel, who glances back, as if intuiting Duris's gaze. The shot closes with their look to each other. The actors are at once performing their roles while cognizant of themselves as performers performing before Honoré's camera.

Duris's look toward the camera serves to acknowledge Honoré and his off-camera presence. In this way, the camera, with Honoré behind it, is part of the always already "making of," the "documentaries of the moments." The cinematic atmosphere that the director establishes for the two men is at once relaxed, playful, and seductive. Not insignificantly, the cinematic play occurs in bed. Considering our earlier remarks in the introduction regarding Honoré's penchant for placing himself within cinematic beds alongside his actors, as well as his commitment to hands-on filmmaking, *Dans Paris*'s credit sequence emphasizes the director's and crew's deep involvement—their embeddedness(as it were)—in the filmmaking process. Honoré's reconstructed and immersive cinematic family—his queer family—is the lynchpin on which his work hangs.

Following the Garrel/Duris portrait, *Dans Paris*'s title sequence continues with the similar pattern in which title cards and images are juxtaposed. Not unlike Duris's and Garrel's title cards, Guy Marchand, Joana Preiss, and Alice Butaud are introduced against Parisian tinted stripes. There are, however, two noteworthy exceptions to the pattern: Marie-France Pisier's title card and the image that precedes Honoré's cinematic signature. In the first, Pisier's credit declares Honoré's embrace of a certain cinematic heritage (specifically that of his youth); on the other hand, Honoré dramatically asserts his cinematic involvement with the film. Pisier's title card, for example, adds an antique blue and crimson stripe to the simple cream and black striping seen earlier. While these colors conjure the national color scheme, the blue on Pisier's card is less regal and more pastel. At the same time, the softened blue is offset by the card's intense red that underscores the frame. Representative of late 1960s and 1970s French cinema, Honoré's film star, Pisier, embodies a significant history, *the director's memory of French cinema*. Like Isabelle Huppert's and Catherine Deneuve's involvement in *Ma mère* and *Les bien-aimés*, respectively, Pisier *is* Honoré's French cinematic family—*sa mère(s)*—and duly noted with her introduction in the tricolor.

Furthermore, Pisier's role in the film is the mother of the two sons, played by Duris and Garrel. Since Honoré's cinematic mothers are often "impure"—as Pisier is in *Dans Paris*—the black line that besmirches the color field should not go unnoticed. Hence, Pisier's matriarchal presence highlights her role in *Dans Paris* as much as it highlights her position in French cinephile culture and the role of French cinephile culture in Honoré's life.

Finally, the image that precedes the title card "Un film de Christophe Honoré" is extremely brief but stands out from the previous montage because it showcases movement. This is to say, while the other images display city movement (traffic along the Seine, pedestrians moving about the Trocadero), they are nonetheless shot on a tripod. Through a very different cinematic gesture, the director's signature is abruptly introduced with a swish pan. Although the lights we see in this cinematic wash are those of Paris, it is significant that the queer filmmaker, Honoré, signs the film with such a tactile and disruptive cinematic flourish—a "swish." The caméra-stylo shot is distinctive for its out-of-placeness from the other images as well as for the way it stamps the director's imprint and underscores his cinematic concept of "moving through."

Later, both *Les chansons* and *La belle personne* similarly introduce their cinematic characters—and by this we mean the actors *and* Paris's urban milieu— through a credit sequence that opens onto the city. Additionally, the two films echo *Dans Paris*'s opening insofar as they historically resonate with twentieth-century modernist culture-industry aesthetics: *Les chansons* continues the use of New Wave font type and editing, while *La belle personne* introduces a familiar printer's typeset, designed in 1970 by Robert Massin for Éditions Gallimard's "Folio" collection. With these aesthetic references in play, Honoré foregrounds the period in which he enters the world (1970) as well as significant French media central to his own art practices—cinema and literature. Honoré's view that the most interesting cinema bears the hallmark of "literariness" is thus brought into sharp relief with the opening of his Parisian trilogy.[5]

DANS PARIS, MAKING A FAMILY

As mentioned in our introduction, Honoré was born in Brittany, well outside the realm of Parisian haute couture. He entered the world just past the crucial May 1968 political and cultural events that took place in France. Growing up as a young gay boy in Rostrenen, far to the northwest of Paris, he looked to the capital city's promises and delights, particularly with regard to the cinema and sexual exploration. Once there, his long-held and rapt attention to an array of theoretical readings, film criticism, art history, literature, and—of course—film viewings intermingled with Paris's vibrant surroundings. The multimedia works he subsequently created must necessarily be seen in light of this move from the provinces to the city. Along with his intellectual appetites and creative interests, his provincial life and family experiences gave imaginative impetus to the way he envisaged Paris's allure. His children's books are insightful in this regard, since they expand on Honoré's interest in friendship, sorrow, courage, and living in a hetero-challenging world—experiences made all the more intense when a young gay man moves to the city. The connection between writing children's books and screenplays is, Honoré notes in *Le livre pour enfants,* directly linked to Honoré's homosexuality. In *Dans Paris,* children's books reiterate the bond between youth and adulthood, especially when one of these books appears as an object of memory-exchange between brothers. Honoré's trilogy is therefore important as a measure of the ways Paris and cinephile culture reenvisage the possibilities for a queer French boy from the country. Although not necessarily *films à clef* (to borrow James S. Williams's phrase), they are sentient films for the ways they explore Honoré's Parisian world and his creative processes within it.[6] With *Dans Paris,* Honoré invites us into the pleasures, disappointments, and aestheticized spheres that compose city life.

Dans Paris opens with Jonathan (Garrel) waking up in bed, where he is sandwiched between his brother, Paul (Duris), and his former girlfriend, Alice (Butaud) (see figures 11.1 and 11.2). Gently lifting himself from the center so as not to disturb his companions, Jonathan reaches for the automatic switch that opens the shades. For a moment, the camera lingers on his sculpted back as he stretches toward the switch. Contemplation of the male body recurs throughout Honoré's work. And though his camera gazes on women's bodies with as much affection, Honoré holds the shot on men in such a way that it caresses the male form. The most obvious examples of Honoré's caressing camera over the male form are in his later films *Les bien-aimés* and *Homme au bain*. The lingering gaze on men's bodies is a staple of his filmmaking. In the meantime, as sunlight fills the bedroom in which *Dans Paris* begins, Jonathan turns toward us and silently casts his look at his partners. Garrel's body in this instance and throughout *Dans Paris* is a vital component of Honoré's filmmaking.

Like Chiara Mastroianni, who plays major roles in Honoré's films (*Non ma fille, Homme au bain,* and *Les bien-aimés*), Garrel belongs to French cinema royalty. Mastroianni's lineage is Catherine Deneuve and Marcello Mastroianni; Garrel is the son of the film director Philippe Garrel and the actor and AIDS activist Brigitte Sy. Film history runs deeper in the Garrel family with Louis's grandfather Maurice, a recognized film actor (1923–2011). Perhaps the most significant

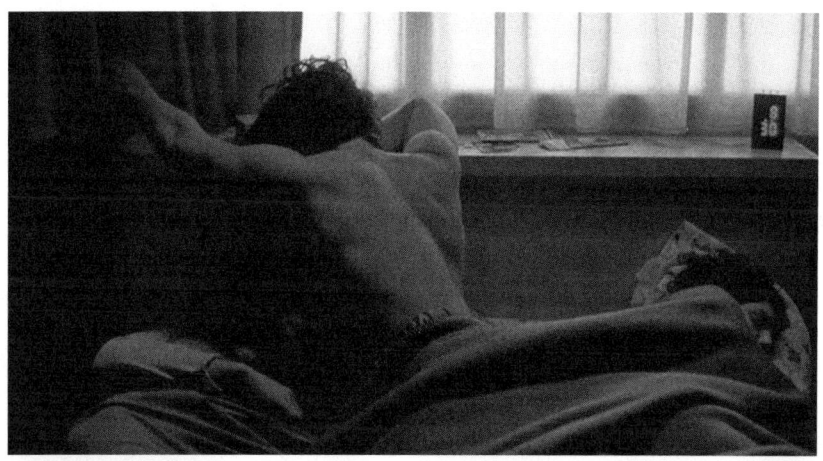

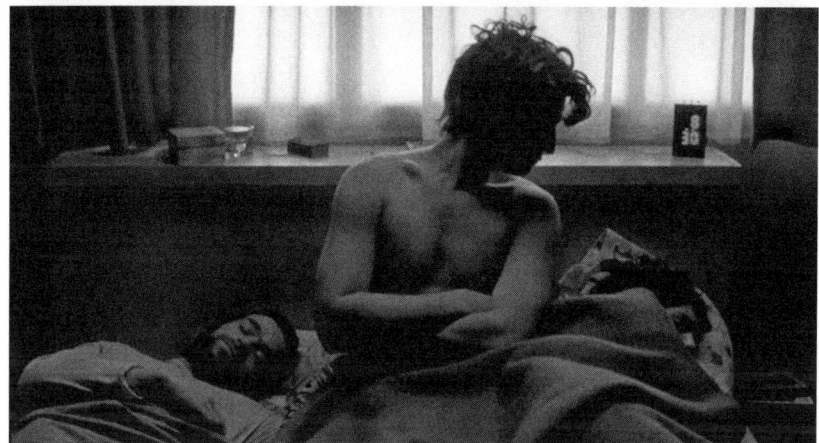

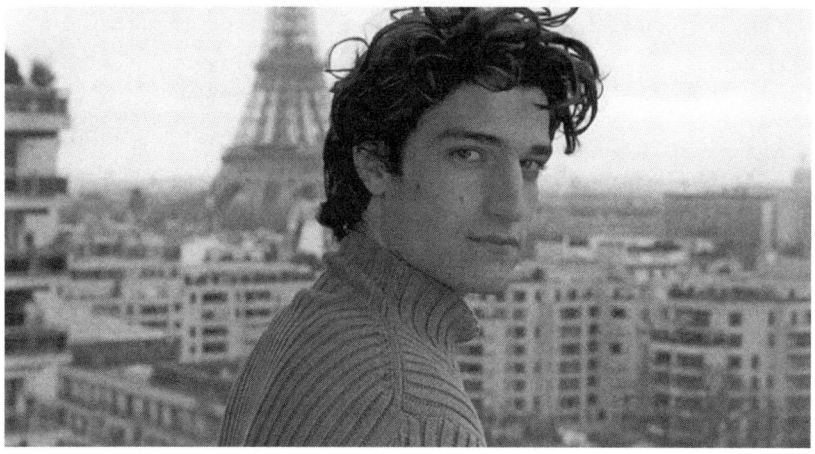

11.1–11.3. Jonathan (Louis Garrel), embodied "omniscient narrator."

extended Garrel family member is Louis's godfather, Jean-Pierre Léaud. Léaud and Jean-Paul Belmondo are the two most highly recognized male actors in New Wave films directed by Godard, Truffaut, and Eustache. Most notably, Léaud's performances in Godard's *Masculin féminin* (1966) and *La chinoise* (1967), Truffaut's "Antoine Doinel" series (1959–1979), and Eustache's *La maman and la putain* (1973) are trenchant predecessors for the way Garrel has developed his acting style. In six Honoré films, Garrel rehearses a Léaud-esque style in which boyish charms are informed by a strategic naïveté. Léaud's performances uniquely signaled France's uncertain and troubled male youth during the 1960s and 1970s. Like Pisier, Garrel's performances embody cinematic history and are instrumental to the way Honoré conceives cinematic technique. In this way, Honoré's films unabashedly refer to Garrel's "familial" cinematic lineage and uncanny physical similarity to Léaud not only in the trilogy but in *Ma mère, Non ma fille,* and *Les bien-aimés*.[7]

But while Garrel cut his teeth in his father's films as well as Bernardo Bertolucci's *The Dreamers* (2003), both Honoré and Garrel have exacted a critical price because of the actor's performance style. The reviews are decidedly mixed. Garrel's Léaud homage is either romantically embraced or viewed as perfunctory and annoying. In a review of *Les chansons,* Peter Bradshaw writes, "Garrel really is turning into the most irritating actor in the world, hyperactively clowning around and generally behaving like the Big Brother contestant from hell."[8] At the same time, Manohla Dargis in her review of *Dans Paris* finds Garrel "lissome [in] body and soul," a "floppy beauty" who "delivers an intensely physical performance that organically conveys a world of impetuous emotion."[9]

Critical responses notwithstanding, Garrel's performance style carries particular historical impact and is valuable to the extent that it provides the contours for Honoré's cinematic explorations. As Honoré's filmmaking transforms and his actors are intimately woven into the ongoing cinematic project, the actor's body serves as a pliable and creative force in his work. "Once I'd shown this adolescent side of [Garrel]," Honoré tells us, "I wanted to push him into adulthood" (JNCH, 188).[10] Not dissimilar to the way Godard engaged Brigitte Bardot's star persona in *Le mépris* (1963), Honoré challenges the star's youthful aura and box-office successes. Duris, we will see, faced similar against-the-grain direction from Honoré.

The "star," as part and parcel of film form, is something of a "double bind." As Pasolini recognized when making *Mamma Roma* (1962) with Anna Magnani, the star may lend a powerful persona to a film and thus broaden its appeal, yet his or her "stardom" often limits provocative cinematic and narrative risks that the director may wish to take.[11] While a member of French-cinema royalty, Garrel presented a challenge to Honoré. Since Garrel has the "face of virility that girls like, and boys too," Honoré concedes, "I found it troubling to make a film much more focused on Louis's face so I made *Les chansons d'amour*. And then I felt I wanted to give him a skill and to stop making him a permanent teenager, which brought me to the film *La belle personne*. In *Non, ma fille* . . . and *Les bien-aimés*, I thought I needed to switch up the process and make it so that he wouldn't be an attraction any more but somebody that nobody cares about. If he's not the subject of the film anymore, how do you work with him to bring out another character that, in theory, the story doesn't need?" (JNCH, 188). But even before these later films, *Dans Paris*'s collaborative relationship between camera and actor highlights Honoré's cinema as a "work in progress," one that is shaped by an intimate dynamic between director, performer, and camera. Garrel's relationship to Honoré's filmmaking thus illustrates the concentrated place for performance in the director's cinematic projects.

ANTICIPATING THE PAST

The opening sequence in *Dans Paris*—a window framed within a frame—draws together interior and exterior worlds, on-screen and off-screen performances, in order to deliver a cinematic trope that ties the trilogy together in several ways. First, the three films are interested in the multiple and imbricated connections between inside and outside, literally and metaphorically. While the two anchor films—*Dans Paris* and *La belle personne*—are framed by sequences that usher us in and out of the trilogy as a whole, the opening montage of the middle film—*Les chansons*—situates us squarely within the center of Paris. In effect, the trilogy's journey traces movement into the city, nestles us within its borders, and then finally moves us outward.

Within the films' urban boundaries, then, characters shuttle between and among their companions, the city and the provinces, and the relationships in which they find themselves intimately ensnared. While *Dans Paris* explores the tension between urban and rural in terms of the affective response to desire, loss, and family, *Les chansons* and *La belle personne* focus on Paris's youth-based culture, reconstituted kinship, and the experience of selfhood. In all three films, character mobility is nevertheless facilitated by desire, particularly an erotic desire that is satisfied, momentarily, through multiple sexual divertissements. Honoré's cinematic and penetrative inside-outside world is, therefore, at once sexually malleable while energized precisely because it is contained within the sensually charged space of Paris. As such, *Dans Paris* and *La belle personne* provide points of entry and exit for Honoré's cinematic Paris, and all his films depend greatly on the back-and-forth movement between Paris and elsewhere, between inside and outside. Paris is each film's spatial focal point, and the city's affective tentacles linger whether the action takes place within it or beyond its borders. The trilogy is the most concentrated effort in which Honoré works through the haptic and emotionally disjointed movements that a cinematic Paris offers.

When we enter the place *Dans Paris,* we also enter an additional passageway: time. Because personal and historical memories saturate Honoré's cinema, spatial and temporal relations are dynamically, structurally, and, in many instances, paradoxically conjoined. Spatially, once Jonathan opens the electronic shade on his window and the film proceeds, we discover that our characters are situated on the edge of the sixteenth arrondissement. The lifting of the curtain, however, proves to be the film narrative's end. This narrative turn on time is only revealed once we travel through the entire, carefully orchestrated, events of the film. Hence, Jonathan's opening of the window *within* the Fourth Quarter (Beaugrenelle) of the sixteenth arrondissement on the Right Bank of the Seine—as seen from the family's apartment window—is a only stone's throw from the fifteenth arrondissement on the Left Bank. In effect, the window that opens our film onto the city's folds within folds is also the window that circularly draws our film to a close. At the same time, *Dans Paris*'s closing-opening/inside-outside sequences look out onto the urban place in which the second film in the trilogy, *Les chansons,* will take place. The trilogy is less a composition made of three discrete units than it is a singularly folded sheet of time and space.

Honoré's trilogy narrative thus seductively maps itself into the circular urban geography that constitutes Paris (*arrondir* suggests "to make round"). "Organized like a centrifuge," Christopher Faulkner notes,

> with its first arrondissement of culture and respectability in the center and the other nineteen spiraled around it, the city expels outward to its perimeter and beyond, the stigmatized and the socially marginal. The geography of the city, first of all, maps the most transparent relations of power—sexually and in terms of gender and class and ethnicity—as well as with respect to extreme forms of transgression, like criminality and madness. Historically, the city has always banished its social waste to its outskirts.[12]

Yet, while we can conceive of the city as "expelling outward," we can also imagine that the city propels inward. In other words, replicating the city's simultaneously centrifugal and centripetal circular design in which quarters tuck into arrondissements, while participating in the city as a whole, Honoré lands his queer characters into the spatial, temporal, and marginalized arcs in which cultural differences weave inward and outward.

In *Dans Paris,* the "present" takes place over a single day, December 23, 2005. The events of this day, however, are not presented in a straightforward manner and are weighed down by memory and sadness. To ground the spectator in *Dans Paris*'s achronological narrative, Honoré creates another framing device with Jonathan as narrator. Once Jonathan leaves his bed partners and opens the blinds onto what we will soon learn to be Paris, the camera follows him through his family's apartment, where he pauses to kiss his father, Mirko (Guy Marchand), who has fallen asleep in his office chair. Jonathan then exits onto the balcony, where the Eiffel Tower is prominently displayed in the background, giving the spectator our first site-specific signpost. With the city location squarely identified as the heart of Paris, Honoré tracks in toward (becomes one with?) Jonathan, who breaks the fourth wall and speaks directly to the viewer. His narration—an address to the absent-present spectator—is, "make no mistake, . . . an apostrophe." He goes on to tell us that he is fully aware that, in a film, "direct speech," such as his, gives off an "odor." Nonetheless, as the film's "narrator" who "can be everywhere at once," his "horribly personal" tale and its apparent stink must be recounted.

Jonathan's introduction continues as we cut to a tracking shot that travels along a country road. We soon discover that this road leads us back in space *and* time to when and where Jonathan's brother, Paul, fled the city for his failed romance with Anna (Preiss), who lives with her young son, Loup (Rambert-Preiss).[13] Over the images of the countryside, Jonathan's voice is heard. Paul's tale is, therefore, via Jonathan's memory, recollected from the city. Importantly, Jonathan's retelling of events is contaminated, carries an "odor" because he is unreliable, if not prejudiced, about his brother's interests in the affair that he ostensibly describes from his role as narrator. He is not once present in any of the events that take place between Paul and Anna; moreover, even when he is in Paris, he meanders somewhere between his family's apartment and the city streets for the better part of the day and sees only small slivers of the circumstances about which he narrates.

Jonathan is thus quite selective about what he tells. For example, he neglects to mention a not-insignificant part of his family history—his sister Claire's suicide. This is no small detail since her death is crucial to understanding Paul's sorrow, on which the story focuses. Jonathan's recollection and retelling, it appears, satisfies his own pleasure and desire to create a tale in which he places himself and his brother front and center. But fulfilling his (familial?) obligation to accurately render emotional impact as it derives from the family's past is a tricky business and demands some fancy footwork. Jonathan shows himself to be adept at the necessary cinematic choreography that evokes the family's more visceral and emotional experiences. Given the familial complexities he hopes to explain (to the extent that "explaining" these things is ever fully possible), Jonathan's narration turns on a cinematic rendering of rearticulated and rehearsed memory. Merged with the film's director through the tracking shot, the narrator's recounting through cinematic means is unavoidable since words rarely fulfill or satisfactorily explain intimate histories and desires. "Fulfillments," as Roland Barthes reminds us, "are not spoken" because "if it is inconsistent to express suffering badly, on the one hand, with regard to happiness, it would seem culpable to spoil its expression: the ego discourses only when it is hurt; when I am fulfilled or remember having been so, language seems pusillanimous."[14] For Honoré, cinematic "language" beautifully entertains Jonathan's discoursing ego so that he might more resiliently express his and his family's "suffering" without words. Hence, Jonathan's "omniscient" and self-centered position as narrator suits quite well his desire "to be everywhere at once." As director of the scene, he ably controls the film's narrative from all angles. He, in fact, see events that take place when he is not there and, not unimportantly, launches the trilogy from within the city in which a series of cinematic memories riddled by bad smells, painful feelings, and complicated but generous self-interest radiate across the film.

LOVE

Midway into *Dans Paris*'s narrative, we return to Jonathan on the balcony, where he tells us about his family's coat of arms. The motto reads, "Take time to ignore the sadness of your family." According to Jonathan, the inscription proclaims his family's "great quality" that is simultaneously their "handicap": this is "detachment." His brother Paul's movement out to the countryside and back to Paris represents this family tradition, since the emotional distress Paul suffers is not necessarily a negative; rather, Paul turns away from his family's deeply entrenched grieving to explore his own suffering precisely because of this family heritage. The emotional price, of course, is that concentrating on one's own self-interests weighs heavily on others. In Paul and Jonathan's family, what may be perceived as arrogant self-gratification—detaching oneself from others yet demanding their full attention—paradoxically sustains intimate relations. Ironically, detachment secures bonds through movement toward, yet away from, one another; it is a life tension that holds the family together. For love to survive, intimate detachment is required. Jonathan's introductory remarks for the film make perfectly clear that Paul's and his own detachment are a form of saying "I love you."

With this key piece of information about the family, we are fully armed to return to Jonathan's inauguration of our tale. Delivered from the balcony in Paris, appearing to be suspended over the city, and guided by Jonathan's voice-over, we embark on our journey to the countryside to witness the fallout from Paul's familial detachment (see figure 11.3). Once there, we open onto Paul and Anna's bed, where we see the postcoital couple. Paul sits up at the side of the bed, distressed, and tries to catch his breath. He barely looks at Anna and rushes to the shower. Through a series of jump cuts, Paul returns to the bedroom and hurriedly begins to dress. Despite his attempt to gloss over the tensions at play in his relationship by donning his "nice white shirt" with an "impeccably ironed collar," Anna astutely notes that his overrehearsed production is "inelegant." Has he lost interest in her? If so, why can he not say so? Since he refuses (is unable?) to respond, Anna promptly provides him with three reasons as to why he leaps into the shower after sex (threes and thirds continue as a trope throughout the trilogy).

First, Anna declares, Paul "fucks for nostalgia's sake." In his "twisted" way, his fucking is nothing more than "being faithful" to a "memory." Anna is merely a "souvenir," a material reminder from an otherwise intangible past. Second, to fuck is easier than admitting that he does not wish to cause her heartache: "Love me too much so you don't hurt me." Penetrating the other's body is less painful than enacting emotional violence against it. As Anna speaks these words, the camera cuts to Paul in the bathroom with his hands covering his mouth, thereby stifling what very well may be an affirmative response to Anna's sharp, if cruel, assessment (the recounting, we should not forget, belongs to Jonathan). But for Paul to confirm Anna's reasoning with words about his actions only perpetuates the limitations of language: "language seems," recalling Barthes, "pusillanimous." Third: Anna tells Paul that in truth he wants her to shower with him because *he* believes *she* "stinks"—that he "prays" for her to wash away her "odor." As Anna points out, however, it is he who urgently washes and straps a necktie around his throat to choke off his own bad smells. It is he, not her, who stinks. He cannot stand to be around himself because, as she calls it, he is a "sack of shit."

Anna, satisfied with her calculations, sits back and lets Paul know that she is prepared to do what he is unable to do. She is prepared, in other words, *to speak* what must be spoken, "to destroy everything." To what extent, however, are her words potent or an accurate assessment of Paul's actions? Is it possible to rationalize emotions in three pointed and specific terms? Can love be categorized, delimited in such a way? Is it possible, through words alone, to "destroy everything" in a relationship? Love? Memories? Or is Anna's linguistic achievement an act of cowardice? Are her assertive words merely signs for the way she wrestles with *how* to express suffering? If love is always already destroyed at the moment that words are used to define and explain it, has not Anna already "destroyed everything"?

Anna's "three reasons" to highlight Paul's "terror" about his inability to express his feelings bring into focus a narrative logic at work in Honoré's films. To intimately touch, and *articulate touch* through words, invariably leads to hurt, loss, and death. The moment touch and language intersect is the moment our characters find themselves on an emotional tightwire. As is often the case in Honoré's cinema (and we discuss in detail later), to overcome the precarious dynamic that occurs when touch and language combine, complex emotions evolve into song and dance. By shifting words into song lyrics, or dancing with the dead through poetic prose and cinematic dissolves, or discharging bodily excess through lyrics in musical numbers (laughter, smells, shit), Honoré puts cinematic gestures to use that open, albeit briefly, channels of communication and reconciliation. Here, we find intimate detachment. Here, we find love.

In the meantime, as Paul's flashback via Jonathan draws to a close, we see Paul drop Anna at the train station on her way to Paris. He states/asks, "So, we are out of love(?)." Jonathan now presents their falling *toward* "out of love" as a nonchronological flashback/flashforward that shows Paul recollecting assorted memories from his time with Anna.[15] If Jonathan is not "present" for these recollected events, he is doubly identified with Paul and shares in his brother's suffering since he now occupies Paul's point of view. The cinematic flashback/flashforward revises and rehearses moments of the breakup as the cinematic narrative shows slightly different angles or actions of the events. The flashback that Jonathan provides, therefore, recalls sequences that show the couple's happier moments as beleaguered with antagonism. This psychoemotional recollection—as Jonathan envisages it—takes its toll on Paul. As the flashback rushes forward, we see Paul reach a turning point where he attempts suicide by downing a handful of pills. He urgently packs the pills into his mouth and, at the same time, attempts to record his death with his Polaroid camera as if a photographic inscription might finally explain his pain. Paul's suicide is a failure because the gesture offers no satisfying description—for him, for anyone.

With Paul's frenetically charged and emotionally fraught backstory complete, Jonathan guides us once again along the same country road but in the opposite direction, back toward Paris. On a cut, we shift from the desolate forest environment to the busyness of Parisian evening traffic as it flows alongside the Seine. Now in Paris, Jonathan and Paul prepare to take a journey across the city. While Paul's journey is an emotional one that finds him saddled to his bed, Jonathan will literally travel about town. Nevertheless, their distinct journeys serve to further intertwine and move the two brothers ever closer.

THE SHIT HOUSE

When we return to Paris from the country, we enter the apartment living room, where Jonathan's movements are on full display for all to see. With Paul now tucked away in Jonathan's bedroom, Jonathan is driven to the fold-away bed in the living room. Given this situation, Mirko, sitting on the edge of the bed, feels free to paternally interrogate Jonathan about skipping classes, his brother's "illness," and why he is out so late at night. Curiously, the only time we see their father share a bed with his sons—or any family member—will be on the edge of the temporary fold-away bed. Unlike their mother, who, later, comfortably moves into her child's bed, their father does not gain entry to the family's most intimate site. Honoré's fathers such as Mirko are often pushed to the periphery, while mother-and-child relationships take priority. In any case, the father's nagging annoys Jonathan. Mirko desperately wants Paul *to talk* because he believes his "illness" is killing him. Jonathan rejects his father's assessment and request to force a conversation with his brother: "I'm going to let him live out his depression in peace." Jonathan's refusal to intervene with words for his brother—*on his father's behalf*—leads Mirko to mistakenly view Jonathan's "worse and worse" behavior as nothing less than "selfish." His father does not relent.

Mirko, for all his shortcomings, reiterates a potent attribute about Jonathan (if not the family itself): his son smells. Specifically, he tells our narrator that his breath stinks while he pries open his mouth to investigate the origin of his son's putrefaction. "You need a dentist." Mirko announces, "Maybe you have something stuck in there." For Mirko, Jonathan's unwillingness to fully communicate ("something stuck" in his mouth?) is directly connected to the fetid odors he radiates. His father is not the last to notice his son's stink. Later, when Jonathan bumps into his former girlfriend Alice, she tells him that she broke up with him precisely because he is "dirty" and that he "stinks," he "always smells of sweat or piss," and he "fucks dirty." As we know from his "apostrophe," Jonathan is not immune to smells that engulf his family.

Time and place corrode the family's bodies. Indeed, Jonathan is not the only rank member of the family. When the brothers' mother (Pisier) pays Paul a visit, she argues with her ex-husband, Mirko, about his troubled finances. Mirko seems ineffectual and impotent alongside her energy. She tells him that he and his sons live in a "shit house." And recalling Anna's earlier remarks, Paul apparently shares the family funk with his brother. Paul, as Anna calls it, is a "sack of shit" who must shower to wash away love's odor because, like Jonathan, his verbal skills are seen as selfish and inarticulate (keep in mind Jonathan's narrative deceit and cinematic rendering of events). The entire family—a world full of love—reeks of shit.

Stink *is* life. It seeps into *Dans Paris*'s familial nooks and crannies; it is Paul's and Jonathan's shared heritage. To be sure, the family's rotten odor may emanate from our "omniscient" narrator, but he is not the only one who stinks. It is no secret to Jonathan that life—erotic desire and death—smells like shit. The brothers' bodily discharges boldly reveal the family's putrescent bodies; they are inexorably decaying. Nonetheless, because of propinquity, the family must tolerate their own stink.

"Smells," Jim Drobnick argues, "defy and transcend (visual) vocabularies regarding sexuality, yet they present powerful, emotionally resonant experiences."[16] Drobnick goes on to discuss contemporary installation artists and their engagement with olfactory experiments as part of their art. As a filmmaker who challenges the limitation of words for expressing desire, Honoré uses smell as a vital component in his cinema, especially because it serves to "defy and transcend (visual) vocabularies regarding sexuality." But how does one evoke "emotionally resonant experiences" through odor in the cinema?

Historically, adding supplemental technologies to the cinematic experience goes back to 1906. Avery Gilbert's chapter "Hollywood Psychophysics" in his book *What the Nose Knows: The Science of Scent in Everyday Life* charts the attempts by various companies, producers, and directors to engage devices that provide the spectator with cinematic scent ("Smell-O-Vision," "AromaRama," Samuel "Roxy" Rothafel, Michael Todd, and John Waters).[17] The cinematic question that Honoré poses, however, is less concerned with giving the spectator the "actual" experience of smell from a scene. To approach odor this way would not be dissimilar to asserting that the words on the screen "match" actual meaning. Nonetheless, encountering olfactory sensuousness is a cornerstone to Honoré's filmmaking. Indeed, it is at the very heart of the visceral nature, the intermingled embodiment, that informs his films.

If stink is life, then art, Leo Bersani significantly notes in *The Freudian Body*, has time and again strived to render and satisfy what is ostensibly a key and "lurid" aspect to life, to our primal instincts—*the smell of sex*.[18] Once man stood erect, Freud teaches, sexual eroticism took shape through a visual exchange. The shift to ocular eroticism from "anal eroticism and olfactory stimulation" resulted in "organic repression" (17). This repression, Bersani explains, led to "our horror of excrement and, at least according to Freud, a repugnance at sex, a shame provoked in us by our genitals and a disgust at genital odors which is so strong in many people that it 'spoil[s] sexual intercourse for them.' And what a loss this was!" (17). How, then, does art—*how does Honoré's cinema*—retrieve the erotic, the primitive instinct, and the sensuality of experience that we have lost through privileging sight? How does Honoré's cinema, tipped heavily to monstration, retrieve the primitive senses and what has given over to the "horror of excrement" and "repugnance at sex"? And, if Drobnick's assertion holds true that "smells defy and transcend (visual) vocabularies," how would smell be visualized, especially within the limitations of narrative cinema?

Bersani makes the case in his analysis of Henry James's "realistic novels" that they "encourage us," through their "extremely tight and coherent structure, . . . to believe in the temporal myth of real beginnings and definitive endings": "[The realist novel] portrays a world in which events always have a significance which can be articulated, and it encourages a view of the self as organized (if also ravaged) by dominant passions or faculties" (82). To be encouraged as such proves vital "in the shaping of the human as a precondition for predicting and controlling it" (83). By arguing for the realist novel as a vehicle through which "predicting and controlling" the "shaping of the human" occurs, Bersani's analysis provocatively echoes the tradition of "apparatus theory" in film studies. His line of thought, in other words, recalls the way that film theorists in this area of study critiqued the realist mode of classical Hollywood filmmaking, in which the cinematic spectator's "passions" were seen to be "organized" and "controlled" by the ideological stitching together of form and content.[19]

Following the study of James, Bersani turns to the queer filmmaker Pier Paolo Pasolini, who, we argued earlier, occupies the queer "double bind" that Honoré similarly shares when his work is critically engaged. Although Bersani does not situate Pasolini's narrative structure in relationship to Hollywood's classical mode of production, his stress on Pasolini's aestheticized *de*narrativizing puts the realist mode and its ideological import in sharp relief. In discussing the Italian director's brilliant and troubling film *Salò o le 120 giornate di Sodoma* (*Salo, or the 120 Days of Sodom,* 1975), Bersani contends that the film's structure of a narrative about the very telling of narratives "is organized to produce a certain type of narrative progression which is itself erotically stimulating" (51). By entering Pasolini's "Circle of Manias, Circle of Shit and Circle of Blood," we encounter the repetition of narrative structure as "mobile repetitions of an eroticized text [that] resist and subvert the logic of narrativity." For Bersani, Pasolini "de-narrativizes" the Sadean text. He argues that *Salo* is, at once, "a philosophical argument which, in a sense, novelistic representation *merely re-presents as traumatically persuasive scenes,* and . . . a self-reflexive discourse, in filmic terms, which repeats and deflects narrative violence in formal recognitions" (54–55; emphasis added). His description assists in returning us to the two distinct yet merged cinematic modes that Gaudreault identified in our introduction as "narration and monstration." François Ozon, we pointed out earlier, is correct when he notes in his film *Dans la maison* that Pasolini is not recognized for adhering to traditional narrative formats. And, as we argued, Ozon's film highlights the way we might view Pasolini's cinema as more "presence" than "representation." What is at stake in both Honoré's and Pasolini's cinema is indeed presence.

By drawing on Pasolini, Bersani provocatively raises the implications of modern civilization's emphasis on the visual at the expense of the "lurid" aspect of sexuality: scent. Indeed, the "horror of excrement" in *Salo* and the odors it strives to emanate—its "presence"—demand that the spectator not merely look at the protofascist's intake of shit; moreover, the spectator is forced to—if only in the imagination—smell shit.[20] But how? Because Pasolini's cinematic form (as well as Honoré's and Fassbinder's) denies a coequal relationship between narration and monstration, "representation" over "presence," we are asked, as Louis Althusser might put it, to "think" with our body.[21]

In *Dans Paris,* for instance, the family's smell proves the most viable way for its members to express themselves. Unfortunately, it is a lesson with which Jonathan and Paul's parents never quite come to terms. Eventually, Jonathan, to quiet his father, reluctantly obliges his request to open a dialogue with Paul. As it turns out, their dialogue cannot escape the familiar stink since the conversation takes place in the bathroom while Paul sits on the toilet, presumably shitting, and Jonathan showers ("Shit! That's cold!" he screams). Their "conversation" at Mirko's behest fails, however, to wash clean the brothers' deeply entrenched smell. Unlike the earlier exchange between Anna and Paul, the brothers' interaction, where bodily cleansing occurs—showering *and* shitting—highlights the spiritual, material, and contradictory connections they share.

To evoke the brothers' fraternal intimacy and its smells, Honoré twice frames the boys in the bathroom mirror in such a way that they reflect each other while remaining distinct entities. While one brother is filmed reflected in the mirror, the other stands directly in front of it, between the camera and the reflection. The framing links their bodies but through a split imago. At the same time, the mirror presents the split yet unified imaginary that Jonathan and Paul share. The brothers are one—cinematically conjoined—yet, at this moment, physically detached. When Jonathan asks Paul what is wrong, his brother can only respond, "nothing." Again, words fail.[22] The brothers' mode of communication is expressed through the mirror's complex reflection, in which the boys are together yet apart (see figure 12). The sequences in the bathroom anticipate the end of the film, where Honoré returns to an intimate doubled framing and the focus is the bed that they de facto share. The bed enables the boys to freely communicate with each other as they once did as children. By film's end, the split imago in the bathroom mirror is thus replaced with the brothers' physical convergence in bed.[23]

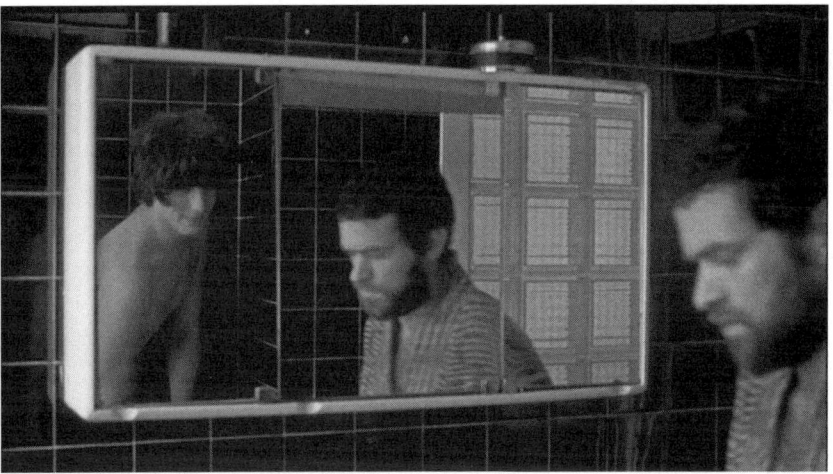

12. Fraternal "split imago" in *Dans Paris*.

PRAYER

From the sequence in the bathroom, the boys make their way back to the shared bedroom, where Jonathan coaxes Paul into some kind of movement. With Christmas so close, Jonathan decides on a childhood tradition to jolt the lethargic Paul. When he asks Paul to "go to Paris," Paul asks, "Why should I go to Paris?" Given that they are already *in Paris,* Jonathan's suggestion invokes a past Paris, one filled with fond remembrances when holidays were alive with family festivities, city lights, and fragrant Christmas aromas. Or so it is imagined. To conjure this past, Jonathan reminds Paul about their boyhood trips to Le Bon Marché Department Store, where they gazed on the holiday window displays. Paul at first refuses to participate in Jonathan's trip down memory lane, even though Jonathan assures him they can make it there in thirty minutes. Paul questions Jonathan's ability to make it to the store on foot, not by metro, in such a short time. Since Paul does not expect Jonathan to succeed in his mission, he finally agrees to participate and offers that if Jonathan makes it to the department store within thirty minutes, he will leave the apartment and meet his brother in front of Bon Marché. Jonathan accepts the wager even though both brothers are fully aware that meeting the thirty-minute time frame is wishful thinking. Jonathan rushes off, cognizant that a difficult task lies before him. Our creative narrator, who always has self-interest at heart, stumbles on another set of scenarios along his route that catch his fancy and distract him from his original goal. This is not to say that Jonathan's satisfying his own self-interests neglects his brother's best interests.

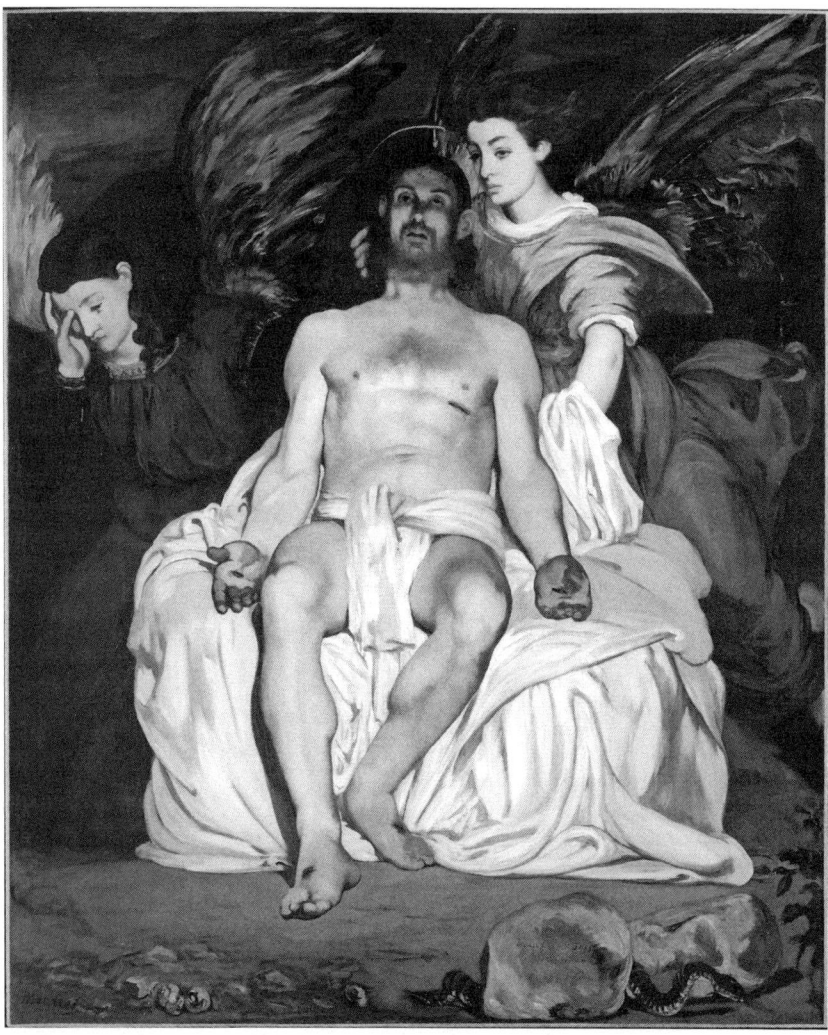

13. Édouard Manet, *Le Christ mort et les anges* (1864), the Metropolitan Museum of Art, New York, H. O. Havermeyer Collection, Bequest of Mrs. H. O. Havermeyer, 1929.

Along Jonathan's journey, the family motto/handicap—"Take time to ignore the sadness of your family"—appropriately reappears for him. Keeping in mind the other family tradition—"detachment"—Jonathan discovers his own self-pleasure as a way to reconvene with, if not resurrect, his brother. On his way to Bon Marché, Jonathan encounters three women—a quick trick with a woman on a scooter, his ex-girlfriend Alice, and a winsome young girl who we see only through reflections in the Bon Marché window. He has sex with all three. Hence, his thirty-minute trip quickly turns into a seven-hour sexual romp across Paris, divided among three

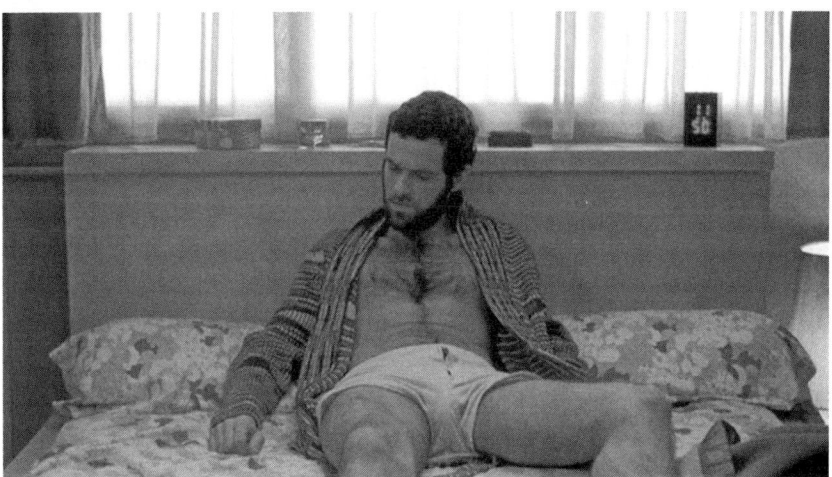

14. Paul-as-martyr occupies a family bed. Jonathan and Anna offer prayers to him from a distance. Throughout *Dans Paris*, a host of angels will join Paul in this bed to give comfort.

romantic rendezvous. With his return later in the evening, Jonathan tells Paul that his sexual interludes with these three women were like "praying" for him: "I shared those girls with you," and "I prayed they'd save your soul."

In the film, prayer—a gesture often made with one's hands clasped together in a triangular formation—functions in parallel with three particularly French phenomena: culture and religion, art and aesthetics, film history and homage. First, the repetition of prayer reminds the viewer that French Catholicism and its emphasis on this intimate gesture that one makes to God purportedly secures redemption in the afterlife (the film's Christmas backdrop highlights Catholicism's central hold on French culture while the holiday's narrative launches the Christian tale of the life-and-death cycle). Mirko's insistence on the family Christmas tree signals an important discussion that we take up later in this volume. Read this way, we can posit Paul in *Dans Paris* as a suffering Christ figure who is surrounded by two intimates—lover and brother—who offer him prayer so as to shield him from further pain. If Paul is presented as a martyred Christ figure (in the Catholic tradition), then Honoré intersects the religious transfiguration with its French attenuation: *laïcité*, or secularization. Sorrow, spirituality, and secular knowledge will return in *La belle personne* as aspects for the (albeit failed) concept of romanticism.

Aesthetically and as a second consideration of prayer in *Dans Paris*, a line may be provocatively drawn to Édouard Manet's *The Dead Christ and the Angels* (1864; see figure 13). Much can be said to attribute a link between this painting and Honoré's work. The striking intertextual allusion is worth noting wherein the two angels that flank Manet's Christ, with their flowing locks and youthful porcelain skin, call to mind Honoré's cinematic "angels" (Anna and Jonathan) who offer versions of prayer for Paul's salvation. In both Honoré's and Manet's work, one angel turns away in despair while the other stays close to comfort him. Manet's rather sensual and muscular Christ calls to mind the similarly bearded Paul/Duris, who remains secured to his bed because of his own spiritual death. The bearded Christ corpse in Manet's painting faces us, directly centered in the painting; the corpse's eyes are propped open, while the body is seated upright on a sheeted bed-like surface. Christ's mouth is agape but is unable to speak. Although Honoré strips Duris's high-polish movieness by dressing him in "mediocre underwear" (JNCH, 188), his sentimentalized body is similar to the martyred Christ figure in that it is nonetheless erotically suggestive.

In this way, Manet's and Honoré's sacrificial men suggest potent and erotically "sentimentalized" figures that are humanized, not victimized; their bodies are at once both spiritual and secularly visceral.[24] Hence, and according to Anthony Julius, "Manet secularised religious painting, and reversed a certain trajectory in the canonic representation of the male death," by corporealizing a spiritual event.[25] Honoré, likewise, invokes the tradition of this particular aesthetic and its religious aura but insists on pushing ever further the terms for its secularization. He commingles familial erotics (especially the male body) in such a way that they are filtered through a queer-spiritual secularization. In this scene, for instance, a long take lingers on Paul's outstretched suffering body as he is about to slowly gyrate to an old Kim Wilde song on his record player (see figure 14). Moreover, Honoré's angels attend to Paul's salvation through prayer that has been eroticized.

Third, Honoré's trinities and prayer also bear a cinematic imprint, a Hitchcockian bouquet or homage. What might be read as cinematic homage brings into play a perverse religiosity. To be sure, Hitchcock—the great visualizer, as Truffaut posits it—was not immune from displaying Catholic impulses, just as Honoré delights in bringing to film his recollection of Catholic rituals of life and death, which he recalls with both fondness and repulsion (JNCH, 171). Hitchcock's cinematic echo is all the more apparent in Honoré's films since their triangular relationships are created through doubled characters. Consider, for example, Hitchcock's multiple triads formed in *Rebecca* (1940) because of Maxim de Winter and (the new) Mrs. de Winter, who is haunted by the dead Mrs. de Winter; or the dissemination of guilt through Guy and Bruno's doubling in *Strangers on a Train* (1951); or Scottie's triangulated arrangement with Madeleine/Judy, who is at once one and the same in *Vertigo* (1958). Hence, like Hitchcock, Honoré's triangles are formed and re-formed with the living and/or the dead. Two become three, doubles yield a third, who joins with the others in the film's action. In *Dans Paris,* a final and significant third will appear at the apex of the cinematic family.

Indeed, it is prayer that triggers doubles into threes. Time and again, Honoré's trinities form through cinematic doublings that explicitly turn on spiritual—if not deviantly Catholic—communication. When Anna, via Jonathan's flashback, had earlier depicted three reasons for Paul's detachment, she tells him that she offered prayer to receive Paul's love. Even though he claims that he offers no prayer for her, we see Paul fold his hands in prayer so as to block his mouth, ostensibly keeping his mouth shut and, perhaps, keeping away his lover's odor. Later, when we see Anna inform Paul that her love for him is like "faith" and that she "prayed" for his love, she decides, "It's not the worst way to save the soul." Paul's "love" is displaced elsewhere, toward his brother and dead sister, Claire. The sister's suicide is the troubling yet guiding force for Paul, and it is Claire to whom he must pray.

What is remarkable about Anna's prayer is that in this retelling, it has been put into her mouth by Paul's double: Jonathan. In whatever way she turns, she is drawn into a thirdness that stubbornly refuses to separate the brothers' doubling. The family odor is thick and impenetrable. In fact, the familial stench is linked through Jonathan's narration of "Anna's" prayer for Paul, a gesture that Jonathan later repeats. Anna's prayer is in effect Jonathan's version of Anna's appeal for Paul's love. From Jonathan's perspective, Paul had no such prayers for Anna. For Jonathan/Paul, prayer demands that one must believe in the other. Paul does not believe in Anna; he believes in Claire (his dead sister), and, most significantly, he believes in Jonathan. Just as Jonathan forges the Anna-Paul-Jonathan triangle, he does so to secure the familial trinity: Claire-Jonathan-Paul.

Later, when Jonathan focuses the narrative on the three scenes in which he cavorts around Paris, he assures Paul that "each and every one" of his liaisons was an offering to "save" Paul's "soul." Paul notes that his brother's prayers bring to mind Anna's "three reasons," the prayers that she hoped would reconnect their love: "Three times I prayed for you today"; "Three times, I believed that I was keeping my brother alive," Jonathan announces. This repetition raises the ante on the terms for brotherly love. By alignment with Anna, Jonathan's three platonic prayers tread close to incestuous affection since, as the narrator, he has treated himself and Anna as the same. They are at once Paul's family, lover, and angel. In this way, *Dans Paris* explores the erotic possibilities that brotherly bonds allow since the fraternal doubling involves a triangulated spiritual imbrication of bodies across cinematic time and space.

PART I

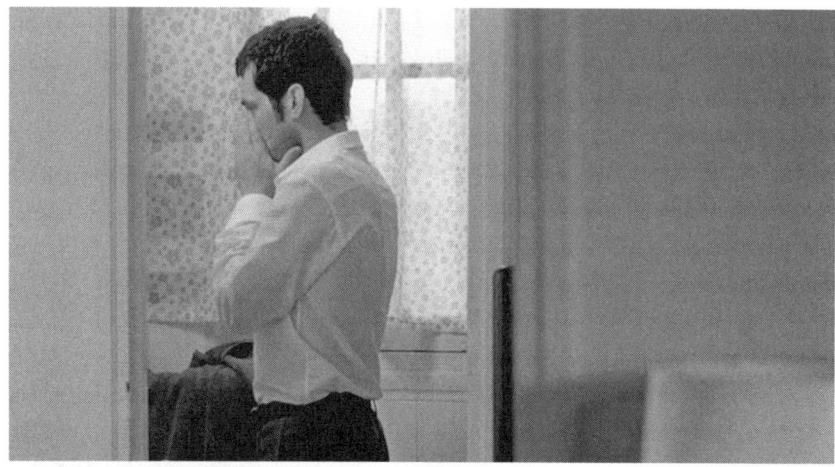

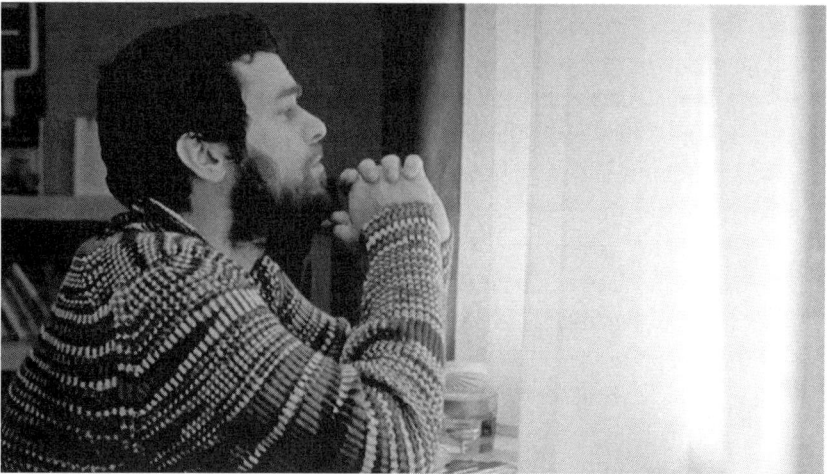

15.1–15.2. Paul in traditional prayer pose.

Finally, and in another echo of the Catholic parable that ghosts *Dans Paris*, Jonathan's three prayers call to mind St. Peter's three betrayals of Christ. Out of fear, out of sadness, Peter's betrayal and detachment from the "brother" he loves so dearly is, when all is said and done, an act of love for self *and* for Christ. Is it not Christ who calls Peter's betrayal in advance? Is it not Peter who subsequently goes on to be Christ's bearer of his legacy so that he might have eternal life? Is it not precisely Peter's lie to save himself that is necessary—nay, required—for this legacy to be handed down to save mankind?

In *Dans Paris*, Jonathan/Garrel and Paul/Duris move centrifugally and centripetally, emotionally and physically, within the city and beyond it. The two are, nonetheless, conjoined with the city of Paris—a third actor to be sure. The cinematic apparatus stitches together the dynamic relations on the screen. Honoré's trinities form from the inside outward—spatially, temporally—and back again. The brothers' doubled bodies, refracted in the mirror, are later rejoined in the bed and thus extend outward and back again. Bodies and their relationships fluctuate in a cinematic current of jump cuts, flashbacks, motivated dissolves, and song. *Dans Paris*'s doubling and triangular formulations are mobile to the extent that they are dependent on memory as it is conceived through cinematic form. Since life is cinema for Honoré, cinematic transformation is a vortex. Father, mother, Anna, Alice, Claire, and others who pass along the way are all transformed by the fraternal doubling and triangular dimensions that it reimagines for and with them. At every turn, new love is expressed, new triangles are formed, while the smell of love's memory continually reeks.

MEMORY AND MEDIATION

The most significant third presence is the brothers' dead sister, Claire, who comes onto the scene when Jonathan and Paul reaffirm their faith and love for each other. Recalling the cinematic portrait that the two young men share in *Dans Paris*'s title sequence, Honoré returns to the bed, where Jonathan recounts a vital piece of family history that paves the way for Claire's illumination of the doubling of her brothers. And we realize that she forms with them the missing and critical element of the film's triangular centerpiece.

On the night before, Paul had once again attempted suicide. In this instance, he jumped from a nearby bridge into the Seine. Because he was dressed in Jonathan's clothing when he jumped (doubled once again), their father mistook Paul for Jonathan as he saw his son leave late at night. As we saw earlier, Mirko berates Jonathan for irresponsibly sleeping late because he stayed out beyond reasonable hours. Unbeknownst to Mirko, and to us, Jonathan had in fact shielded his father from Paul's actions. Rather than being irresponsible, Jonathan had instead nursed his water-soaked and chilled brother upon his return. For all of Mirko's demands that Jonathan help deliver Paul from his "sickness," Jonathan—*silently*—has in fact saved his brother's life. Once again, the father remains ignorant about his family's goings-on, and, thus, he is situated outside the family's intimacies. Mirko's wish for clarity through words ultimately gives no access to his own family dynamics.

If Paul and Jonathan's "secret" is hidden from their father and only revealed through a flashback, then Honoré identifies familial intimacies as an affective cinematic memory. Sentient intimacy is, in other words, envisaged through very particular cinematic means (flashbacks, soundtrack). The trilogy films, for example, often bridge spatial and temporal detachments with song and/or ghost-like hauntings that draw bodies physically and emotionally together. Distance is overcome through mediation between the characters and the dead or, in some instances, through media technology or through a combination of the two. In all instances, this involves a trinity. For instance, when Jonathan's former girlfriend Alice reappears at the family home after her afternoon tryst with Jonathan, she provides Paul the opportunity to reconnect at last with his departed sister, Claire. Though "not the best conversationalist these past few days," Paul is nostalgic for Claire when he tells Alice about the way his sister used to weep for an entire day. Her tears were "for no reason," he explains. They were "for an old sorrow" that Claire experienced during a "previous life, in the Middle Ages, or the times of idle kings." She was, for Paul, a weeping "Divinity." Her inexplicable, lost past nonetheless revealed itself through her tears, which Claire welcomed as her "cousins." Her tears, in other words, were more nurturing and healing than were her immediate family members. As Paul is so fully and recently aware, families nag and demand. Tears comfort.

As Paul's prosaic recounting unfolds, he tells Alice that his frustration with Claire's sadness was not so much caused by her endless tears; instead, he felt "humiliated" that he could not help her. Her sadness felt as if it were a "test" that only made him realize his "helplessness against others' suffering." No words, he realizes, alleviate the other's sorrows. It is arrogant to imagine one has an ability to erase someone else's "heartache." If anyone feels this most profoundly, it is Paul. Alice, attentive to Paul's story, surmises that sorrow is instilled at birth, like eye color; it fills our every day because it is a memory long ago inscribed into our very being. Paul agrees and reckons that happiness can only be found in self-sorrow, since, as for Claire, it brings people into "communion" with one another precisely because sadness is universal. Claire's suicide was desperation; the "old sorrows killed her." Ever-lasting grieving is what we die from.

With Claire finally conjured, Paul reaches out to Anna. They communicate in a final gesture, from a distance, through technology and cinematic form—they sing to each other over the telephone. The song, "Avant la haine" (Before the Hate), rehearses their wish to let go, while simultaneously yearning to stay together. Alex Beaupain's melancholic mix of Jacques Brel– and Françoise Hardy–style music and lyrics tell of the difficult back-and-forth pull that the lovers experience as they begin their farewell (Beaupain's contribution to Honoré's cinema is taken up in the next chapter). As with other songs in Honoré's films, the lyrics describe a sensual process, often involving description of tastes, smells, and multiple bodily sensations. The lovers *touch* from a distance and through song. Through the mediated connection, the lovers gently and expressively put their relationship to rest.

Putting to rest a relationship is, of course, not dissimilar to laying to rest a loved one. Both events involve loss and mourning. For Honoré, the complex psychological and emotional mechanisms, associated with the erotic and death, intersect through song. Yet ends of relationships and death in his films do not mean "the end" once and for all. For Honoré, memory—particularly memory prompted by death—lingers and is envisaged cinematically. The trilogy is a major work that places song and death side by side; they work together in a symbiotic partnership. In this way, Honoré poses possibilities for what appears impossible. He moves bodies toward one another, tears them apart through death, and discovers cinematic reconciliations between the dead and the living.

Since to love invariably involves detachment, song reaches for an expression of the inexplicable suffering that is love itself. To say "I love you" in an Honoré film, in other words, recalls Barthes's note in *A Lover's Discourse* where to say/write "*I-love-you* is on the side of expenditure. Those who seek the proffering of the word (lyric poets, liars, wanderers) are subjects of Expenditure: they spend the word, as if it were impertinent (base) that it be recovered somewhere; they are at the extreme limit of language, where language itself (and who else would do so in its place?) recognizes that it is without backing or guarantee, working without a net."[26] Such is the tenuous, yet oddly life-affirming, atmosphere we discover in Honoré's cinema.

FAMILY ROMANCE: A NOTE ON MOTHERS

The mother in *Dans Paris* (Pisier) has a central role. Through her brief presence, Honoré evokes the strongly affective position and cultural obligations that rest on the figure of the matriarch. Future work on the filmmaker undoubtedly requires detailed analysis of Honoré's approach to the mother as she appears in such films as *Ma mère, Non ma fille tu n'iras pas danser,* and *Les bien-aimés*. The mothers in these films pivot on self-determination and their negotiation of vexed family matters. The trilogy does not afford the same opportunities to study mother figures as fully. Nevertheless, the mother in *Dans Paris* stresses the crucial role that mothers play in Honoré's cinema.[27]

Whether it is for Paul to communicate with his father, his brother, or his girlfriend, he finds himself trapped insofar as he is unable to use words to express or describe emotion. The boys' loved but impure mother (the brothers refer to her as "the Saint-of-a-Whore") most visibly asserted herself in their past without words when she, one day, "slammed the door shut" and left the family for a "Canadian lumberjack." While Jonathan cavorts across Paris ostensibly to alleviate his brother's pain, their mother, at her ex-husband's request, pays Paul a visit. Although her visit to comfort Paul during his depression proves frustrating, she laments her son's silence—"Nothing to say?"—and Mirko gleefully takes pleasure in her failure to encourage Paul to speak. Later, however, Mirko stumbles on his son and ex-wife rolling with laughter on the boys' bed. If the father insists that Paul speak, his mother has, without much effort (intuitively), recognized that Paul's "nothing to say" does not mean he has nothing to express. Paul and his mother vibrantly communicate when she guides him toward the past, toward the moment when they shared childlike giggles in her (little) boy's bedroom.

Hence, failure to express feeling—clearly, definitively—is overcome without words and rehearsed through what we have discussed as cinematic "monstration." Honoré's cinematic mother plays no small role in facilitating such a dynamic. Jonathan, as our "omniscient narrator," learning well from his mother, understands the necessity of turning over language-based storytelling to cinematic showing. Specifically, the emphasis in distinction between word-language and cinema-language is Honoré's thematic centerpiece when exploring the difficulty of fully expressing emotion in relation to the erotic tension that demonstrative behavior provokes within the family environment. Indeed, the emotive impasse in his films emphasizes the familial discourses that pulsate with incestuous possibilities.[28] Paul's giggling and rolling in bed with his mother, for instance, suggests the fuzzy incestuous line that Honoré subtly, yet in discomfiting ways, crosses with his cinematic families.

The familial/-r bed on which we see the intimate mother-son play thus returns us to the title sequence that opened our discussion. We return to the film's "beginnings," in Thierry Kuntzel's terms, in order to consider the way the "link[s] in the chain that constitute the film" resonate with familiarity across *Dans Paris* and specifically in relationship to Honoré's own insertion into the cinematic family romance. The bed, on which mother and son frolic, echoes the bed where we first encountered Paul and Jonathan in the film's credit sequence. Paul and Jonathan's bed-sharing, in short, holds the film together. A shared bed is the film's focal point, where brothers, lovers, mothers, and film history sensually connect. Anna was also drawn into this bed from a distance when she and Paul serenaded each other from their phones, as was Alice and, as always already, Claire. Honoré's beds are the place where new French families emerge and come together. They are the sites where "family" and French film history touch and communicate with each other.

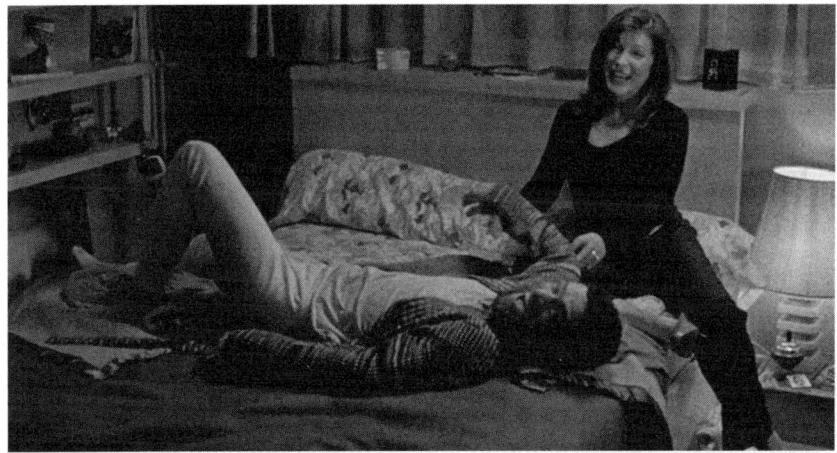

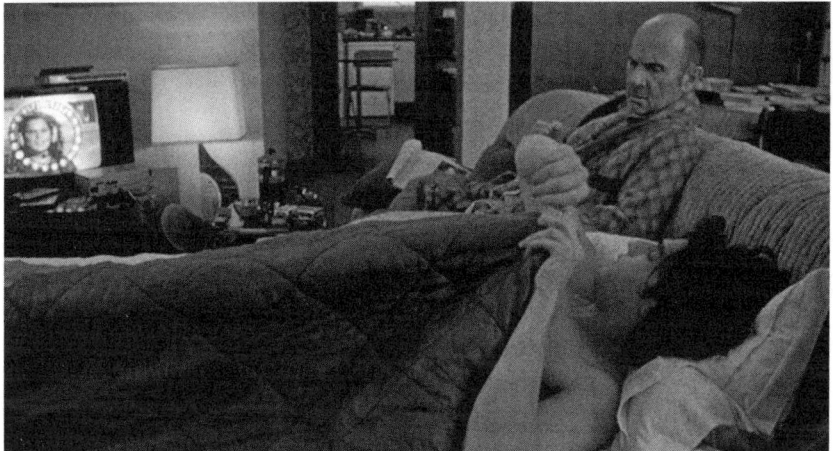

16.1–16.2. While Honoré's cinematic mother (Marie-France Pisier) frolics with her son, Paul, in the family bed, his cinematic father (Guy Marchand) is relegated to Jonathan's temporary fold-away bed in the living room.

If beds are treated, Honoré tells us, "like dining-room tables" in his films, they are so because they are the site where elaborate histories and memories gather. Hence, Pisier tumbles around in Honoré's bed with France's young heartthrob Romain Duris. Not unlike the way Honoré does with his other cinematic mothers—Catherine Deneuve, Isabelle Huppert, and Chiara Mastroianni—he feasts and delights in sharing historical and incestuous histories.

If the bed is, as Paul calls it in *Dans Paris,* "a nice and sensible family tradition," it is so to the extent that its wrinkles reveal the emotionally charged and eroticized bodies that have rolled across it. The very definition of family, however, is in flux as Honoré unpacks it. Indeed, the bed is where Honoré firmly situates himself in the filmic enterprise. By connecting beds across cinematic scenes and film history, Honoré not only draws himself into the cinematic world but also brings into relief the incestuous delights that develop as he commingles with actors, French New Wave filmmakers, and a range of multimedia arts.

JOURNEYS

As the day in *Dans Paris* circles back to the film's beginning, the narrative ellipses are slowly filled in. Our return to the beginning of the film leads us, of course, back to the brothers' bed. From here, a final significant doubling occurs, and a new familial triangle is formed. Honoré maximizes the brothers' doubling when Jonathan, on his way home from his sexual escapades across the river and into central Paris, plunges into the Seine. The jump not only mirrors Paul's attempted suicide (when, we recall, he was dressed in Jonathan's clothing); Jonathan's action,

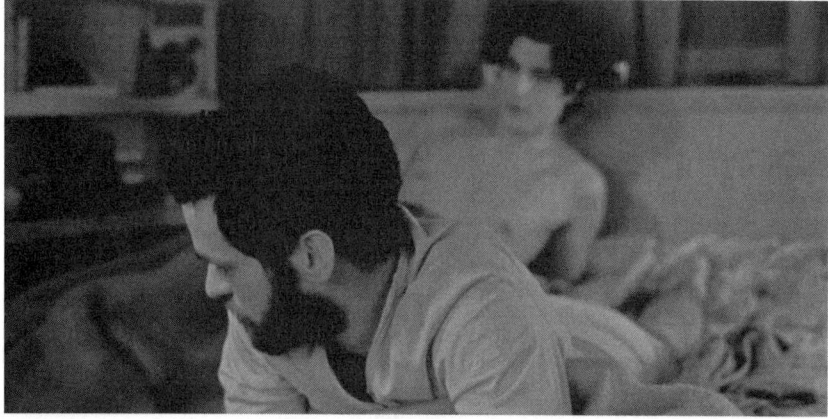

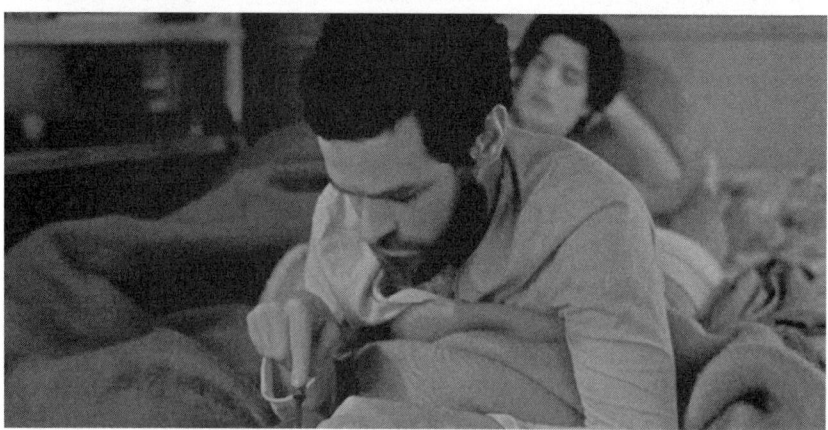

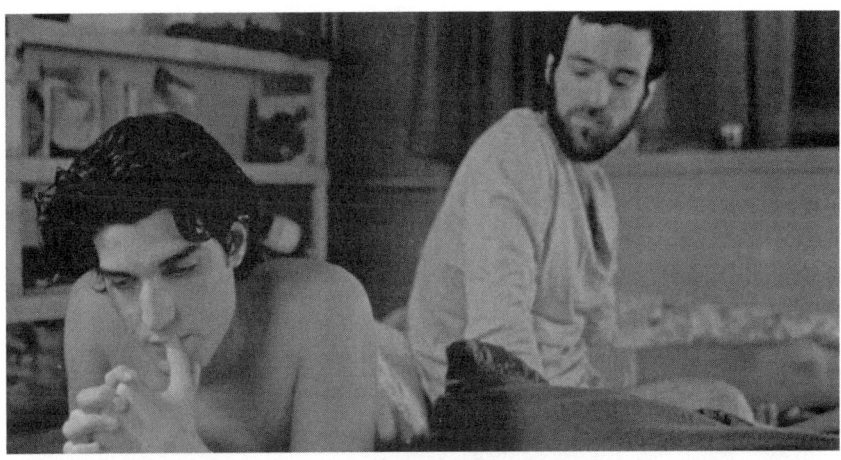

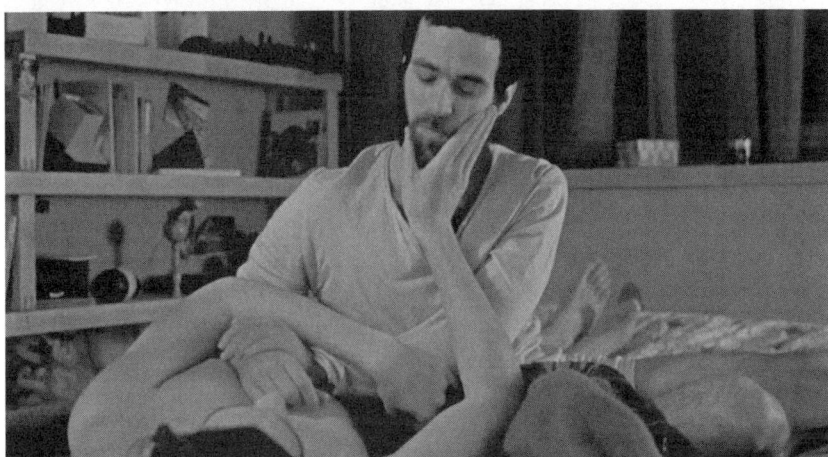

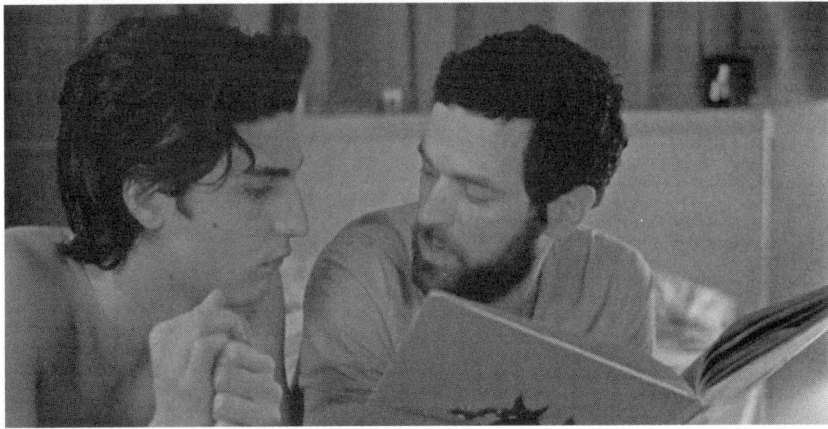

17.1–17.5. Brothers tenderly conjoin in bed in *Dans Paris*.

moreover, folds the brothers' lives into each other. He jumps not to mimic but *to feel* his brother's sorrow. Echoing the earlier sequence, Honoré swaps Jonathan's brotherly nursing and hands it over to Paul, who now assumes the role of caretaker as he warms and dries Jonathan's shivering body. Through love and the promise of death, the brothers are one.

As Jonathan and Paul lie in bed to discuss their mutually complex sex life and self-inflicted near-death experiences, Jonathan suggests that Paul's return home was not a choice that he himself would have necessarily made. To return home, Jonathan argues, is only another form of failed suicide, purgatory. (See figures 17.1–17.5.) "If I were you, anywhere but here," Jonathan insists. Paul responds, "But I'm not you, my life's not yours." Jonathan punctuates Paul's remark with a slap to his ass and declares, "And my life's not yours." Jonathan quickly adds, however, "Too bad."

Indeed, *Dans Paris* has convinced us otherwise. The brothers are linked as one; each brother's life belongs to the other. When Honoré frames the two boys during this conversation, he choreographs the dialogue in such a way that their declared independence from each other is a deceit. The film's framing, in effect, contradicts the words we hear. Following the brothers' less-than-truthful remarks to each other ("my life's not yours"), Honoré positions Jonathan at the head of the bed, shirtless. Paul also faces the camera, but he is positioned closer to the camera in the foreground, bare legged. Situated this way, Jonathan's and Paul's bodies intersect midway. The camera remains locked on them as Paul begins to cut pieces of cheese that he offers his brother. As they shift about on the bed, a new framing occurs in which they appear as twins conjoined at the neck. Paul then shifts onto his back, while Jonathan regales him with his afternoon trysts. On the cut and as they chat, Jonathan moves to the foreground, while Paul moves toward the rear of the frame, where he rests against the headboard. Throughout, they remain cinematically/corporeally connected within the frame.

Still physically connected, Jonathan and Paul wrap up their adult storytelling and all its attendant angst. While rolling around the bed, Jonathan stumbles on a children's book stuffed under his bed. The book is *Loulou* by Grégoire Solotareff. At Jonathan's behest, Paul reads the story to his younger brother as he has done so many times before—they know it "by heart." A story of friendship, fear, loss, and trust, *Loulou* tells the story of a small rabbit and a wolf who, with all natural odds and logic against them (they are a rabbit and wolf living in the forest, after all), realize the value in protecting one's friends from fear. This is not to say that sorrow and fear do not coexist—certainly they do. *Loulou* teaches that friends' (brothers') relationships may run into difficulties when one or the other friend creates fear and sorrow for those whom he or she loves.[29] This often happens—as the wolf does in the book—when one friend ventures into the world and leaves the other behind. Nevertheless, their bond remains secure. It may be disrupted and rattled, but it remains secure.

CODA

As Jonathan makes his way home, and just prior to his own-but-shared suicide attempt, he passes two film posters: for Gus Van Sant's *Last Days* (2005) and David Cronenberg's *A History of Violence* (2005). Pausing before each, Jonathan turns toward the camera and grins—a cinematic wink—at the spectator.[30] Given Honoré's pleasure in homage, his use of film posters here marks a long cinematic tradition in which filmmakers point to their own aesthetic histories and influences. On the city streets, Honoré directs Louis-Garrel-as-Jonathan so that he passes through and revises a history of cinema. His movement through the city further anticipates his move into Honoré's next reenvisioning of Paris: *Les chansons d'amour*.

But the film posters in this scene also nod to the words of the Nietzschean epigraph noted earlier. If *Dans Paris* stresses the impossibility of words to get at "the" truth, and that the "mobile army of metaphor and metonymy" render themselves, at the very least, exhausted, *Last Days* and *A History of Violence* rehearse similar theoretical terrain. Mumbling and music replace clearly articulated dialogue in *Last Days*, while duplicitous words and the tremor of sexual violence lie at the heart of a family's unconscious in *A History of Violence*. But in both these (queer) auteurist films, emotions and the experience of death *are* expressed. In some ways, Van Sant's and Cronenberg's film posters wink at Honoré since all these filmmakers—before and after him—murmur and resonate with the historical past and what is to come.

II

Les chansons d'amour

NARRATIVE ARC

The themes of family, love, and loss continue in *Les chansons d'amour*, part 2 of the trilogy. The film opens with a romantic threesome—Ismaël, Julie, and Alice. Their romance is a triangle whose emotional tentacles reach deep into Julie's family to ultimately draw Ismaël into complex negotiations with her parents and siblings. After experiencing a series of ups and downs in the romantic triangle, Julie dies suddenly and unexpectedly. Because Honoré casts *Les chansons* as a "film with song"—not a musical in the traditional sense—characters turn to song as the only available form of communication to express their grief. Since words fail them when love and death come into the picture, it is only through song that words, *lyrics*, can render inexplicable and visceral experiences. With Julie's passing, those whose lives she touched—even at several removes—are opened onto new forms of intimacy. In this way, erotic desire and loss play out through song in such a way that they serve as prompts for characters to act on unanticipated encounters.

PART II

THE POLITICS OF LOVE

Les chansons d'amour is about love, loss, and family relations. It is deeply connected to the film's composer, Alex Beaupain, and Honoré's queerly lived cinematic lives since it draws on the very themes they suddenly experienced once settled in Paris. The film, Nick-Rees Roberts notes, is "dedicated to a friend ... and to a fellow filmmaker who had died from AIDS."[1] Unnamed by Rees-Roberts, the friend—Aude Monnin—was a dear and cherished friend of both Honoré and Beaupain. *Les chansons* is offered in her "memory." The "fellow filmmaker" to whom the film is dedicated is Jean-Claude Guiguet (1948–2005). The title card that indicates that the film is a gift to their departed friends reads, "Ce film est à mémoire d'Aude Monnin, il est dédié a Jean-Claude Guiguet." Hence, both Jean-Claude and Aude are essential to Honoré's conception of *Les chansons*.

Guiguet was a filmmaker and screenwriter as well as a professor at La Fémis. According to his obituary in *L'Express,* "his passion for cinema was born with a vision when, at fifteen years old, he saw Luchino Visconti's *Les nuits blanches*."[2] Like Honoré, a cinephile born during adolescence, Guiguet went on to write for *Cahiers du Cinéma* and other film journals and collaborated as second assistant director on Paul Vecchiali's *Change pas de main* (1975). Along with several notable feature films (*Le mirage,* 1992; *Les passagers,* 1999), he is highly regarded for his short film about AIDS, *Une nuit ordinaire* (1996), which is included in the short-film collection *L'amour est à réinventer* (1996). The film's dedication to Guiguet is given in thanks for his work and for inspiring Honoré's filmmaking.

"In memory of Aude Monnin" involves a more intimate history for Honoré. Although the filmmaker and composer remain discreet about the relationship, it is certain that Beaupain, Honoré, and Monnin were extremely close for many years.[3] With the three being friends since the early 1990s, Aude's death in 2000 was particularly devastating for both Honoré and Beaupain, especially since Beaupain and Monnin were engaged to be married. In 2000, while celebrating at a nightclub, according to Marie-Laure Delorme, Beaupain's "fiancée collapsed" and was never revived. When she died, Beaupain was greatly affected and, like Honoré, confirms that *Les chansons* is a film about mutual pain and loss.[4] In effect, the scene in which Julie dies mirrors a personal and tragic event.[5]

The film is cathartic, then, in the classic sense of the term. Indeed, Honoré describes *Les chansons* this way: "[It was] inspired by the death of somebody whom I loved as a friend and whom the composer Alex Beaupain loved as well. When that person passed away, Alex wrote some songs, and I referred to the feelings of my grief in my novels. But we came together with the idea of transforming this grief into the joy of making a movie."[6] In an interview with

Aloysius J. Gleek, he says, "*Les Chansons d'amour* tells such a personal story that I knew it by heart. The issue of the story was never raised in fact, only the idea of *how* to deal with it without becoming petrified, how to tell it and make it work in a musical structure that reflects on the whole film."⁷

Les chansons thus cinematically performs the *how*, the director's process of mourning. Through this process, Honoré and Beaupain create a gift for the woman they loved and lost. Before her death, Monnin had also produced a gift for her friends. In 1998, she completed two thesis projects ("mémoires") at l'École des hautes études en sciences sociales, l'École normale supérieure. The titles for her projects—"Les cadeaux dans les relations familiales" and "La fidélité chez les homosexuels"—underscore what are undoubtedly strong thematic links shared within Honoré's circle in which homosexuality, family, and intimacy shaped the friendships.⁸ Through the "film with song," the beloved—Aude (like Claire in *Dans Paris*)—is cinematically conjured. She haunts Honoré and Beaupain's "idea of transforming [their] grief into the joy of making a movie."

Les chansons' dedications also afford us the opportunity to consider Honoré's relationship to "the political." By acknowledging Guiguet's death by AIDS and his own queer relationship with Monnin, Honoré's cinematic gesture marks only one of the ways he politically intervenes in French queer culture. *Les chansons* hit several tender spots regarding homosexual relationships and the family—domestically and abroad.⁹

When Honoré was asked, following the release of *Les chansons,* as a "twenty-first century filmmaker who films today's world" whether he is "is fully implicated in it," he responded, "Yes, I feel this need to deal with the modern world very strongly."¹⁰ To be "fully implicated" and to engage politically as the "homosexual narrator," especially in relationship to AIDS (but not exclusively), Honoré approaches "the political" through several mediated registers. In other words, he turns to a range of discrete media conduits to express and "deal with the modern world."

On at least three separate occasions since *Les chansons*' release, Honoré has signed his name in public protest. In 2009, along with other filmmakers and culture-industry producers, he signed his name to protest the Sarkozy-supported HADOPI law).¹¹ The law—ultimately struck down in 2013—placed strict requirements on Internet "end users" and did little for filmmakers' ability to control the terms for their work's distribution and subsequent remuneration. When the law was appealed, its emphasis shifted from legal ramifications for creator and end user to placing the onus on "commercial piracy." In 2010, Honoré petitioned in *Le Monde,* along with more than six thousand other writers, the decision of the General Council of Seine Saint-Denis that sought to reduce subsidies for a Montreuil book fair, dedicated to children's books.[12] And in 2012—again in *Le Monde*—Honoré coauthored and signed with other significant French cultural figures a treatise that denounced "homophobic" declarations and French law that prohibited same-sex marriage, prevented adoptions by homosexual parents, and refused medical assistance for homosexual partners who sought to have children.[13] Honoré continually positions himself in political debates through multimedia venues in which—and this is a critical component of his cinematic enterprise as a whole—"the political" is experienced as multipronged. It is best engaged and most saliently realized when its channels of communication are creatively and judiciously strategized.

In 2002, for example, Honoré directed a public service advertisement, "SIDA [AIDS]—Bedroom." The advertisement introduces us to a young heterosexual couple, who after frolicking in bed discuss whether they should test for HIV. In the end, they leave together to take the test.[14] While Honoré's cinematic advertisement is clear and concise in the arena in which social messages are best received, "the politics" of AIDS is delivered differently in *Les chansons*. As he makes clear, cinema that mobilizes a "message" fails *as* cinema (JNCH, 199). Through a range of mediated contexts, Honoré's work reveals "the political" as complex, varied, and aesthetically challenging. There is not just one way to get at "the political."

Hence, Rees-Roberts is not entirely accurate when he contends that *Tout contre Léo* is Honoré's only AIDS film. Rees-Roberts argues that the director's subsequent films are a genre of cinema he identifies as "not-about-AIDS." He further argues that Honoré's later work is of a group of films "that either consciously chooses to banish grey areas around HIV within queer subcultures . . . from its visual production, or one that is unable to address the issue head-on." Instead, Rees-Roberts applauds Ducastel and Martineau's *Jeanne et le garçon formidable* and *Drôle de Félix* as "an AIDS cinema" because these films "[eschew] sentimental pathos in favour of bitter-sweet camp (combining a darkness of humour with a lightness of touch)" that proves to be "indeed artistically and politically viable."[15] We suggest otherwise. Honoré's cinema is "about AIDS"—"artistically and politically." But it scores the topic quite differently than Ducastel and Martineau do. His films need to be viewed in the larger context of a queer auteur whose work in relationship to "the political" stretches broadly and across wide swathes of media production.

Les chansons, therefore, is not intended as Demy pastiche and a "politically viable" film to reckon with AIDS in the way that Ducastel and Martineau's films do. Although Honoré is often accused of making "obvious" references to Demy and Godard, Ducastel and Martineau's *Jeanne* is far more literal and direct in its appeal to Demy. Their film drives home an important point about AIDS in France in 1998. For the purposes of creating a message as such, the film engages the visual and musical tropes associated with Demy while drawing on documentary-like footage from ACT-UP demonstrations in Paris. Put together this way, *Jeanne* strictly adheres to a linear narrative structure while, at the same time, introducing whimsical Demy-esque song and dance. Honoré was determined that *Les chansons* would treat the film's "topical dimension" (AIDS) without "making a documentary or militant film."[16] Ducastel and Martineau's "bitter-sweet camp" pushes itself toward a "message film" with music—the very direction that Honoré resists.[17]

Honoré is unequivocal about the way he approaches Demy and the way his elder's cinema surfaces in his films, especially *Les chansons*: "I love the work of Jacques Demy, to me he is a godfather of French cinema. You can't make a French musical without acknowledging Demy, but I didn't want to make a copy of *The Umbrellas of Cherbourg*."[18] The implication is clear: Honoré does not make Ducastel-Martineau-style films that "copy" Demy—in terms of either aesthetic form or uninteresting "harmonious sexuality." And he points out, "As far as Demy is concerned, we're not looking for the same things. I like to have actors sing because *I like it when they can't sing*. I like to see their vulnerability in the singing segments. It feels like they forget they're acting, and as a result they're focused on something other than the psychology or the blocking, and that lets me film them in laid-back situations. In Demy's films, the song is much more operatic. He was much more under the influence of Michel Legrand than I am with Alex Beaupain" (JNCH, 195; emphasis added). Unlike Ducastel and Martineau's *Jeanne*, for instance, in which the singing is highly polished as it is in Demy's films, Honoré's singing is visceral and integrated into the cinematic moment. The film's less-than-polished *thereness* sensually imbricates body and emotion. "Film with song," as we discuss, is yet another cinematic experiment that, like Honoré's evocation of smell in *Dans Paris,* seeks to make spectators *feel* or, indeed, think with their body.[19]

In short, Honoré's homage to Demy is love from a distance. His love for Demy is equal to the emotional "detachment" that inspired Jonathan's love for this own family in *Dans Paris*. By Honoré's refusal to use cinema as a message that directs the audience *to know* once and for all, his queer homage invites the spectator to think in unforeseen ways.

PART II

FILM WITH SONG IN THE CITY

In what way is song a critical and visceral component of French cinema, especially for French queer cinema? In *Dans Paris,* the city's landscape gathers within Honoré's cinematic temporal and spatial folds, whereas *Les chansons d'amour* parlays Paris through another particularly French cinematic means: song in film. Song in French film breaks out differently than it does in an American musical. A song in, say, *Coeur di lilas* (Litvak, 1932), *L'Atalante* (Vigo, 1934), *Le jour se lève* (Carné, 1939), *French Cancan* (Renoir, 1954), *Une femme est une femme* (Godard, 1961), *Lola* (Demy, 1961), *Jules et Jim* (Truffaut, 1962), or *Cléo de 5 à 7* (Varda, 1962) expands mise-en-scène rather than mimics the Hollywood-musical narrative form. If Hollywood musicals engage "folk tradition," as Jane Feuer describes it, to nostalgically "[link] community to entertainment" through "integrated" or "backstage" generic formulas and offer what Richard Dyer argues is a unified productive-community response from a capitalist society, song in French film may be said to diffuse the cinematic community (character and spectator) and its cultural experience. Put another way, song in the French tradition is atmospheric, not narrative driven.[20]

In a discussion of French women "realist singers," Kelley Conway usefully introduces the term "affective landscape" to describe a cinematic "world," an "atmosphere."[21] Drawing on Dudley Andrew's readings of "poetic realism" in French cinema and Pierre Mac Orlan's writings from the early twentieth century, Conway shows how the French realist singer—particularly when in the role of the prostitute—is conceptually bridged with the city's gritty urban milieu: "Mac Orlan's linkage of the realist singer and the geography of Paris is quite explicit."[22] At the same time, the singer's body pushes beyond the city's "geography," since the song reveals the singer's/prostitute's limited access and means to successfully make herself heard in hetero-bourgeois culture. In French cinema, then, when queer characters (such as prostitutes) sing, they do so because the place in which they perform no longer sustains or provides *enough* space to express desire that does not meet standards of propriety.[23] Dialogue is simply not enough. Song spreads affective qualities that give shape to cinematic mise-en-scène; it is a vital element of French cinematic staging since it is not merely a device for narrative advancement or show-stopping spectacle. French songs in film are nothing less than—*but significantly more than*—cinematic wallpaper. Whether the songs are presented as part of a theatrical event (*French Cancan, Une femme est une femme*), dropped into the narrative (*Jules et Jim, L'Atalante*), or a combination of both (*Cléo de 5 à 7, Lola, Le jour se lève, Coeur de lilas*), French song is crucial to the way mise-en-scène elaborates an "affective landscape." In Honoré's filmmaking, song is thus a crucial aspect to his cinema of monstration.

With *Les chansons*—a "film with song," as Honoré terms it—the histories of French *chansons* and cinema mix in such a way that these culturally institutionalized media provide Honoré with the formal means to reimagine emotional and sexual desire. The certain *Frenchness* that classical *chansons* and cinema bring to mind, however, is disrupted in yet another way in *Les chansons*. In this film and others, Honoré's queerly erotic renegotiation of the family, his amalgamation of American-British-French-sounding pop music (often composed by Beaupain), and his marginalized characters (Bretons, gays, prostitutes) trouble the idea of a national sensibility or community as such.

In this way, Honoré's turn to song in film resists nostalgia for early French cinema and, hence, also resists nostalgia for cinematic Frenchness. Yet, at the same time, Honoré is cognizant of the history that precedes him. Phil Powrie maps this history of music in French film in the following way: (1) popular song or chansons (1930–45), (2) operetta or French swing (1935–55), (3) jazz and *yé-yé* (1955–70), and (4) the compilation score (1980–present). As his analysis suggests, "popular music in French cinema" and its negotiations over French national identity were put under pressure during the twentieth century, giving way to "the slow disintegration of specifically French cultural forms."[24] The ideal French community—a bond formed between film song and spectator—begins its "slow disintegration," according to Powrie, in the postwar era.

Powrie's argument itself is somewhat nostalgic for the 1930s "community" to which he lays claim.[25] If his terms for "community" reside in film song that "[allowed] spectators to celebrate not just emotion, but a *community of emotion*," then his argument hinges on a longing for a community shaped by nationalist interests.[26] As Conway effectively counters, even if performers in films from this period "evoked an imaginary community, . . . [it] no longer existed, if it ever *had* existed."[27] In fact, if community did arise as part of the cinematic *chansons* experience, it was a community that had no fixed identity along class, gender, sexuality, or racial lines. Honoré's contributions bring this unfixed relationship between screen and spectator into twenty-first-century parlance. While his films sit squarely within this historical cinematic phenomenon, Honoré's "film with song" surprises—detaches—the spectator from a form of narrative that would otherwise verify "reality" for a single-voiced community. As Powrie sees it, the 1930s witnessed the spectacle of French community at its fullest, and it evaporated when American pop saturated French culture. However, the likes of

Jacques Demy and Honoré fuse these cultural exchanges through cinematic song in ways that are more queer than nostalgic.

Indeed, Honoré invites the history of French song into his cinema as a critical tool that draws spectators into querying their everyday relationship to national popular culture, not unlike Alain Resnais's use of song in *On connaît la chanson* (*Same Old Song*, 1997).[28] Resnais stunningly—if not chillingly—dubs snippets of French-song recordings as if they were thought bubbles (at times shared) that surface suddenly and unexpectedly from a character's mouth, whereas Honoré includes contemporary Beaupain compositions in order to evoke an echo of a French-song past. By doing so, he signals Beaupain's compositions as queer infiltrations on sentiment (national, emotional, and otherwise). If Resnais's film contains his bourgeois characters in a claustrophobic and neurotic end-of-the-twentieth-century Paris, then Honoré's film enables his twenty-first-century queer youth—no less ideologically contained—to go out into the streets and move through them, sensually, erotically, and uncertainly.

The communities presented to us in Honoré's films may walk in the historical shadows of French "song in film," but they do so in order to filter these cinematic remains in a culturally mobile fashion. Hence, if films such as *Les chansons* and, later, *Les bien-aimés* nod to a particular brand of French cinema and song—a history saddled with national consecration—then Honoré's homage is one firmly committed to intimate detachment.[29] Like the family in *Dans Paris* who embraced "detachment" as a form of love and familial bonding, Honoré's filmmaking similarly embraces the ghosts of French song in film. Honoré's homage breathes unsettling life into the historical debris of popular culture and the spaces it once occupied. Hence, when in *Les chansons* Jeanne (Chiara Mastroianni) invokes memories about her dead sister, Julie (Ludivine Sagnier), she does so through a song she performs in "Pépinière Park." The eponymous song title is charged with Jeanne's emotional longing for her sister as well as evoking the figure of the historical chanteuse. There is no park named "Pépinière" in Paris (although one does exist in Nancy). Yet, significantly, a music hall named Pépinière that hosted "soldiers and domestics" did, in fact, exist in Paris during the early twentieth century.[30] Homage through song is not, in other words, a longing for a nostalgic return to a past dressed in period-piece mise-en-scène; rather, Honoré's mise-en-scène evokes a historical moment in which "films with song," such as *Les chansons*, find themselves once removed yet indelibly stamped.

More immediately, Honoré's community of film characters who sing in *Les chansons* forge an on- and off-screen family. The director, friends of the director, actors, spectators, the memory of a lover, and an inspiring filmmaker are drawn in and toward historical *Frenchness* insofar as Honoré infuses this cinematic world with historical intrusions such as the youthful pleasures associated with American-British pop music. Honoré's cinematic youth assume the twenty-first-century version of Godard's "Marx and Coca-Cola" *enfants terribles*. Whereas Powrie argues that postwar cultural mixing dismantled French historical memory *as* French, Honoré discovers new French "communit[ies] of emotion" precisely through global commodification and its perverse romanticization.[31] *Les chansons* delivers on and rearranges the invariable clichés to which global commodity culture leads, by identifying queer French bodies and erotically entangling them within pop-culture packaging. Song in film is the hinge on which the hetero-national package is queered.

These implications for song in film are significant for the personal and professional relationship between Alex Beaupain and Honoré. Born in 1974 in Besançon, on the opposite side of France from where Honoré was born, Beaupain is the middle sibling of three, with a sister and a brother. The son of a schoolteacher and a worker for France's mass-transit rail system, SNCF, Beaupain learned piano as a child. He left for Paris when he turned eighteen. Growing up with Jacques Brel's 1960s songs in the air, Beaupain's compositions, on the one hand, fall into the tradition of French love songs associated with Françoise Hardy and Julien Clerc; on the other hand, his songs reverberate with Serge Gainsbourg's seductive and smoky moods. In 2012, François Hollande selected Beaupain's song "Au départ" (a song included in *Les chansons*) as part of his presidential campaign. Beaupain is the president's "favorite singer."[32]

Honoré and Beaupain's friendship is long-standing and professionally productive. Besides the work on the trilogy, Beaupain composed the songs for films such as *17 fois Cécile Cassard* and *Les bien-aimés*. Although Beaupain's songs for *Les chansons* were composed in advance of making the film, he firmly conceptualizes the placement and implications of the film's thirteen songs. "There's the idea of a path through the film," he asserts. He continues,

> The songs and the moments when the characters sing them are never innocuous. Nor how they sing them: alone, as a duo, as a trio, as a family. The film starts with fairly light-hearted songs. And we slowly move towards a more intense and lyrical musicality. We worked a great deal on the *aural atmospheres* according to how the scenes would be built up, whether they would take place out of doors or in a bedroom. But these orientations occurred in a totally natural manner, probably because Christophe, in writing his screenplay, had already thought out precisely how to integrate the songs in the scenes.[33]

With song marked as a trenchant cultural signifier in French film, a mise-en-scène imbued with an "aural [and visual] atmosphere," *Les chansons* draws attention to Honoré's cinematic choreography, in which the director "thought out precisely how to integrate the songs in the scenes." The multilayered cinematic atmosphere is crucial to the way bodies move in his films. Although Honoré's eye on dance is more specifically focused in films such as *Non, ma fille tu n'iras pas danser, 17 fois Cécile Cassard,* and *Homme au bain, Les chansons* (like *Dans Paris* before it) concentrates on a "non-dance" choreography that directs body movements in tandem with the camera or, in a key instance, attaches the body to the camera apparatus. It is true that most astute directors may be said to "choreograph" a scene so as to articulate character relations sans dialogue. (Consider, for example, Vincente Minnelli's stunning "pas de deux" performed by Gloria Grahame and Dick Powell in *The Bad and the Beautiful* [1952] in their Beverly Hills Hotel bungalow or the couples whose emotional and physical connections are rearranged through a rondelet as directed by Rainer Werner Fassbinder in *Chinese Roulette* [1976]). Honoré's particular terpsichorean impulse is to choreograph cinematically erotic solutions for bodies that are at play in the delimited space of the bed. We will return to this.

In short, *Les chansons* broadens the arc of loss, love, and death by giving it expressive form through song, by choreographing it in relationship to camera and body movements, and by intertwining it with twenty-first-century media technology. Hence, the film expands on *Dans Paris*'s thematic thrust insofar as it eroticizes family relations while bringing sexualized love between men into the picture. *Les chansons* introduces newly formed family relations that are tactile; they are multisensory and, through cinematic song, work to reform the place in which historical and national memory is held. While *Dans Paris* introduces Paris's central place in the characters' world, *Les chansons* foregrounds the hypermediated city as an active participant that is deeply implicated in the narrative action. Twenty-first-century Paris is a key player in the film since it assumes the role of the omniscient narrator that motivates, distills, and prompts the fluid nature of the relationships through which our characters move. Paris thus takes over the role of narrator from Jonathan in *Dans Paris;* and, like him, the city is everywhere in *Les chansons.* Paris enables *the way* characters can or cannot move; it drives the energy that gives life and takes it away. The city provides the cinematic mise-en-scène in which expressive song emanates from within its skin. As such, Paris is the emotional and erotic heart of the film.

Through this clichéd conceit associated with the "City of Love," Honoré doubles the romanticized city with the lead female character, who dies midway through the film. "Paris is a woman" is that other formidable cliché.[34] Does *Les chansons*, therefore, suggest that Paris and French culture are dead? Does the link between Paris-Julie-"woman" repeat stereotypes that serve men's fantasies about seduction, women, and sexual desire? In part, yes, but not entirely. A French community and its terms for *Frenchness* that purportedly once existed in concert with French song in film is rechanneled in *Les chansons d'amour* as something less than nationally pure. *Les chansons*' French community upends the heterocentric ideals that determine national identity. In poisoning French culture with its very own traditions, Honoré resists oversimplifying Paris and those who populate it. "Poison," for Honoré, has its charms.

THE HEART OF PARIS

As the film's players and producers are introduced in the title sequence, Honoré's camera tracks along a brightly lit avenue during a winter evening in Paris. Immediately, we are moving through the city (figures 18.1–18.32). The titles engage the same Godardian font, Antique Olive, that earlier introduced *Dans Paris*. The montage sequence that composes *Les chansons*' introductions—an aesthetic carryover, stitched in from the concluding shots of *Dans Paris*'s closing credits—takes us on a journey through an array of Parisian street scenes so that we are drawn into the overlapping worlds that make up the tenth and eleventh arrondissements. Both districts carry import for Honoré in several ways.

First, the eleventh arrondissement is the area of Paris that Honoré calls home. Since the millennium, both the tenth and the eleventh arrondissements have become gentrified with young artists and professionals (such as Honoré) while maintaining a diverse cultural demographic.[35] These two closely connected arrondissements are also home to monuments that mark French revolutions, albeit quite different in their historical scope: Place de la Bastille and Place de la République. The statue perched atop the July Column in the Place de la Bastille plays no small part in *Les chansons*' story and is no less significant as a point of identification with the director (see figure 18.6).

Designed by Auguste Dumont between 1833 and 1836, *Le Génie de la liberté* is an oddity in French art history and its emplacement in the French capital. As Valérie Montalbetti notes, Dumont's statue is "a rupture with art tradition [because] Liberty is symbolized by a masculine figure"—a symbol historically reserved for the female form.[36] The *Génie*, "slender, arms extended, wings extended, balanced on the left foot, ... floats in the air."[37] Not only does the *Génie* perform an airy dance, a dance not unimportantly tilted to the left; for Honoré, the lithe statue marks an

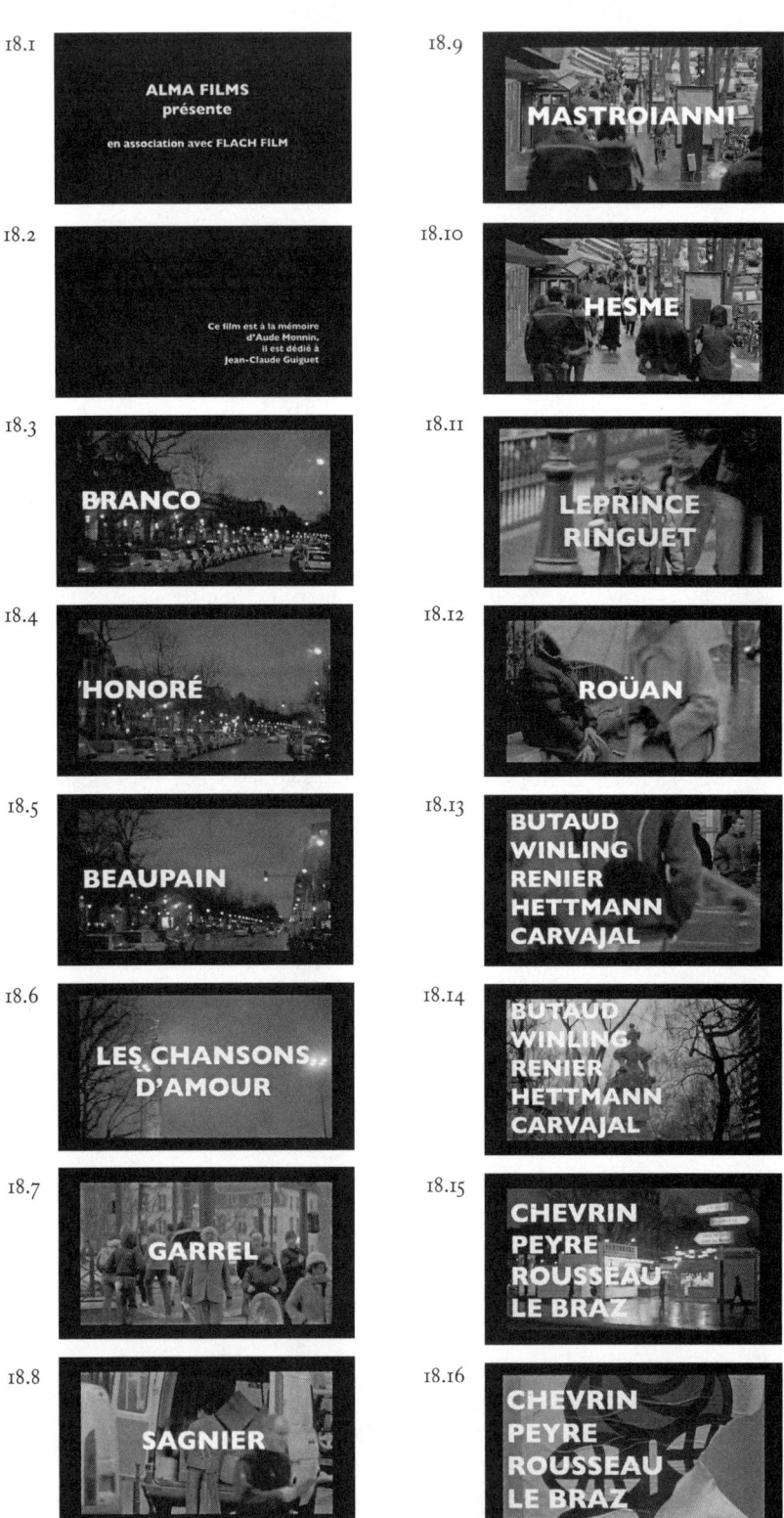

18.1–18.32. *Les chansons d'amour*'s opening montage with credit sequence.

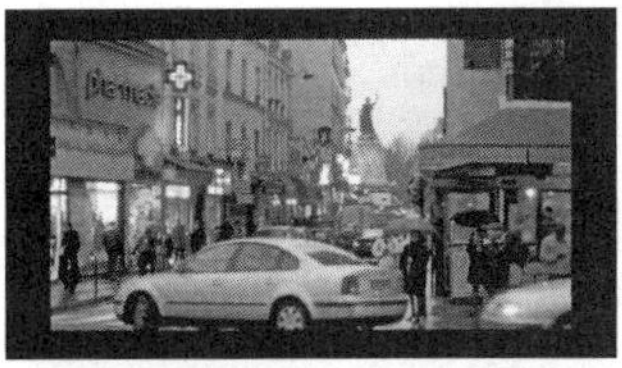

18.17

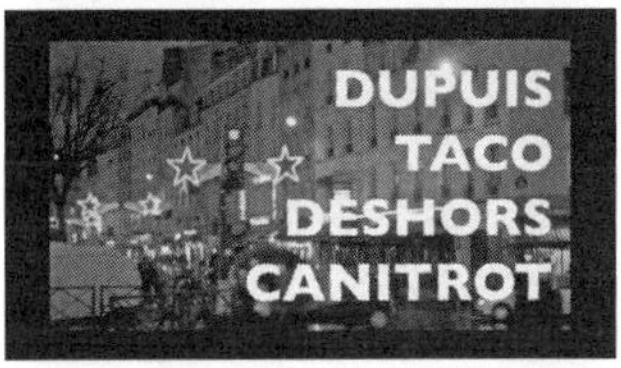

18.18

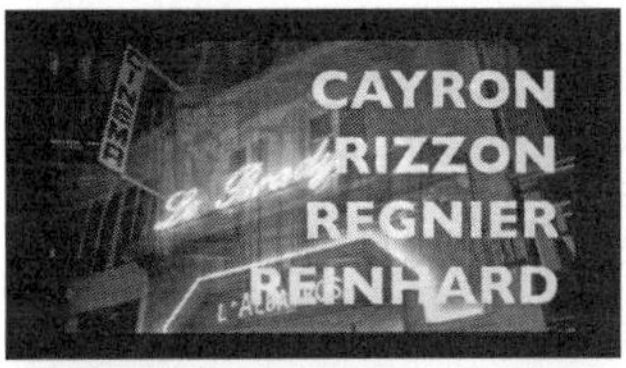

18.19

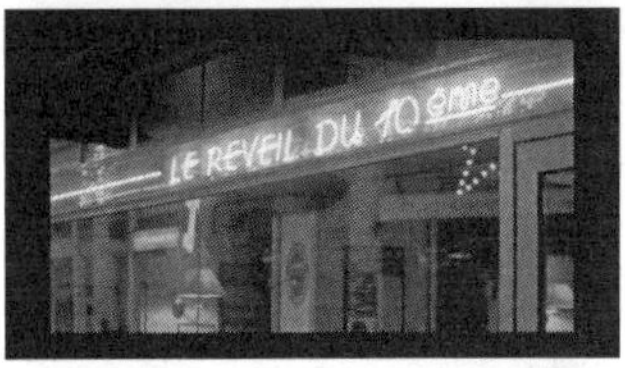

18.20

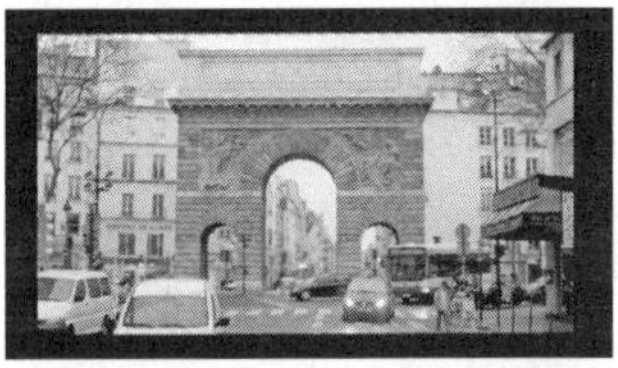

18.21

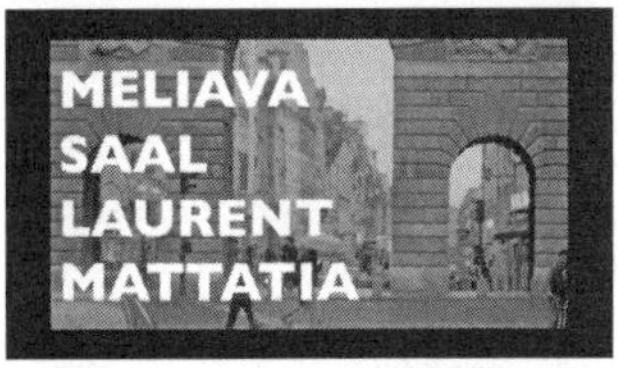

18.22

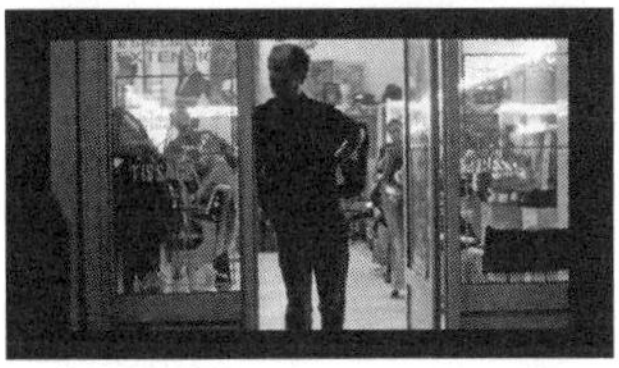

18.23

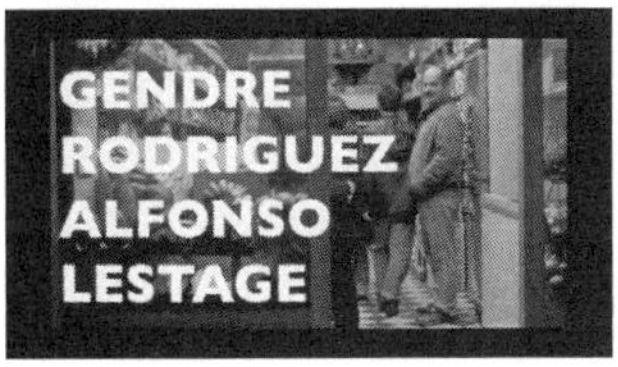

18.24

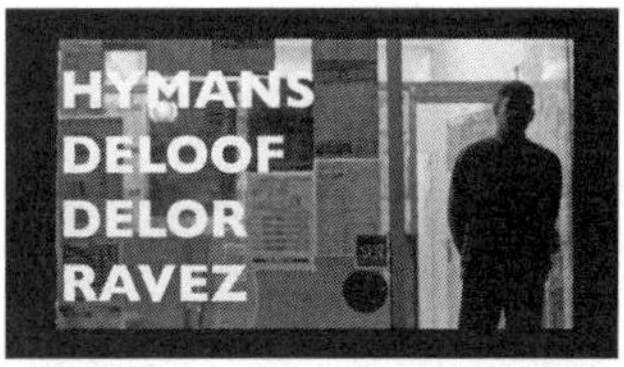

18.25

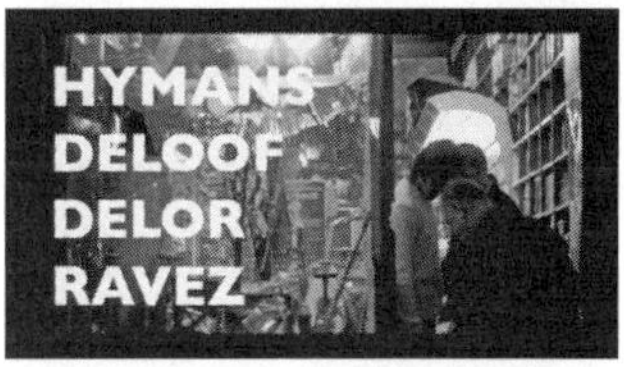

18.26

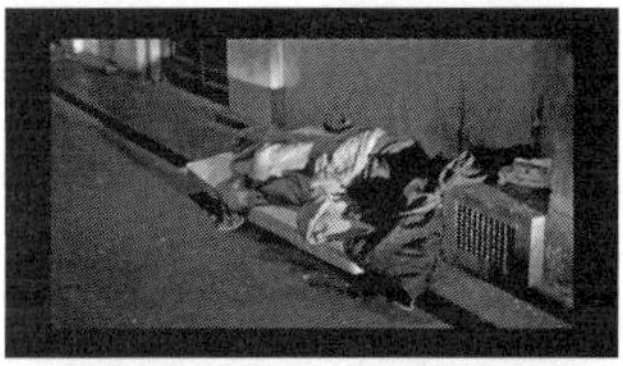

18.27

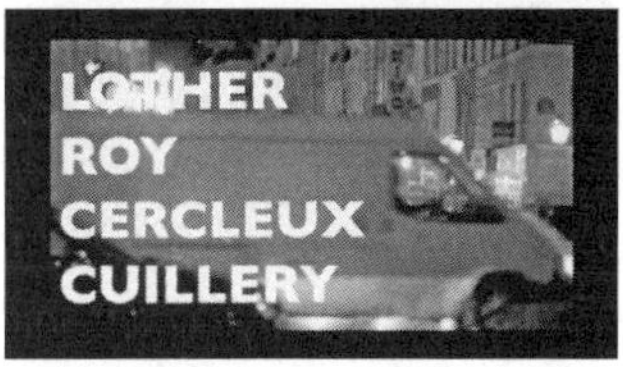

18.28

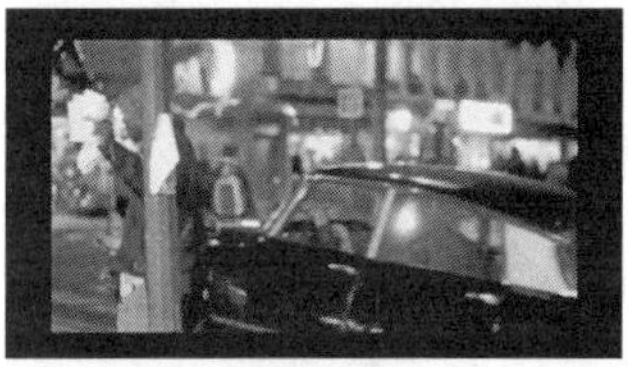

18.29

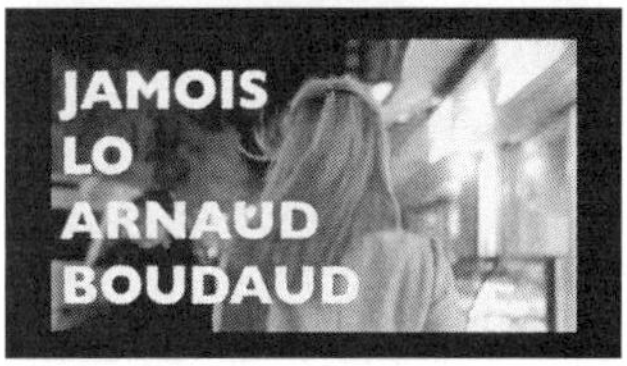

18.30

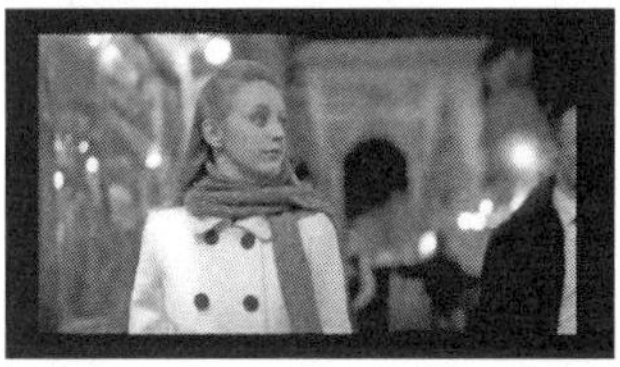

18.31

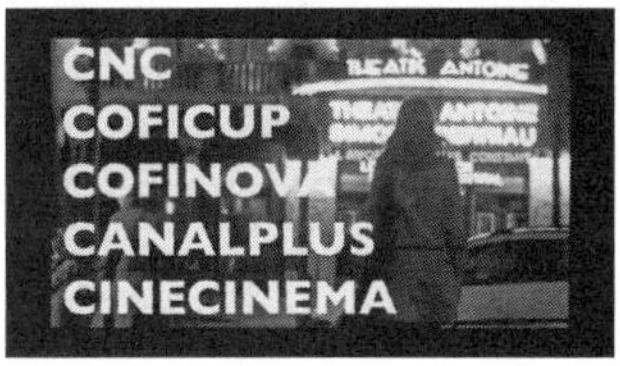

18.32

area in Paris where revolutionary liberty coincides with less traditional modes of creative practice. The graceful yet disciplined *Génie de la liberté* serves as a materialized signature on the Paris skyline and later assumes a protective stance over *Les chansons*' family, the Pommerayes (perhaps heirs to Nantes's Passage Pommeraye, which features as the arcade in Demy's *Lola*). In *Les chansons*, the family sings the statue's praises in the song "La Bastille." Honoré, the cinematic "*génie*," aptly measures up to the dancing angel that overlooks the districts on which he inscribes his multimediated cinematic signature. Place de la Bastille and the two queer angels who call this district home—*Le Génie* and Christophe Honoré—anchor the credit sequence since they immediately identify the location where our story takes place.

Second, the montage sequence points to French culture in the tenth and eleventh arrondissements as something beyond tourist hot spots. The districts are presented here as multicultural, where a wide range of bodies stream across the screen. The interconnected arrondissements are thus the stages on which Honoré's urban *corps de ballet* display complex everyday movements.[38] If the Eiffel Tower situates *Dans Paris* as unequivocally *in* "Paris," the street scenes of *Les chansons* are a more multiracial and not so obvious Paris, one that involves vibrant trade, an amalgam of commuters, and young artists. To be sure, Honoré's Paris is far from the pristine one of tourist campaigns, Hollywood films, or even recent French films. Honoré instead shows a Paris where streets mix offbeat theaters, cinemas, and brasseries, as well as workers, shoppers, and the city's homeless, who rarely appear in sanitized versions of the city. Honoré's Paris is a sentient city. The smells, the sounds, and the uneven flows that urban life provides our characters are not only atmosphere in which they live/perform; in the city, these sensorial attributes also soak into the characters' very skin (we will shortly see how Honoré suggests this cinematically).

Finally, as the film's credit sequence collects the sites of the arrondissements, it announces itself *as* cinema, as Honoré's cinematic dream-memory. Without overtaxing a Freudian reading, the filmic dream—*Les chansons*—may be said to conjure latent imagery from a cinematic past so that it seeps into Honoré's cinematic present. Honoré's film thus calls to mind Freud's "Mystic Writing Pad" insofar as the remains of cinematic memory haunt the text's undercurrent.[39] For instance, *Les chansons* references *Une femme est une femme* (1961) by shooting sequences where Godard filmed in the tenth and eleventh arrondissements (Porte Saint-Martin, Boulevard de Sébastopol, and Rue Saint-Denis). Godard's Paris returns transformed in *Les chansons*. With our gaze directed toward specific locations where Godard traced cinematic scars on the Parisian landscape, we encounter Honoré's reenvisioning of his forefather's cinematic dream-place.

As we continue our stroll through Paris's tenth and eleventh, we catch a glimpse of a neon sign that very precisely confirms the world we are describing: "Le Réveil du 10ème" (The Awakening of the 10th). Awakening into Honoré's Parisian arrondissement is awakening into a cinematic dream, a surrealist "dream-journey."[40] Here, in *Les chansons,* dream and coming to life converge. As the Parisian montage draws to a close, the camera catches up with Julie Pommeraye as she delightfully jaunts down the street. As she is about to arrive at a movie theater, Honoré cuts to an overhead shot of her passing a public phone booth—a relic from a bygone era whose offspring, the mobile phone, plays no small part later in the film. Over this image, a title appears, again Godard's Antique Olive font. Now, however, the title on the screen bears the imprint "Première partie: Le Départ." Here, with Godard's representative typeface embedded in the scene, another cinematic trace appears: Jacques Demy's *Les parapluies de Cherbourg* and the title cards that divide the film into three acts (see figures 19.1–19.3). Through style and form, Demy's and Godard's influence on Honoré's filmmaking is put on full display, yet here Godard's integration with Demy is ushered in through a very gay filter, especially in act 3. In the film's final segment, Honoré queerly punctuates the third act's introduction ("Le Retour") by showing two boy lovers head into the night.

As we cut from the overhead shot of Julie walking down the street, we see her purchase a ticket to see the film *Fragments sur la grâce* (Dieutre, 2006—a film appropriately distributed by Celluloïd Dreams). As the narrative commences, a young man approaches Julie from behind while she waits in line to enter the theater. As he passes, he utters, "Excusez-moi, j'étais après lui" (Excuse me, I was after him). The young, charming, but disruptive spectator continues to pass each of the moviegoers, tapping them on the shoulder with the same comment. As it turns out, the man interrupting the spectators is the director Gaël Morel, with whom Honoré shares a friendship and for whom he wrote the screenplay for *Après lui* (*After Him,* 2006). The cinematic wink in the imperfect tense ("I was after him") takes the form of a tap on the moviegoers' shoulders while it does the same to the spectator of *Les chansons.* The scene, noted in our introduction, is a form of homage in which we are reminded that we are about to enter the future anterior, the always already of film history.

THE MECHANICALLY REPRODUCED WORLD

Les chansons tells the tale of a young Parisian couple who seek to define their terms for love as a couple in the modern world. They seek to reshape traditional coupledom by exploring its wide-ranging contours. Their quest is certainly not new in the history of cinema, and as they discover, it is no easy task to reconstitute

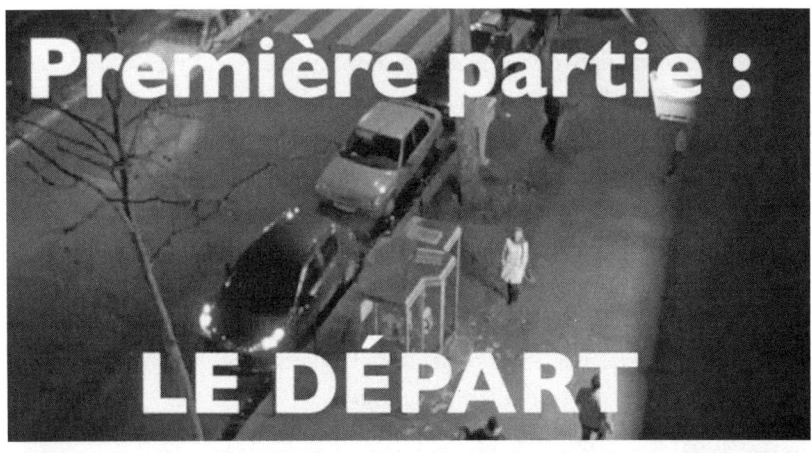

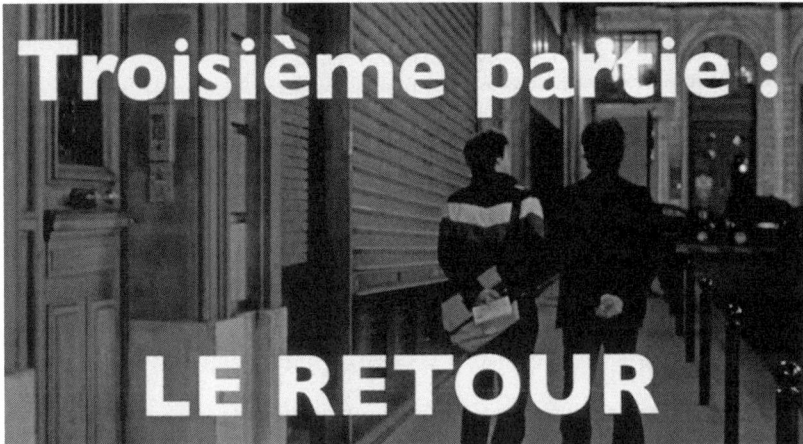

19.1–19.3. The title cards that divide *Les chansons d'amour*'s three acts bear the imprint of Godard's and Demy's cinema. Act 3 is queerly marked as we see Ismaël and Erwann form the film's gay couple.

long-inculcated ideologies about romantic love. The contemporary world in which they find themselves, however, does provide specific means for the way they respond to their youthful quest. Their emotional bonds fray as their search is intensified while they navigate a noisy culture besotted with hypermedia technology and multinational commodification. Yet this noise glues their relationship together in unexpected ways and offers fresh perspectives on love. *Les chansons* thus opens with the great-grandparent of the twenty-first-century multimedia experience—cinema. The twentieth-century medium is cast as a critical wedge, in both form and content, for Julie and Ismaël's relationship and the way they communicate. Yet twenty-first-century technology intervenes and strongly encourages Honoré's prerequisite, emotional detachment. The awkward promises that instant communication and gratification give way to, however, prove to be a blessing and a curse.

Whereas *Dans Paris*'s triangular relationships take flight from a fraternal doubling, *Les chansons*' point of departure works from the inverse position, where our narrative is introduced by a preliminary ménage-à-trois: Julie (Sagnier), Ismaël (Louis Garrel), and Alice (Clotilde Hesme). Two doublings emerge from the triangular framework that initiates the film. Whereas *Dans Paris*'s tale of doubles and threesomes moves out from the center of Paris and back again in order to grapple with emotional and physical stress, *Les chansons* directs its cathartic energies inward and toward the city's center. Emotional excess is thus contained within the city's boundaries. The confined urban space, however, lends Honoré's characters a stage on which they may dance and float—evanescently, cinematically—alongside *Le Génie de la liberté*. Like the statue, they reach toward the sky yet are always grounded in the city (recall Jonathan's appearance of floating above the city while he introduces *Dans Paris* from the balcony of his Parisian apartment). The delimited dance space, nonetheless, nurtures complex frameworks of desire.

Within Honoré's Paris-centered narrative of *Les chansons*' threesome, two erotic relationships diverge to become queerly transfigured. A third figure, Julie/Paris, moves through the film's center, its very heart. This cinematic coembodiment is crucial for how Honoré approaches love and death. The Julie-Ismaël-Alice triangle that begins the film's erotic discharge is one that mobilizes or, in fact, reconstitutes the first doubling since it zeroes in on Julie and Ismaël's romance. This doubling is short-lived because Julie dies almost as soon as she and Ismaël break from Alice. Is it this return to a traditional romantic couple that immediately triggers death? To a certain extent, yes. But Julie's presence remains and is *felt* as much as it is *seen* throughout the film. On the one hand, coupledom and its constraints remain as a permanent cultural fixture; on the other hand, the failing of coupledom to live up to cultural ideals serves to generate transformation of the ways it is envisaged and lived. To these ends, with Julie's premature death, a second doubling occurs precisely because of the threesome: this is the gay relationship of Ismaël and Erwann (Grégoire Leprince-Ringuet). Julie's death, in effect, in drawing to a close the traditional heterosexual couple, enables new erotic possibilities. The titles of Monnin's theses, "Les cadeaux dans les relations familiales" and "La fidélité chez les homosexuels," may be provocatively recalled since the death of the friend extends the gift of new and transformed family relations.

To get to these erotic reformulations, Honoré takes us through the movies and new media technology. Once Julie purchases her movie ticket for *Fragments sur la grâce*, she calls Ismaël on her mobile phone. The phone-call sequence cuts between Julie in front of the movie theater and Ismaël in his office, where he produces a local newspaper with Alice. Both Ismaël and Alice are situated in contemporary surroundings that are lit by cool blue lighting and where computer technology fills every corner of the room. From the outset, the threesome is viewed as one that forms within a hypermediated environment. Moreover, the sequence establishes Honoré's erotic triumvirate as bonded by both cinematic form (cross-cutting) and the mise-en-scène (new technology) that define this particular generation. As such, movies, mobile phones, computers, and iPods carve out the spatial and temporal dimensions in which modern Parisian relationships take place within the city's *architecture ancienne*. Although technology provides new models for communication, erotic desire and love are not made easier because of it. In fact, the immediacy that mobile phones and computer technology provide may appear to put people *in touch* instantly, but they can never make up for corporeal, sensual touch. Nevertheless, both bodily and mechanically reproduced touch are modes of communication that reach for meaning but never fully deliver on it. Honoré is interested in exploring the sensual possibilities of disparate emotional and physical connections between body and machine, even as those connections fail.[41]

Indeed, while new technologies enmesh *Les chansons*' characters within complex erotic divertissements (incestuous inclinations, vicarious erotic longing, multiple sex partners), their use of technology is inadequate when compared with "old" forms of art such as literature, pantomime, and song. Hence, Honoré involves the "old" and the "new" to avoid both modernist nostalgia and starry-eyed celebration of every new technological device. Therefore, when Julie calls Ismaël from her mobile phone, we see him nonchalantly clicking a computer mouse and vacuously staring into his computer screen. To his right, Alice stares into space listening to her headset. Our characters are not so facile, however, that they completely absorb themselves in the sphere of technology. For example, when Ismaël jokes with Alice that the music she listens to is overromanticized tripe, she melodramatically performs the pop song's silly emotional ploys. Ismaël responds in a disturbingly playful way when he threatens to cut out her tongue / *la langue*—the very organ necessary not only to speak words but to taste, lick, and touch. Linked to speech and the erotic pleasures, Ismaël's gesture to cut away Alice's vital organ anticipates Honoré's thematic centerpieces around the tongue's / *la langue*'s wide-ranging forms as a mode of communication and as an erotic zone. But Ismaël's "playful" act signals his unconscious desire to castrate Alice. It is a shortsighted gesture on his part, as we will see, because Alice's tongue is multitalented in terms of how she communicates with others and the gifts she offers them. Alice's "thinking with her body" (to recall Althusser's concept) leads Ismaël and others along unexpected and rewarding paths. Honoré, through the tongue / *la langue*, opens affective communication in *Les chansons d'amour*.

In the meantime, on the phone, Ismaël asks Julie what movie she is seeing. We do not hear her response, but as soon as Ismaël discovers that she is seeing a movie without him, he springs to life from his dulled state of mind in front of the computer. Julie, who is "sick of going to the movies alone," refuses to tell Ismaël the title of the film. As he becomes more agitated, Julie finally tells him the film title. He lets her know, "I'll be offended if you see that movie without me." Keeping in mind that the movie Julie waits to see is *Fragments sur la grâce*, Ismaël's concern points to his anxiety of being left aside by his lover as much as it points to his fear of being left out of the film experience.[42] For Honoré, these experiences are one and the same.

CHOREOGRAPHING TONGUES IN BED

Les chansons' threesome is first seen in Julie and Ismaël's apartment following two Beaupain-scored songs, "De bonnes raisons" and "Inventaire." Although two distinct pieces of music, the songs are linked by a pause in which we cut from the city's streets to the couple's apartment. The break between songs and the movement from exterior to interior divide the scenes in such a way as to demarcate Ismaël and Julie's uncertain feelings about the third person—Alice—who occupies their romantic lives. Sung on the street, "De bonnes raisons" establishes the couple's intimate connection with each other. Following a key trope in *Dans Paris*, the song introduces the themes of angels and prayer and anticipates Julie's later omniscient and cinematic transcendence—a heavenliness—through death. During the song, for instance, Julie places her hands in prayer and sings "Gloria" while Ismaël "sings praises" to his "holy dove," Julie. At one point, he moves behind her and positions his hands to create angel wings for his beloved. With the sudden break in music between exterior and interior,

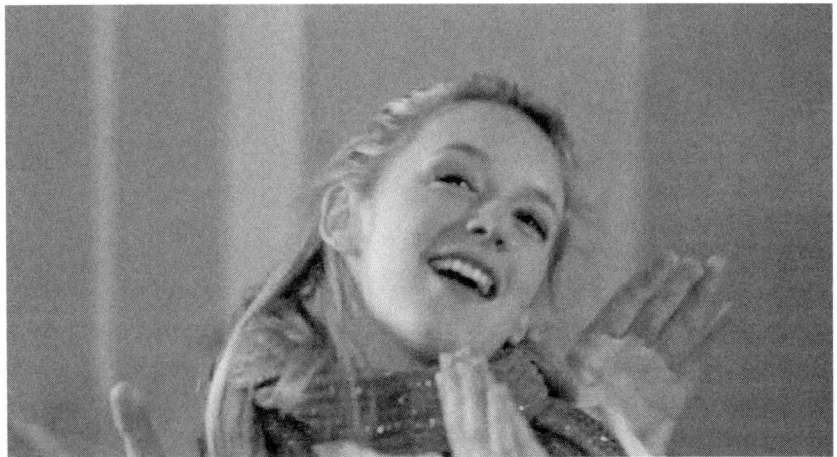

20. Ismaël's angel, Julie.

Julie then performs "Inventaire," in which, in contraposition to her earlier declaration of love, she expresses her unease with their threesome arrangement. Singing about Alice's "panties left on the floor," Ismaël's doubly kissed lips, and discovering another's "pubes in the shower," Julie questions the emotional commitment she is prepared to make in the current setup. "Inventaire" also signals Ismaël's frustration with Julie's mother, who constantly intervenes with "seven phone calls a day." The mother's disruptions foreshadow other subtle and not-so-subtle intrusions that recur later between Ismaël and Julie's extended family.

While Julie sings, we see Alice making her way to the apartment. She passes the movie theater that Julie has left and where Julie and Ismaël met and broke into song. When Alice arrives, she comes prepared for an overnight visit, carrying her pajamas and a free-spirit attitude that ignores the fact that she has troubled Julie and Ismaël's romance. At first, Julie is annoyed with Alice's arrival, but the emotional temperature warms as we cut to our characters in bed and their bodies entwine.

The threesome's bed scene begins with blond Julie and brunette Alice undressing. With their backs to us, they perform what could be described as a nonmusical version of Howard Hawks's opening duet from *Gentleman Prefer Blondes* (1953), in which Marilyn Monroe and Jane Russell sing "Two Little Girls from Little Rock." As Ismaël feigns naïve *dis*interest in the two women who sit on the bed's edge, they slowly disrobe and throw seductive glances toward him. The bed is once again Honoré's icebreaker since its inviting sexual possibilities melt away the emotional chill—if only for a moment—that Julie feels. The bed also draws on past cinematic threesomes such as those seen in Godard's *Masculin/féminin, Une femme est une femme,* and *Deux ou trois choses que je sais d'elle* (1967) or Truffaut's bookish bedroom intimacies in *Domicile conjugal* (1970). And as in those earlier New Wave films, Honoré's characters read books in bed that humorously identify the subject's position within a scene, while, at the same time, the titles suggest the bed's sensual promises or, in the case of Ismaël (like Jean-Pierre Léaud before him), his blundering attempt to link the political with the erotic.[43] Not only does Honoré's scene mimic the cinematic bed in which Godard and Truffaut situate young lovers reading, but the organization of the threesome in Honoré's film mirrors Godard's seating of characters side by side in a movie theater, in effect reading the movie screen. Whether listening to music, reading books, watching television, or frolicking with friends (and the director), Honoré's bed is a multimediated erotic experience. In *Les chansons*' bed, the three jockey for position, which ultimately sees Ismaël pushed to the outer edge. With Alice in the center and Julie to her right, the two women playfully chat about contraception and their views on sex.

Although Alice claims that she believes in "nonsex," sexual pleasure with Julie is "okay" because Julie is "like [her] sister. It's not really sex." The familial reconfiguration thus raises the specter of lesbian incest, so that newly engaged "nonsex" points directly to the erotic power that underscores family relations. Is Rees-Roberts correct, then, when he states that lesbianism in *Les chansons* is a "regressive vision of female sexuality" that recapitulates "the normative politics of heterosexual experimentation in *Ma mère,* in which Huppert and Preiss's 'lesbian' sex scene was for male eyes only"?[44] Is Honoré's inclusion of lesbianism a perfunctory and hetero-masculinist gesture in *Les chansons*? Or do Honoré's sororal relations more provocatively raise the stakes on queer family and kinship? To be sure, Ismaël is ostensibly the hetero-male who observes Alice and Julie's lovemaking. Yet Terry Castle, in her magisterial *The Literature of Lesbianism,* informs us,

> Lesbian images have proliferated far and wide in modern Western culture at least in part because such images have always been—for reasons yet to be satisfactorily explained—deeply titillating to men. . . . However sordid or gross some of the results—and many underground images of female same-sex love are cankerous indeed—male pornographers must be credited with giving female homosexuality over the centuries a starkly palpable representational life. By their graphic insistence that such intimacy was possible—*in the flesh*—they helped make the lesbian topos part of the mental landscape of modern civilization.[45]

And where, according to Castle, does this "palpable representational life" in which "women meet and love" take place? In Paris, "of course" (38). Castle explains,

> For whatever reasons—whether due to that strain of worldliness and moral realism present in French society since the Middle Ages, the relatively high status of women, or the freethinking intellectual traditions associated with the Enlightenment and French Revolution—French writing of the past three or four centuries has been distinguished by an unparalleled sexual frankness and sophistication. So often indeed has female homosexuality been thematized in French literature one may be forgiven for imagining love between women almost a kind of French invention, like champagne or foie gras. (38)

On the one hand, Honoré's portrayal of sororal lesbianism may be viewed as part and parcel of the "unparalleled sexual frankness and sophistication" in historical French literature, poetry, *and* cinema, where female homosexuality plays a prominent role. On the other hand, and specifically, Honoré's film draws on twenty-first-century questions and debates about queer identity and French family dynamics, especially as these concerns directly affect the matter of *homoparentalité* that is so close to the filmmaker's heart. In this way, *Les chansons* highlights the dimensions of homosexuality as it relates to the erotic possibilities available to the traditional "family." Honoré's film brings into focus, in other words, queer incest.

Rey Chow explains that "the taboo against incest itself has been primarily based on a heterosexual conceptualization of sexual and family relations . . . thus helping to derealize gay and lesbian erotic and kin formations."[46] In her discussion of Tsai Ming-liang's *The River* (*He liu*, 1997—a film, we recall from our introduction, that Honoré so admired in his 1998 *Cahiers du Cinéma* polemic), Chow tells us that *luanlun* (the Chinese term for incest) suggests the "overturning of kin or, more precisely, of hierarchically arranged social relations." Significantly, this cultural "rationale is intertwined with a heterosexual paradigm of sex." Chow asks, "If same-sex sex is not recognized as real sex to begin with, what would be same-sex incest?" (182). For Chow, in *The River*, when father-and-son sexual relations unexpectedly occur, tenderness is exchanged rather than Oedipal punishment that "can only result in suicide, physical blindness, and general destruction." In a Chinese cultural context, Tsai's *The River* presents the "dissolution of the kinship system based on seniority and hierarchy" (192).

Similarly, the history of French cinema maintains the hierarchical structures that define hetero-inflected incestuous desire. In "Daddy's Girls," Ginette

Vincendeau traces a pattern of French filmmaking during the 1930s that "revolves around the seduction of 'fathers' by the 'daughters'" in which the "[Oedipal] 'master narrative' privileges a strong, often eroticized, relationship between a mature man and a young woman, but also eliminates—actually or symbolically—the mother figure and replaces her ... with a daughter figure."[47] Although Vincendeau rightly reveals the dominant power structure in these films that invariably works to the benefit of men, the relationships as such are not literally incestuous. The "widespread pattern" that Vincendeau identifies suggests what Kelley Conway sees as a "formation of *quasi*-incestuous couples consisting of mature men and very young women."[48]

In Honoré's queer France, sororal incestuous desire is crucial to the "dissolution" of hierarchical kinship, as Chow shows in her reading of *The River*. Like Tsai Ming-liang's film, *Les chansons* enables a queer kinship that is held together by its very mobility and detachment. To borrow Chow's terms for *The River*'s cinematic residents, *Les chansons*' queer characters live in a "transient abode" (195). To be sure, Alice and Julie's sisterly love turns the heterocentric claims for incest, as determined by hetero-conceived logic, on their head. If indeed heterocentrically determined incest "derealize[s]" the possibility for "gay and lesbian erotic and kin formations" because its normative structures dictate it as such, Honoré's newly formed relations marked *as* familial are precisely the point where queerly eroticized kinship is energized and made mobile. The nominal terms associated with family—"daddy," "sister," "brother," and so on—are now queerly reframed within "gay and lesbian erotic and kin formations."

To seal the queer kinship, as soon as Alice indicates her sororal relation with Julie, the two women kiss, which in turn leads Alice to slide down and under the sheets, where she performs cunnilingus on Julie. The "nonsex" between women is in fact an encounter with *la langue* that intermingles their bodies and emotions, which, importantly, puts Ismaël in an awkward familial position—literally and figuratively. This will not be the last time he is marginalized in the film, nor is it the last time Julie will be unsure about her "sororal" relations with Alice. Unsure how to respond to the women's mutual satisfaction, Ismaël scrambles to occupy himself and, as Godard's boys were often want to do, picks up his book and cites irrelevant political passages. If Honoré's rendering of female homosexuality is by and large for Ismaël's male gaze, it positions "le non-sexe" (*not* "not-sexe") that includes his gaze, in Castle's terms, as cocreator of the "lesbian topos [that is] part of the mental landscape of modern civilization." And, not insignificantly, this takes place in France ("of course"). Hence, even as Honoré invites the male gaze into the queer-incestuous lesbian scene between Alice and Julie, Ismaël is left uncertain about his place in the cogenerated sexual sphere of the film.

Uncertainty and questions are the grounds on which queer identity and erotics emerge in *Les chansons*.

While Julie enjoys Alice's sisterly tongue from under the blanket—the tongue that Ismaël jokingly threatened to snip off in an earlier scene—Julie asks Ismaël to "guide" the event so that he might take a more active role in the threesome's lovemaking. Ismaël's active role in the affair is indeed always on slippery ground. On the one hand, he thrills at the opportunity to have two women fawn over him and perform sexually for his voyeuristic delight; on the other hand, he fears the emotional and "sisterly" connection that Julie and Alice comfortably enjoy insofar as it might alienate him. Soon after their time in bed, in an outburst at a bar, Ismaël claims that Alice and Julie "beguile" him with kisses in order to "eliminate" him from the relationship. He insists that their relationship is "no three-ring circus" because, as he informs Alice, "touching [Julie] means fucking me." Both women smirk at Ismaël's androcentric proclamation. According to Ismaël, their "contract" (Julie calls it their "gentlemen's agreement") does not allow for his being sidelined. He is the center and, as such, rightfully exercises his patriarchal prerogative. And, for the time being, the cinematic point of view revolves on his narrow masculinist perspective since Julie, enamored by his terms for heteronormative romance, falls back into her culturally inculcated role as the woman who can only love but one (man). Julie and Ismaël's heterosexual relationship is revealed, not unlike the troubled idealism that circulates around *Frenchness*, as shaken in its ideology. Although Julie undoubtedly finds herself drawn emotionally and sexually to Alice, the heterosexual social contract weighs heavily. The price for her refusal to embrace a love that is directed by her desire becomes a missed opportunity that proves fatal. Thus, Julie inhabits the troubled bind in which women are ideologically ensconced: that is, hetero-masculinist romance with its attendant, erotically sublimated, familial obligations. Alice's response is quite different and resets the terms for romance across identity positions.

Back in bed with Alice, Ismaël delivers contrived words of love that suture Julie into this (heterosexual) accepted model of romance. Alice is rightfully annoyed that Julie's attention on Ismaël throws off her oral dance; she quickly realizes that her position in the triangle has come to an end because Julie and Ismaël support something she rejects: soppy coupledom. Alice moves beyond the petty romantics and will be in the position to formulate new and ambiguous combinations of bodies for her and others. In several ways, Alice's good-humored movement through the city and across its bodies represents the narrative's fairy—the imperfect gendered "génie"—who capriciously spreads her pixie dust across the city so as to open broad avenues toward erotic love. In concert with "*Le Génie*/Honoré," the short-haired "*la Génie's*"/Alice's whimsical relationship to love creates an environment in which the threesome's breakup takes on something of a celebratory mood.

Later, on the way to a bar named Les Étoiles, the trio sings, "Je n'aime que toi." While Julie and Ismaël sing about their love for each other and the discomfort that comes about when expanding the boundaries of the couple, Alice jocundly dances between them. As Alice dances, she sings, "I am the bridge between your banks / Running from side to side / Cross over and give me thanks / Kiss and let me be your guide." Her free spirit marshals the film's life force and journey because, as we will see, she easily glides between time and space, emotions and bodies. "Je n'aime que toi" also highlights the desire for physical sensuality via the tongue and through the senses, particularly smell, as a way to substitute the limitation of words. If Julie has a difficult time finding the words to express her frustrations with Ismaël and Alice, lyrical renderings assist her in discovering fresh expressive forms. Smell, as we saw in *Dans Paris,* is cinematically evoked as a major component of the erotic triangle; *Les chansons* similarly invokes olfactory experiences but channels it through song. At one moment in the song, for instance, Julie smells Ismaël's fingers and suddenly casts a sharp glance at Alice. Here, Honoré cuts to Julie in a "fixed-tracking shot" (à la Demy's *Les parapluies de Cherbourg*)—a shot in which the character is embedded on a dolly on which the camera is simultaneously attached. On the fixed-yet-mobile mechanism, Julie sings to Ismaël, "I smelled your fingers, swine / Where did you get that odd smell? / It's definitely not mine."

Honoré's frame yields two turns on movement with different implications for the women who are the focus of Ismaël's life. In this shot, it appears as if Julie is floating within the scene as she emotionally distances herself from it.[49] At the same time, Alice continues to jovially flit around the frame. Julie's movement is both contained and mobile since she is strapped to the very (ideological?) apparatus that moves her through the frame. While Julie's lyricized anger simultaneously moves and contains her within the song space, Ismaël walks toward her, his feet firmly on the ground: "You're the same. She has touched you too." Alice, of course, rolls her eyes at such petty gamesmanship that the romantic hetero-couple is determined to engage. For Alice, life is quite simple: she loves both equally. Rather than foolishly waste energy, they should utilize her as their bridge; they should "rub along her flanks" and "enjoy the ride." "Je n'aime que toi" does not, therefore, merely push mise-en-scène to its outer limits; it simultaneously presses it inward. Song, in other words, penetrates the bodies while spreading the cinematic space—including their smells—that they

PART II

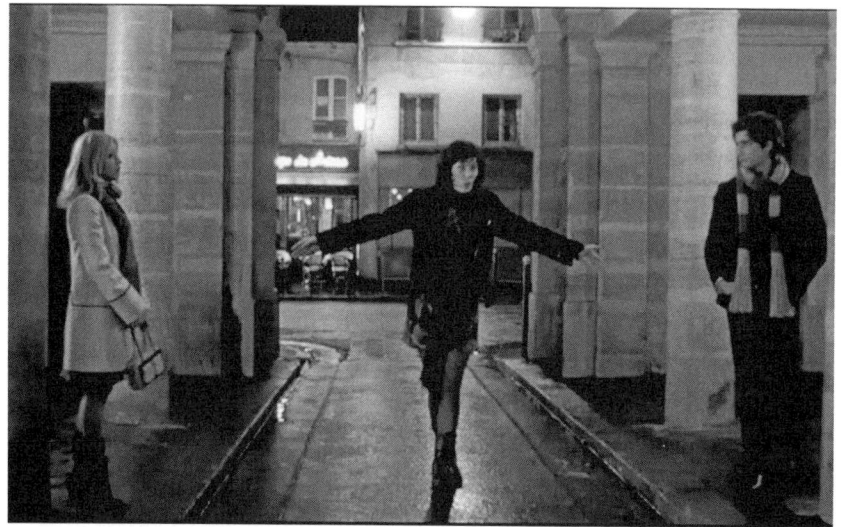

21. Alice acting as "the bridge" for Julie and Ismaël.

occupy. Song, like Alice, bridges interior and exterior, whether from street to apartment or ego to unconscious.

After the song and dance has more or less put the threesome to rest, Alice goes her separate way once they reach the bar, where she scopes out new romantic fun. With her bridge constructed through song, dance, and Julie's and Ismaël's bodies, she now extends outward and in multiple directions, one of which ultimately brings together Ismaël and Erwann.

BRIDGES

In musical terms for both the French and English languages, "*le pont*" and "the bridge" are defined as a short passageway or interlude that disrupts while nonetheless holding together a piece of music. It moves the work from one place to another. In English, the bridge or "middle eight" (named as such because it is measured by eight bars of music) introduces a variation in the repetitive motif of popular song. In French, *le pont* connects the first and second themes of a sonata-allegro. This is not dissimilar to the way the bridge in *Dans Paris* and Les Étoiles, the bar in *Les chansons d'amour*, are sites for transition. In *Les chansons*, the bar-as-bridge serves as cinematic and music-filled dream-space, a heavenly bridge between time and place, love and death. And Alice, who stands in as Julie and Ismaël's "bridge," similarly furnishes a disruption for the heterosexual motif in the film's narrative.

The soundtrack that plays across *Dans Paris*, scored by Beaupain, evokes Miles Davis's haunting melody of absence and loss from Louis Malle's *Ascenseur pour l'échafaud* (1958). Similarly, in *Les chansons*, "Brooklyn Bridge," the longing ballad that Beaupain wrote and performs onstage at Les Étoiles, conjures a bridge elsewhere to overcome loss. At Les Étoiles, the film's makers meet and recall the passing of their friend Aude. Along with Honoré's ethereal and magnetic mise-en-scène, Beaupain's music provides the setting for the journeys that are about to occur.

The nightclub's energy engulfs our characters, who soon embark on unexpected events. Indeed, Alice quickly molds the scene and herself with a new (male) partner, Gwendal, and she instantly warms herself with his body. In the meantime, Julie and Ismaël wrap themselves together in their purportedly secure coupledom. Alice is now separated—physically—from Julie and Ismaël. She will remain, however, a spiritual conduit that will directly impact her former lovers' immediate future as well as the futures that await them. Alice generates two coterminous futures around Julie's death: that of Ismaël and that of a Paris no longer guided only by hetero-romance. In each case, the terms for erotic love are transformed. Her generosity is, therefore, at once powerfully illuminating and (de)constructive, because her actions highlight the absurdity of hetero-romantic constraints while they reveal alternative passageways where Eros and Thanatos intersect.

Through a deus ex machina at the bar, Julie suddenly becomes ill while listening to Beaupain's "Brooklyn Bridge." Her hands turn cold even though she is snuggled into Ismaël's arms. Feeling faint, she exits for the toilet; Ismaël soon follows. Here, he discovers Julie staring into the mirror and suffering a nosebleed. As it turns out, the life draining from Julie is a result of a failing heart, whose weakening, we will learn, is caused by unspecified medical reasons that have triggered a heart attack. Her heart has, we have also learned, suffered emotionally due to the strain put on her by cultural rules and regulations that delimit her desire. As her body discharges heat and blood, Julie's heart finally gives out in cardiac arrest. She stumbles to the club's exit while Ismaël hurries to collect her belongings at the coat check. When he reaches the exit, Julie is passed out just beyond the club's doors. A young woman desperately applies CPR while paramedics and police arrive. Once Ismaël identifies himself to the police, they usher him to a patrol car, ask him official questions about drug and alcohol intake, and then request him to wait in the back of the car. Time stands still. The music stops. Cold statistical dialogue and medical machinery replace Beaupain's melancholic melody from the bar.

With time and space dramatically and momentarily frozen, Ismaël waits. Honoré inserts black-and-white photographs that are intercut to reveal Julie's final moments on the ground. Here, we see several sets of rubber-gloved hands urgently attend to and attach tubing to the traumatized young woman. In another cutaway photograph, Julie is carried on what amounts to another cinematic bed—the ambulance stretcher.[50] Covered with a silver-foil blanket, her wrapped body recalls Andy Warhol's *Silver Clouds*. Honoré's choreographic gifts are fully displayed in this sequence since he manipulates both the paramedics' disciplined bodies and the formal elements of the cinema. Cutting between the chilling photograph of Julie's medically wired body with the moving images of five paramedics, placed in long shot, Honoré's compositional skills underscore the emphasis on structure for an "affective landscape." Hence, in the long shot, we see paramedics and their rigorously rehearsed dance while they remove Julie from the street and then lift her onto the stretcher. With Julie placed in her mobile "bed," Honoré directs the paramedics' clinical maneuvering as a manly *corps de ballet* in which they delicately yet precisely guide Julie's ailing body. Their by-the-book medical staging, which is meant to prepare the process for death, is presented as an aestheticized performance.

Soon, the police return to the awaiting Ismaël. Treated less humanely than Julie's corpse, Ismaël is ignored by the police and receives the tragic news that his lover has died only when the officer radio-calls in her death. Alone and seated in the back of the police car, Ismaël simply hears, "Delta Charlie Delta."[51] Stricken with grief, he clasps his hands over his mouth and groans in anguish. He is silenced. No words can express his loss. The event's suddenness and the shock it creates establish a critical turning point, a crossing-over, for Ismaël. Time and space briefly halt. Just as Honoré's cinematic world abruptly shifts its aesthetic contours, Ismaël's present oscillates between motion and motionlessness, between *what was* and the unpredictability of *what will be*. Tossed into mourning and the obligatory details involved in wrapping up Julie's life, Ismaël is made to navigate through Honoré's film form and content, which mixes a disturbingly beautiful photographic and cinematic collage of color and black-and-white images. Caught between frozen and fluid time and space, Ismaël's world is fractured and displaced.

PASSAGEWAYS

Disoriented, Ismaël carries away Julie's belongings from the police station on the following morning. He takes stock of his transformed Parisian milieu while, at the same time, realizes he must make the unfathomably painful call to Julie's parents. With the song "Delta Charlie Delta," he reflects on the journey he is forced to take "along the road" once shared with Julie. As Ismaël sings, Honoré again uses still photographs as well as cinematic flashforwards to show the future in which Ismaël and Julie's family mourn as well as to collapse the fraught dimensions of death's aftermath, in which Ismaël spins. No longer dancing with Julie or wrestling with her about seemingly petty romance matters, Ismaël's "single song" is suddenly one "for a single man." "Delta Charlie Delta" recounts his life-changing experience that has been so inelegantly summed up through radiotelephony code: Delta Charlie Delta—"the song of approaching death." With three short and efficient terms, death is curtly announced.

In a scene from the flashforward sequence during Ismaël's song "Delta Charlie Delta," we see Julie's family at the cemetery. Again, cutting between photographs and moving images, Honoré wends his camera amid the mourners. Here Julie's younger sister, Jasmine (Alice Butaud), has a panic attack because she cannot find the book she has been reading, Henri Michaux's *La nuit remue* (*The Night Stirs*). Distressed, she and her sister, Jeanne (Mastroianni), search for the book. Once it is found, we cut to the image of a passage from the novel: "Many people have a soul that loves to swim. They are commonly called lazy. When one has the stomach to swim, and the soul departs the body, a freedom is produced that I can't describe; it is abandon, it is pleasure at once sensual and spiritual, *it is detachment at once intimate*" (emphasis added).[52] Honoré displays Michaux's metaphoric chain in order to stretch the paradoxically mobile and sensual themes that intersect with his cinema, the words recalling Jonathan's and Paul's courageous leaps into the Seine so as to swim away, paradoxically in order to move closer to those whom they love: "it is detachment at once intimate." Not unlike Hitchcock, who on so many occasions stamped his film's themes quite literally on the mise-en-scène, Honoré permeates his characters' worlds with the written word.[53] In *Les chansons*, the novel's passage(way)—placed as it is at this moment of Julie's death and in the hands of one of her sisters—serves as a reminder for those who surrounded Julie, that describing one's experience is less important than swimming through it.

Swimming through, or the ability to malleably express emotion and desire through one's body and in relationship to other bodies in the wake of loss, is central to Honoré's cinematic concept in *Les chansons*. "I have the impression," he notes,

> that [the characters] react above all at different speeds. Ismaël ... walks along blindly but he keeps walking in spite of everything. From the very beginning of the story, I have filmed in motion and I refused to halt that motion in spite of the sudden tragedy. And then Erwann ... quickens his pace a little. Jeanne ... on the other hand, is condemned to be immobile, she remains a fixed point. The tragedy freezes her. As for

> Alice ... she walks alongside Ismaël, then she turns away from his path to follow another story with this Breton guy that she meets.[54]

Indeed, the ever-agile Alice swims through as she follows another "path," but she is at the same time both a swimmer and also the vessel to which others may cling and swim alongside. When Julie becomes ill and dies, Alice is initially oblivious to her "sister's" demise. When, for instance, Julie is collapsed in front of Les Étoiles and we hear Ismaël give police the cold facts about Julie—her name and age—Honoré cuts to Alice while she lightly moves about the bar with the other patrons, kissing Gwendal and listening to the music. She is no less saddened than Ismaël, however, when she finally hears about Julie's passing. Shortly after the night at the club, Alice and Ismaël are back in the newsroom, where words drive their word-based business to ostensibly make sense of the world. They soon realize that "making sense" of the world with words alone comes up short when expressing grief. Soon, the two friends caress each other tenderly, hopeful that touch will relieve their heartache. As they entwine, the lovers' lyrics dig deep to express corporeal delights so as to sensually engage each other. The inexplicable terms for Eros and Thanatos feed their demand for sexual intimacy. Together they sing "Il faut se taire" (Silence Is Necessary).

If, as Godard taught, words fail to articulate meaning as such, Honoré demonstrates this in relation to emotion. "Il faut se taire" redeploys the tongue's use through punning on the homonym "tongue" ("langue") and "language" ("langue"). Hence, since "[their] tongues are tired" ("[ses] langues se fatiguent"), the lovers' lyrics punctuate "promises without a voice" ("des promesses aphones"). "Let's spare the tongue against language" ("Pour se faire langue contre langue"), they sing, while they grope, so as to "preserve" their "saliva," which they can "finally take down [their] throats, like sweet poison" ("Gardes ta salive / Que je puisse enfin la faire couler dans ma gorge / Comme un doux venin").[55] During the number, Alice and Ismaël caress each other, guided by lyrics that emphasize expressive *sound* for their feelings over functional communication.

Throughout *Les chansons*, Beaupain's lyrics emphasize the tactile body and its array of functions (feet, asses, blood, breasts, saliva, tongues, odors) as forms of communication. Forgoing words to express the inexplicable or, rather, hoping to express the inexplicable through song, lovers rely on the form's queer-abilities to get through to each other. Cinema's "sweet poison" is thus visceral because its affect reaches toward that which is ultimately unreachable through words alone. The "film with song" is thus an intimate cinema; it is also an impure cinema, sweetly poisoned by transcultural and sensual circumstances. Later, when Ismaël and

Erwann finally come together, song "naturally" occurs. When they roll together in bed, their lyricized corporeality purges Ismaël's longing for Julie. As the boys undress, tongues intertwine, and they tumble through the sheets, they sing as Alice and Ismaël had before. To *lyricize* corporeality, or to make corporeality musical, Honoré evokes the spirit of inexplicable desire or the "queer spirit" to which Demy introduced him. Honoré's film with song is a platform for a sensually intimate cinema in which bodies and mise-en-scène penetrate one another.

If, as Honoré notes, Alice and Ismaël erotically fold their bodies into each other and *actively move* through the frame precisely because of death, Jeanne remains immobilized by loss. Her movements in the film are stifled, frozen. With Julie's death, Jeanne assumes her role as the dutiful daughter. She regularly and annoyingly checks in on Ismaël, she tidies the apartment that he and Julie kept, and she insists that he articulate his feelings more cogently for the sake of her and her family. To articulate as such is "to hold it together." Her wish to control her emotions translates into controlling the way others manage their own. Jeanne's fixedness is presented not only through her taut movements and gestures; her immobility and her lack of flexibility are equal to the demand she makes on others to speak about their loss. Her insistence *to speak* embodies a cinema that stultifies (e)motion. Like narrational-driven cinema that often locks the camera in place, Jeanne's desire to "talk it out" suffocates cinematic affect.

During the song "Au parc," Honoré situates Jeanne amid the finely shaped and meticulously maintained trees familiar in Parisian parks. Like the city's winter trees and the precision with which they are planted and pruned, Jeanne is frozen. If Alice, Ismaël, and Erwann embody Paris's effervescence through movement and song, Jeanne stands in for the rigidity for which French culture is also known. The only moment that Jeanne's controlled nature is loosened is when she sings her sad song while the city's controlled nature serves as her backdrop. But even when Jeanne is emotionally moved to sing, only the camera is mobile. She remains frozen in place.

BOYS

Alice's "boyfriend," Gwendal (Yannick Renier), whom she met at Les Étoiles, becomes something of a one-night-stand drag. But their short-lived relationship leaves a promising legacy insofar as Gwendal's younger gay brother, Erwann, crosses paths with Ismaël. Out of concern for Ismaël's ongoing depression and worried about him spending time alone in his and Julie's apartment, Alice arranges for him to stay at Gwendal and Erwann's home. Erwann is a critical figure in

Les chansons because he suggests a mirror onto Honoré's view of himself as a gay Breton. Erwann is at once as naïve as he is determined in love and the fulfillment of sexual desire. He is enthusiastic about and familiar with surrealist poetry as well as classic rock and Broadway soundtracks. Smitten with Ismaël, the young Breton discovers his troubled guest sleeping in his bed. Surrounded by the mise-en-scène of a young gay man from Brittany (Queen album covers, *That's Dancing* posters, novels by Edmund White and Jean Genet), Ismaël awakes in an uncanny environment and to Erwann's boyish face. Mocking Erwann's odor of lemon crêpes, his Breton colloquialism, his taste in music, and his fisherman's sweater, Ismaël's urbane disposition brings into relief the awkward experience that a queer boy from the provinces (Honoré?) encounters when he arrives in the big city.

Erwann's cinematic presence and the space he occupies in it remind us of Honoré's declaration in *Le livre pour enfants*: "Bretagne est mon décor." And, as such, it is the mise-en-scène that enables his all-important trinity: "Homosexuality, Brittany, Adolescence." The actor who plays Erwann, Grégoire Leprince-Ringuet, was first seen by Honoré in André Téchiné's film *Les égarés* (*Strayed*, 2003; Téchiné apparently discovered him in a choir). Honoré describes his casting decision this way: "Grégoire represents a certain idea of youth without falling into the clichés or sexual fantasies of our times. His beauty has an open and unostentatious side to it. I wanted the character to be a young man who has no doubts about his homosexuality but who hasn't had an affair yet. Erwann isn't tormented by his sexuality but by his feelings. Grégoire displayed a form of simplicity and kindness that quickly convinced me that he was the right actor for the part."[56] Given this description and what we have come to learn about Honoré thus far, and given the significance of personal events and experiences that give life to *Les chansons*, Erwann's nearly queer angelic presence (he sang in a choir, after all) in concert with his comfort about his sexuality testifies to Honoré's imagined self. Erwann presents us with a shadow of the young queer Breton who has made his way to Paris to discover love and life.

For Ismaël, his awakening in Erwann's bed is thus uncanny because, on the one hand, the queer boy's mise-en-scène trades on a seemingly disparate worldview that is quite different from his own hetero-romanticized one; on the other hand, his awakening in the queer Breton scene is also safe, comforting, and strangely home-like.[57] Wrapped in the gay boy's Breton fisherman's sweater to keep warm, Ismaël is drawn into an intimate yet inscrutable queer and surrealist moment between awakening (*réveil*) and dream (*rêve*) in the eleventh arrondissement. "Dream and the uncanny," Douglas B. Wilson tells us, "both provide (to borrow from Freud) 'the royal road to the unconscious.'"[58] And because the scene in which Ismaël awakens is uncanny in this way, he confronts significant questions about his manhood, his long-rehearsed heterosexual script, and intimate relationships that involve bodies, erotics, and love.

Ismaël, although flattered by Erwann's persistent advances, remains uncertain about whether he is capable of love in any form whatsoever. Julie's death haunts and bars him at every turn; contact with her family perpetuates her lingering effects. Moreover, her haunting bears the ideological constraints of heterosexual romance, in which both she and Ismaël were confined. He now finds himself torn between the "rules for love" and the intimacy he shares with Erwann. Here on earth, Julie's sister Jeanne, annoyingly and without invitation, continually appears at Ismaël's apartment under the auspices of concern for his well-being. With the family in agreement, Julie's father (Jean-Marie Winling) insists that Ismaël receive her life insurance. And her mother (Brigitte Roüan), out of the blue, calls on Alice for no other reason than to ask her (or so she says) to watch over Ismaël. In effect, their largesse, which is meant to draw Ismaël ever closer into their familial lair, instead pushes him further away.

In pushing aside the family's pouncing and their longing to keep Julie alive through Ismaël, he discovers new pathways via Alice. To echo Mary Ann Doane, Alice awakens Ismaël to *the desire to desire* alternative intimacies that Julie's family seek but have no imaginative roadmap for how to achieve. Ideological hauntings are a powerful force. Hence, while Ismaël pushes Erwann away, the distance between them in fact draws them together. Like the sisterly love that Alice felt for Julie, Ismaël and Erwann develop a brotherly erotics, not dissimilar to that shared by Jonathan and Paul in *Dans Paris* (Ismaël continues to wear Erwann's sweater). In *Les chansons*, however, the terms for brotherly designs are sexually enacted.

In Paris, the push-and-pull "detachment" in which Ismaël and Erwann participate is precisely the act that brings them together. Detachment *is* seduction. And, most clearly and as we have seen, overcoming distance as a negation of detachment succeeds through media technology. In *Les chansons*, communication devices network people into unexpected yet self-determined relationships. A transformative moment that substantially bridges Ismaël and Erwann's relationship, for instance, is when they sing to each other over their mobile phones. Unlike in *Dans Paris*, in which the song over the phone inaugurates a thoughtful and mutually agreed to separation between Paul and Anne, the song "La distance" in *Les chansons* cements the couple's mutual care for each other. At the same time, it serves to keep alive, albeit disjointedly, the boys' emotional and physical connection. And like in *Dans Paris*, their technologically mediated duet prompts mediation with the person who has died. While the song "La distance" draws Erwann and Ismaël ever closer, it also drives Ismaël toward his final farewell with Julie.

Thus, slowly detaching from Julie and moving closer to Erwann, Ismaël glides toward Julie in a cinematic conjuring that finally sets both her and Ismaël free. Not insignificantly, her spirit makes its return once the boys have sex. Together for the first time, the boys undress and roll through the sheets, where Ismaël soaks in Erwann's caresses so as to "hunt" down and "fight" the ghost that haunts him. Repeating Alice and Ismaël's use of song to orally cleanse, the boys fondle, embrace, and bring together their tongues (the *langue/langue* homonym reappears) so as to "wash" (*lave*) their bodies and purge the "soiled" memories clean that stain them ("lick me clean" / "Du bout de ta langue nettoie-moi partout"). The physical connection through their pliant mouths provides the necessary poison to alleviate sorrow and loss.

Moreover, Honoré strictly choreographs Erwann and Ismaël's lovemaking in bed; "every single gesture was mapped out."[59] Sentient and mobile bodies press into each other in a rigidly contained space, thus, paradoxically, freeing their emotions. Tightly framed in close-up, the boys tumble together and deeply insert their tongues to excavate desire and sadness. The carefully plotted movement, in concert with Honoré's penetrating camera and Beaupain's lyricized mode of expression, draws together self-interested desire with mutual pleasure. Honoré's choreographed beds most fully display the ironic sentiment that anchors his films: intimate detachment.

In a cut from Erwann's bed to Ismaël's apartment, we discover that the boys' lovemaking has extended beyond one singular moment. While they sleep, the apartment door opens, and the Pommerayes' family dog trots over to Ismaël's hand and licks it (an unexpected tongue application as a form of communication). Immediately, he knows that Jeanne has again asserted her uninvited presence. When Jeanne discovers Erwann in Ismaël's (and, to her mind, Julie's) bed, she is stunned. She quickly exits. Ismaël rolls from bed, revealing Erwann's bare ass, and chases after her.

On the street, Ismaël catches up with Jeanne and asks, "Can we talk?" The discussion, such as it is in Honoré's world, fails to find common ground since the two are unable to communicate the different ways they grieve. When Jeanne tells Ismaël that his grieving process is "violent" because it is "self-centered," Ismaël realizes that this is the time and place to break with Julie and Julie's family since it is they who are violently self-centered and refuse to see their own behavior as such. In hoping to "understand" Ismaël, Julie, and Alice's threesome, Jeanne presumes Ismaël's "boy in his bed" is the reasoning behind his and her sister's arrangement, why he and Julie did not want children, and why Julie was unhappy. Ismaël is left speechless.

Alice finds herself similarly disposed when, as we noted earlier, Julie's mother summons her to a café to ask her to "watch over Ismaël." Furthermore, and in a motherly tone, Julie's mother inquires whether Alice and Ismaël remain "emotionally" together since she has moved out. Alice finds the question "weird" and that Julie's mother's wish to "help" Ismaël oversteps her presumptive mothering role. Gently, Alice informs her, as Paul had earlier reminded us in *Dans Paris*, that it is not possible to help those who do not seek it.

Jeanne and her mother's insistence on "understanding" Ismaël, and Jeanne's reminder to him that she and her family have afforded him every opportunity "to speak" about his sorrow—as well as the private details between him and her sister—begs the question about "self-centeredness." The mother's remarks tellingly echo Mirko's view about his son Paul in *Dans Paris*. How is it possible to respond to those who believe they have access to the other's emotions when, in truth, their insight to the other only reveals their own self-centered needs? By what logic does Ismaël and Julie's relationship provide an invitation for the nuclear family to participate in its intimacy? Are not the sister's intrusiveness and the family's unrelenting wish to be inserted into Ismaël's "emotional" life—*to make him speak about feelings*—the selfish acts here? Honoré in effect turns the tables on the gift of sympathy and generosity. *Les chansons'* disassembling and reassembling of familial relations pointedly make the case for love on *undecidable* and variable terms.

Ismaël's break from Julie's family leads directly to the break he finally must make with Julie. But unlike his feelings for her family, he loves Julie, and their farewell is understood as one that is fait accompli but never to be permanently erased. Honoré treats Ismaël's moment of "happy grief" with a cinematic ghosting of Julie. Like Claire before her in *Dans* Paris, Julie is summoned from the dead so that Ismaël (like Paul before him) may be forgiven for the wrongs he may have committed—knowingly or unknowingly. By evoking dead loved ones, the living can move forward with their lives.

When Ismaël and Jeanne separate on the street, we cut to Jeanne's melancholic song for her sister, "Au parc." As described earlier, the chanteuse recalls the past of an imaginary Parisian park, "Pépinière," where she longs for her playmate Julie. In the park's highly manicured winter scene, Jeanne stands alone—frozen—while other children play and create childhood memories. Julie remains a memory that leaves Jeanne forever sad. Ismaël will also fall into song once he and Jeanne depart each other. But, in his longing, Julie joins him in song and encourages his moving on.

In Montparnasse Cemetery, Ismaël visits Julie's gravesite. He lingers a while as night closes in; Montparnasse Tower's early evening lights glow behind him. Soon, his weeping turns to song while he makes his way to the exit. While he is leaving, Julie's ghost joins him and strolls just beyond his right shoulder. "What sudden desire or fear brings you here?" she inquires as the camera tracks slowly in front of the couple. As she fades into the night's blackness, Ismaël continues on his way, certainly feeling her presence surround him. We, in fact, will see her sentient presence as Honoré dissolves to a large close-up of Julie that floats over Ismaël as he walks away from the camera (and her). Even though she knows why he has come so late to reconcile loss and love (Julie, of course, has no way to intervene in circumstances at this point), she nonetheless nudges her "angel," Ismaël, to confront his "fate." It is time for Ismaël to move along, to choose. (See figures 22.1 and 22.2.)

Julie's double—Paris—merges with her, while the song she sings fades and the scene segues from the cemetery to Ismaël's walk along the city streets. If Julie's prompting fails to make the case that it is time for him to move on and into the bed of a new love, Paris will reinforce her message. Recalling the montage that opens *Les chansons,* Ismaël's point of view takes note of the city landscape, in which signs that read "Brittany," "Yes, You Can!" and "Cry Me A River" speak directly to his circumstances. The city's pointed suggestions, in intense neon light, along with Julie's mediated presence, motivate Ismaël to return to Erwann's arms, where the young Breton clearly understands the relationship's terms: "You want a body, that's okay," he sings to Ismaël. For the time being, love returns in Paris.

Les chansons' own cinematic shadows are precisely a conjuring of the dead—Guiguet and Monnin. In their memory, Honoré grieves, a "happy grief," for his loss but reckons with his sorrow as a generative force. "Communicating" with the dead, cinematically, derives from the moment of his realization "Bretagne est mon décor": "Brittany becomes obvious because that's where I come from, and particularly in my relationship to death, I think there's something very Breton about the idea of communicating constantly with dead people, because living people constantly ask dead people to forgive them for something or other" (JNCH, 176).

Honoré's films are a cinematic séance.

PAPA'S KISS

We close part 2 with some remarks on one final cinematic bed: the family's living-room sofa. In *Dans Paris,* the living room served as a makeshift bedroom where a family member's private life may be, for assorted reasons, both temporarily relegated and put on display. At Julie's family's apartment, located not far from Place de la Bastille and *Le Génie,* the living-room space opens out

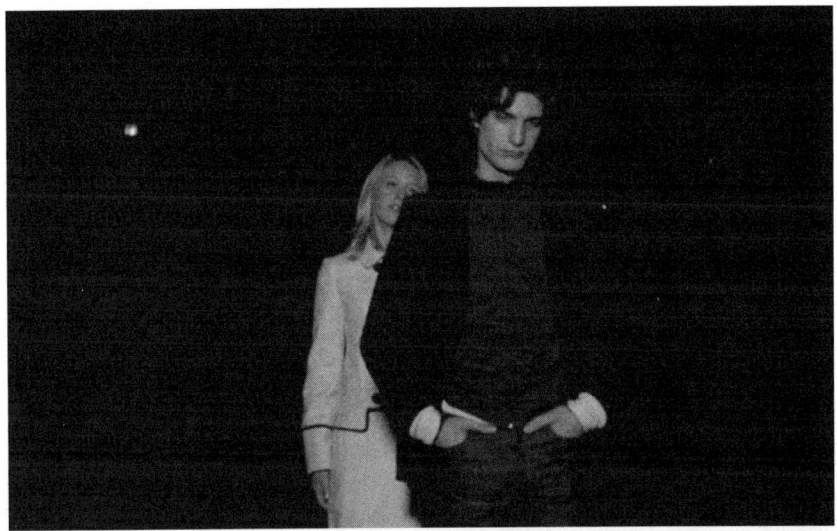

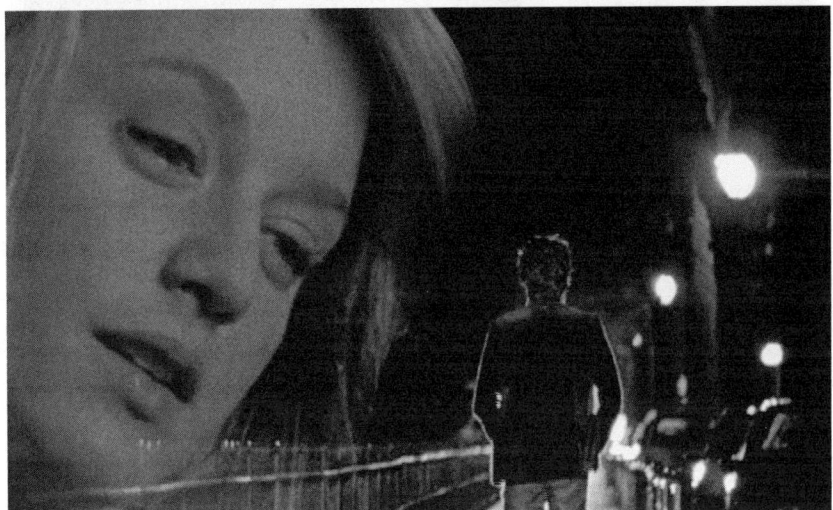

22.1–22.2. Julie's specter prompts Ismaël to move along and to make choices.

from the dining room, where we first meet Julie's family. Set during the holiday Epiphanie: Fête des Rois (Epiphany: Feast of the Kings), we first see the family convened around the dining-room table, where Ismaël performs a game of charades for the family audience. Performing gestures that interpret "amazement," "surprise," "horror," and "despair" (the latter choreographed by using a napkin as a noose to hang himself), Ismaël presciently, wordlessly demonstrates what will amount to the various stages that will mark his relationship with Julie's family.

At first, her family's charming and close connection is warm and inviting; but, as we have seen, their charm quickly wears off, and their desire to possess him leads to intimate suffocation and, ultimately, despair.

While Ismaël entertains the family, Julie becomes annoyed with his antics and begins to clear the table. Jeanne follows her to the kitchen, where she briefly comments on her own failing relationship with a married man. In turn, Julie confides about the threesome (her idea, she tells Jeanne) and how it has made romance with Ismaël more complicated than she had expected. Although Jeanne's affair with a married man barely raises an eyebrow between the blood sisters, Julie's ménage à trois piques Jeanne's prurient interest. From the hallway, their mother overhears their conversation and is drawn in, titillated by her daughter's admission. The conversation between mother and daughters draws the specter of familial erotics and lesbian incest into the family scene. It represents Honoré's emphasis on sexuality as core to the familial dynamic.[60]

Entering the kitchen, the sisters' mother prods Jeanne into leaving so she can take up a detailed conversation with Julie about her amorous arrangement. She is clearly intrigued yet hoping to remain mother-like in her inquisitiveness (i.e., erotically neutral); it becomes clear that her motherliness is formed by an erotic impulse transferred into her desire to talk about Julie's sex life. By pressing Julie to speak more and more about the sexual parameters of her relationship, her mother inserts herself into the threesome fantasy. At the same time, Julie freely explains how the three arrange themselves in bed, the possible roles the three-way offers, and the pleasure she takes in the sensual encounters. Once the two women exhaust the conversation and decide to end the descriptive possibilities of Julie's sex life, since it leads to disconcerting heart palpitations for the mother, they retreat to the living room, where the familial erotics are restaged in yet another domestic space. If Honoré's beds are treated as dining-room tables, the action in this sequence moves the family from one dining-room table to another: the sofa bed (JNCH, 191).

When the women return to the family gathering, they find the father seated on the couch while Ismaël continues his game of charades, cradling a sofa pillow as if it were a baby. His performance appropriately, if sardonically, emphasizes the Epiphany since it is the holiday that commemorates the Magis' visit to the Christ child. The sequence suggests an unsettling celebration of the child since the epiphany/Epiphany occurs by witnessing the aura of familial erotics that play out against the holy-day backdrop. While the father chuckles at Ismaël's performance, Julie looks on, bemused. Ismaël carries his bundle back toward the dining-room window, where Jeanne is smoking, and asks his "child" to burp for her. With a mock discharge from the baby, he scolds the "little bugger" and tosses him/it out the window. Julie's mother laments, "I love that cushion." "Are you crazy?" Jeanne declares about the fake "little bugger." We learn later that, according to Jeanne, Ismaël is the "little bugger" who is the reason why he and Julie had no children. Hence, both Jeanne and Julie's mother foreshadow and project their dismay onto the family sofa cushion that represents the child who will never be, as well as the child they will soon grieve.

In the living room, the family celebrates the holiday's climax with the traditional cake ("une galette des rois") in which a small porcelain figurine ("une fève") is contained. The room in which this cake is served is plainly decorated and anchored by a large divan-like sofa. It is on this makeshift bed that the Pommeraye family gathers while the cake is served (see figure 23.1). Hanging above the couch-bed is a painting of storks—a mother and her baby waiting, standing side by side.[61] As the family assembles and cuddles on the bed, Ismaël is seated separately from the sofa and in the frame's margin; he is a nominal member of the family, but, since he and Julie are childless, he is always beyond its bloodline.[62]

The familial erotics are made even more cinematically dense when Honoré treats the sequence as an incestuous homage to two Jacques Demy films: *Les parapluies de Cherbourg* and his 1970s musical fantasy *Peau d'âne* (The Donkey Skin). Honoré intermingles with his own film Demy's two films, one of which is Demy's explicit exploration of an incest fantasy—the king (Jean Marais) seeks to marry his princess daughter (Catherine Deneuve) in *Peau d'âne*—capitalizing on the Catholic family holiday tradition insofar as this particular holy day involves the crowning of a princess. The other homage is to the Epiphany scene in *Les parapluies de Cherbourg*. In *Les chansons*, daddy's princess proves to be Jeanne because it is she who discovers "la fève" in her piece of cake. The girls' father is thrilled when his "sweetie pie" finds the hidden gift and is crowned as his princess. In a close-up that replays Dencuve's crowning in *Les parapluies,* Jeanne wears the traditional crown. Once she is crowned, the father summons the entire family to snuggle with him on the couch-bed—sans Ismaël (and the beloved cushion-cum-"the little bugger"), who refuses to join in since he finds the familial overattachments suffocating (see figures 23.2 and 23.3).

Taken together—the family scene just described and Honoré's queer homage to his dead "godfather" (Demy)—*Les chansons* incestuously echoes Deneuve's role as Geneviève in *Les parapluies* when her would-be suitor, Roland Cassard, joins her and her mother for dinner and she discovers "la fève" in her piece of cake and dons the Epiphany crown. Deneuve's holiday crowning in *Les parapluies* is repeated in *Peau d'âne* when she assumes the

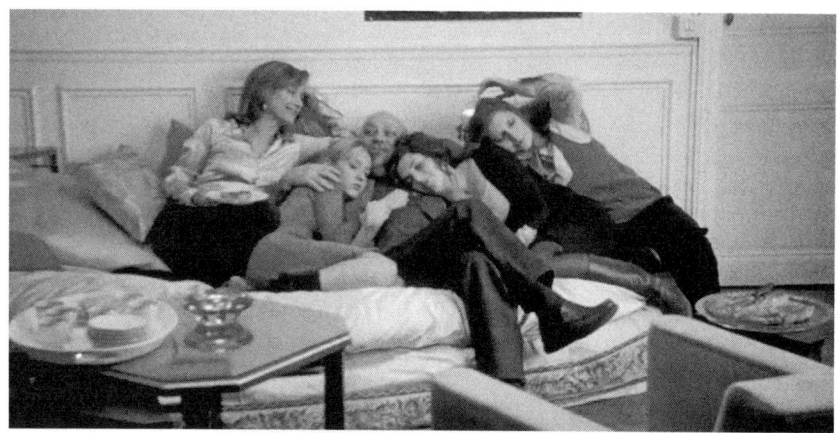

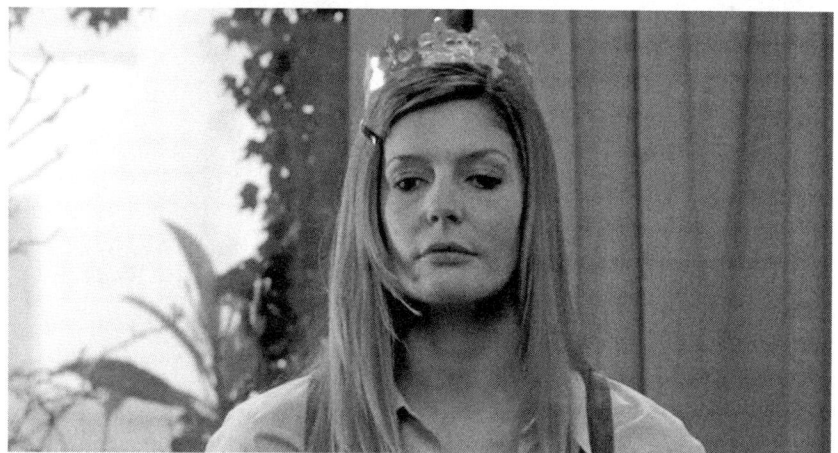

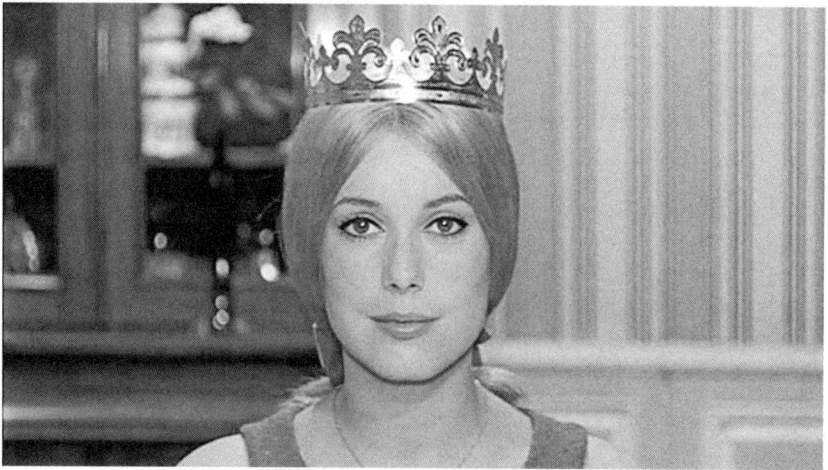

23.1–23.3. Honoré's cinematic families are an incestuous affair.

role of the princess who is the target of her father's marital designs. Deneuve thus in both Demy films memorializes the role of the lucky one to receive the charged gift of being a princess on display for male desire. In *Les parapluies* and *Peau d'âne*, her crowning as the family's princess is strictly for patriarchal delight (the older Roland Cassard and the queer patriarch-king, played by Jean Cocteau's lover, Jean Marais). Honoré, in pressing cinematic homage further on history/incest, positions Jeanne (portrayed by the daughter of Deneuve and Marcello Mastroianni, Chiara Mastroianni) as the family member who now bears the princess crown. Honoré's actors, indeed, *en famille*, erotically intermingle with the history of cinema. If the family who propels the film's narrative is unable to imbibe in their sexual desire for the other, Honoré arranges the cinematic bed as a sensual alternative.

In *Les chansons,* this family celebration is haunted by two imaginary child-figures—the holy child and the future child (the "little bugger") denied to the Pommerayes. Heterocentric fantasy and its attendant imaginary press on the tensions that delimit family erotics. If the tension that this scene reveals rests on the reproducibility of the child to define family *as such,* then the Pommerayes' fulfillment of the heterocentric model is put at risk. The family thus occupies a place of longing: longing for the child and longing to be sexually gratified by one another. The Epiphany is family tradition as sublimation. The family's "epiphany," then, is their desire transferred through holiday cake and hugs. As the family gathers onto the sofa/bed, the sexual tensions of the day are roped in and contained by the king who desires his "princess" and the queen who lives vicariously through her daughter's reconfigured sisterly love with Alice.

LOVE ME LESS, BUT LOVE ME A LONG TIME

The final image we see in *Les chansons d'amour* is that of Ismaël and Erwann standing on the second-floor window ledge outside Erwann's apartment. With Alice secretly keeping watch below, a large cinematic spotlight encircles the boys as they sing about their affection for each other. But their "love song" insists on the porous boundaries for love: "You want a body, that's okay," sings the young Breton, who happily announces that he "smells of rain, the ocean, and lemon crêpes." Indeed, Ismaël longs to hear "I love you" but only to the extent that he *feels* (that is, smells and tastes) Erwann's love from both near and far. Once on the window ledge, the boys embrace, and a light (a streetlight? the stars? the moon? a 10K spotlight?) shines on them. Just as

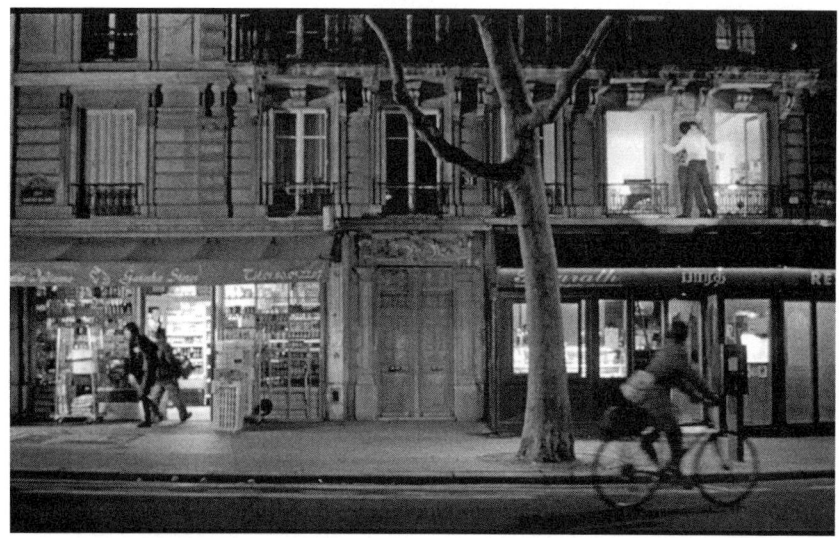

24. "Love me less, but love me a long time."

Erwann is about to speak words of love, Ismaël looks toward the sky, as if to check for Julie's presence. Ismaël quickly covers his lover's mouth before he can utter the words that Erwann believes Ismaël "needs to hear." With Erwann's mouth shushed, Ismaël kisses the boy. As the camera cuts to a long shot of the two in embrace, and the perfectly formed spotlight encircles them, we hear Ismaël's distant whisper: "Love me less, but love me a long time." Below, in the market, Alice looks on, and a worker exits and strolls onto the street. Life and love in the eleventh go on.

III

La belle personne

NARRATIVE ARC

La belle personne is the final film in the trilogy. It is based on Madame de Lafayette's novel *La princesse de Clèves* (1678), a canonical text in the French lycée curriculum. Honoré marshals cinematic monstration in the spirit of this novel that explores networks of passion that are often facilitated without words. *La belle personne*'s narrative centers on Junie, a young woman transferring into a new high school, following the death of her mother. Here she immediately makes a host of new friends, one of whom—Otto—falls in love with her. Other students notice Junie's sullen yet radiant beauty, as well as her seductive insouciance. They, like Otto, are quickly drawn to her subtle charms. Most complicated, though, is the passion that develops between her and her Italian instructor, M. Nemours. The film follows Junie while she navigates the tricky path of desire—between lovers and friends—as it intersects with the cultural rules and obligations that a young woman is expected to follow. The film, like the novel, stunningly articulates the *unspoken*. Where words fail, Honoré's youths communicate through media technology, international languages, and—most importantly—the look.

PART III

ARRONDIR

From the open window in the tenth arrondissement where we leave Ismaël and Erwann in a tentative but full embrace, we move toward the world of *La belle personne*. Here, Honoré circles back toward the sixteenth arrondissement, where we left our ensemble in *Dans Paris*. "It's true," Honoré claims, "that *Dans Paris* and [*Les chansons d'amour*] are variations on a common theme." Moreover, he confirms that together they are "part of a trilogy" in which he "[tackles] three themes: a look at Paris, a look at French cinema, and a look at the sentimental portrait of youth."[1] *La belle personne* is the third film—not insignificantly, the third "look"—in the trilogy.

If the first two films are exemplary for the way Honoré draws on a range of multiple art forms and cultural signifiers, *La belle personne* broadens his very French historical palette. On the one hand, classic literature, poetry, love letters, librettos, theater, pop songs, photography, and cinema dance across the film. On the other, Honoré is steadfast and conscious of his work as film-*as*-art, that is, as an art that incorporates the other arts. Like the characters to whom we are introduced, the history of art media—including film—is intimate, if not incestuous, in Honoré's oeuvre. In other words, *La belle personne* reaffirms Rudolf Arnheim's hypothesis in the essay "A New Laocoön: Artistic Composites and the Talking Film" that "the art of the motion image is as old as the other arts, it is as old as humanity itself, and the motion picture is but its most recent manifestation."[2] Honoré further abides by Arnheim's theoretical premise that each art form contains—and must fully demonstrate—its unique aesthetic properties without giving way to cinema's primary concern: the visual (224). For the cinema to maintain its specific and discrete formal dimensions, therefore, it must necessarily display the particularities of each work of art that becomes involved in film production. In this regard, sound (music, dialogue, and so forth) is front and center when used in concert with film. *La belle personne* is a major work in its achievement of cinematic monstration.

If the various arts are to intermingle in film, they can only do so if their specific properties register sui generis. For Arnheim, therefore, the "100% talkie" is a dismal failure in the cinematic arts since it hides the distinct qualities that enable the cinema to effectively communicate the cinema as art. In fact, "dialogue paralyzes visual action" (228). By naturalizing the relationship between the visual and sound through dialogue, cinema then only mimics theatrical presentation. Sound, in this instance, is more an aesthetic disservice than a dynamic companion to the visual. Arnheim is clear that each art form must maintain specific and discrete boundaries to manage a "parallelism of complete and segregated representation" (228).

La belle personne

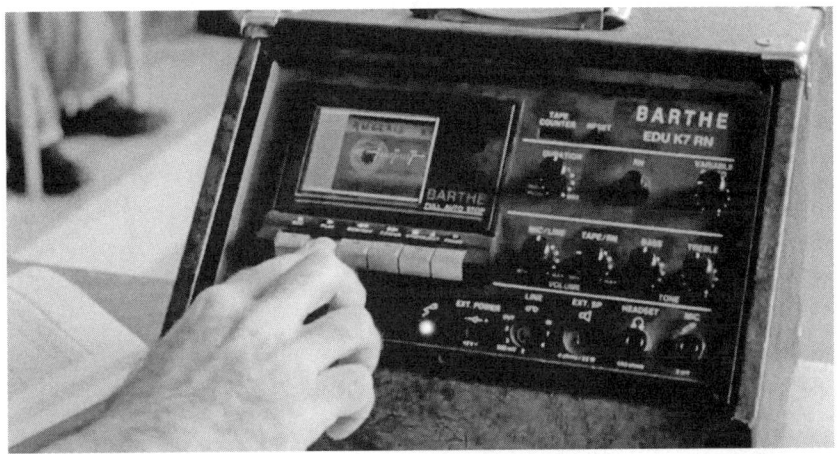

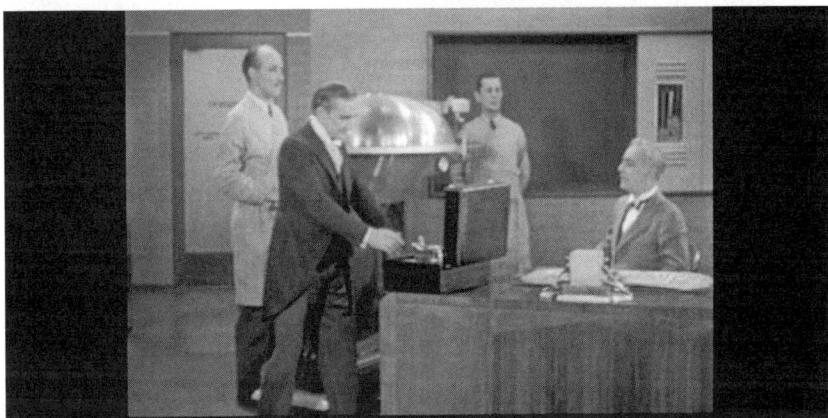

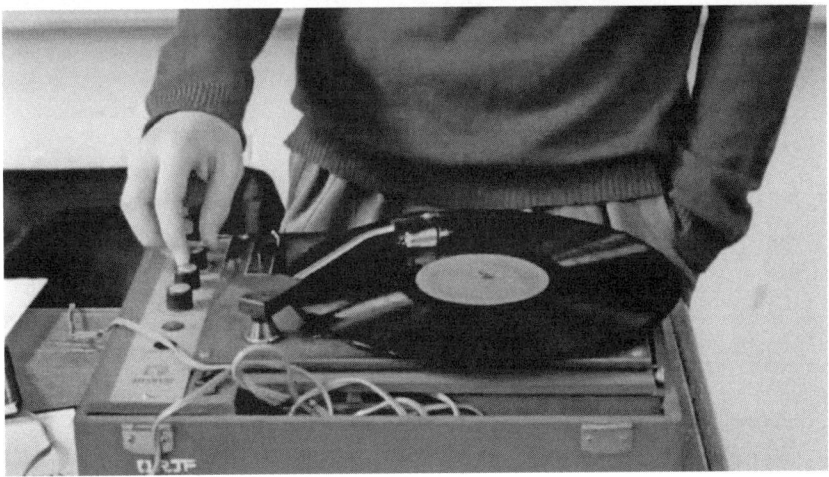

25.1–25.3. Modern cinema. *La belle personne* and *Modern Times* (1936).

In *La belle personne,* Honoré directs his film in close approximation to Arnheim's theoretical premise, a premise that turns to the filmmaker that Arnheim champions: Charlie Chaplin. Although Arnheim does not directly comment on Chaplin or his critical experiment with sound and film, *Modern Times* (1936), in "The New Laocoön," Chaplin is elsewhere a convincing figure for Arnheim's theory on cinematic aesthetics.[3] Like Chaplin's strategic structuring of silent-sound film and gesture in *Modern Times,* Honoré engages the mechanically reproduced arts (records, tape recordings, photographs) in *La belle personne* not only to create an ambient diegetic sphere in which characters bodily communicate and emote; the mechanized media in *La belle personne*'s diegetic space are revealed as well-defined sources that animate rather than "[paralyze] visual action" (see figures 25.1–25.3). In this way, both *Modern Times* (consider the use of the on-screen record player that serves as the salesman's voice) and *La belle personne* rely on the specificity of sound and the primacy of image while ensuring that when they commingle, they announce themselves distinctively yet emerge as a creative whole.

As we have seen, to speak through words and to intend those words to convey concise meaning is no simple matter. To push the language of words and its boundaries, Honoré expands the terms for language, through cinema. In *La belle personne,* Honoré's "young aesthetes" (to borrow the author Dennis Cooper's terms) emotionally pivot on multiple languages and mediated forms.[4] The various arts we encounter in the film, in other words, "speak" to *and* for the characters' emotions and desires. And, as in the first two films in the trilogy, media technology plays a critical role in the ways contemporary youths manage these traditional aesthetic forms and modes of communication. Honoré's chains of communication are at once as immediate as they are historical.

STAGING

We are introduced to the world of *La belle personne* when two enormous nineteenth-century heavy wooden doors are pulled open to give entry to a lycée. As this wooden curtain slowly opens, a Parisian street is revealed in which young people pass by and congregate. Set back in the school's foyer, the scene is shot in long take, counterposed to the montage sequences that open *Dans Paris* and *Les chansons.* The opening of the doors shows the exterior through a frame within a frame, thus reiterating Honoré's theme of inside and outside, as when Jonathan opens the electronic shades on his apartment window. The dramatic opening of the frame within a frame also recalls Jean Renoir's precise mise-en-scène and layered framings where multiple actions occur, suggesting active off-screen space. Outside,

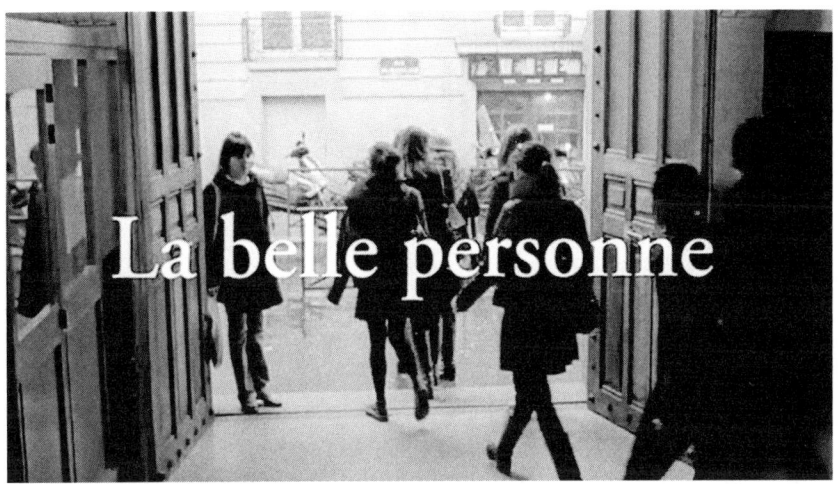

26. Moving between interior and exterior in *La belle personne*.

the Paris streets teem with activity that will soon flow into the lycée halls, while the dramas that occur in the school will, in kind, pour into the streets.

As the scene continues, we soon hear a school bell, indicating a transition between classroom periods. We also hear ghostly, ambient voices that permeate the giant foyer—voices that are soon embodied by students who enter and exit the building and congregate on the street. Over the long take, the credits roll in a font type that is readily familiar to French students since the 1970s. The typeset mirrors Gallimard's Folio Editions, which was introduced in 1970 and, since then, has been inscribed on the publisher's vast library of French novels required for the curriculum of most lycées.

"Liberally inspired" (the end credits tell us) by Madame Lafayette's *La princesse de Clèves* (1678), the film honors what Robin Buss considers to be the novel's major contribution to French literature: "an overriding concern with psychological analysis, a certain 'purity' of language and classical simplicity of plot."[5] More pointedly, and more apposite for Honoré's translation of the novel, Buss suggests,

> [The novel's] structure, the characters, the treatment of love, politics, and above all, of serious moral issues, appear full of ambivalence. There is an intellectual framework behind the touching emotions and presumed moral values, which is puzzlingly at odds with them. *The Princesse de Clèves* is a romance against love, with a hero who is an anti-hero and a heroine who is a victim of circumstance, whose life is destroyed by passion, and yet who

convinces us throughout that she retains control of her fate. The plot and the language are so direct that they become opaque and invite questions, both about the nature of passion and about the nature of power. (3)

And while our heroine's life is not "destroyed by passion" in the film, her life and passions do make way for "puzzling" effects and "invite questions" about youthful desire. As Buss suggests, and Honoré expounds, the novel's "purity of language" is tantalizingly "opaque" and is never as "direct" as it appears. Keeping alive Honoré's inquiry into the representations of language, *La belle personne* transfigures the novel's narrative while maintaining the seductive nuances associated with it and *la langue française*.

Once the credits for *La belle personne* come to an end, we cut to a close-up of a finger pressing the "play" button on the 1970s-style cassette recorder, from which a generic British-English-language lesson is heard (see figure 25.1). The perfunctory, extremely dull, but ever-so-direct recorded dialogue we hear is that of a man and woman discussing the man's new job. As we listen to the tape, we are introduced to the film's cast of students through a series of close-ups in which the students halfheartedly listen to the silly dialogue. The students, at once classical and contemporary in their style and comportment, roll their eyes and cast knowing glances at one another. Dismissing the mechanized drone from the language-machine, the students' *looks* toward one another tease the spectator with anticipation about the unknown and unforeseen intimacies and intrigues they share.

Complementing the students' youthful, elegant, and stoic French visages, their soft porcelain skin is framed by thick flowing hair. Honoré's student portraits trade on the paintings of Jacques-Louis David and Gustave Courbet in such as way as to accentuate the students' transhistorical beauty.[6] They are as exquisite as they are erotic. They are as self-aware as they are vulnerable. They are as astute in gamesmanship as they are fragile in their fall from grace.

As the camera moves about the room, we see a traditional classroom that contains none of the more advanced "smartroom" technology of the twenty-first century. Instead, a blackboard, wooden desks, and large thin-paned windows compose the room's décor. Whether in math, history, literature, or language class, Honoré's settings are saturated with the passage of time. The institution in which knowledge is inculcated and disseminated from the past is filtered through mise-en-scène, and particularly costume and gesture. Yet, while the repetitive nature of classroom teaching reaffirms France's well-rehearsed curriculum, its instructive force is no guarantee that students play out their lessons in the same fashion from generation to generation.⁷ Honoré's high-school cinematic atmosphere is a dynamic field through which time passes, erodes, and transforms.

To be sure, the film's mise-en-scène is critical for Honoré's adaptation from novel to cinema. Vis-à-vis his staging, costume design, and narrative adaptation, Honoré's imprimatur weaves through the film's passages. *La belle personne* follows in the footsteps of *Dans Paris* and *Les chansons* insofar as it recognizes its own modern-media place in relationship to a very discrete and sensual historicity (French New Wave cinema, *yé-yé* music, and Gallimard's typeset design for literature). *La belle personne*, especially, draws on long-standing traditions of French literature, theater, and dance. And whereas the deep modes of communication in *Dan Paris* and *Les chansons* never find exact footing because they fall short in their ability to communicate precisely, *La belle personne*'s precision of language, as Buss points out in relation to *La princesse de Clèves*, unravels because its exactness is so artfully crisp that emotional communication is made opaque. Mechanical articulation is, in other words, too precise.

But the film is not a period piece that restages Lafayette's novel word for word, scene by scene. The novel itself artificially conflates historical periods by condensing over one hundred years of royal courts into a brief narrative. Instead, Honoré's cinematic impressions are not dissimilar to Pier Paolo Pasolini's thoughts on making *The Gospel According to St. Matthew* (1964): "I did not want to reconstruct the life of Christ as it really was, I wanted to do the story of Christ plus two thousand years [*sic*] of Christian translation."⁸ Honoré thus offers *La belle personne* through four hundred years of aesthetic traditions and translations. Seen this way, the film is a French mise-en-scènic palimpsest in which *La princesse de Clèves* as well as Racine's play *Britannicus* (1669), Donizetti's *Lucia de Lammermoor* (1835), and Mallarmé's poem "Le cygne" ("The Swan," 1885) haunt the scene. Language and meaning are mired in a densely aestheticized historicity.

ADAPTATIONS

La princesse de Clèves tells the story of the young and beautiful Mademoiselle de Chartres. Such beauty stuns Henri II's court since she "exhibited true perfection [and] inspired awe in a place where people were so much accustomed to the sight of beauty" (29). Mlle. de Chartres was, in brief, a work of art with her "whiteness of complexion" that gave her "unparalleled radiance"; "her features were regular and both her face and figure full of grace and charm" (30). At the same time, her beauty holds her captive to those who desired her—including women—in the king's playground. Mlle. de Chartres finds herself intimately entangled within the court's intrigues and power plays, which invariably involve a woman's shrewd negotiations. "There were so many different factions and parties," Lafayette writes, "and women played so great a role in them, that love was always allied to politics and politics to love" (34). Mlle. de Chartres's mother, Madame de Chartres, does her best to guide her daughter through the imperiled politicized romances that await her and advises her to choose a suitor for more than lust and overromanticized passion. Mme. de Chartres is particularly concerned with Duc de Nemours, whom many members of the court considered "nature's masterpiece." Nemours "showed extraordinary skill in all that he did. . . . His whole being had a presence which ensured that wherever he appeared, all eyes were drawn to him" (25). His reputation indeed preceded him: "There was no lady in court whose pride would not have been flattered, were he to feel some attachment for her" (25).

Such was the concern that Mme. de Chartres felt for her daughter. To her mind, the abject Prince de Clèves more properly suited her daughter's place in court than did the seductive Nemours. Fortunately for Mme. de Chartres, when the Prince de Clèves first meets her daughter, he is so taken with her beauty that he immediately blushes at the sight of her—an embarrassment that Mlle. de Chartres quickly yet hesitantly notes. Nemours, on the other hand, displayed no unease when he gazed on her beauty. And unlike Nemours, the Prince is decidedly short on description in the novel. What description the author provides remains solely in relation to what the Prince *sees*: Mlle. de Chartres's beauty. Her beauty is what defines *his* existence and very presence in the rooms he occupies. He has no unique or outstanding qualities when compared with Nemours. The Prince de Clèves is a nice guy—a banality that appeals to Mme. de Chartres's designs on propriety. Thus, the arranged marriage between the Prince and Mlle. de Chartres satisfies the required court etiquette. With Mlle. de Chartres's marriage to the Prince and Mme. de Chartres's death after the marriage, the now Mme. de Clèves must self-direct her principles so as to avoid the petty squabbles and gossips among her peers, while discovering ways to channel her desire for "nature's masterpiece," Nemours.

As Mme. de Clèves soon realizes, etiquette is not so powerful that it can withstand passion. Hence, the novel's intricate narrative and staging hinges on Mme. de Clèves's doings without *appearing to be* doing anything at all. Fully aware of both her courtly obligations and her love for Nemours, the narrative traces her stratagems for fleeing the sites to which she is frustratingly drawn. The novel is prescient in its portrayal of the ways women must pilot their wishes and desires through the cultural morasses that shape their world; it is a narrative model that places women at its center. As such, rather than rehearse a tale in which a woman gives herself over to her sexual desires, which invariably involves a giving over to the man who desires her, the novel and the film instead explore the intricate decisions a woman is forced to make within specific cultural constraints. Crucially, the tension foisted on women to make decisions, one way or another, is precisely the narrative tension on which Honoré concentrates and continues to develop more fully in *Non ma fille tu n'iras pas danser* and *Les bien-aimés*. At heart, both Lafayette's and Honoré's texts explore the aporia in which female characters shuttle to and fro within the confining scene in which they search for escape. What may strike many readers and viewers as indecisiveness on the part of both the Princesse de Clèves and Junie is in fact strategic maneuvering in making choices in dangerous and constrained circumstances.

Bringing the spirit of Lafayette's novel to film, Honoré translates her version of France's historical monarchy into the twenty-first-century classroom through a cinematic legerdemain. For example, he suggestively refashions teenager garb. Large scarves, loosely fitting chemises, and faux-fur-trimmed winter coats are the wardrobe simulacra of a royal court. Lafayette's novel is already an aestheticized history that takes liberties in conflating figures such as Henri II (1519–1559) and Louis XIV (1638–1715) and the courts they ruled. *La belle personne* was filmed at the Lycée Molière in Paris, and the school's Italianate architecture contains a large courtyard encircled by several levels of passageways that give entry to the classrooms where art, history, and romance languages play out. The original planting of Italian poplars in the school's courtyard re-created the traditional Florentine atmosphere that so appealed to the French monarchy.

The structure of the lycée, designed by the French architect Joseph Auguste Émile Vaudremer (1829–1914) in 1888, recalls Renaissance Florentine palazzos and institutional buildings that first ushered in the tranquil and secure setting of the courtyard.[9] Vaudremer's historical ties to Italy as the winner of "laureate du premier grand" in 1854 and his residency at the French Academy in Rome at the Villa Medici, are particularly noteworthy. His contribution to the Lycée Molière is all the more significant to France's own entangled historical connection to Italy since it follows in the centuries-long cultural and political tradition that launched when Henri II married the Florentine Catherine de Medici. The specter of Italian culture in *La belle personne* nods to France's desire to mimic "la gloire" of the Roman Empire and Renaissance enlightenment.[10] Indeed, Honoré's classrooms and courtyard reverberate with Italian chatter that echoes the dissipated voices of those diplomats, artists, and ambassadors who once forged French-Italian alliances or, in the case of Vaudremer and Lafayette, carried French and Italian aesthetics between one another.

Lycée Molière is significant on another count for our discussion. From its beginnings, the lycée committed itself to the advanced education of women. The *Centenaire du lycée Molière: Memorial 1888–1988* notes the many women who passed through its doors and gained degrees in medicine, history, natural sciences, the arts, and mathematics. Having the Lycée Molière for *La belle personne*'s backdrop bears considerable weight on the film's characters and the events in which they are embroiled.

Lafayette's key characters appear on Honoré's scene, showing that the students' contemporary lives are never far removed from the historical texts that they study and the institution in which they participate. Honoré's recorporealized revisions are as intricate as they are broad in their intertextual shadows. For instance, the "princess," Junie (Léa Seydoux), is a composite of desired women in French creative works. She is at once a realization of Lafayette's eponymous character as well as of Racine's beauty Junie in *Britannicus*, who finds herself "caught between" a lustful man, Nero, and a dull but sincere man, Britannicus. In *La belle personne,* the quietly astute Junie makes note of her literary heritage when she first meets Otto, her naïve lover-to-be. Ever shy, Otto comments that he has no literary predecessor as prevalent as her namesake. Representing the Prince de Clèves, he (Grégoire Leprince-Ringuet, the actor to whom Honoré introduced us in *Les chansons*) is corrected by Junie when she reminds him that a children's book exists with a title that bears his name: *Otto: The Autobiography of a Teddy Bear,* authored by Tomi Ungerer. Ungerer's reputation as both a children's book author and adult-erotica illustrator mirrors Honoré's own aesthetic preoccupation within the psychological vortex that commands children's literature and adult sexuality. Accordingly, when Junie later hands Ungerer's book to Otto, her gift serves as a prelude to a sexual encounter between the two.[11]

The historical Franco-European linkages weave deeply in *La belle personne*. The Italian instructor, for example, is named Nemours and played by Honoré's mainstay, Louis Garrel. Because the Italians and Italian culture played no small role during Henri II's reign (1547–59), Honoré blends the French-speaking Nemours's seductive bodiliness with Italy's seductive linguistic qualities.[12] M. Nemours thus requires his students to recite and translate Italian verse that resonates with ardor as if to ignite his *and* his students' unexplored erotic wishes. With his flowing black locks Nemours is debonair as much as he is detestable for his cavalier demeanor and chauvinist behavior. Like his novelistic counterpart, the cinematic Nemours's charm is linked to his position of power, which draws women unreservedly into his lair, only to be discarded for his next love affair. Playing on Mme. de Clèves's intuitive persona, Junie is Nemours's match since her own seductive distance and sense of obligation to Otto causes Nemours to remain uncertain about her feelings for him. Her refusal to fulfill his desire drives him further into a passionate impasse.[13]

When Junie first attends Nemours's Italian class, he immediately, like the Duc de Nemours before him, unabashedly falls for her. His attempts at eroticizing pedagogy turn back on him since Junie's reading aloud the Italian poetry assigned in class will leave him passionately longing for a love that will, although mutual, never be satisfied. Nevertheless, Junie's provocative beauty and sotto voce stir him to break off all—and there are many—relationships he has under way. Her presence in Nemours's class is further complicated when the coolly assertive student Henri (Simon Truxillo) gives a class presentation that includes Maria Callas's aria "Il dolce suono, mi colpi di sua voce," from Donizetti's *Lucia di Lammermoor*. In the opera, Lucia, because of distressed desire and lost love, descends into madness that leads to her death. Love's madness—as only Callas can deliver it—deeply resonates from within the artist's performance. The diva's sublimely aestheticized emotional turmoil fills the classroom while it *describes* Nemours and Junie's fraught attraction. The aria paints the scene so that the music seeps beyond the frame's edges. Whether it is because of Donizetti's libretto, which is steeped in sacrificed passion and death, or the unequaled voice of Callas, Junie breaks down in tears and exits the room. Like Lucia, she is burdened by sorrow in mourning the loss of her mother. And like Lucia, the men and circumstances that delimit her freedom to choose love and life on her own terms further burden her loss. Junie's response to the aria—a performance penned by an Italian that is based on a tale by a Scotsman and, here, is mechanically reproduced for our Parisian students on a record player—draws Nemours closer to her sensitive beauty. Honoré's cinema, which highlights the mechanical components involved in creating the recorded image-sound event, delivers on expression that cannot be realized through dialogue alone. The "100% talkie," as Arnheim recognized, would not do so well in a cinematic world such as *La belle personne*'s.

Along with these principal characters, secondary but no less significant characters from the novel—Henri, Catherine, Madame de Tournon, Estouteville, and Sancerre—recur in *La belle personne*. Honoré's figures bear the markings of Lafayette's text, inscribed by the histories that are the fodder for her fictionalized representations. The lycée's curriculum to be sure appears as a defining powerhouse of international studies, aesthetics, cultures, and languages. Students take an endless stream of classes that include French, English, Russian, and Italian. And even when other disciplines are taught—math and history, for instance—they are presented in the film as disciplines predicated on discrete forms of language with their own long histories. The classrooms are thus the sites where age-old languages and cultures, once profiting by dreams of empire and marriages-of-convenience, intertwine yet set in motion new terrains of power and passion. As in days of court and empire, the modern youths encountered in *La belle personne* communicate with no shortage of language skills and cultural references that the Princesse de Clèves similarly put to use when she steered her way through her own thorny institutional obstacles. But since "direct" language only complicates matters, Honoré shifts the language of history as such to a mise-en-scène that encompasses multiple intersections that are exacted on languages and cultures. Language is thus temporalized while it is spatialized. And, of course, cinematic monstration is the mediated language on which so much emotion rests.

According to Carl Jenkins, the "idea of French exception," and its commitment to "*grandeur,*" is dependent on the monarchical tradition that looks to Roman antiquity as its cultural measuring stick. French language is deeply ensconced in the "French exception" idealist principles insofar as linguistic precision came to be historically recognized as part and parcel of an advanced civilization. By 1635, Cardinal Richelieu established the Académie Français, where an "authoritative" French dictionary was created, thereby "stabilizing" the French language so that it "went hand-in-hand with the attempt to codify the composition of literary works and establish the theory of a new art."[14] Such nationalist and aesthetic impulses are all well and good, but regional patois and the limitations on the verbal quality of expression ultimately, as we have seen in Honoré's work, come up short.[15] Hence, Honoré's students immerse themselves in the rigors of multiple languages and multicultural studies and their creative forms so as to resculpt French nationalist aspirations through various aesthetic languages: poetry, music, literature, photography, and cinema.[16] To aestheticize or make language cinematic, Honoré's students communicate through the look. It is not uncommon, for instance, to see the students pass knowing glances toward one another as they did when the film opened during the English-language class. In other words, the look *at* the other—a form of communication rehearsed to challenge the tyranny of words, as well as the institutional authority that assesses and "stabilizes" verbal meaning—anticipates and reveals the intimate involvements into which *La belle personne*'s characters are drawn.

In what way does the language of "the look" move transhistorically in *La belle personne*? How do we take stock of, comprehend, and interpret the cinematic look that Lafayette conjured with the written word? If the king's court "owed its splendor and majesty to the vast princes and peers of exceptional quality, ... the ornament and wonder of their age" (Lafayette, 24), and was dramatized by various factions in which the court served as the place where "love was always allied to politics and politics to love" (34), and, furthermore, it was a place in which the stakes on love—its rivalries and jealousies—were raised, are these theatrics found in the French court any different from the emotional intensity we encounter in this contemporary French classroom? How then, as Robin Buss calls it, did *"love at first sight"* play out? How is it possible that sight—and not words—"[become] the channel and the figure for [lovers'] desire" (4; emphasis added)?

What is striking about *La belle personne* is that Honoré picks up on Lafayette's literary achievement by adapting the plot with a less-than-literal translation. Instead, he employs cinematic forms of communication to convey that which Lafayette makes available through the written word. *"The Princesse de Clèves,"* Gilles Taurand reminds us, "is also the story of silences and a game of glances. . . . [Honoré's] film beautifully participates in these games of looks that are ultimately more ardent than words, since they are behind the success to retain desire."[17] The remarkable literary command that Lafayette employs to demonstrate the expressive exchange of the look in literature requires an art form such as the cinema to successfully translate her linguistic turns. Honoré's cinema thus steps in as the ideal medium through which the transformation of literariness into cinematics might occur. As such, his cinematic enterprise channels a range of multimedia in a way that their discrete aesthetic layers *describe* meaning more than they define it or, as Lee Edelman would have it, "inscribe" meaning as such. Arguably, Honoré's cinema points out what we already know insofar as the novel's words are only always already descriptors. Yet, when cinema combines its own unique properties with, for example, opera, literature, poetry, history, and mathematics, the multimedia event swirls about the students' world with unanticipated results. The possibilities for the students to express across languages are rescored and repitched so that their emotional registers are aestheticized for the cinema. If the "opacity" of courtly language and its academic tradition only make human communication impregnable, the multiple forms of expression made through the creative arts give life to intuitive and sensuous *knowingness.*

THE LOOK OF LANGUAGE

After we pass through the large, wooden doors of the lycée and enter the English-language classroom where the students' knowing looks are first put on scene, accompanied by the tinny-sounding cassette recorder, the next class we encounter is History, taught by Nemours's current lover, Florence (Valérie Lang). We enter her lesson midstream as she is discussing, among other things, Martin Luther's and John Calvin's dissemination of ideas through print. While the students listen to Florence's narrative, they direct their gaze toward their teacher with pens at the ready, earnestly intent on capturing her every word. Youthful

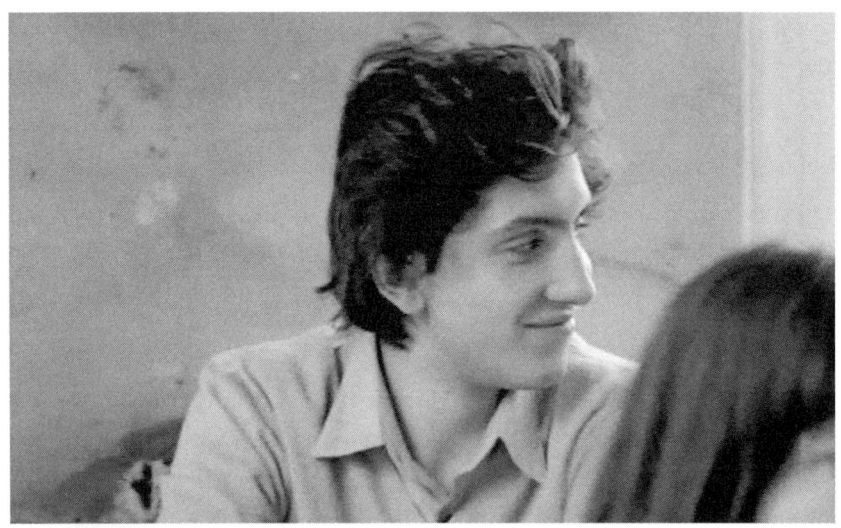

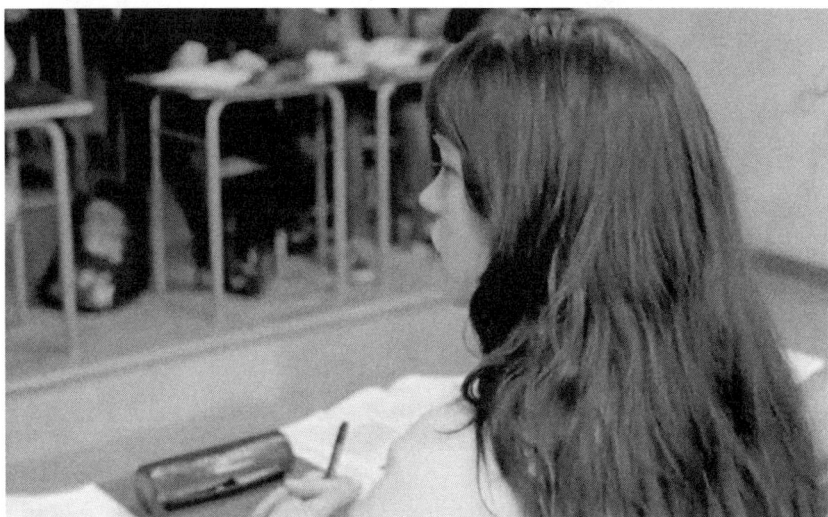

27.1–27.4. Knowing looks: Matthias, Junie, Otto, and Henri

intrigue and shrewdness, conjoined with vanity, however, soon lock horns with Florence's assumed authority. When, for instance, Henri challenges his instructor's interpretation of Calvin's theory that "predestination" suggests that the "individual can't change anything," Honoré cuts to a series of close-ups. In these shots, we observe Otto and then his peers as they quickly direct their gaze onto the theatrical confrontation between student and lecturer. When Henri further challenges Florence, and after she reminds him that no one person holds the

La belle personne

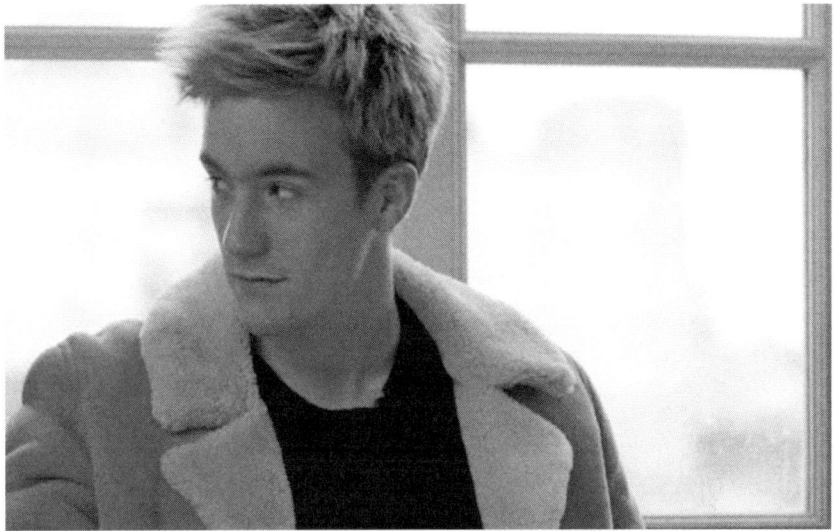

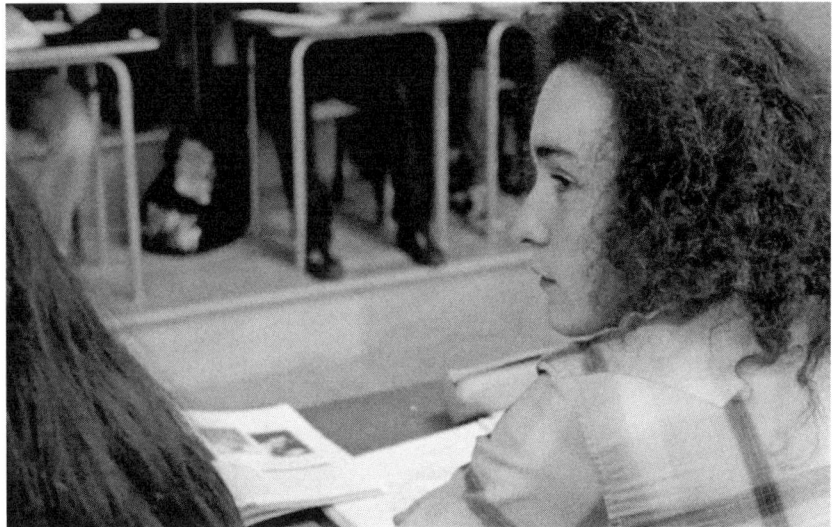

key to truth *as such*, the ever-smug Henri pauses and then boldly asks if she is married. When she responds, "No," Henri is persistent in his line of questioning: "Do you have a boyfriend?" Florence responds in the affirmative (all the students know, as we will soon enough, that Nemours is her lover). He asks, "Do you love him deeply?" Again, she responds in the affirmative. When he posits that her "deep" love for her boyfriend is inseparable from the very possibility that she could just as determinedly "hate" him, Florence declares that such a proposition is not fathomable. For her, love is love—*tout court*. "Well, if that's really the case," Henri prods, "can we stop with all the bullshit about two ways of seeing everything?" Florence is stumped. She will soon realize Henri's point when the affair with Nemours to which she so solidly clings suddenly destabilizes and "hate" and "love" share the dais.

From Florence's world history, we move on to mathematics. On the blackboard, a complex algebraic equation is set alongside its even more complex translation in words. The language of math carries its own significant currency in the French literary arts. In 1960, the author Raymond Queneau and the chemical engineer and mathematician François Le Lionnais founded the literary group Oulipo (Ouvroir de littérature potentielle [Workshop of Potential Literature]). Their aesthetic concerns involved utilizing mathematic language and stratagems as a literary device.[18] Along with the likes of the writer Georges Perec, who endlessly mines language for its descriptive possibilities, Oulipians engaged palindromes and mathematical problems associated with maneuvers on the chessboard to exhaust literary aesthetics—that is, they sought to exhaust words. Founder Queneau was no stranger to the cinema; among other things, Louis Malle adapted his novel *Zazie dans le métro* (1960) to film. *Zazie*'s cinematic revelry distinctively displays an Oulipo aesthetic dream and reformulation of logic.

In *La belle personne*, the amalgam of geometry and argumentative clauses scribbled on the math-class blackboard thus follows in the wake of Oulipo's aims insofar as they mirror the students' aesthetic and emotional frissons. When Jacob (Jacob Lyon) is called to the board by the instructor, Estouteville (Jean-Michel Portal), to work on solving the math problem, Otto turns away from his notes and directs his sights on Junie, who sits behind him and off to his right. While Jacob calculates, she vacantly—or is it thoughtfully? (point-of-view is everything here)—stares at her colleague's "workings" (as his teacher calls it). Her pen balances on its tip so that it rests against her notebook; it appears as if she is about to write but is unable to do so. She is positioned, from Otto's perspective, as a painting or sculpture, frozen in time and space.

Not insignificantly, Estouteville is the classroom instructor; his name is directly inherited from Lafayette's novel. In the novel, the character is presented by M. de Clèves in an aside to Mme. de Clèves. The tale he tells is about the widowed, yet discreet, Mme. Tournon, a lady of the court whom Mme. de Clèves highly regards. In the film, Otto (in place of M. de Clèves) recounts the tale of the school librarian, Mme. Tournon (played by Clotilde Hesme—Alice, our "bridge" between lovers in *Les chansons d'amour*), and her love triangle with Estouteville and Sancerre (the former gym teacher at the lycée, played by Honoré's brother,

Julien; see JNCH, 190). Honoré portrays Mme. Tournon's smartly played romance as a film within the film; it is a cinematic parenthesis distinctively marked by a "home-movie" quality, as shot in Super 8mm. Both the smaller film gauge's texture and its rapid cutting express the *hotness* that envelops the tale. The film within the film, which is shot on a fast-film stock and whose grainy texture and sharp hues of orange, yellow, and blue flash across the screen, appears to burn through the primary film. In any case, Estouteville, a "nice guy" and not dissimilar to Otto and M. de Clèves, is in love with Mme. Tournon, only to discover that she has been simultaneously carrying on an affair with his very good friend Sancerre.

From the back of the math class, the romantically singed Estouteville giggles to himself when he asks the youthful slacker Jacob, "Can you explain to us your workings?" With a thick head of black curly hair and wearing a T-shirt that parodies the Hollywood sign with the word "Crazewood" etched across its front, Jacob explains the cumbersome mathematic symbols he parses for the class: "So . . . we stated $U(x)$ equals $0/x$ and $V(x)$ equals exponential of $1/x$." As Jacob describes his "workings," Otto once again turns his look to Junie. When Junie shoots a sharp glance back at Otto, we hear Jacob inform us, "the derivative of the function equals the product of the two functions and the derivative of a function product."[19] If language is as opaque as we have come to learn in Honoré's films, it is perhaps the art of mathematics (a Oulipian vertigo) that most effectively and aesthetically displays one's emotional "workings": "the derivative of the function equals the product of the two functions and the derivative of a function product."

Following the mathematician René Thom's and Oulipian practice, although in a different context, Jean-François Lyotard questions the common assertion that mathematical language is a "stable system." In fact, Lyotard contends that mathematical language is far from determinist since it "[allows] a formal description of the discontinuities that can occur in determined phenomena, causing them to take unexpected forms: this language constitutes what is known as catastrophe theory."[20] Tangents, digressions, and unpredictability are the hallmarks of all languages, no matter how rigidly defined and perceived. Honoré trots out many language possibilities in his classrooms, where desire teeters on the verge of brilliant "catastrophe."

FROZEN

Poetry is an ideal mode of expression in which the idea of language evokes phenomena so that, borrowing from Lyotard, they "take unexpected forms" on the verge of "catastrophe." In *La belle personne*, Honoré turns to Mallarmé to demonstrate the point. In a tight close-up of the smitten Otto, we see him direct his gaze to the left while we hear students reading aloud the opening stanza from Mallarmé's "Le cygne":

> Le vierge, le vivace et le bel aujourd'hui
>
> Va-t-il nous déchirer avec un coup d'aile ivre
>
> Ce lac dur oublié que hante sous le givre
>
> Le transparent glacier des vols qui n'ont pas fui
>
> The virgin, vibrant, and beautiful dawn,
>
> Will a beat of its drunken wing not suffice
>
> To rend this hard lake haunted beneath the ice
>
> By the transparent glacier of flights never flown?[21]

While the poem is read, Otto turns his attention to his notebook, where, rather than mark his thoughts about the poem, he hastily scribbles a note to his own (perceived-to-be) innocent swan, Junie. Seated a row behind the long table at which Otto is located, Junie stares intently toward the front of the room. Otto slides the note to his companions, who messenger it along the table as we continue to hear Mallarmé's stunning paean to innocence, an innocence transparently trapped and facing imminent death. Before the note reaches Junie, however, the ever-mischievous Henri intercepts it.

While Henri takes over Junie's response to Otto, Honoré cuts to the class instructor, who peeks out the classroom-door window during the recitation and observes two young students passionately kissing. Pressed against a winter tree and framed by a frosty winter's landscape, a young black man tenderly kisses a white female student. The stark, gray-cream-colored winter's scene and the high-key lighting focused on the students' bodies put into sharp relief the morphed skin colors that take shape through their interracial kiss. A transfigured French history and culture—racially, aesthetically—is well under way in Honoré's twenty-first-century courtly classroom. The cut from the teacher's point of view, in which she sees the innocent youth before her, heightens the mix of warm naïveté and chilled maturity that Mallarmé's script provides the students of *La belle personne*. Such painful promises for these students' future is not lost on their instructor. As she looks back to her students, her eyes "sigh" (not dissimilar to Estouteville's gesture of the giggle) with a mix of envy, delight, and knowingness.

The instructor returns her concentration to the classroom and asks Matthias (Esteban Carvajal-Alegria) to continue reading aloud. Matthias continues to read, and, as if to mock Otto's own virginity and his youthful relationship to Mallarmé's sharp-edged poetry, the poem's recitation cuts against Otto's naïve devotion to Junie. Otto's bathos also encourages Henri to return the note to Otto with stinging sarcasm: "You idiot! That's it. You haven't done anything!" Otto is no Mallarmé. From Henri's perspective, Otto is short on life experience and has not the convictions of his overromanticized beliefs. When the disappointed Otto shoots a frustrated look at Henri, Henri responds with a glance that speaks youthful hubris and ennui. Otto's self-assured counterpart Henri, however, soon learns vis-à-vis the passing of notes that a similar and painful lesson about lost innocence awaits him. In a short time, we discover that Henri's cynicism veils a delicate soul, one that is similarly overromantic.

CINEMA: LETTERS AND IMAGES

The Princess de Clèves's narrative folds, creases, and hinges on the activities involved in securing mutual but unfulfilled desire especially, but not exclusively, in the relationship between Nemours and Mme. de Clèves. As the reality sinks in that satisfying desire's passion appears more and more unlikely, Nemours becomes desperate to make tangible Mme. de Clèves's affections. Similarly, she remains on tenterhooks not only about Nemours's intentions but about how to navigate her own passions for him within the court's codes and regulations, as well as those laws that define her marriage. In a spin of stolen portraits and misdirected letters, communication between lovers and the court's subjects takes place in the novel as through Max Ophüls–like cinematics, wherein Lafayette's description of events suggests a camera floating along extended passageways and magisterial halls. Lafayette's narratological *la ronde* directs characters inward, then outward and, finally, away from one another. The courtly dance they perform to achieve their goal thus brings bodies together, pulls them apart, all the while sustaining the thrill of pleasure that is desire—*unfulfilled*—within the confines of the royal court.

In Honoré's revision, *La belle personne* uses photographs to replace the seventeenth-century portrait, while a mislaid letter in a movie theater propels our protagonists into a miasmic swirl of uncertainty and intrigue. When Junie first arrives at the lycée, the Oulipian mathematician—Jacob—is also the school photographer who snaps each student's photo. The library, directed by the desired and desirous Mme. Tournon, is where the young photographer's student portraits are exhibited. Words and image yet again find a venue where aesthetic possibilities mix. After Jacob gives Junie a copy of her portrait, she inadvertently leaves it behind in Nemours's class as she darts from the scene during Callas's aria. Honoré's Nemours sees an opportunity to hold on to a material remnant of the young woman for whom he yearns (as Lafayette's Nemours had done when he absconded with Mme. de Clèves's portrait), pilfers the photo, and then denies doing so when he later returns Junie's notebooks.

A class field trip to the cinema, chaperoned by Nemours and Florence, however, further inflames *la passion de drame* among the students when an unaddressed and unsigned love letter falls from a character's pocket. This letter, in turn, lands in Junie's hands. Things are somewhat less complicated in the novel since the mislaid letter is addressed to Nemours by one of his spurned lovers, yet it is also unsigned. The gender dynamic of the letter in the novel is decidedly female-male and heterosexual. In *La belle personne,* however, Honoré degenders the letter. It is not clear, in other words, to whom the letter is addressed and who wrote it. The gender-anonymous letter unleashes classic dramatic conflict and presumption that fully resonate with centuries of melodramatic activities while drawing in a queer dalliance.

The movie theater is a crucial site for this vexed transaction because it is where an aesthetic foreplay is enacted that leads to the film's most complex results. Just as the cinema swaps places with the bed in *Les chansons d'amour,* in *La belle personne* the archival center of French cinema—the Cinémathèque—is swapped with the lycée, restaging the classroom intimacies *and* the look (see figures 28.1–28.2). Moreover, by screening a film within the film at this location, Honoré situates himself in the folds of film history, since this location houses the history of French cinema—a historical archive of cinematic memory. The movie screen serves as a blackboard that reiterates the pedagogical and aesthetic goals that Honoré's lycée offers. In both theater and classroom, multiple language forms expand across the space, leading to provocative and discomforting interpretations.

At the Cinémathèque, the students, along with Nemours and Florence, watch the African film *Yaaba* (Ouedraogo, 1989). Not dissimilar to *La belle personne*'s narrative currents, the film within the film (*Yaaba*) tells the story of the ways misinterpretation and miscommunication invariably lead to misguided judgments about others. And, like Honoré, Idrissa Ouedraogo is a filmmaker who is keenly aware of languages' limitations. As one who studied film at the Sorbonne and l'Institut des hautes études cinématographiques, Ouedraogo not only seeks to reach audiences among the forty-two languages that compose the African continent; he also explores cinema's formal aesthetics in order to interweave his experience with African and Western cultures. In this regard, his film questions the use and value

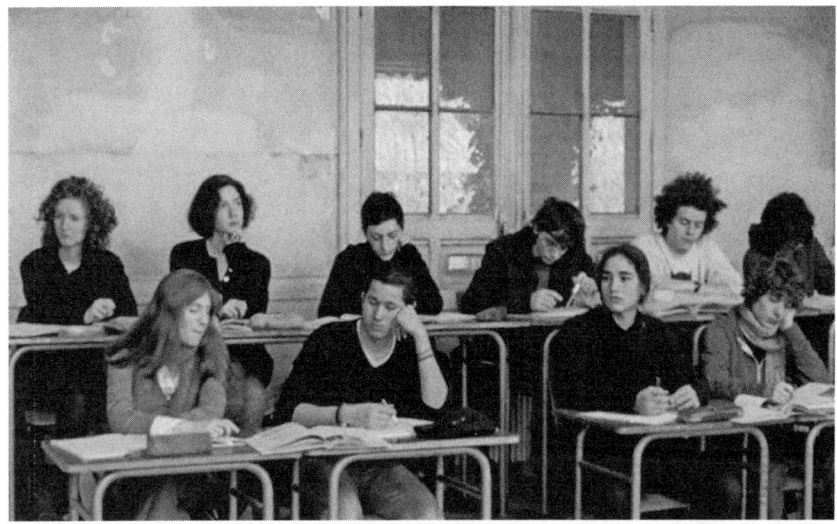

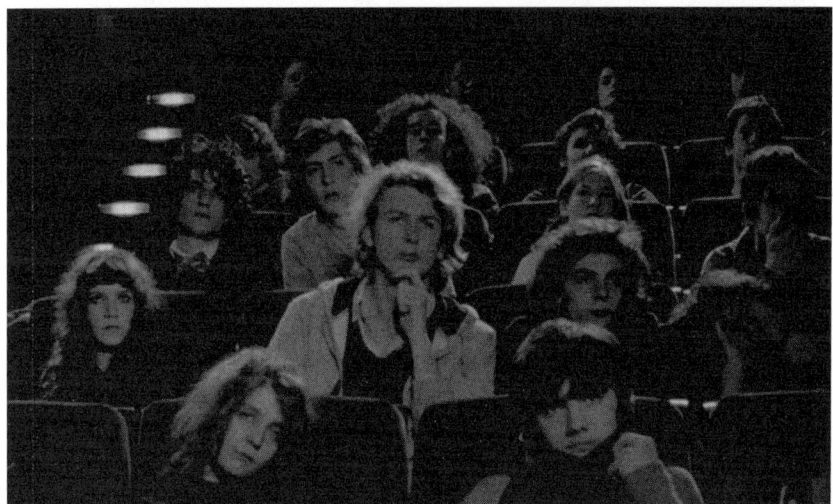

28.1–28.2. Honoré's classrooms. The screen more successfully grabs students' attention.

of tradition when it stymies unanticipated love and friendship, whether in Burkina Faso or Paris.[22] As such, in order to reach multiple listeners and viewers, *Yaaba* presents an elegant example of the cinema of monstration.

In *Yaaba*, a young village boy, Bila (Noufou Ouedraogo), and an older woman, Yaaba (Fatimata Sanga), develop a friendship that is considered toxic because Yaaba is perceived to be a witch and the cause of the village's misfortunes. As

Bila's relationship with Yaaba develops, some villagers "other" him (at one point, he is mocked as effeminate). Later, when Yaaba dies, the villagers revise their sentiment toward her since she has a hand in saving the suddenly ill Nopoko (Bila's cousin, played by Roukietou Barry).

Yaaba's opening shot also serves as its closing shot. The repeated sequence is a long take in which we see Bila and Nopoko playfully running out into the distance, away from the camera. We learn, by the film's end, that these events follow Yaaba's death and Bila and Nopoko's narrative journey in which they have learned to accept difference in all its manifestations. During the course of the film, they successfully change the village's prejudicial views about Yaaba. Like *Dans Paris, Yaaba*'s cinematic structure circles back to where life and death are no longer demarcated by strict and clearly established beginnings and ends.

Ouedraogo's film, the film screened within the film, thus reverberates with the critical attention to form that Honoré seeks for his trilogy; *Yaaba* cinematically reannounces the remarks that the director Gaël Morel makes in *Les chansons d'amours* when he bypasses the movie-ticket line: "I was after him." Here, the *film* screened within the film positions Honoré's cinema as something more than a teleological addition to the "history of cinema." Rather, by signaling a film such as *Yaaba*, whose narrative endlessly rewinds, Honoré intermingles historical cinematic dialogues. Given the layering of subtitles and international production that *La belle personne* integrates—African, French, and (for some viewers, English)—Honoré positions his own filmmaking within the archive's screening room, where cinematic practices conjoin. If a single film is, as Honoré asserts, "nothing but recollection," then filmmakers consciously and/or unconsciously repeat and contribute to the history of cinema in unexpected ways (JNCH, 183). For him, to be a "unique" filmmaker is to bear the imprint of what came before and what will come after.

The scene's arrangement is predicated on the interpretive possibilities and, hence, possible miscommunication that international translations permit. Whereas the lycée's classroom stresses words—written and aural—the Cinémathèque fuses words and (moving) images. In this way, Honoré's camera looks at spectators looking at film that, in this instance, contains an African-language soundtrack. Echoing the earlier scene in which the audio-cassette recorder introduced English-language lessons, a movie projector at the Cinémathèque now assumes a similar pedagogical role. And, just as in the traditional classroom, the cinematic classroom enables a secondary form of communication among the students: the look. Their look is, however, doubly occupied at the cinema since it involves the screen and their peers. The cinema is a very active classroom for words and images.

The cinematic classroom, therefore, invites us into yet another set of divergent cultures and languages. As with other classrooms in *La belle personne,* the movie theater facilitates an encounter with cultural difference that nonetheless bears resemblance to the students' own lived contexts. For example, the scene from *Yaaba* that we see along with the students derives from a subplot in the film in which Koudi (Assita Ouedraogo) steals a moment to rendezvous with her lover, Tibo (Amadé Toure). She is a married woman whose husband neglects her emotional and sexual needs and, by the film's end, must courageously assert herself against the moral condemnation that the villagers foist on her. During this particular scene, Koudi is dancing at a wedding celebration when she surreptitiously slips away into the bush with her lover.[33] As she and her lover make their way into the bush, Yaaba and Bila witness their actions. Bila tells Yaaba that Koudi is "not a responsible woman." Yaaba remains silent and ushers the young boy away from the scene.

The screening sequence in *La belle personne* is complex in the way it implicates character(s)/spectator(s). This cinematic interaction brings into play the characters in *Yaaba, La belle personne,* and, certainly, "us"—in short, the *films'* spectators. In other words, Honoré forges multiple cinematic worlds that deeply intertwine even as they embrace different cultural aesthetics and traditions. For instance, as we watch Koudi act on her desire with her lover, Honoré cuts from the scene in *Yaaba* to a shot of Junie leaning cozily into Otto. The cut occurs after we see and hear that Koudi is "not a responsible woman." We then see Junie shift herself from Otto's arm, sit upright, and pay strict and direct attention to the events on the screen. Junie's alertness recalls earlier images of her as she focuses intently on events in the classroom.

The images on the screen awaken Junie for two reasons. First, Koudi's actions parallel Junie's world to the extent that her attachment to Otto has been encouraged yet policed by her peers as well as the cultural demands placed on her day-to-day life as a young woman (ideals of marriage, monogamy, love, and so forth). Koudi's marriage is one predicated on a tradition that is sustained under strict cultural surveillance and rules of heteronormativity. And while both women (and, of course, we must not forget Mme. de Clèves) are in conflict with cultural obligations, these very expectations and institutionalized repetitions are precisely where creative strategies are most often generated. Facilitating desire, *pleasure,* through surveillance and ideological containment is well understood through a Foucauldian lens: "What makes power hold good, what makes it accepted, is simply the

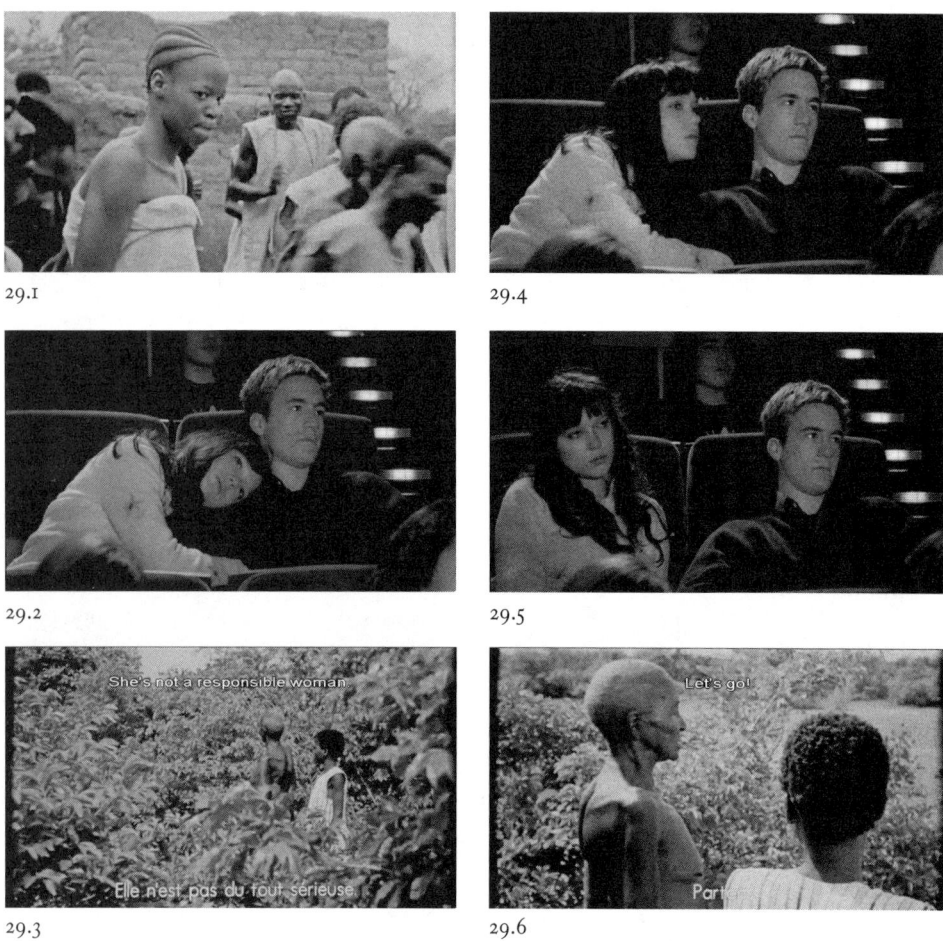

29.1–29.12. A triple layer of spectatorial suture occurs in *La belle personne* at a screening of *Yaaba*.

fact that it doesn't only weigh on us as a force that says no, but that it traverses and produces things, it induces pleasure, forms of knowledge, produces discourse."[24]

From Honoré's perspective, the Princesse de Clèves, Junie, and Koudi are each caught within similar demands that exist cross-culturally. This is especially true for the patriarchal establishments they must navigate. Here, Honoré's editing proves significant (figures 29.1–29.11). Through the shot/reverse-shot sequence that intercuts between the films (Junie sitting at attention and Koudi's rendezvous with Tibo), we, along with Junie, are sutured into the ideological matrix that the cinematic exchange sets forth. We are no longer ideologically secured (as the theory of suture would have it); instead, we are ideologically fractured. The editing's destabilizing effect on the spectator(s) "produces things, it induces

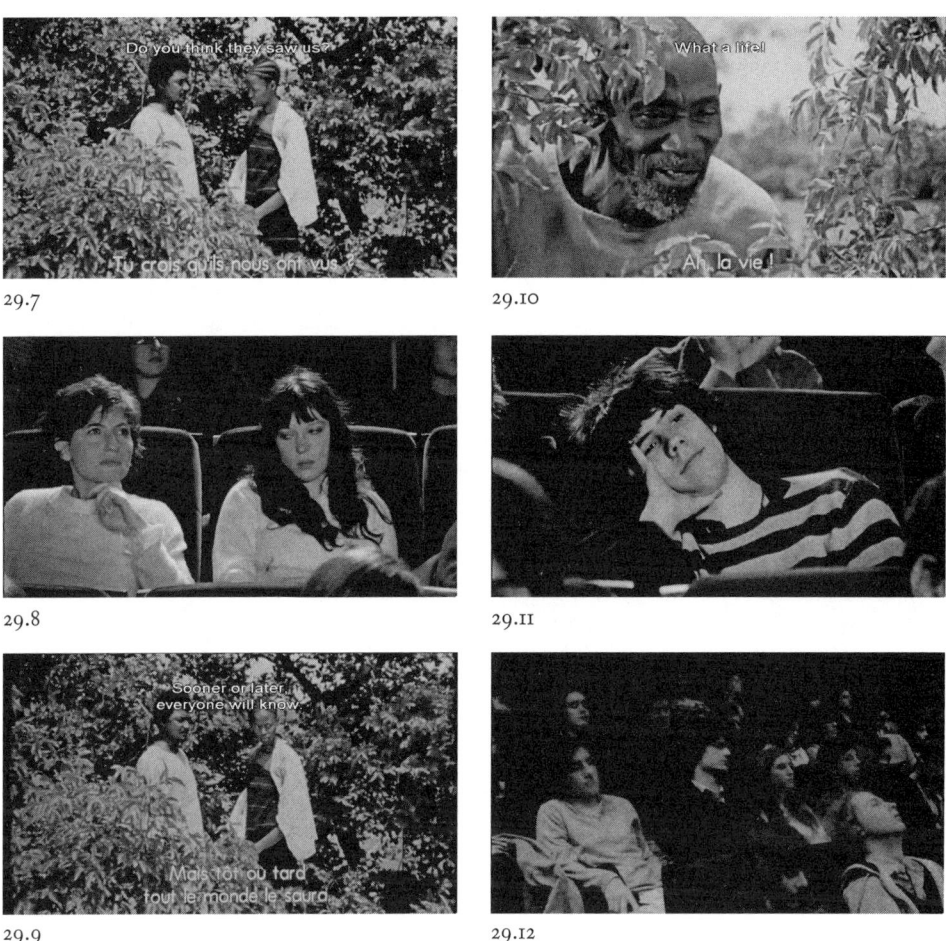

29.7 29.10
29.8 29.11
29.9 29.12

pleasure, forms of knowledge, produces discourse." The final image we see from the sequence in *Yaaba* is of an old man spying on Koudi and her lover. As he exclaims with pleasure, "Ah! Life!" we cut to the satisfied smile of a student. Universalism is only reliable as a concept when it enables cultural difference.

Second, *La belle personne*'s encounter with the cinema disorients the spectator at another level. Ouedraogo's film joins the texts of Lafayette, Donizetti, Luther, Mallarmé, Racine, and the Oulipos as part and parcel of Honoré's cinematized world. The ideological repetition to which we, and the characters, are beholden and subsumed may in fact be a limitation, but it is a limitation that releases imaginative forces. Historical, cultural, and aesthetic texts are thus the reimagining of the banal everyday, precisely at the site of bodies, bodies that actively participate in these textual matrices, such as those explored in Honoré's films. His queer texts—in *homage*—expand boundaries even as they bear the burden of the future anterior. Intertextuality is not only a game of "spot the reference." Honoré's aesthetic guides and opens cinema but does not determine its interpretative outcomes once and for all; instead, his films make way for choice.

Therefore, while *Yaaba* continues on the screen, *The Princesse de Clèves* (among other texts) remains in play. At *Yaaba*'s screening, Nemours swaps seats with Matthias so that he is able to see the screen clearly. Unbeknownst to us, their movement triggers a letter to fall from Matthias's pocket and into the seat that Nemours recently occupied. These turns of events befuddle things further because Nemours's seat exchange moves him closer to Henri's sister, Marie. Marie, we have discovered earlier, is a student with whom Nemours once had a sexual affair. Mutatis mutandis, the misplaced note leads to a Hitchcockian miscommunication and unintended consequences, as we will see. The staging of the screening event is key for the way these intricate exchanges play out.

Once the film ends and students gather their belongings, the letter is discovered where Nemours was seated (and Matthias was before him). In the novel, one of Nemours's many lovers has written him a letter that encourages their love affair even though she understands that his extracurricular affairs will invariably continue. Sharing him, according to the letter's author, is better than not having him at all. At one point in the novel, the lover's letter falls from Nemours's pocket and lands in the hands of another Nemours-smitten lady of the court. Aware—as many of the court are—of Nemours's desire for Mme. de Clèves, the lady in question sniggeringly delivers the note to Mme. de Clèves. "Without knowing what it was she had read," Lafayette writes, "*all she could see* was that M. Nemours did not love her as she believed" (91, emphasis added). Although the woman in love who scripted the misplaced letter displays, first and foremost, irrefutable "will power" (according to Mme. de Clèves), the young princess is heartbroken and furious. As far as she was concerned, Nemours "loved other women and was deceiving them as he was her." If "seeing" ("all she could see") *is knowing* in the novel, it is also as imprecise as words and, certainly, as deceptive. Emotions and psychology—even when the written word appears to make it so—render knowledge a foggy enterprise.

Fully aware of the obfuscated vision that results when mixing texts, Honoré ratchets up the short-circuited communication lines that such a simple letter creates. Shifting to the contemporary scene in which passion and uncertainty similarly recur, the letter reappears in *La belle personne,* but from an unnamed lover; it is discovered by Nemours's former student-lover Marie. Marie's conjecture about who sent the letter takes on something of a Faulknerian grain of sand that triggers an avalanche and collapses an empire. By erasing the letter's addressee and signatory, presumptions about the author's gender raise the stakes on love and identity. The letter reads, "I love you too much to let you think I could live without you. If you deceive me, I don't care as long as you have the sincerity to tell me. Hide me, I don't care, come find me even for a minute, even for a second. I am patient. While I wait for you I'll recite your body by heart, your so soft arms, your lips, the smell of your hair. And your knees. To mention even your knees, I'm in love."[25]

Marie, who finds the letter, initially believes it to have been written by one of Nemours's female lovers. She is already upset with Nemours since he inelegantly broke off their relationship. As Marie hands the letter to her fellow students, and as it makes it way among them, gossip quickly spreads. Since the letter was discovered on Nemours's seat, where it appears to have accidently fallen from his pocket, the students assume that Junie wrote the letter to Nemours. This infuriates Marie. Once the letter reaches Junie, however, she is convinced that it is written by one of Nemours's former female lovers (Marie? Florence?).

As it turns out, the letter in fact is written by Martin, who, in yet another turn of events, is Matthias's lover—an affair that takes place behind the back of Henri, Matthias's boyfriend. Matthias suddenly realizes that the mislaid letter written by Martin belongs to him. He urgently approaches Nemours. Matthias implores his teacher to inform everyone involved that the letter belongs to him, Nemours. He makes this request so that Henri does not get wind that Martin's love note is for Matthias. If Henri discovers this to be the case, he will be livid. This is because of events that we discover through a flashback. Now the ironically simple letter introduces, for the first time in the film, the story of the not-so-simple affair between Matthias and Henri and between Matthias and Martin. While Matthias explains to Nemours why he needs his help with the lie, we see the events that led up to this awkward state of affairs. Within the flashback, Henri dramatically draws Matthias into an illicit kiss in the boy's bathroom. Via Matthias's description of events, we see in flashback his subsequent and clandestine affair with the sporty Martin. Henri soon learns of the affair. Following a basketball game, Henri sneaks up on Matthias and Martin as they make out behind a parked car. With Martin's bare ass cupped in Matthias's hands, Henri snaps a photo of the two lovers and threatens to post it on the school website.

With the flashback filling in the background for Matthias's plea to Nemours, the teacher agrees to his entreaty. He then must convince Junie that the letter originated from Matthias's lover, Martin. Surprised by the news (she was unaware that her cousin, Matthias, was bisexual or gay), Junie finally believes Nemours. While Nemours explains the convoluted events to Junie, the scene cuts to a close-up of her digesting the Byzantine tale she hears. Cinematically drawing out the letter's palimpsestic qualities, Honoré now superimposes Martin's letter over Junie's close-up (see figure 30). Through the dissolve, it is clear that Junie overread the ungendered letter; a subtle knowing smile crosses her lips as the dissolve comes to an end and we return to the present conversation with Nemours. While the acrobatic rewriting of events concludes with hopes to shield Matthias, Martin, and Henri, when all is said and done, the entire scheme collapses, dramatically and tragically.

The gymnastics are for naught because Henri, already aware of Matthias and Martin's affair, violently attacks Matthias in a classroom, where he grabs scissors in an attempt to stab his lover (Callas's operatics haunt this queer romance, to be sure). The operatic climax for the gay lovers stuns the students. Henri is led off by the police, and Matthias's friends and family are left to nurse his injured eye. The deposed Henri is subsequently shunned. One of his friends redirects the violence toward Matthias by stabbing Henri's eyes in the photographic portrait that hangs in the library gallery.

The promise that the look once held is now dramatically attacked. For Henri and Matthias, while their look toward each other sets in motion a sensual romance, it also sets in motion irretrievable damage to the very eyes that seduced them. The letter sequence is a critical centerpiece to *La belle personne* because the

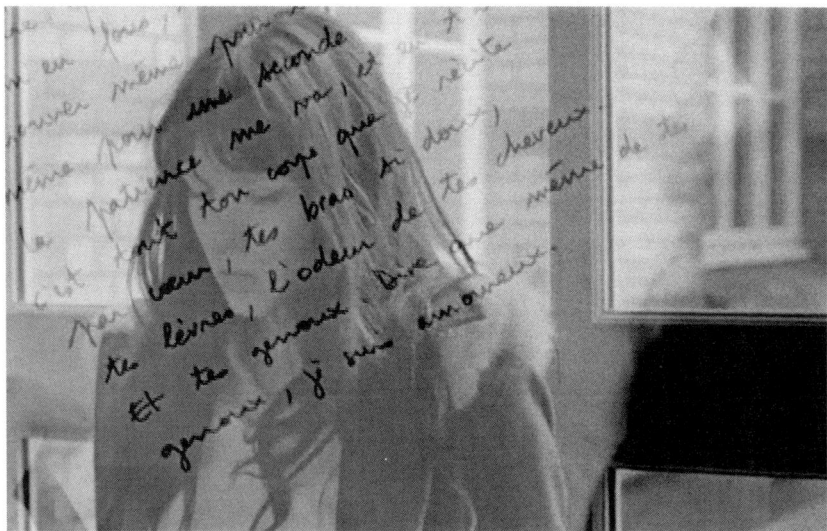

30. Cinematic palimpsest.

failure of letters and images—love letters, international cinema subtitles, photographs, *le regard d'amour*, as well as Honoré's own aestheticized look through the camera—unleashes a stunning cascade of circumstances in which youths' crisscrossed desires cinematically intersect and converge.

THE ROMANTICS

It is appropriate that as this study draws to a close, we return to Nietzsche's reckoning with language and Kuntzel's model of close film analysis that opened our book. It is important to draw out the implications for these theoretical positions in relationship to the queer bodies that compose Honoré's cinema. What can be said, in other words, about the trilogy's dynamic of gender and sexuality as it is pressed within the language of history and aesthetics? In what way does Honoré embrace yet critique art as romantic transcendence? Specifically, do Honoré's portraits of youth—especially young men—merely rehash nineteenth-century Romanticism? And, if so, is the trilogy ultimately a conservative artwork that ignores the undeniably complicated relations of gender in the twenty-first century? *La belle personne* and the trilogy as a whole provide complex responses. Honoré's romantic youth lead us in unexpected directions.

In *Human, All Too Human*, Nietzsche looks to Byron's "Manfred: A Dramatic Poem" to highlight the poet's Romantic sensibility: "sorrow is knowledge." Byron writes, "Sorrow is knowledge, they who know the most / Must mourn the deepest o'er the fatal truth: / The tree of knowledge is not that of life."[26] For Otto in *La belle personne*—as well as for Paul (*Dans Paris*) and Ismaël (*Les chansons d'amour*)—sorrow does not merely drive Honoré's narrative. Sorrow is a guiding element—a certain impulse generated through knowledge—that Honoré embraces and revitalizes. Yet, if sorrow is knowledge, Honoré's view, we argue, is Nietzschean since it is resistant to neat and resolute conclusions. Significantly, and as we hope our consideration of the trilogy suggests, "sorrow" pervades Honoré's formal cinematic dimensions in unsettling yet rewarding ways.

In *La belle personne*, the noise generated by Honoré's ebullient bunch can easily lead the spectator to pass by one of the film's more critical characters, Otto, and the Byronesque sorrow he exudes. Otto is at once a child and a mature young man; he is naïve yet poised as the film world's moral guardian. And as the film's resident romantic, he has a delicate sensibility that verges on what is clearly already very fragile ground. Importantly, he carries on the lineage of young men we have thus far encountered in Honoré's trilogy. These three young men—Paul, Ismaël, and Otto—are ensnared in sorrow, grief, and a pursuit of knowledge.

Ultimately, each one is a portrait of the romantic young man caught amid those who believe, like Byron, that "sorrow is knowledge."

On the one hand, and as representative French citizens, these young men embody national secularism (*laïcité*) through their devotion to art and culture. In this way, they resist religiosity in favor of a quest for self through art. They, in effect, recognize what Nietzsche identifies as "the false assertions of the priests that there is a God who desires that we do good, [He] is the guardian and witness of every action, every moment, every thought, who loves us and in every misfortune wants only what is best for us" (60). Through art, not God, then, Honoré's young aesthetes grapple with existence. Yet, on the other hand, their romantic secularism remains haunted by the religion of priests: Paul's prayer, Ismaël's appeal to angels, and Otto's martyrdom.

By studying the Romantics at the lycée, Otto discovers secular knowingness through classroom lessons in which art promises a rewarding and fulfilling life, one that purportedly breaks from theological indoctrination. As such, art, and the value assigned to it in culture and education, assumes the role of the priests and their "false assertions." Art displaces religion. Otto's and Honoré's other new romantics wrestle with their French-defined male subjectivity at the point where the secular remains inseparable from the religious (it is worth recalling the cultural tension that Honoré experiences in his relationship to Breton Catholicism; JNCH, 171). Hence, Paul, Ismaël, and Otto "mourn." In Honoré's films, "to mourn" involves a search for knowledge so as to make sense of the sorrow from which there is no escape. Cinematically, Honoré situates the trilogy's romantics in a winter's scene, mapped by barren trees and gray skies. Within this backdrop, Honoré's youths discover that sorrow, indeed, is knowledge.

But Nietzsche (and Honoré) suggest a complicated approach to the "tree of knowledge," one that is certainly a more poisonous "antidote" to Byron's romantic reasoning. Through Horace, Nietzsche "conjure[s] up ... solemn frivolity" in provocative ways ("at least for the worst hours and eclipses of the soul"): "why torment your mind, which is unequal to it / with counsel for eternity / why not come and lie under this tall plane tree, or this pine" (quoted in Nietzsche, *Human*, 61). "Any degree of *frivolity or melancholy*," Nietzsche continues, "is better than a romantic return and desertion, an approach to Christianity in any form: for given the current state of knowledge, one can no longer have any association with it without incurably dirtying one's intellectual conscience and prostituting it before oneself and others. Those agonies may be painful enough: but without agonies one cannot become a leader and educator of mankind; and woe to him who wants to attempt it but no longer possesses this clean conscience" (61).

If Paul, Ismaël, and Otto find succor in Byron's romantic mourning, they foolhardily ignore the Nietzschean double move on sorrow and suffering: "frivolity and melancholy." The boys' introversion remains sullied by secularized Christianity. (For Nietzsche, "romantic returns" are only and always "an approach to Christianity.") To be sure, the mournful young men, and their sorrow with which we sympathize, resembles that most sentimentalized historical portrait: the suffering Christ figure on the cross. Embraced by Christianity and ritualized through liturgical song in the Catholic Church, Christ represents the ultimate performance of sentimentality and serves as the perfect romantic ideal in which sorrow is knowledge. Through cinematic imagery and sound, Honoré's boys echo the sentimentalized Christ figure as a model for stimulating sentimentality for themselves.

In *Dans Paris*, for instance, it is to Paul that lovers, family, and friends pray. Recall the Manet painting that Paul appears to mime as he "dances" to secular pop music in bed (see figures 13 and 14). At the trilogy's heart, *Les chansons d'amour*, recall the mourning that Ismaël sings to his lost "angel" (see figure 20) and, in the final sequence, his assumption of a Christ-like pose when a giant spotlight reveals his outstretched arms as he kisses his new lover (figure 24). Finally, in *La belle personne*, Otto sings of lost love just at the moment when he prepares to sacrifice himself in the name of unrequited love. Otto thus gives himself the ultimate gift—death—in order to transcend the agony that lost love has presumably caused him. Death, as we have seen, remains a possible "out" for Paul and Ismaël as well. Otto, we will see, follows through on this promise.

Honoré's romantic trinity—Paul, Ismaël, and Otto—thus express their sorrow through the poetry of song and imagery that have borrowed from liturgical song and religious icons. Structurally, their songs form a cinematic triptych when viewed across the three films. While song is cathartic, and the boys' Christ-like posturing unequivocally announces their sentimentalized bodies, the tropes lead them into realms of ever more complex uncertainty. This is even true of Otto's death in the final segment of the trilogy since, as *Dans Paris* made clear, death is never quite the end of the story. The song that Otto offers is the ultimate, if clichéd, romantic gesture: suicide in the face of unrequited love.[27] Here, song is romantically transcendent as much as it is viscerally conclusive. The romantic's self-sacrifice dramatically insists that those who are touched by his act will remain forever emotionally inscribed by his grandiose gesture. Through song, therefore, the boys self-indulgently display their "agonies" as "a romantic return and desertion" (Nietzsche, *Human*, 61).

It soon becomes apparent that Honoré turns to a self-determined group of women to identify characters that are more strong willed—*more knowing.*

Honoré's women also act on the possibilities of the impossible but through different means and ends. The Alices in *Dan Paris* and *Les chansons* and Junie in *La belle personne* are the ones who make room for Nietzsche's more dynamic translation of sorrow and knowledge. Honoré's framing directly establishes a historical connection between the trilogy's romantics and the "trees of knowledge" in such a way that it is the women in his films who grasp the complex possibilities available in the double move, "frivolity and melancholy."

A WINTER'S MISE-EN-SCÈNE

Does Honoré, therefore, misdirect our sympathies? Has the purportedly mistreated Otto seduced the spectator by reaffirming indoctrinated Christian beliefs revised as secular romanticism? Does Honoré sentimentalize the suffering male figure to which we are accustomed in classical and art-house film narrative?[28] Has he not offered Otto as yet another Christ figure who "died for our sins," thus suturing the spectator into "false assertions" by the high priests of art? In this way, has Honoré confirmed Vincendeau's criticism, that his "women are inadequate mothers, neurotic girlfriends or easygoing playmates" for the pleasure of the director's romanticized men?[29] If not, what is the "antidote" that Honoré delivers to penetrate the complex dance of gender relations?

Since Honoré's romantic young men fall short in meeting Nietzsche's appeal to "lie under [Horace's] tall tree" and allow "frivolity *or* melancholy" to wash over them, they delude themselves that they have chosen "alternative" forms of existence. "To choose" the "alternative," however, is not necessarily the surest sign of strength, nor is it the guarantee of fulfillment. Honoré's boys are unable, in other words, to see that the "trees of knowledge" merely offer a choice of poisons. To put it simply, the trees we see in Honoré's cinematic world provide few choices and rewards. The trilogy's overall winter landscape, filled with barren trees, does not bode well for a youth's existential quest.

By following Nietzsche, we can identify two often-conflated trees that Honoré places in the mise-en-scène—the "tree of knowledge" and the "tree of life." The trees do not simply serve as the background where "right" and "wrong" are determined. Instead, the frozen trees—not unlike the students in *La belle personne* and the characters who dance across the trilogy—are caught between the secular and the religious, between autumn and spring. Nietzsche understood that the allegories about the "tree of life" and the "tree of knowledge" both offer poisonous fruit. Whichever way one turns, to choose invariably inscribes one within Christian indoctrination and idealism.[30] Nevertheless, one must choose.

To choose, therefore, is never an easy matter and is always riddled with risk. But in choosing, human strength is constituted, or not. "Examine the lives of the best and most fruitful people," Nietzsche writes in *The Gay Science,* "and ask yourself whether a tree that is supposed to grow to a proud height can dispense with bad weather and storms; whether misfortune and external resistance, some kinds of hatred, jealousy, stubbornness, mistrust, hardness, avarice, and violence do not belong among the *favorable* conditions without which any great growth even of virtue is scarcely possible. The poison of which weaker natures perish strengthens the strong—nor do they call it poison."[31] Honoré's trilogy implicitly involves itself with Nietzsche's realization that one chooses one's "poison" (named thusly or not; consider the lyrics of "Il faut se taire" in *Les chansons*).[32] Pointedly, the films preview the effects of choice particularly for women who resiliently prove to have an inordinate strength against certainly less-than-"favorable" conditions.

Women—especially Paul's mother in *Dans Paris,* Alice in *Les chansons,* and Junie in *La belle personne*—have reconciled themselves to accepting the rewards and the consequences that poison/choice allows for. They understand it as the only option they have available to them. Unlike the men who seek to negate its ill effects by romanticizing an antidote through dramatic and sentimental *gesture toward death,* the women recognize that the fruit borne of the trees of knowledge and of life offer, as Manfred Riedel puts it, "precisely not life but death."[33] For Honoré's women, to know initiates gestures and actions akin to a shuddering, a *frisson.* These women adroitly adjust to civilization's doctrines and the male-inflected emotional confines it establishes. As such, their performance rubs against the order of things; it creates mobility within palindromic cultural logic (similar to the Oulipian equation we encountered earlier in the classroom). Movement may at times be subtle, constrained, but it is far more empowering than aestheticized despair. With Honoré's ubiquitous winter-dormant trees as the background, women sing, dance, and look within the cinematic frame, often and seemingly going nowhere with few results. Yet even a palindrome that appears to circle in on itself and be limited in its affective range reveals imaginative possibilities that the Oulipo writer François Le Lionnais calls "acrobatic."[34] Palindromes are "stigmatized" by people of "'serious' literary ambition," but the constraint on language that they are said to deliver underestimates what Marcel Bénabou sees as their "commodious way of passing from language to writing." Palindromic constraint, Bénabou continues, "goes beyond rules which seem natural only to those people who have barely questioned language, it forces the system out of its routine functioning, thereby compelling it to reveal its hidden sources."[35] Rather than secure a (male) romantic design on knowledge-life as the explanation for death in which their (male) companions "prostitute" their "agonies," women *choose* to prostitute themselves. Fully aware of the limitations they inhabit, Honoré's women choose to "reveal [constraints'] hidden sources."

CHOICE

How does Honoré make cinematic his young aesthetes' poisoning, their choosing between the "tree of life" and the "tree of knowledge"? To which tree do they turn? And in what way do they choose?[36] If a Nietzschean critique bears out, the forbidden fruits from both trees of life and knowledge invariably lead to death—in one form or another. And if death and immortality assume two sides of the same coin, as Honoré's films suggest, the trilogy critically and aesthetically explores this existential impasse.

Set in the halls of the Lycée Molière, where "life" and "knowledge" rattle youth, *La belle personne* puts into relief the long-standing conflation between the sacral and secular, a conflation that, according to Nietzsche, confuses while it substantiates our faith in the allegorical trees. Indeed, as Peter Thacher Lanfer shows, the epistemology of the trees is lengthy and intertwined with the Western "pursuit of wisdom." Lanfer marks, for instance, the discursive shift from the traditional Judeo-Christian literature to the "gnostic passages that demote the Tree of Life in order to elevate the Tree of Knowledge."[37] For Nietzsche, because Christian doctrine saturates all corners of so-called secular civilization, all discursive versions of the trees and their fruit merely ground man's delusional beliefs: "Probability but no truth, appearance of freedom but no freedom—it is on account of these two fruits that the tree of knowledge cannot be confounded with the tree of life."[38] To blur the two allegorical trees in any shape or form in the name of gaining wisdom is a dupe; to conflate them gives purchase to false consciousness (to borrow a Marxian axiom).

If Honoré's boys prostitute their agonies as self-interested dramatics "before oneself and others," Junie—and the other women of his films—revise the terms for prostitution. To prostitute is not a question of morals. To ignore that one is always in the position of prostituting oneself is disingenuous. The question at hand is *how* and *why* one, in fact, prostitutes. Hence, in *La belle personne,* when Otto commits suicide (preluded by a song), Junie looks on bewildered. Whom was his overromanticized plunge to death meant to move? Does Otto's prostituting of his agony involve a "clean conscience"?

In the trilogy, Honoré invites us to look, along with him and his cinematic troupe, at actions, movements, and the choices made within the film's "frozen" landscapes. What we see, then, are the results of *the ways* one chooses to

La belle personne

prostitute or (in Thomas Elsaesser's terms) to move within the "double bind."³⁹ Here, within the mise-en-scène filled by winter's "trees" that are frozen between autumn and springtime, lies the aesthetic and philosophical rub. Three specific scenes in *La belle personne* rehearse the paradoxical dangers, the "double bind," in choosing from the poisoned fruit that the trees offer. Throughout the trilogy, trees surround the scene in which characters face significant and transitional moments; the trees in *La belle personne* stand out for the direct involvement in the decision-making process. Hence, recall Jeanne in *Les chansons d'amour* as she mournfully sings in "Pépinière Park," where she is framed by elegantly planted winter trees; or recall Ismaël as silhouetted trees watch over him in Montparnasse Cemetery, where he finally releases Julie's spirit so that he may move on to Erwann. Earlier, in *Dans Paris,* Mirko drags home a (soon-to-be-dead)

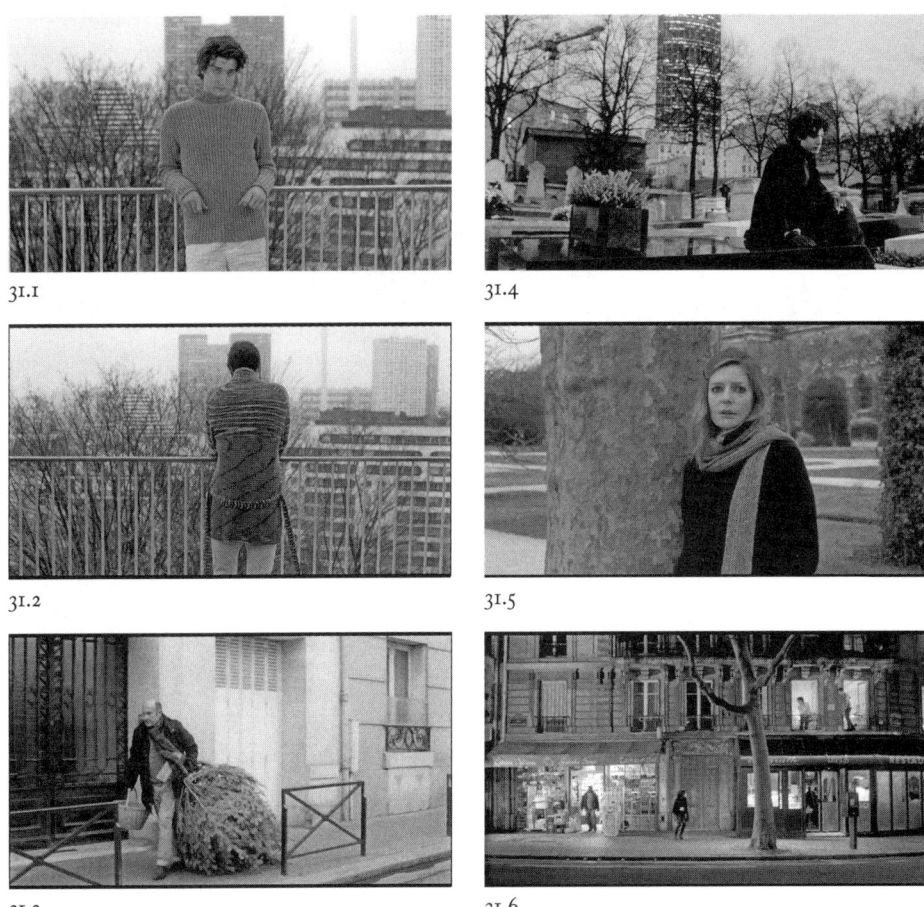

31.1–31.6. Between trees of life and trees of knowledge in *Dans Paris* and *Les chansons d'amour.*

Christmas tree with hopes that it will bring life to his decaying family; and Paul manages his fraught relationship with Anna against the rural, crisp, and chilly wooded landscape. Indeed, Paul's brother, Jonathan, inaugurates the film's narrative by centrally staging himself on his apartment's balcony with the bare branches of the city's trees behind him. Multiple examples of winter trees correlate to character choice over matters of life and knowledge in Honoré's trilogy.

The three scenes we now consider in *La belle personne* specifically realize the complex intersection between the allegorical trees and the act of choice (figures 32.1–32.3). As such, the scenes demonstrate the vital relationship between performance and mise-en-scène that Honoré consistently brings to his work. Each sequence described here intimately involves Otto's relationship to self and to the other, Junie. Sequences 1 and 3 echo each other insofar as Otto's choices are played out at the same location. Sequence 2 draws Junie into the mix and frames the vexed trees of life and knowledge at the juncture where Eros rubs against Thanatos—one leads to the other for Otto. We begin by examining the connections between Otto's actions in sequences 1 and 3 and then turn our attention to sequence 2, where Junie's and Otto's actions set the stage for two different existential exit points.

After we learn that shy Otto is smitten with Junie, the mysterious new girl in school, his pals tease and taunt him. The first passage where we see Otto come face-to-face with the symbolic tree is after class, when Henri and Matthias usher him to the balcony's edge that overlooks the lycée's courtyard. As Otto exits the classroom, the boys snag him. In a medium shot, the camera follows the boys as they move toward the balcony. Positioned to either side of Otto, Henri and Matthias firmly hold their friend and direct his gaze across the courtyard. With the three boys' look directed outward, the camera frames the boys in the foreground while the courtyard's actual trees fill their line of vision in the background. Henri and Matthias prod Otto to make his move on Junie, who, in a cut, is seen traversing the balcony across the way. "Go on," Otto's comrades tell him. "It's now or never. Go for it," they insist. In the film, this is Otto's first encounter with the conflict between "life" and "knowledge." At this moment, his view of Junie, the focus of his hopes, is filtered through trees. Encouraged by his friends, here Otto makes the first choice in which his romantic ideals are put to the test (figure 32.1).

We later return to that location on the school balcony after Otto's romantic hopes are finally dashed. It is crucial for the way Honoré links Eros and Thanatos that Otto returns to the scene where he made his initial act to choose in his pursuit of Junie. Toward the end of the film, a romantically beleaguered Otto makes his most dramatic decision. The tree that offers both vexed knowledge and life starkly fills the scene. Disenchanted with Junie's ambivalent affections

La belle personne

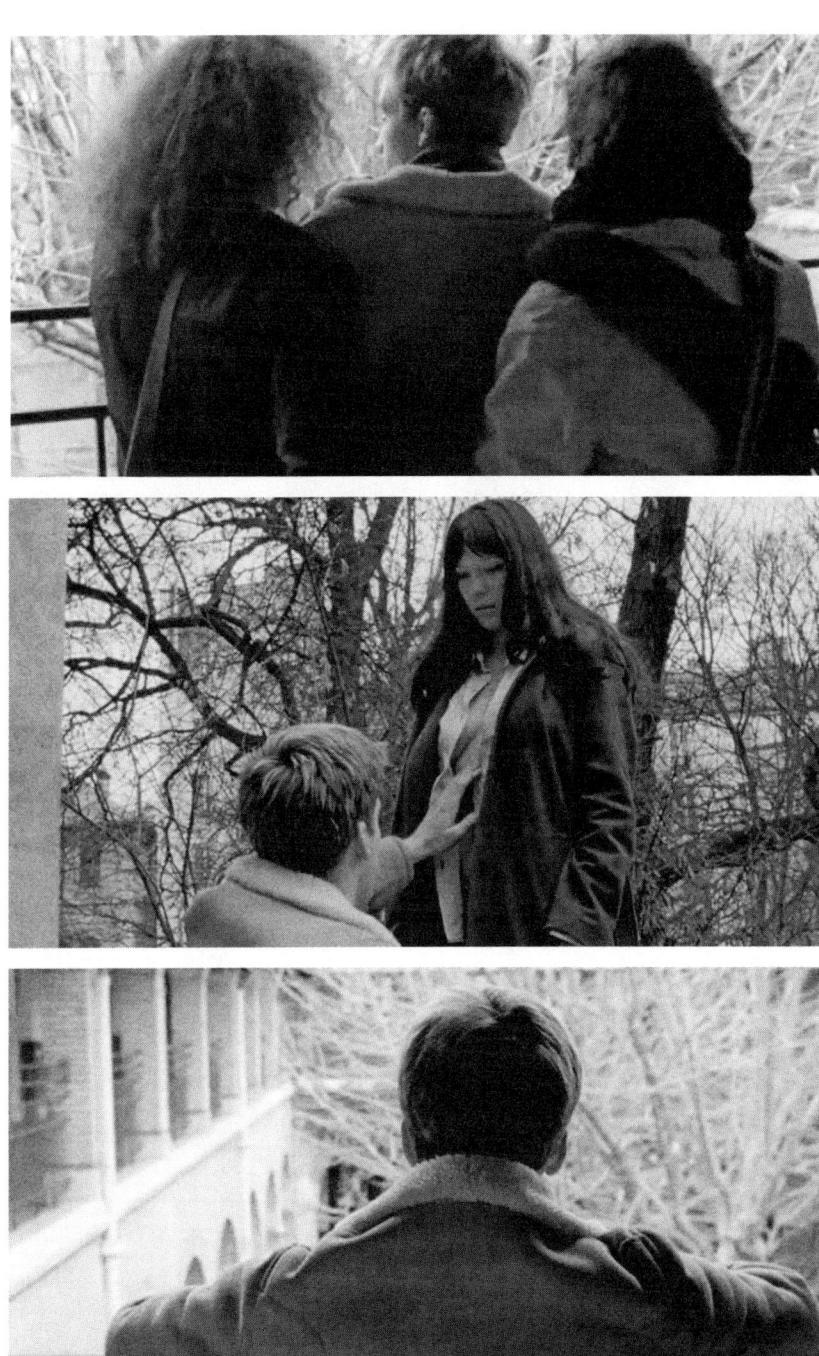

32.1–32.3. Trees and choice in *La belle personne*.

for him—affections at once erotically intimate yet chillingly indifferent—Otto makes his way back to the place where he found the courage to follow his heart (figure 32.3). Through the film's one song, "Comme la pluie," he laments the series of events that have unfolded while he has been steadfastly true to Junie.

Alex Beaupain's music and melody are equal to any love ballad. The lyrics, however, are disturbing and suggest a troubling undercurrent to the sentimentalizing assigned to romantic boys. As the soon-to-be-tragic figure, Otto, wanders the grounds of the lycée where Junie and her friends congregate, he sings how he wishes "to beat her, give her pain" so that "no one would want her." On his journey back to the balcony, while the song continues, Otto sees Junie hanging out with friends in the courtyard. While he sings about "tears" that she will never offer him for his pain, we see Junie turn away from Otto and giggle, presumably over her lover's adolescent appeal to love. Beaupain's musical arrangement ramps up as we hear a violin dramatically impose itself, as if to match Otto's anguish and the urgency for the choice he believes he must make. As he moves to the second floor, his poetic lyrics suggest that the only reprieve from the pain he feels is through the cover of night, where the "stars like crosses" lure him to his required sacrifice; the daylight is too painful. Stepping onto the balcony railing, he sings of this pain. While framed once again by the tree that seemingly led him to the tortuous love he feels for Junie, Otto jumps into the courtyard.

The body hits with a thud. Stunned students, including Junie, turn to the corner, where they see Otto's lifeless body that now lies in a puddle of deep red "blood" ("Not blood, red," Godard famously reminds us).[40] Similar to the sequence that saw Julie pass away in *Les chansons,* Honoré cuts the sequence to emphasize the distinct range of emotions created by the character's death. The first cut, following Otto's leap, shows students suddenly look off-screen to the courtyard's corner after they hear the unexpected sound. They move toward the event's site as Honoré cuts to an over-the-shoulder shot that peers down onto Otto's lifeless body. The following cut disrupts the spatial and temporal moment to pull Junie out from the gathering noise. Here we see her in a medium-long shot, alone in the courtyard with her back to us, staring down at Otto's splayed body. Returning to the scene where all students have congregated around Otto's final performance, we cut to a tightly framed close-up that includes four students with Junie tucked in between them. As the shot continues, she quietly withdraws from the group, keeping her eye on Otto, and she steals away from the confined space. An over-the-shoulder point-of-view shot offers one last look at Otto. The final cut in the sequence returns to the medium-long shot wherein the frame and space are cleared of all but Junie and Otto. Junie, now facing us, slowly walks away from Otto's body and exits the frame.

CHILDREN'S BOOKS

Otto's grand gesture before the courtyard tree—his turn on "prostituting" his agony—comes on the heels of yet another event in which the tree of life and/or the tree of knowledge weigh heavily on choice. But in this instance, the choices made now involve both Otto and Junie. What becomes apparent through this sequence is that the acts engaged by Otto and Junie delineate two very different realizations for the actors who perform in the scene. The mise-en-scène significantly frames the way we understand Junie's and Otto's final decisions in the film.

Junie's struggle over Nemours's and Otto's passion for her are caught between desire and cultural obligations. It is the conflict so magisterially presented in *The Princesse de Clèves*. In many ways, the men who pursue Junie represent two different models of eroticized masculinity. On the one hand, Otto's youth and inexperience are charming and benevolent but lack a seductive *je ne sais quoi* that only comes through a remarkably lived life. On the other hand, Nemours's allure is precisely his worldly sensibility (one might argue, *too* worldly). His emotional connection to Maria Callas's performance and fluency in the romance of the romantic languages erotically dovetails with his well-known sexual prowess. The many who have involved themselves with Nemours are unequivocally drawn to his range of linguistic expertise. Junie gives pause to reactively falling prey to what paradoxically adds up to Nemours's and Otto's shortcomings. They both perform to excess those attributes that Junie finds attractive in them.

The Junie-Otto-Nemours relationship returns us to a concept we charted earlier: the triangle. In *La belle personne*, Honoré's dynamic among three characters plays out through the movement of a triangle that reforms into shifting doubles. And like the earlier films, love and death are the forces that manage the triangle's existence. Junie, however, is the engine that drives the passion. It is she who sets the terms in the relationship.

What does Junie offer her suitors? For Otto, she gives her body. Otto has a sense that their relationship is becoming more and more vague. Their romantic rendezvous in a private enclave gives him a glimmer of hope. Junie approaches Otto outdoors in a tucked-away corner near the lycée. Seated on a ledge, we see Junie approach him from a high-angle shot. As with many scenes in Honoré's films that portray character transition, the director favors a camera position that shoots diagonally into the scene; the setup, in other words, creates perpendicular angles in the background while forming something of an isosceles triangle, not dissimilar to what Alan Williams refers to as the "Lumière diagonal."[41] This particular shooting arrangement that Honoré puts to use is worth noting since it is a signature shot in his films. Whereas Douglas Sirk and Vincente Minnelli turned to staircases and their diagonal intersection into a shot to heighten moments of emotional or psychological transformation, Honoré triangularly corners his characters, setting a stage in which action is all but required.[42] Within the triangulated frame—the double's third, Nemours, haunts the scene—Junie approaches Otto. From her bag, she hands him a thin children's book, the one literary work that carries his name: Tomi Ungerer's *Otto: The Autobiography of a Teddy Bear*.

Ungerer's children's books are important textual signposts for Honoré since his books subtly rehearse the erotic potential in a child's experience with friends, family, and themselves. *Otto*'s tale is one that delicately, but not oversentimentally, explores the painful journey that takes place as one lives in the world—a world filled with cruelty that is equal to love. And since Otto shares his name with the book's title, Junie's gift also reminds Otto that, like his own Oulipian-palindrome name, the hurdles and pleasures that constitute existence are choices made between life and death. In other words, our uniqueness and the events that give it shape are as vital as the existence we all share. Difference and sameness are not disparate entities. *Otto* is a not-so-gentle reminder from Junie that her young lover's romantic views are as narcissistically clumsy as they are precious.

While Otto glances over his new book, Junie moves onto the ledge where he is seated. The camera cuts to a low-angle shot where we see Junie now standing above Otto. Behind them, a large winter tree fills the background. As Otto turns toward Junie, she opens her coat and blouse to reveal her breasts. Moving between the bildungsroman children's book and Junie's inviting body, Otto caresses her breasts. He stands, begins to kiss Junie, and moves her toward the wall, where he continues to make love to her. Before the cut, Junie turns away from his kisses, but the actions in the scene indicate that they will fulfill the act. Behind them, the winter tree remains in full view (see figure 32.2).

Otto and Junie's kiss ends on a match cut, where we see Martin holding Matthias against a mid-twentieth-century stone wall that supports the entry to Junie and Matthias's apartment in the sixteenth arrondissement—a rather treeless environment as Honoré casts it. The cut is intriguing since the one tree we see in the sixteenth is a potted palm tree enclosed behind the building's lobby window. The juxtaposition between shots is striking for the divergent urban foliage that Honoré sets up to frame his protagonists' performance where life-altering choices are made. If the gay boys find love where trees bloom eternally—yet certainly artificially—the heterosexual couple occupies a site where the winter tree mirrors the tension involved in choosing between life and knowledge. In all cases, however (gay, straight, and so on), to choose one over the other is a false distinction. The indoor trees, as well as the trees planted in "nature," do not suggest that choosing life over knowledge (or vice versa) enacts anything worth the heavy contemplation in actually making the choice in the first place.[43] Confounding the trees and their poison, Nietzsche tells us, is a "false assertion." Junie recognizes that it is impossible to separate "life" from "knowledge"; instead, she drinks the trees' poison. But, "perhaps," she does not call it this.

ONWARD

> There standeth the boat—thither goeth it over; perhaps into vast nothingness—but who willeth to enter into this "Perhaps"?
>
> Nietzsche, *Thus Spake Zarathustra*

An oft-made criticism about Nietzsche's "will to power" is that it is nihilistic. A similar, and certainly overly simplistic, claim might be made about Honoré's women such as Junie. Along with female characters in Honoré's other films *Ma mère, Non ma fille,* and *Les bien-aimés,* Junie's actions conceivably appear self-centered, disjointed, or cruel. Junie's perceived indifference, her emotionless response to others, and her refusal to explain herself might easily confirm her as one who is, if not nihilistic, then narcissistic. For some viewers, the distinction is moot. But a more nuanced reading of Honoré's women and their choices—their actions in the world—renders these depictions of women and their gestures as a "will to power." In seeking to complicate those who critique Nietzsche's "will to power" as equal to nihilism, scholars such as Sheridan Hough set out to "explain Nietzschean reflectivity as a non-nihilistic activity, one that manages to do its dismantling work while still allowing us to inhabit particular 'ways of life.'"[44] Apropos for our study of Honoré and specifically *La belle personne,* Hough focuses on "Nietzsche's customary epistemological trope . . . of the voyager at sea" (56).

Hough's reading is useful, as is the telling subtitle to her book: *The Self as Metaphoric Double.* Throughout our study, we emphasize Honoré's splitting and merging characters into doubles and, indeed, triples. To double metaphorically (whether from Nietzsche's perspective or Honoré's) is insufficient if only understood as a language game. Language sui generis, we have seen, is never satisfactory. In order for the "self as metaphoric double" to realize its phenomenological possibilities, language and the material world must necessarily work in dissonant concert. Though we have not emphasized it here—and though it is no less significant a metaphor for Honoré's cinematic imaginings that draw on the city of Paris, winter landscapes, and youthful pleasures—water moves his characters to act in the winter chill.

The draw to water for Honoré's characters is in its appeal to crossings. From bridges, water offers an escape from life's sorrows. The River Seine's inviting flow is seductive for Paul in *Dans Paris*; in *Les chansons*, Alice is herself "the bridge between [the lovers'] banks." In *La belle personne*, Junie sails away from land with a "clear conscience." For Honoré, journeys begin and end (and then begin again) with water. Honoré's women evoke the spirit of Zarathustra (noted in the epigraph to this section) as they navigate the uneasy rapture of the sea and head toward "perhaps."

Following Otto's suicide, Junie and Nemours convene to address their love. In a hotel room on the outskirts of Paris, they discuss their possible outcomes as lovers. Torn, Junie tells Nemours, "Imagining you could no longer love me is far worse for me than what you call 'the rules' I set for myself." Her "rules," of course, have been played within the well-established thicket of cultural expectations for women. Wisely, Junie recognizes that her rules are the tools for her life experiments; and although "far worse" than "imagining" that Nemours will no longer love her, Junie remains fully aware of his own rules about philandering and male privilege. With no consummation at the hotel, Junie and Nemours agree to meet a few days later. Junie sets the time frame.

Nemours returns to Junie and Matthias's apartment. He waits. Finally, Matthias meets him out front with a message: Junie left the day before their agreed-on appointment. When Nemours inquires about her destination, Matthias tells him that he cannot say. She has gone far away, and, he continues, "You shouldn't wait for her." Most importantly, Matthias transmits the message that Junie never wants to hear from Nemours again. A saddened and bewildered Nemours turns and walks away while the camera tracks with him along a darkened and chilly Parisian street. On a cut, we see Junie in bright daylight. She stands aboard a ship that has just departed a port that is clearly situated well beyond the city's limits. Her back to us, she stands motionless, carrying her travel bag. While the ship pulls away from the dock, the slow movement of the boat is animated by the camera's fast-motion effect. Junie looks out onto a radically different landscape from the one she left—a verdant and pastel landscape dots the scene while small port buildings can be seen against the rolling hills and blue sky. The city's somber winter scenes that she left behind are put into sharp relief with the winter sunlight that illuminates her exit. With Nick Drake's elegiac song "Day Is Done" providing the closing soundtrack, Junie heads out to sea.[45]

Hough argues, "there are two senses in which 'being at sea' is metaphorically significant" in Nietzsche's writings (56). The first involves "self-conscious seeing." "A person on the water," Hough continues, "even when stationary, is constantly aware of her relation as viewer to what is seen: as the ship moves what is seen, what can be seen, moves as well. The connection between the trope of the sea and that of vision is important; on the water the land-dweller's visual habits are self-consciously altered. Of course, this initially self-conscious seeing, this awareness of seeing from a particular, perhaps temporary, point-of-view, is part of Nietzsche's account of perspectivism" (56).

Much of our argument about Honoré's films rests on "perspectivism," a "self-conscious seeing," a cinema of the look, of looking,—that is to say, a cinema of monstration. Honoré's films, in other words, dynamically engage perspective (of "land-dwelling" spectators and their "visual habits") through cinematic aesthetics. From the sea, Junie does indeed *see* "from a self-consciously altered" perspective; Honoré's Nietzschean lens thus revises "visual habits" toward "a particular, perhaps temporary, point-of-view."

In *La belle personne*, Junie's movement outward by sea foregrounds water's significance throughout the trilogy but underlines its required place in revitalizing *the way* we see. Hence, while the myriad urban landscapes ground characters in Honoré's cinema, they do so to the extent that they do not necessarily disorient them. Instead, the landscapes in which water invariably flows—bridges, courtyards, passages within novels, city streets—provoke choice. Water is clearly a deciding factor in Honoré's cinema. And, following Hough, Honoré's films suggest "a second important feature of [Nietzsche's metaphor of] being at sea" (56). Our cast has maneuvered their way through tricky everyday obstacles over very urban ground. The water that runs through and ultimately around this ground is alluring precisely for the "altered" perspective it offers, whether in, on, or over it (Paul's and Jonathan's dives into the Seine, Julie's and Ismaël's traversing the bridges over the city's river, and Junie's journey across the sea). At the same time, like the seafarer who suddenly realizes his minuscule place in the world aboard his "frail and tiny" ship, Junie et al. long for "assurance and stability." Involvement with the water is when "loss of ground is felt most keenly," and, as Hough concludes, "the person who calls her values into question ultimately wants to make solid claims about the moral position, but that very 'voyaging,' the reflective process she has embarked upon, has destroyed the ground she once inhabited" (56).

Hough's language is provocative for a study on Honoré's perspective since the director tantalizingly turns to the cinema's aesthetic properties less to disorient than to destabilize. Honoré's mise-en-scène, editing, and cinematography communicate matters of choice, matters of (in)decision. Junie's voyage takes us—and the trilogy—outward with a self-determined point-of-view, always keeping in mind the "destroyed" ground she has left in her wake.

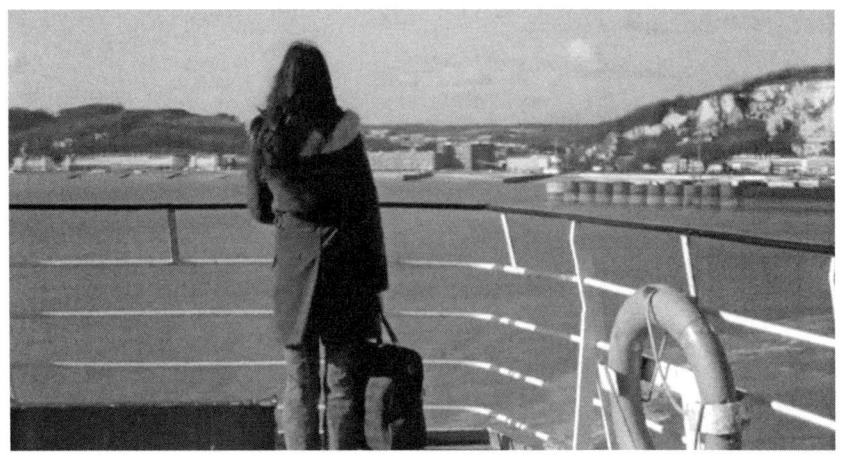

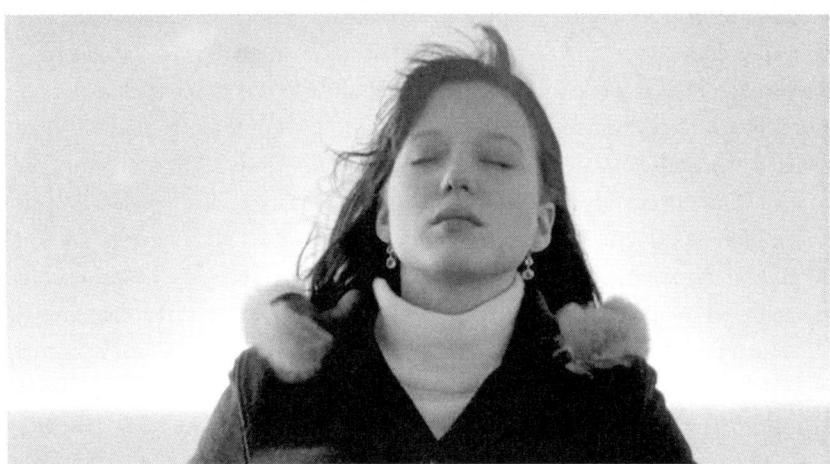

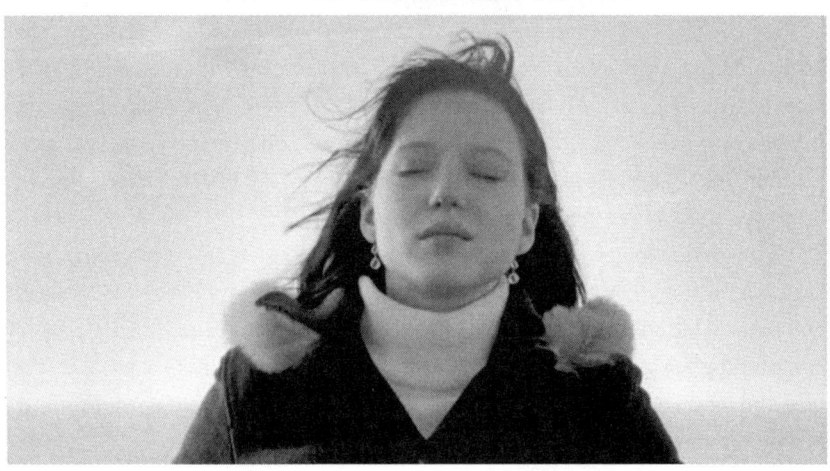

33.1–33.3. Onward and "perhaps." Junie's perspective and choices made in *La belle personne*.

INTERVIEW WITH CHRISTOPHE HONORÉ

Translated by David Powell

Two interviews with Christophe Honoré were conducted with Julien Nahmias on April 24 and November 2, 2012, in Paris. At the time of the interviews, the director was in preparation for the film *Métamorphoses*. The separate interviews are indicated by date. Notes attributed to the translator are marked as such; all other notes are those of Gerstner and Nahmias.

APRIL 24, 2012

BEGINNINGS

JN: You come from the village of Rostrenen in Brittany. The region seems to hold an important place in your artistic creation, especially recently with the focus on the Breton tale in *Non, ma fille tu n'iras pas danser*. Can you tell us what being Breton means for you and how you are influenced by your regional culture?

CH: It's not really a relationship with a regional culture; it's just that I come from there. Childhood is an important part of my fiction writings, both film and literature. Apart from that, Brittany offers the advantage of being a region heavily steeped in Catholicism with a peculiar relationship to death. I'm just as fond of Brittany as I am repulsed by it. I remember that as a child, I had the feeling that staying in Brittany was like being in a tomb.

My family isn't at all religious. I was at once fascinated and terrified by all these wayside crucifixes, churches, and all the crosses that you encounter just about everywhere in Brittany. Anyway, Brittany is full of legends in which dead people come visit the living; it's a land of ghosts.

Sometimes in interviews I highlight my Breton side or even just Brittany because I find it a bit annoying when I'm labeled a Parisian middle-class Bohemian filmmaker. It makes me laugh because I came to Paris when I was twenty-five. And I still feel very provincial and not at all Parisian, whether it's at social events or just my relationship with the city. From this perspective, I feel I'm more Breton than Parisian, but I'm not at all in favor of independence for Brittany. [*laughter*]

JN: How did you come to film?

CH: I don't know. Quite honestly, I'd be lying if I said I had very clear childhood memories concerning film. It always makes me laugh to hear directors like Claude Lelouch say, "I saw *Snow White* when I was four, and ever since then I've wanted to be a director!" Everyone knows that's completely false. People don't have these kinds of memories; they're just things they make up later in life.

My family aren't at all movie people; they're craftsmen in a village of two thousand inhabitants, where the movie theater, called the Brest, showed movies Friday and Saturday evenings. I can remember very clearly how excited I was as a child when I was allowed to watch movies on TV in the evenings. The television wasn't always available. I can remember when I was in the seventh grade,[1] I would go to my aunt's in Nantes for the summers and would take advantage of the movies, where I'd spend my afternoons. I very soon knew that I wanted to be a filmmaker, but I'm not at all clear on how I came to settle on that. It could just as easily have been music, painting [*trails off*].

JN: Were those artistic studies more available to you at the time than film?

CH: Yes, because you can become a painter in Brittany, as so many painters have done. You can be a musician in Brittany, with the Transmusicales, for example.[2] There are also many writers in Brittany. At the same time, while I knew when I was thirteen that I wanted to be a film director, I didn't know that I would become one. After all, I made my first film when I was thirty. I don't know how I could have been so stubborn in my perseverance for artistic ambition.

As early as middle school, I was writing a movie column in student papers. I belonged to theater clubs and the high-school film club. No one really knows where this film-buff thing comes from. I think it's got something to do with the forbidden.

Anyway, it's easy to see that for all film buffs (and it's not a coincidence that many film buffs are gay—homosexuality and a love of film are connected, especially in France) there's an idea of the secret, the illicit, something that's not for us but we go watch anyway. Clearly there is a notion of voyeurism.

When you start to get obsessed with film, as I was when I was a teenager, you can't get away from four films a day, or from pushing the real world away, so you hide out in movie theaters. Sometimes I could do it, especially since I lost my father when I was fifteen years old; it's true that losing your father offers a kind of free space. For me movies were always my free space. Maybe I would have become a filmmaker[3] even if my father had lived—I don't know.

JN: You are the author of a significant literary output, including novels for adults but also numerous books for children that broach subjects as diverse as the death of a parent, AIDS, same-sex parents, suicide, family secrets, or a doll's upbringing. What things brought you to write for children?

CH: It was totally by chance. When my father died, I felt utterly incapable of saying anything. So I started writing poetry and short stories. I felt no vocation for writing for children. I was very politically active during that time insofar as I was a counselor in a vacation resort. I say "politically active" because I believed in the idea of the new education, education for the people.

Soon after, I became the director of a vacation resort, a vacation resort for disadvantaged people. It was working with this group of poor and culturally underprivileged people that I began to get interested in children's literature.

When I was little, I didn't have any children's books. I had some *Astérix,* some *Tintin,*[4] that kind of thing, but I wasn't brought up with kids' books. So it was a big surprise for me, at the age of eighteen, when I realized there was a whole literature just for kids. It was a new kids' literature. Anyone interested in this literature can read almost all the important books within six months. That motivated me enormously to write. In fact, I quickly realized, for instance, that there weren't any books like *Tout contre Léo*. So, then, I was truly original!

JN: Do you find there's a specific kind of writing necessary for this literary genre?

CH: Yes, it's a closely defined sphere, a branch of literature closely monitored by law. You can't write just anything in kids' literature; it's a literature of constraint, and that really attracted me to it. I thought, here's a possibility to be innovative through children's literature. It was also much less intimidating for a big reader like myself who was very much influenced by Georges Bataille, Maurice Blanchot, and the *nouveau roman* authors.⁵ When you read their novels, they don't really give you any energy for writing. They're such inhibiting and demanding writers that you think, "Whatever I plan to write is going to be worthless!" But with children's literature, I felt like I could invent a form all my own.

That's why when I came to Paris, I did some work for *Cahiers du Cinéma*, and at the same time I published my first young-adult novel, *Tout contre Léo*. Actually during the time when I was waiting to make my first film (more or less between 1995 and 2000), I wrote many children's books, which kept me from writing bad screenplays, or at least from writing screenplays that I would never get to produce. Rather than writing screenplays that I would shove into a drawer or making shorts, I siphoned my desire to tell stories through kids' books. That was my way of testing my stories; it was an artistic experiment. It still is.

I find it very satisfying to write books for children. In that five-year period during which I wasn't making films, I think I published my three young-adult novels and maybe ten children's books.

JN: Where, in your opinion, does the difference lie between children's and adult literature?

CH: For me, the difference is to be found on the level of the constraint imposed by the genre itself. I'm not necessarily happy with my adult novels, not even with my films. My children's books, however, I feel are pretty enjoyable. There's something in this literature that belongs to me which in the end few people have. Mainly it's a matter of the narrator. It might seem like a technical concern, but broadly speaking children's literature is not so much about the ability to deal with homosexuality or AIDS any more than all the other books that broach these topics; it's more about being able to write something like a book like *Tout contre Léo*. This book is about AIDS, but I find that when you look at it just a little from a literary perspective, you realize that the story doesn't come from someone outside the narrative context. And for me, that's really important. The real difference in young-adult literature, the only thing that is forbidden in the end, is talking about yourself.

Children's literature is complicated because it's adults talking to children, and even more so because the adults are strangers to the children. In interesting children's books, we understand that the person talking to us isn't just anybody but someone like our grandfather who is telling us a story that seems to come from a long time ago. You communicate with children by lying, by pretending to be a child.

For *J'élève ma poupée* (a book I shouldn't have written ten years ago), I needed to be able to write a children's book in which I was an adult but also a bastard.[6] And so when I bawl you out throughout the whole book, you don't buy it. All that totally complicates things for children's literature.

I know that my ideal book for kids, which I'll definitely never manage to write, would be an autobiography for children, meaning managing to talk about myself with the utmost sincerity, all the while aware that I'm talking to children but without putting them in the role of phony adults.

JN: In your 2005 *Livre pour enfants,* which might be an attempt at a children's autobiography, as you were just saying, you describe yourself with "Homosexuality, Brittany, Adolescence." Can you explain this "triptych"?

CH: The plan for *Livre pour enfants* was really to write a self-portrait. I came to literature at a moment when a new trend held sway in French literature, which is I think a true trend: "autofiction."[7] I particularly admired Christine Angot, who gave me considerable energy to write, even if my novels don't resemble hers at all. I'd always thought that one day I would have to work in the vein of autofiction. I went more in the direction of self-portrait, which for me is quite different.

The point of this book is to try to define myself, knowing that each definition given in the book is a false definition that ends up being canceled out by the next one. So, in this "absurd" trinity—"Homosexuality, Brittany, Adolescence"—it seems to me anyway, there's something in this combination that defines me well.

I'm not really a militant homosexual in my books. I don't think so at any rate. I think I belong to a generation of gays that don't need, perhaps mistakenly, to assert their homosexuality. None of my books or my films tells a coming-out story. For me, this is not a subject anymore. I feel it's no longer interesting to elaborate on what happens afterward. People often tell me, "Your characters don't have any problems with their sexuality!" And it's true; they have a certain uncomplicated sexuality that interests me.

In my films, sometimes there are homosexuals, sometimes not. I don't say to myself, "Oh, homosexuality is missing here!" It's the same thing for my children's books, in which I don't avoid gay narrators or fathers.

Since I always try to stay close to my own experience, Brittany becomes obvious because that's where I come from, and, particularly in my relationship to death, I think there's something very Breton about the idea of communicating constantly with dead people, because living people constantly ask dead people to forgive them for something or other.

And adolescence makes sense because I see clearly that in a definite way, I'm not someone who is very much interested in mastery, which for me would be connected with being an adult. On the contrary, I much prefer the idea of incompleteness, the idea of desires that can be at once deep and quick, fleeting. I feel like I have a kind of adolescent aesthetic, whether in my novels, my theater, or my film.

JN: So you're also a gay narrator in film?

CH: I think I am, even if I find it annoying to be reduced to that. For instance, I remember an essay in *Cahiers du Cinéma* on *Les chansons d'amour* that said that the only interesting thing the film had in connection to the New Wave [is] that it's the New Wave as seen by gays. And *that*, that annoyed me!

Obviously there's something there along those lines, all the more so since the New Wave was pretty much homophobic and the only gays in the New Wave (Jacques Demy mainly) were always very much hidden and involved in transformism.[8] Not that that's not interesting, but it annoys me if the film is reduced to that.

JN: The teenager played by Grégoire Leprince-Ringuet in *Les chansons d'amour* has classic homosexual literature in his library, like the novels of Edmund White and Hervé Guibert. Do you think that literature still has this identitary impact on younger generations?

CH: Well, I can just say that was very much the case for me. Before I was in a place to be able to say I was really homosexual, I read lots of gay authors. I remember very clearly discovering Hervé Guibert in eleventh grade, then reading Jean Genet. I know for sure that when I started to get interested in films by André Téchiné, Patrice Chéreau, Luchino Visconti, Fassbinder, Pedro Almodóvar—when I was fifteen or sixteen, I wouldn't have said so—it was because these directors were gay; at the time, I didn't know they were. But I felt there was something that spoke to me, the way the actors were filmed, the notion of the illicit. All this has so much to do with illicitness. These were often rather dark, very tortured works, because it was about people who experienced their homosexuality in a conflicted way through their films, at least at first viewing.

Anyway, I very much think that art is a way to project oneself into one's sexual and romantic life. It must be the same thing for heterosexuals. I can also see it with Facebook, where I'm frequently contacted by people who have read my novels or seen my films and who, after a few exchanges, need to talk to me about their sexuality. It's quite clear that there's something for them there that gets somewhat mixed up between their appreciation of a film like *Les chansons d'amour* and being able to say, "I'm gay." It's indeed pretty identity based for them.

DOING AND QUEERING FAMILY

JN: A central theme emerges from your literary production: family, whether it be from the angle of siblings or that of often conflictual relationships between parents and children. Do you also broach representations of the family in film from the angle of the adolescent revolting against his family?

CH: I wouldn't agree with that because I think there are almost no novels that do not talk about family. I'm often rather embarrassed when people tell me I talk so much about family. I do write more stories about families than about the business world, for example. However, I have no score to settle with my family; I really don't think so. I sometimes very much appreciate people like Hervé Guibert, who wrote an incredibly violent book called *Mes parents*.

When my mother goes to see *Ma mère*, she does not say to me, "What are you doing talking about our relationship or about any inappropriate gestures I might have made?" even if afterward, all alone, she thinks all this is a bit odd. In any case, we've never had that kind of conversation. As I come from a family that splintered because of my father's death, this may also give me another kind of freedom. I'm not at all in a situation of "Families, I hate you!" I'm not in a rebellious mode toward my family. Maybe that comes from my homosexuality.

I remember that when I was fifteen or sixteen, I thought I was going to be gay. It was also just as clear that I was going to have children. I've never associated the notion of being gay with not having a family. So maybe in my novels and films I prefer to show that a family is not necessarily connected to a predetermined setting: daddy, mommy, children. More to the point, I invent all kinds of families; as a result, it can seem to be an attack on family values.

JN: Also, as a result, you create erotic tensions at the very heart of the families you describe.

CH: Yes, I can easily see that in the relationship between brothers in *Dans Paris* or in the relationship between sisters in *Non, ma fille*. There is a type of sensuality within the family that interests me. I have this idea that sexuality is a family issue. It's something that is taken care of without questioning. Obviously I go all the way when I make a film like *Ma mère*.

Anyway, you can immediately see it when you spend the night at a friend's house when you're young that, in other people's families, there's an extra excitement, an apprehension. Prohibitions about having sex are different depending on whether you're in a strange family context or in your own family context. I think people's sensuality is shared, and you figure that out when you meet your lovers' siblings. I want to get past the idea of fraternal tenderness, mother-child tenderness, and so on, so that we can see how the family is also a matter of sexual upbringing.

JN: While you claim responsibility for this adolescent figure, you paradoxically take on a "classic" voice in order to succeed in the world of Parisian cinema, meaning in particular *Cahiers du Cinéma*. Was this obvious to you that you needed to become part of this cinematic institution branded as a voice of the New Wave?

CH: I remember all too well when I was in junior high that I'd go to buy *Cahiers du Cinéma* in a little newsstand in the village. For me, that was an occasion. I came to *Cahiers du Cinéma* because I started to get interested in François Truffaut's films, and I'd seen that he'd been published there. After that, I did have a very classic education, an academic French education: *Cahiers du Cinéma*, a filmmaker's retrospective. It seemed obvious to me when I got to Paris that I should hand in my résumé at the Passage de la Boule Blanche,[9] with my heart in my throat.

JN: What did it mean for you to be a film critic?

CH: It was more important for me than making a short film. I realize it's my failing, my handicap, because I always do this in my films. I've always thought that making films involved thinking about others' films and about defining a particular idea about cinema. That's always been the assumption of *Cahiers du Cinéma* (much less so these days), which is to say, "Okay, maybe it's a good film, but it's of no interest to us because we're trying to stand for a particular idea about film." I acquired this standpoint quite early on as a film buff. I was very dogmatic when I was a student film buff, and I still am today. Succeeding in Paris is very important for me.

I never wrote bona fide reviews for *Cahiers du Cinéma*. I never wanted to become a film journalist because I got to a point where it was becoming a profession in itself. Before, it was a transition job for directors. I think it was Truffaut or Godard who said, "Writing a film review is already making films." What I really did was more like a film column.

The job of a film critic has changed quite a lot. I feel very keenly that I'm a dinosaur in that respect. I have it in my head that film critics had the same education as me and, therefore, they had read their Rossellini, they had learned their Rivette by heart, and that they were not taken in by the manipulation of film.

JN: Speaking of that, as a spectator, you sometimes call to mind contemporary cinematic production in a wise and sometimes controversial way. In fact, you've written an article, published in *Cahiers du Cinéma* in 1998, called "The Sad Morals of French Cinema."[10] Apart from the hostile feelings it may have brought up for you, does it suggest that your critical mind is permanently active?

CH: At the time, I never thought that the column would have such repercussions. But I could write just about the same thing today (I would be less severe with Robert Guédiguian). Today, I still criticize the idea of fabrication, the false values of French cinema. This is a French "cinema of power" that I cannot stand.[11]

I often give my opinion. There are only a few of us in the cinema world to do so. I have the reputation of the little bastard who, for all intents and purposes—out of bitterness, jealousy, and I don't know what else—speaks badly about others. As a result, I've never gotten a César, and I've got a bad name within the French cinema world. At the same time, however, I'm lucky that my films have been rather well received by the critics and have pretty much been financial successes. Thus, for the moment, no one can really make trouble for me because of it. I prefer to like films rather than not like them.

I've always stood up for new film directors that I find very interesting, such as Mia Hansen-Løve, Bertrand Bonello, Jean-Paul Civeyrac, Gaël Morel, Sophie Letourneur [*trails off*]. The only thing people remember is that I think that Maïwenn's films are dreadful and very bad news for French cinema. It annoys me that films like *Polisse* [Maïwenn (Le Besco), 2011] are valued.

Another example is *The Artist* [Hazanavicius, 2011]. I criticize the fact that they're claiming that it's an auteur film. For me, it's a commercial film. I find that it has had a certain success; but when it's touted as an auteur film, that's where I draw the line. It's a film made for the industry; it's not at all marginal. It's actually structured on the very idea of classicism!

JN: Throughout the interviews you've given in the past ten years, you are often defined as a "child of the New Wave," which in France is not always a compliment. How do you explain this still rather enduring rejection from what the cinema of the New Wave has been?

CH: I think I have become a child of the New Wave, in particular with *Dans Paris*. This was really a return to French cinema for me, an attempt to make a very French film, a way for me to say that the golden era of French film is the New Wave. Now, it's also true that this is something that foreigners can't quite understand, that this is not a universally accepted idea. The majority of current producers consider that the New Wave killed French cinema. It's the same thing for most actors. An auteur film today is always assimilated into the New Wave except that very few directors are interested in the movement. It was more or less in this sense that I could be said to be indulgent.

I said that my critical eye is a handicap, because I make films in reaction to other people's films. Sometimes I also find myself to be indulgent with a particular idea of French cinema. Sometimes that keeps me from getting on with things, but this comes from my adolescence as a film buff with people like Truffaut, Godard, and others. I admired their journey. I think I understood their thoughts about film and why we make films. It's no picnic, making movies. But at the same time, the way film was being made in the 1960s doesn't work today. You can't hope to do the same thing today, because they have already done that.

Then, when I saw the attacks levied against *Les chansons d'amour* or *Dans Paris,* I decided, "Okay, let's go on sticking their noses in it!" And *La belle personne* came specifically from that. Three times might have been a bit hard on that position, and it earned me a label. I'm not a child of the New Wave insofar as I am more of a grandchild, which would allow me to be much freer in relation to them.

In one sense, I find it interesting to revisit the ideas of the New Wave today by applying them to a screenplay, so that it's not the subject of the film that makes the film; instead it is the production. People don't understand this idea anymore; consequently it's an idea that is essential for me. That's why I stand up for people like Jim Jarmusch, Nanni Moretti, Pedro Almodóvar, and others, the great auteurs for whom there is no subject in a film; the subject is the production. Without talking about postmodernism, we could say that we've moved on to something else and that each one of us has to reexamine our thoughts about that something else by holding on to some humanist values concerning production. Today very few journalists know anything at all about production. The number of people who write for newspapers without knowing anything about film is astounding!

What a film director can do is to work on form, to try and find form in little things that are current, forms that in any case could represent the present. That's the lesson of the New Wave. I can better relate something about the world by going around filming my girlfriend in the streets of Paris than by making a film about schools, prisons, the police. This is a particularly French idea; Americans have never had it. When New Wave critics went to see the great American filmmakers to brag about their production practices, the Americans said that it was quite simply a matter of telling a story well or not. I really treasure this lesson I learned from the New Wave. Because for me, as soon as I feel that a subject is taking over in my films, I tend to sabotage my screenplays; this gives me some space, some freedom to invent form.

*Non, ma fill*e is without doubt the most extravagant in this respect, where I am working on the idea of a family story in which a character tries to break free from his or her family as well as the issue of motherhood today. When I realized that I was making a film that was actually a society piece for *Elle*, I resolved to drop this Breton legend right in the middle of it so that I could show the viewer, "No, that's not what it is!" I know very well that I get on the viewer's nerves doing that.[12] It's the same thing I'm working on in *Les chansons d'amour* or in *Les bien-aimés*. The idea is to push the viewer to stop deluding him- or herself about the story or the language and to get back to the role of the spectator who is faced with forms and that it's the form that creates interest and reflection.

JN: It's often said that you had a direct legacy from Jacques Demy—probably because of the musical genre—which could conceal other important influences in your work, such as Jean-Luc Godard or Jean Eustache. To which New Wave auteurs do you feel closest?

CH: Someone I became quickly fond of was Demy, but definitely because of the gay angle. The first film of Demy's that I saw in a cinema was *Trois places pour le 26* [1988]. And for me, *Lola* [1961] is a fabulous gay film. Clearly, it's not a coincidence that all gay men love *Les parapluies de Cherbourg* [*The Umbrellas of Cherbourg*, 1964] or *Les demoiselles de Rochefort* [*The Young Girls of Rochefort*, 1967] despite the fact that there isn't a single gay person in either one. It's because there is indeed a queer spirit there that isn't just the "Fée des lilas" ["Lilac Fairy"] thing or the predominance of pink in *Peau d'âne* [*Donkey Skin*, 1970].

After that, I turned to Truffaut, just about the time when his correspondence was published and when he died. Reading Truffaut—especially his articles in *Cahiers*—is like reading a manual for how to become a film director. Soon after Truffaut, it was Godard and then Rivette. I remember writing about Rivette's *La religieuse* [*The Nun*, 1966] when I was in my last year of high school, connecting it with Alain Cavalier's *Thérèse* [1986], which had just come out. It took me a long time to like Rohmer. For quite some time, he didn't do anything for me. The first one I saw wasn't the best; it was *L'ami de mon amie* [*Boyfriends and Girlfriends*, 1987], which was difficult to get into regardless. I remember rediscovering Rohmer with *La femme de l'aviateur* [*The Aviator's Wife*, 1981] when there was a retrospective in Rennes. I loved that film and *Le genou de Claire* [*Claire's Knee*, 1970], too. I really learned to like Rohmer a lot when I started making films. He's a very difficult director to understand, a total production director. I think I wasn't sufficiently prepared for Rohmer.

Whereas with Godard, even if in theory he's very complicated, he's in fact very seductive for the adolescent film buff. When you're with him, you think, "Wow, that's great. We can do anything!" I found the punk side of Godard seductive. I always like Godard, even his difficult films, like *Soigne ta droite* [*Keep Your Right Up*, 1987] That was intense.

It's true that there's a kind of education associated with these directors. It's clear that afterward I was more interested in them than in directors like Claude Sautet, who seriously gets on my nerves.

JN: How do you work with the legacy of the New Wave? Is it more in the screenplay, in the production, in the editing that you recollect that cinema?

CH: I'd be lying if I said that I took another look at four Godard films before starting a shoot. I refer to him very often with the actors because we frequently talk about New Wave directors; but we forget the inventiveness of New Wave actors. I know that I have a taste for actors' enthusiasm [*lyrisme*], and I need a mixture of spontaneity and musicality/sensitivity [*lyrisme*].[13] And that's why when I came upon Louis Garrel, I adopted his lyricism. I feel like this explains to actors what I expect of them, a kind of availability, but not in the naturalist sense. I'd never show a film by Maurice Pialat to an actor.

Yet I don't hesitate to make reference to New Wave filmmaking, whether it's in the editing or in the filming. I make movies because I've seen other movies. It's inevitable; there aren't that many possible situations in film. When you're setting up a shot, someone else's shot very often comes into your head. And if it's a New Wave shot that comes to me, I'm not going to change it because they've already done that. On the contrary. It's amusing to see what could happen these days with another actor or with different lighting. And that's where it's going to play out.

I think [the New Wave] did exactly the same thing with Renoir's or Hitchcock's films or, say, what Rohmer did with Mizoguchi's films. Hitchcock did the same thing with Griffith. As I see it, for filmmakers working in the film industry, it is nothing more than thinking about the films they saw when they were teenagers. Film is nothing but recollection. That's why I get so annoyed when other directors contend that they've invented something and claim they've never seen any films. I feel it's just as idiotic as when someone who starts writing a novel set in the beginning of the twentieth century among aristocratic circles in an atmosphere of memory and says, "Wow, terrific! I'm inventing something new!" [They say it as if] they haven't read Proust. It's totally ridiculous.

JN: Apart from the auteurs of the New Wave, do you feel close to French gay underground cinema from the 1970s epitomized by Lionel Soukaz, Philippe Vallois, Paul Vecchiali, or even Guy Gilles?

CH: I don't know them. I didn't know them when I starting to make films. I know that there was a Guy Gilles retrospective at the La Rochelle festival a few years ago and as a result they edited a DVD boxed set.[14] That's how I got to know him. I've never seen a single film by Philippe Vallois. As for Vecchiali, I remember seeing one of his films when I was a student; it was called *Encore* [*Once More*, 1988], about AIDS. It was done in long take, which I found very impressive. I also remember a film called *Le café des Jules* [1989], which I loved. That's where I spotted Brigitte Roüan, whom I then picked for *Les chansons d'amour*. But I don't know his films very well. I saw *Femmes femmes* [1974] when it first came out on DVD not so long ago. But I wouldn't say that those directors were an important influence in my development.

JN: It's surprising you don't know Philippe Vallois's *Johan, mon été 75* [*Johan, One Summer 1975*, 1976]. It has so many important resonances with *Homme au bain*, in particular in regard to the treatment of the image of the masculine body, of dance, or even of evoking homosexual desire.

CH: I admit that [*Johan*] is a gap in my culture. For gay cinema, it's the same thing. I discovered Warhol and Morrissey rather late. I was very impressed by them. *Homme au bain* was very connected to *Flesh* [1968], as was Jonas Mekas.

JN: Maybe it was also because underground gay film was not very available in France at the time?

CH: Absolutely. I remember when I came to Paris in 1995, there was a gay film night at the l'Entrepôt cinema. That's where I discovered Rémi Lange, who's made *Omelette* [1998]. I was really very impressed by this film. I think Lange had seen those films.

JN: In the '80s and '90s in France, there was a swell of new, younger directors who broached the gay theme, like André Téchiné, Patrice Chéreau, Gaël Morel, Jacques Nolot, or even François Ozon. How do you see yourself in relation to them?

CH: The gay directors I knew then were Téchiné and Chéreau, who weren't really in underground film. I liked them very much. That was totally a cinema "du milieu." I think I developed my aesthetic in opposition to them. I'm Téchiné's and Chéreau's "son," and like in any classic relationship, I feel like my films became the rejection of theirs, especially in regard to homosexuality. They're people I quite respect. It was a way for me to find a legitimacy for my existence.

I admire *Les roseaux sauvages* [*Wild Reeds*, 1994], his last films less so. It's a pity he didn't become the French Clint Eastwood. I think he is a great classic director. I understand that this annoys him. He wants to be an innovator in film, and I'm not so sure.

I ran into Chéreau, who asked me to read the script for *Intimité* [*Intimacy*, 2001]. I remember a meeting with him where I'd given him my opinion on a couple things. I loved *Ceux qui m'aiment prendront le train* [*Those Who Love Me Can Take the Train*, 1998]. It touched me in an extraordinary way. I had a love affair with this film. I saw it countless times. I wrote a column in *Cahiers* about it for which I was pretty badly criticized because other critics had never been quite frank with Chéreau. Now that I'm making films myself, I would be even more embarrassed by this film, by the form of his film.

François Ozon, who must be about my age, started long before me. He was already an established director when I started making films. For that matter, I think he was somewhat irritated when several gay directors showed up as competition for the top spot. We don't really make the same kind of films. I don't think he likes the New Wave. In fact, I think he hates it.

I had very much liked *Gouttes d'eau sur pierres brûlantes* [*Water Drops on Burning Rocks*, 2000] and *Les amants criminels* [*Criminal Lovers*, 1999], too, because this was where he showed he was at ease with his artificiality. I like when he accepts his "story" side. He really likes his shots to be orderly and clean, without any excess. Furthermore, he is the camera operator.[15] Personally, I really like giving a feeling of chaos, which, I hope, ends up giving a bit of grace.

I'd like to work in the comic genre and to twist it the way he does in *8 femmes* [*8 Women*, 2002] or more recently in *Potiche* [*Trophy Wife*, 2010]. I don't really know how to do that very well—maybe because I come from a more working-class background than he does. That's why I have more of a tendency to take on elitist-type things.

JN: Do you not consider your recent collaboration with Mikael Buch on the screenplay for the comedy *Let My People Go* [2011] to be part of your oeuvre?

CH: These are two very different things for me. When I'm a screenwriter, I'm nothing. I'm not really the author. I'm presently working on the script for Louis Garrel's first feature film, and once more I feel like I'm a technician.[16] I generally help friends out. I write fairly easily; and I give them text, and they do with it whatever they like.

JN: Do you find it pertinent to define yourself as a gay or a queer artist?

CH: I don't find it discreditable. I remember that when Guillaume Dustan launched his gay section at Éditions Balland, he wanted me to write a book for them, and we met. I wasn't really that excited about what he was writing. Today, I would be less critical. I told him that a gay section was a bookseller's problem: it means something if booksellers are putting books into gay sections. These days, I'd be less uncompromising about it because I find it annoying to be harassed for it. For instance, the "Gérards of cinema,"[17] a rather humorous type of thing, really irritated me when they did a parody of *Homme au bain*, saying, "Oh, Christophe Honoré made us a film about suburban fairies!" After that I felt super gay. This started up again this year with *Les bien-aimés*, with a kind of "we've had enough of fairy films" attitude. It's quite clear to me that there is homophobia in the film industry. I haven't suffered too much from it, but someone like Gaël Morel has. [He experienced a homophobic response] when his film *Après lui* [2006] got criticized in *Le Monde* for not knowing how to direct film actresses like Catherine Deneuve and that he should go back to filming the prepubescent teenagers that turned him on.[18] I also remember when *Ma mère* came out, a film critic at *Technikart*[19] said that Honoré's production was driven by his cock! This kind of comment would push me to proudly declare myself a gay director and to get my back up against the homophobia that it comes out of. Nobody ever criticized François Truffaut for making heterosexual movies when he filmed Deneuve, with whom he was sleeping. If I make a film with François Sagat, inevitably it must be because I'm sleeping with him, and that's why I want to make a film with him, or that I want to sleep with him or put my actors' asses on display!

It's also true that there are financial pressures. When I was making *Les bien-aimés*, producers did tell me, "This is too gay, whereas you could have had a hit if it had been more straight!" How could anyone say that these days? They think it; they're really convinced of it.

I don't feel I've ever made a "big old gay film." I really like *Homme au bain*, because it's a film that paints homosexuality in such a good light. On the other hand, I was pretty much criticized in the gay media for this film, which is funny. Anyway, there's rarely solidarity in the gay community.

I thought we'd moved on to other things after Téchiné and Chéreau, just as they had followed on after Pasolini and Fassbinder. I thought that the sex issue was more about class struggle, for instance, especially for Fassbinder. I thought that being a gay worker or middle-class person was not exactly the same thing. Or for Pasolini, in a sort of hedonism, it's more youth and beauty that took over. I tend to be more influenced when I'm working on gay themes rather than defining myself as a gay auteur.

JN: In an interview for *Têtu* magazine [September 2011], Louis Garrel calls you a "repressed straight." What do you make of this joke?

CH: I think he understands the relationship between the two of us. I have no kind of desire to do any producing with him. Maybe that annoys him a bit. He'd like me to give him more credit sometimes. He can easily see that it's more often the girls that are valued in my latest films. I do have a more sensual relationship, especially with Chiara or Ludivine, than with Louis, even in how I direct actors. The fact that I'm a father has an unsettling effect—it disturbs people who know me. But if we have to get back into that again, that's inconceivable! It scares me a little.

JN: Are you interested in queer studies insofar as it might apply to French culture?

CH: Very little. I read somewhere that I was attacked in queer studies, which is often a little radical. I think I was criticized for being bourgeois. I was also criticized in another article for a kind of bisexuality shared by everyone consensually.

I don't know Guy Hocquenghem's or Jean Genet's work very well, to speak only of these two. Only occasionally have I been interested in reading them. At present, I'm working on a play about the New Novel for the Avignon Festival [*Nouveau Roman*]; it includes Robert Pinget, the only gay in the group but in the closet. In this play, I took a university paper on queer studies that develops the fact that Pinget's only subject was homosexuality. I use this text rather violently: I put the actor playing Pinget on stage completely nude while another actor reads the queer-studies paper. Naturally, everybody knows that sexuality is one of the sources for all artistic creation. All the same, my own sexuality isn't social. I'm also working on a novel that's really about the subject of a homosexual narrator who's starting to become paranoid.

It's still a little complicated for me because I don't think that homosexuality is a subject in itself. Homophobia can be a subject. I've written another play, *La faculté*, which will be mounted this year in Avignon produced by Éric Vignier.[20] It's a play about a homosexual crime that everyone considers to be a racist crime, with the notion that the racist side is more important than the homosexual one.

I often feel a homophobic aggressiveness—not in my personal life, of course. I live in the eleventh arrondissement of Paris, I work on film [*pause*]. So nobody's ever really given me a hard time. But I do feel that critics are often just there about to check off the homosexual parts of my films.

JN: Throughout your filmic production, a family of regular collaborators has formed around you, especially Louis Garrel, Chiara Mastroianni, and Alex Beaupain. Was this something you were already hoping for when you started making film? What dynamic does having this kind of complicity bring to your writing or to your filming?

CH: It wasn't always already there. Between *17 fois Cécile Cassard* and *Ma mère*, I don't think there is a single actor in common between the two. On the other hand, I did take Romain Duris, from my first film, for *Dans Paris*. It wasn't so much the idea that I could work better with the same actors; for me, it was an additional difficulty, a challenge. Working again with an actor is more difficult than working with a new actor, no matter what people think. Of course, it's easier from the perspective of a friendly relationship. However, desire, seduction—everything that's fairly mysterious and obscene in the rapport that develops between every actor/actress and the director—can crumble.

Any film with a new actor is about both chipping away at the wall bit by bit and acknowledging that you're looking at him and he acknowledges that *he* really wants you to look at him. Once the rapport crumbles, you can't rebuild it; that would be ridiculous. So at that point, you've got to try something else. So, I have the feeling that this is going to take me further in my work of directing actors than to work with the same ones. For instance, I find that in *Les bien-aimés*, Chiara Mastroianni wouldn't have been able (me either) to play that role that way if this had been the first film we'd made together. It requires more feverish and more vulnerable acting.

I could write a lot of characters like in *Les chansons d'amour* and have them played by other actors. That would be enough and would create new characters. However, I'd have to admit that when I'm writing the screenplay, I'm thinking of my actors like Louis Garrel, and so that forces me to reinvent my characters.

I discovered [Garrel] when filming *Ma mère*. I discovered his comic talent off-stage, and as a result, I made *Dans Paris* so I could benefit from his energy. Once I'd shown this adolescent side of him, I wanted to push him into adulthood. He also had a new face of virility that girls like, and boys too. I found it troubling to make a film much more focused on Louis's face, so I made *Les chansons d'amour*. And then I felt I wanted to give him a skill and to stop making him a permanent teenager, which brought me to the film *La belle personne*. In *Non, ma fille tu n'iras pas danser* and *Les bien-aimés*, I thought I needed to switch up the process and make it so that he wouldn't be an attraction any more but somebody that nobody cares about. If he's not the subject of the film anymore, how do you work with him to bring out another character that, in theory, the story doesn't need?

Working with actors is all about [film] form. Working with actors a second time forces me to think about formal considerations. With Romain Duris, we did *17 fois Cécile Cassard*, in which he has this twisting temperament: he sings, he dances, bringing out his rather feminine side. Even more, he plays a gay, which he'd never done before that. Then [in *Dans Paris*], I wanted to get rid of this absurd seduction that Romain has in the shot when I put him in bed with mediocre underwear and T-shirt and, then, we'll tell him "don't move." We'll lock him up, there won't be any girls, and there will be Guy Marchand, just to see how that could work. I wanted to slow him down. I know that I want to work with Romain Duris again on something else.

Still, I get the feeling that there is a danger for the public in repeat work with the same actors. *Les bien-aimés*, for instance, didn't work as well because many people wondered whether it was the same thing as *Les chansons d'amour*. Newness is a premium with most directors. Jacques Audiard, for instance, never works with a single actor that he's worked with before. You always have to find new faces. Personally, I hate this type of feat, both as an actor and as a director. So I'd have to say that in this matter I'm out of fashion.

JN: Talking about working with actors who've already got a cinematic history, you've chosen for roles as mothers Marie-Christine Barrault, Marie-France Pisier, and Catherine Deneuve, keeping their characters from films done with Truffaut or Rohmer. Do you filmically construct these families with this heritage in mind?

CH: In these cases, I try to invent my own form. It's true that for the women of that generation, these actresses are of course the matriarchs of the films and, thus, they're more likely than not to be playing the roles of mothers. And another thing, these aren't exactly exemplary characters: Marie-France Pisier plays an absent mother; she blows through, gives out erotic impulses in this apartment, and then goes off. I felt this strongly with this actress. It's the reverse with Marie-Christine Barrault; she's a castrating mother who doesn't want her daughters to be any different from her. Catherine Deneuve is a loving mother who always seems happy but isn't all that happy. I put together this role for her because I quickly knew that she wanted to be in the film.

JN: Was it the same sort of cinematic genealogy that you had for Chiara Mastroianni in *Les chansons d'amour*, where, just like Catherine Deneuve in *Les parapluies de Cherbourg*, she ends up with an Epiphany Kings' crown on her head?

CH: During the filming, I wasn't necessarily thinking about the Epiphany Kings' cake in *Les parapluies de Cherbourg*, but when I saw Chiara with a crown on, I thought I couldn't not keep that. But she doesn't have the same role at all; she's not the main character of my film. It's not an allusion; I'm not really very fond of that, contrary to what people think. I'm not that kind of fetishist director. For example, I'm not really that much of a fan of Quentin Tarantino. My approach is more Rivette, like when he said, "You have to leave bad shots in the film; they're just as much a part of the film as the good ones." This is why I don't want people doing a "the making of . . ." of my films. In my films, the "making of" is already included. I rather like leaving in the ideas that were going through my head at the time, the books I was reading then, something I'd heard the night before. I rather like the idea that my films are the documentaries of the moments when we were filming. And since I have no attachment to the screenplay, I often rewrite a third time to adapt it to the actors.

JN: You have, besides, filmed your brother Julien Honoré, in *Non, ma fille*.[21] Was that your way of injecting family realism into the film? Are you conscious of how much autobiographical material you bring to your films and how indiscreet that may be perceived to be?

CH: I really wrote that role for him. I have three brothers. I wanted him to have the same role as what he had in our family: the funny guy who never took anything seriously, whereas in reality, he's rather more serious than the others. I found it amusing, and at the same time, I was very demanding with him because I kept saying to him, "But isn't that what you do when we're with Mom?" What I was more or less saying to him was not to be an actor, and that's pretty violent and cruel.

I have no problem accepting that my actors' truth is not what they live in their everyday lives. Their truth, that's my way of seeing them. For my little brother, of course, my way of seeing is the truth, since I was already born when he was born and, moreover, there's a big age difference between us.

I used Julien a lot when writing *Dans Paris* and *Les chansons d'amour*. I stole his convoluted diction, the way he has of being lyrical and deadpan. I gave the role to Louis Garrel afterward because I'd have a hard time seeing my brother in a main role in my films. Once again, it's kind of obscene to destroy your rapport with your little brother. I don't feel sufficiently prepared for that.

NOVEMBER 2, 2012

DEATH, LOVE, AND DESIRE

JN: In Georges Bataille's adaptation of *Ma mère*, you deal directly with the theme of incest and with obscenity within the family. The families in your films most often function on the verge of sexual promiscuity. How do you capture these intrafamilial tensions on the screen?

CH: I don't really know. And anyway it's easier to capture it cinematically than to get it in real life, insofar as it's among actors and they're not in the same family. It doesn't go by way of a storyboard or rehearsal. It really comes from expanding a dialogue, for example, in *Les chansons d'amour* or *Les bien-aimés*, where Catherine Deneuve starts talking to her daughter about the STDs she'd had. I have this idea that the family is a privileged locus for talking about one's sexuality rather than a place where one defines one's sexuality. Obviously this is exactly the opposite of what most people think.

Most of my stories take place in a family landscape. The first link that connects characters is often a filial sort of link, and I rarely bring outsiders into this family. The most blatant for me is, like in *Dans Paris*, the sensuality you can have between two brothers or father and brother, where they share the same bed, the same clothes. The bed is no longer a place of intimacy and secrecy but one of sharing. From a cinematic standpoint, I seem to deal with beds as if they were dining-room tables. There are always many people around them. You can see it in the bed in *Dans Paris,* for example: everybody ends up there. The bedroom for me would be a guest area. It also works through a change in décor.

The apartment in *Dans Paris* is entirely re-created, even if it's a real apartment. Since I like to do bed scenes and because you always have to have some critical distance to film them, they are always bedrooms that aren't really bedrooms.

JN: Families in your films are always tragically marked by the grief of one of their close friends, and this often happens in the beginning of the narration. Other than the autobiographical dimension, can you tell me how death can be a creative element for you?

CH: I've realized it over the years. My stories weren't tragic in the sense of a tragedy in which you always expect catastrophe as the endpoint of a plot line. Rather, I'm attracted by stories that start with a catastrophe (in this case death), and then I see what can be done with that. They're survival stories, which makes them more optimistic in my view. I don't really have any explanation for these things. For instance, I notice that I'm not very happy when I end a film with a death. For me, it's one of those important things in *Les bien-aimés,* that the death of Chiara does not signal the end of the film; this certainly poses questions for those who see the end of the film as an epilogue. In that case, two-thirds of *Les chansons d'amour* would be an epilogue! For me, it's more the idea that death triggers the story.

JN: In *Homme au bain,* the estrangement of the beloved is experienced as grief by the character played by François Sagat. He hopelessly attempts to substitute this with other boys. The Breton folk legend in *Non ma fille n'iras pas danser* is also about the relationships between desire for the other and the death of the object in love. Are the relations between Eros and Thanatos still pertinent do you think, and how do you manage to make them current?

CH: Yes, anyway, I do think it's still pertinent today—experience tells us it is. The feeling related to a breakup is in any case very close to that related to the grief of injustice, anger. It's difficult to explain because it's not a theory for me, even if I feel I'm getting close to something Roland Barthes might have written. Afterward, it's always a little too easy to give it an autobiographical explanation. Sorrow generates fiction. Converting your sorrow into "happy" sorrow, thus into fiction, is sort of my philosophy of life; it may be somewhat silly, but it seems rather essential to me. It's clear to me that death in my stories does not equal ending life. It's clear to me in my next project—an adaptation of Ovid's *Metamorphoses*—and it's no coincidence that in Ovid's text, when someone dies, he doesn't really die: he's transformed into a tree or a flower. There's a reference here to the Orpheus philosophy: Life-Death-Life. In any case, I tend not to treat death or a breakup as bad news. In the end, the permanence of things—in the permanence of a feeling of love—there is more morbidity, more lugubriousness, more desolation than in breakups. There's also certainly something there that belongs to the time period.

JN: You often talk about how AIDS affected a whole generation and its influence on our relationship to feelings of love. Could you expand on this idea and tell us how this epidemic colors your artistic creation?

CH: It colors my creation quite simply through an idea of emptiness. What stimulated me in literature, in cinema, in dance, and in the theater when I was a teenager were these people—Hervé Guibert, Bernard-Marie Koltès, Dominique Bagouet, Serge Daney, Jacques Demy—who should have been the ferrymen; they all died from AIDS. As a result, in contrast with other beginning artists who had the expectation of passing the baton—it's obvious for New Wave directors, who chose for themselves either Renoir or Rossellini as their father—I am of a generation of gay artists who were not able to talk with their elders. I think this brings about many things, especially the idea of starting out from chaos.

On the other hand, I don't think that AIDS has affected only the queers of my generation; I think it touches [us] in a broader way, because of the indoctrination we get in childhood that sex is connected to danger, that the stranger is connected to danger. There was a sense of terror in the late 1980s and early 1990s. I think that parents were entirely terrified about the thought of their children's sex life. It's always been full of danger, with the possibility of a baby, etcetera; but it's not exactly the same thing for a girl to think that she could get pregnant as it is to think that she could die from AIDS. I think that the discourse of terror has produced a generation who has, curiously, overinvested itself in feelings. In *Non, ma fille* or *Les bien-aimés*, it's clear that my characters are a little unsettled because of these inverted values, turning feeling into something solemn and serious.

JN: You have collaborated with, among others, Dennis Cooper and Adam Thirlwell, American and British authors who broach the issue of sexuality and pornography. How do you visualize the representation of sexual relations on screen? Do you see it as choreography as Dennis Cooper thinks about it, as in the matter of anilingus?

CH: That's really not a challenge that has been so much undertaken by the people of my generation but, rather, in French cinema, by people from the previous generation (Breillat, Vecchiali, Chéreau). They strongly challenged the issue of sexual representation and freedom from conventions, which they accomplished with the idea of moving toward more realism: actors really have sex, and so in theory, you "give birth" to shots that are cinematically different. I think I'm less naïve than they are: it's not really the act that interests us. The issue for people like me, Ozon, or Gaël Morel would be, "Is penetration really the most interesting thing to film?" Isn't it more disturbing to film a guy shaving a boy's butt or, like in *Ma mère*, a girl putting her finger in a boy's anus and then making her mother smell it? That way it's more a story about sexual practices. I tried to get away from that insufferable '80s thing, especially in heterosexual relations, where they showed sexual violence: all the women were getting sodomized, as if sodomy were the worst violent sexual act that you could do to someone. That's a superconventional thing about sexuality—I was going to say right-wing thing. So I'm all about variety in sexuality, putting the sexual where it's least expected.

To get back to the question, I think that I confronted the issue too early with my second film [*Ma mère*]. I wanted to take issue with this theme. It was rather violent because I hadn't thought to hire porno actors. I didn't at all want to do a "for real" thing; rather, I wanted to evoke a sexualized atmosphere, to build it, to put it onstage. It was pretty trying. It's not easy to do because despite everything, it's always going to be uncomfortable—lots of people on the set.

The reading that was done of this film afterward devastated me. The work was totally discredited. It took me a long time to get back to sex scenes. That's why I was glad to do a film like *Homme au bain*. Hiring someone like François Sagat was interesting. I didn't use him anything like the way Catherine Breillat did with Rocco Siffredi [*Anatomy of Hell*, 2004].

JN: From the teenage body of Grégoire Leprince-Ringuet to the bodybuilder physique of François Sagat by way of Romain Duris, you've given your public a great variety of men's bodies to look at. How do you work with these bodies?

CH: Everyone knows that bodies change according to the time period. There are types of bodies. It was interesting in *Homme au bain* to try and show that homosexuality could be communicated through very different bodies. In this film, François Sagat is treated like a dinosaur. He's part of an already outdated idea of homosexuality inherited from the '90s. François takes it on very nicely. He's someone who dreamed about models like Claudia Schiffer when he was a teenager. He used this superfemininity in his case to invent a supermasculinity. He ended up taking on a daintiness linked to his sexuality by fashioning the threatening body of a superman. Today, even if he is the subject of many gay men's fantasies, François's body is clearly completely out of sync with the generation of gays in their twenties and thirties, where the convention is almost like showing a lack of gratitude: the less effort you spend on your body, the punier it is, and then that becomes the trend, at least in Europe. Thus, I filmed a muscle body at the center of a story where it was already outdated. François Sagat's passivity (in any case, he's known for being mostly a bottom in porno films) is always a kind of "butch" passivity, a little slutty. Even he gets a kick out of it. On the other hand, the passivity of bodies like Omar's [Omar Ben Sellem] or Dustin's [Dustin Segura-Suarez] never incorporates the fact that it might discredit them. I think that François is convinced that this passivity discredits him as a man.

I'm no sociologist or philosopher, but I try to see how people are; consequently, it interests me to film different bodies. It interests me to film someone like Louis Garrel today. If I'd been making films in the '80s and filming Depardieu, it wouldn't have been the same body as Garrel's; and similarly in the '60s, filming Belmondo or Delon wouldn't have been the same body either, even less so Gabin or Jouvet in their time. I like that men's bodies evolve in films, just like women's bodies. As a director, at the very least you must be accurately attentive to this evolution of bodies. This works mainly by the choice of actors. Oddly, it doesn't work by desire. I do not desire Louis Garrel; if I did, I wouldn't have made another film with him. The desire for an actor has nothing to do with sexual desire, contrary to what was written by some critics for *Homme au bain*.

MUSIC, MUSICALS, AND DANCE

JN: How do you broach the subject of the musical in film? Are the Hollywood classics a reference for you?

CH: One day I'd like to make a Bob Fosse–style musical, but that's currently not possible in French film. I'm hearing that there are loads of plans for musicals. For example, Jacques Audiard would like to make one. Claire Denis, too. So much the better if *Les chansons d'amour* or *Les bien-aimés* managed to bring back a taste for this genre, even if in my opinion they're not musicals. Music doesn't really fit well with the French variety of realism.

JN: Starting with your first film, *17 fois Cécile Cassard*, music and song have always been present, and in this case with the re-creation of the song,

"Lola" sung by Romain Duris. At what point in the creative process do musical ideas come to you?

CH: It's rather strange because deep down, I don't like music. I'm neither passionate about music, nor do I have any musical training. Music doesn't come to me naturally. Before doing my first film, I was on a Pialat kick: [his] music pulls the spectator away from the film. Ideally, a silent movie has greater value for me than a musical film. Bit by bit, I noticed that my mise-en-scène was pretty much in sync with musical spheres and that it would be a pity not to take advantage of that. It turns out that my films have a fair bit of music in them. It really happens during the editing. There's very little music that I think about during the filming or even when writing the script. On the other hand, I've actually had music playing on the set for some sequences to give the actors a rhythm without, however, using it later on. Clearly, for *Les chansons d'amour* and *Les bien-aimés*, it was very different because we had to conceive and work out the music and the songs well before the filming.

JN: What difference is there in having the actors perform the songs in your films, something Jacques Demy, for instance, refused to do?

CH: As far as Demy is concerned, we're not looking for the same things. I like to have actors sing because I like it when they can't sing. I like to see their vulnerability in the singing segments. It feels like they forget they're acting; and as a result, they're focused on something other than the psychology or the blocking, and that lets me film them in laid-back situations. In Demy's films, the song is much more operatic. He was also much more under the influence of Michel Legrand than I am with Alex Beaupain.

JN: How does your collaboration work with Alex Beaupain?

CH: I don't listen to him, whereas I think that Demy listened tremendously to Legrand. His opinion doesn't interest me much. We're very good friends; that's why I can say that.

Above all, I give precedence to the acting, which might make his work very difficult for elaborating the melodic line. Even during the sound mixing, I sometimes undermix the voices, which produces something like mush, and for him, this is not always very satisfying musically. I'm not looking for a masterful musical sequence in my films; I'm more likely to steer Alex toward things he doesn't want. For instance, I told him he wasn't going to do the music for *Dans Paris* because I needed jazz. He hates jazz, and in the end, he did it for me. Our friendship sometimes lets me ask him for things he doesn't want to do.

JN: Recently you've staged the video of a song by Alex Beaupain, "Avant la haine." Was it a rewarding experience for you to take on a music genre?

CH: It's simply a matter of friendship and a combination of circumstances. It doesn't bring me anything; it's a day's filming. It's a kind of a pain in the ass to do music videos. I was happy to do it for him because it helped him out. I was happy to film Camélia Jordana. However, I am quite in awe of the work of some video directors like Romain Gavras. My video doesn't compare to this kind. I'd be very embarrassed to have to do a video with Mýa.

JN: You also use preexisting pop songs like "Amoureux solitaires" or "Ma biche" in the short *Hôtel Kuntz*. In that piece, the use of a song—first sung then screamed by the male lead—creates a disconnect and, then, some discomfort. It's a queer performance. Do you purposely twist primarily heterosexual love songs that way?

CH: I can't remember how I came to this song, "Ma biche." I think it was an association between the words *biche* [doe] and *faune* [faun], given that it was a request from Olivier Dubois [the main actor] to stage it like [Diaghilev's] *L'après-midi d'un faune*. I wanted to find an absurd element. If I remember, he sings it by ending with a piece of clothing on his head and howling. I thought this went very well with this actor.

What's interesting with popular songs is that when people already know them, and then you hit them with something that doesn't at all correspond with what they might have felt in the song, that creates, in my opinion, something surreal, trivial, and obscene that must be there to complete the film. I really like this short. I haven't done many. My first one, *Nous deux*, for example, is a veritable catastrophe.

JN: A moment ago, you were talking about the choreographer Dominique Bagouet. How would you characterize your association with the world of contemporary dance? Do you direct your actors the way a choreographer would?

CH: I was in a modern dance group when I came to Paris, then in a company that my girlfriend founded. We would often go to see performances, and we put on a little show; I enjoyed all this. As I'm curious, I have a spectator's rapport with dance. I have too much respect for modern dance to claim to be a choreographer in my films. It is true though that I like to have bodies move around in a certain way and with a certain rhythm.

JN: How did modern dancer Cédric Andrieux, who formerly danced with Merce Cunningham, happen to come to be on the set of *Les bien-aimés*?

CH: I noticed him in his sole appearance with Jérôme Bel.[22] I found it quite beautiful. I really like when films are a meeting place for people coming from different worlds. I found it interesting to entrust him to Chiara Mastroianni; I don't think there is an actress in the world any less excited by dance. Cédric and I visualized the choreography together. We also had to make do with Chiara's strengths because there was no way we would use a stand-in.

JN: Your characters, especially in *Les chansons d'amour* or *Les bien-aimés*, walk around a lot in the streets, whether it be Paris, London, or Montreal. Are these walking tours conceived like a dance, too?

CH: As a matter of course, I enjoy having my actors in movement when they're in the frame. I think that I make films about walking. I am a bit like Rousseau in that sense. The camera movement that I use the most in my films is a reverse-tracking shot [in which the camera faces and is] in front of the characters who are walking and talking. There are so many scenes of this type in *Les bien-aimés, Les chansons d'amour,* or *La belle personne*. I like it because, first of all, it requires an absent technical crew, thus liberating the set a bit. It also requires the director of photography to be restrained when installing lights, and, anyway, everything will be constantly changing. In that way, there is something along the order of freedom, and the actors are accurate when they walk and talk. It might be an easy way out, but I'm not the only one to do it! In addition, you have to make the link with the impermanence that my films convey, about people who don't really know where they are. I don't ever make films about wandering people; they're always people looking for a place. They aren't necessarily running away either. They're traipsing around.

JN: You often say you're a provincial living in Paris and not a Parisian. However, your take on Paris shows a deep knowledge of the neighborhoods and the atmosphere that might have a rapport with them. Few films have shown the essence of the tenth arrondissement or the sixteenth arrondissement as well as *Les chansons d'amour* or *La belle personne*. Do you agree that you use Paris not as a setting but as a character in its own right, which would then be an extension of the actors' performance?

CH: That actually comes from my stubborn and obstinate side of preferring to film continuously, despite what my assistant directors and producers want to do. What this means is that most of the time when you want to film in Paris, a city that is extremely complex for filming within the terms of the permits, you have to make considerable compromises, which then incurs erroneous geographic link shots (filming a calm street in the fifteenth district when the people are sitting in a café in the tenth). I'm kind of a pain about this stuff, but it's important to me. Consequently, Paris is like a character, and I very much respect the topography of locations. I try to make it so that places join up without any geographic fiction. Depending on the arrondissement, you aren't always working with the same police personnel or the same suppleness in what concerns the permissions agreements. For instance, on a film like *Les bien-aimés,* there was a change in [Parisian administration], and it was even more complicated than in my previous films. So I rewrote many of the scenes in *Les bien-aimés* because I could no longer go down the streets the way I had originally planned or into the apartments that corresponded to the streets. Chiara's apartment does in fact look out onto the street that she goes out onto.

La belle personne wasn't originally supposed to be in the sixteenth arrondissement because I'd found a high school in the twelfth that I liked very much. Once we realized it wasn't going to be possible to use that school, I found Lycée Molière, and as I'd already scoped out the streets in the twelfth, my crew suggested I keep that set of locations. I said, "no way," and we did all the filming in the sixteenth. This also forced me to redo all the work with the extras and the school's population. The film plays with timelessness. There are very few cell phones. The English teachers work with audio-cassette players, but truthfully, that's how they still do it in that school today! We didn't deface anything in the school; it really is in a very bad state. On the other hand, I had a good time furnishing a classroom with sculptures; that way, I told myself, a bunch of artistic things could crisscross.

I wanted to make a convent out of the location, but schools are outside the real world anyway. They're little ghettos in a city where there's very little movement. I also had fun getting some timelessness into their clothes. I certainly did not want to do a "hip young kids" film. I remember when I was a teenager, we didn't always like contemporary pop music, and we went looking for music from another generation. We also were working with the colors in the film so that it wasn't obvious whether we were in the 1970s, the '80s, or 2010, which is often the case in my films. In my opinion, interiors only look like 2010 in decorating magazines. If you go to your parents' house or anyone's house, there are always traces of the '70s, the '80s, etcetera.

JN: Was it also inspiring and easy for you to work on the New York urban fabric in *Homme au bain*?

CH: I filmed in New York City without any permits. This comes from the stroll I took with Chiara and Justin and from the places where we were invited to talk about *Non, ma fille.* I have an old and battered DV camera, and the idea was to work on a Jonas Mekas–type diary: you don't try to compose shots but to take a series of bad photos.

POLITICS AND QUEER CULTURE

JN: You're politically engaged, and you don't hesitate to say so, even if it's only by cosigning the artists' letter of opposition to the HADOPI Law[23] that appeared in *Libération* in 2009. Was *La belle personne,* an adaptation of *La princesse de Clèves* (which suffered heavy criticism from then-president Nicolas Sarkozy) a cinematic political act on your part?[24]

CH: I don't think of myself as an engaged director in the Sartrean sense. To stay with this thought, I'd say I'm much more in the spirit of the *nouveau roman.* These were people who were thoroughly engaged in their lives but who never, at any point in their lives, delivered a message. I consider myself a "manifesto" director. I'm more interested in responding to the disastrous atmosphere of the first years of Sarkozy with a film like *La belle personne* rather than making a film on a ministry.[25] I try to find more poetic answers. I'm not someone who lives in a bubble, but I wouldn't ever at any moment want my films to deliver a message. I'd feel like I was dealing in propaganda. I really think that what makes me sick the most in film is when a director takes over. I try to make films in which I delegate my power as much as possible. I really have a hard time with directors, especially French directors, with whom—from my perspective—I only see them taking over, either the actors or the spectators or the self-righteous approach. Abdellatif Kechiche,[26] for me, is a good example. It's the exact opposite of my films, and for me, that becomes a cinema of surveillance cameras and thus not at all what I want to do.

JN: As a director-citizen, what do you think of French universalism and the famous "Liberté, Égalité, Fraternité"?[27] Is *Homme au bain* your "défense et illustration"[28] on republican values in their gay Black, White, and Beur[29] version?

CH: I don't think about any of these things when I'm casting. I got over that watching Benetton ads in my youth. I think that to send a self-righteous message by putting a white person, a black person, and a yellow person together to show your antiracist politics and open-mindedness is an aesthetic vision of absolute stupidity and absolute ugliness. I *never* think about the sociological representation of my characters when I'm casting.

JN: Was filming the Parisian suburb of Gennevilliers[30] a challenge for you, especially the idea of the possibility of an openly homosexual life in situ?

CH: *Homme au bain* is a utopia, but there is nothing sociological about it. If there is a black man and an Arab man in a film, it's only because I did a large general casting call and that these particular people interested me as individuals. I didn't hire this black actor to represent black gays. For me, that would be an absolute disregard for the people that I'm filming, as it would be limiting them by their social or ethnic representation. That's not realism. It's not a photo of verisimilitude. I don't want to consider the problem of this ideological foolishness, like when I'm criticized for filming only white sons or daughters in *La belle personne*. This is where American foolishness is sometimes a bit frightening, but at the same time, it creates interesting things because they have a much wider diversity in their "livestock" than in France thanks to positive discrimination.[31] In France, when I organize a casting session, I encounter very few black or "beur" actors.

JN: Were you aware, then, when you were filming *Homme au bain* that in choosing François Sagat, you would be working on clichés of ethnic gay film? Sagat started out in Citébeur productions, and in those films he incarnated a gay beur from the projects.

CH: Yes, I knew about his beginnings. I was very attracted by the idea of going to Gennevilliers to film and to bring a body like François Sagat's, who, for the little thugs in the area who spend their time at the gym, was the ideal guy, exactly what they wanted to become. It amuses me very much to think that these people start dreaming about becoming something like a porn-star bottom from homo porn, clearly unaware! In a way, it's a bit of perversity on my part. After all, François is from Royan. He's a guy from the Vendée. He has nothing to do with the Parisian banlieue. I like Satyajit Ray not because he makes films with Indians or that as a gay man I can identify with the female characters or the heterosexuals in American films. As a matter of fact, maybe I'm superuniversalist! I film human beings. I don't film social or ethnic categories.

JN: How do you understand the political ambiguity in the aftermath of May '68 in France? Do you see any connection between the events of '68 and the way universalism is culturally and politically engaged in France?

CH: I don't connect May 1968 with universalism. I grew up in a period where we had to pay for May '68, pay for the *nouveau roman*, and pay for modern cinema. We figured that they were either ideological or artistic dead ends. We had to go back to good old novels with stories; the only valid cinema was an intelligent, popular cinema. Ideologically, it was a return to reality and not a utopian culture.

I strongly refuse this discourse and condemn it as very reactionary, conservative, and reconstructionist. Thus, in my films, I've revalorized the New Wave, modern cinema, the *nouveau roman,* and a certain idea of the sexual utopia of the '60s.

JN: Some French feminists, like Geneviève Sellier, blame the New Wave for having a masculine and heteronormative perspective, probably a reflection of French society of the '60s. Do you agree with this analysis?

CH: They're right. The New Wave is clearly a right-wing, macho, and homophobic movement. For Truffaut, Godard, or Rohmer, a man's position is a place of power and rarely a place of nervous agitation. They're not engaged directors and happily not; and that's how the representation of man's power got turned around, like in *Sirène du Mississippi* [Truffaut, *Mississippi Mermaid*, 1969]. However, they did create narrative structures that are much richer than the analysis of their themes. I'm not interested in doing a sociological reading of these people.

JN: Have you been influenced by Jean-Luc Godard's political cinema, and if yes, do you continue to be so?

CH: Godard's political cinema is different because at one time he wanted to stop making bourgeois films; otherwise he felt he was a traitor. You can easily see it in *Made in USA* [1966] or *Two or Three Things I Know about Her* [1967]. The strength of *La chinoise* [1967] is not in his Marxist discourse, which is a little ridiculous today. The strength of the film is in the editing, in the friction between false documentary and realism, the work with the actors or on the color. And that's where people like Godard haven't always been very clear in these questions, in all these questions; for example, we don't really know what they're saying about Palestine and all that. It's not very clear. Nonetheless, for me, he's still the superlative director because he is head and shoulders above others in form and in aesthetics.

JN: Do you have a Balzacian notion of your oeuvre, like Jacques Demy, or does that come gradually?

CH: I remember that when I was a teenager, I was very struck by that dynamic for people like Demy or Truffaut, who built a Balzacian-like structure in which everything fits together. But they're postwar directors who thought they had to re-create a history, to re-create a French narrative. For my generation, there's no more interest in doing that, on the contrary. All directors who claim to relate the world the way it is, masterfully and in a linear way, are wrong. I feel I am, because of my generation, condemned to impurity, to incompleteness, to diffraction. I totally accept this, and I cultivate it when I'm about to design a production in the theater or the opera *Dialogues des carmélites*[32] or even when I write a children's book. I am well aware that what's happening here is something along the lines of my own modernity, which does not correspond with the modernity of the

New Wave. Directors are no longer witnesses of the world, as they might have been in the time of Rossellini, since before a film even comes along, there are already forty thousand people who've recorded it, filmed it with their cell phones, etcetera. *Allemagne année zéro* (*Germany, Year Zero*, 1948) wouldn't have any other justification. You can't do anything more than take the chaos into consideration. Apart from the Parisian trilogy [*Dans Paris, Les chansons d'amours, La belle personne*] which were made within six months of each other and also give an idea about youth at the time Sarkozy came to power, my films aren't made with or against each other.

APPENDIX A

FILMOGRAPHY

NOUS DEUX (2000)

Directed by Christophe Honoré
Written by Christophe Honoré and Gilles Taurand
Produced by Sépia Productions
Director of photography: Jean-Marc Fabre
Editor: Guy Lecorne
Sound: Bernard Borel
Production designer: Françoise Doré
Costume designer: Pierre Canitrot
Composers of original music: Alex Beaupain, Pierre Beaupain
Cast: Philippe Calvario (Laurent), Geoffrey Greenhill, Julien Peny, Emma Piesse (Kate)
France, 35mm, color, 15 mins.

DIX-SEPT FOIS CÉCILE CASSARD (*SEVENTEEN TIMES CECILE CASSARD*, 2002)

Directed by Christophe Honoré
Written by Christophe Honoré
Produced by Sépia Production, ARP—Association des Auteurs Réalisateurs Producteurs (Paris), Art France Cinéma
Producers: Philippe Jacquier and Béatrice Mauduit
Assistant director: Sylvie Peyre
Director of photography: Rémy Chevrin
Editor: Chantal Hymans
Sound: Michel Casang, Valérie Deloof, Thierry Delor
Original music: Alex Beaupain

Production designer: Laurent Allaire
Costume designer: Pierre Canitrot
Casting: Richard Rousseau
Cast: Béatrice Dalle (Cécile Cassard), Romain Duris (Matthieu), Jeanne Balibar (Edith), Ange Ruzé (Erwann), Johan Oderio-Robles (Lucas), Tiago Manaïa (Tiago), Jérôme Kircher (Thierry), Julien Collet (Stéphane), Jérémy Sanguinetti (Julien), Marie Bunel (teacher), Fabio Zenoni, Robert Cantarella
France, 2002, 35mm, color, 105 mins.
Distributed by ARP Sélection

TOUT CONTRE LÉO (*CLOSE TO LEO*, 2002)

Directed by Christophe Honoré
Written by Diastème and Christophe Honoré
From the novel *Tout contre Léo* by Christophe Honoré
Producers: Sophie Deloche and Serge Moati
Assistant directors: Sylvie Peyre, Louise Narboni, Dominique Perrier
Director of photography: Rémy Chevrin
Sound: Michel Casang
Editor: Chantal Hymans
Production designer: Marie-Hélène Sulmoni
Costume designer: Pierre Canitrot
Original music by Alex Beaupain and Doc Mateo
Casting: Richard Rousseau and Marion Touitou
Cast: Yaniss Lespert (Marcel), Pierre Mignard (Léo), Marie Bunel (mother), Dominic Gould (father), Rodolphe Pauly (Tristan), Jérémie Lippmann (Pierrot), Louis Gonzales (Yvan), Joana Preiss (Yvan's mother)
France, TV movie, December 8, 2002, digital, color, 88 mins.

MA MÈRE (*MY MOTHER*, 2004)

Directed by Christophe Honoré
Written by Christophe Honoré
From the novel *Ma mère* by Georges Bataille
Produced by Gémini Films (Paris), Madragoa Filmes (Lisbon)
Producer: Paulo Branco
First assistant director: Sylvie Peyre
Director of photography: Hélène Louvart

Editor: Chantal Hymans
Sound: Jean-Claude Brisson
Production designer: Laurent Allaire
Costume designer: Pierre Canitrot
Makeup: Delphine Jaffart
Casting: Richard Rousseau
Cast: Isabelle Huppert (Hélène), Louis Garrel (Pierre), Emma de Caunes (Hansi), Joana Preiss (Réa), Jean-Baptiste Montagut (Loulou), Dominique Reymond (Marthe), Olivier Rabourdin (Robert), Philippe Duclos (father)
France, Portugal, Austria, Spain, 2004, 35mm, color, 110 mins.
Distributed by Le Petit Bureau

DANS PARIS (INSIDE PARIS, 2006)

Directed by Christophe Honoré
Written by Christophe Honoré
Produced by Gémini Films (Paris)
Producer: Paulo Branco
Assistant directors: Sylvie Peyre, François Tessier
Director of photography: Jean-Louis Vialard
Sound: Frédéric de Ravignan, Thierry Delor, Valérie Deloof
Editor: Chantal Hymans
Production designer: Samuel Deshors
Costume designer: Pierre Canitrot
Makeup artist: Caroline Philiponnat
Original music: Alex Beaupain
Casting: Richard Rousseau
Cast: Romain Duris (Paul), Louis Garrel (Jonathan), Joana Preiss (Anna), Guy Marchand (Mirko, the father), Alice Butaud (Alice), Marie-France Pisier (the mother), Héléna Noguerra (girl on the scooter), Judith El Zein (girl who believes it will rain), Annabelle Hettmann (girl in the window), Mathieu Funck-Brentano (boy with the cigarette), Lou Rambert-Preiss (Loup)
France, 2006, 35mm, color, 90 mins.
Distributed by Le Petit Bureau

LES CHANSONS D'AMOUR (LOVE SONGS, 2007)

Directed by Christophe Honoré

Written by Christophe Honoré
Produced by Alma Films Productions (Paris), Flach Films (Paris)
Producer: Paulo Branco
Assistant director: Sylvie Peyre
Director of photography: Rémy Chevrin
Sound: Guillaume Le Braz, Thierry Delor
Editor: Chantal Hymans
Original music and lyrics: Alex Beaupain
Production designer: Samuel Deshors
Costume designer: Pierre Canitrot
Casting: Richard Rousseau
Cast: Louis Garrel (Ismaël Benoliel), Ludivine Sagnier (Julie Pommeraye), Chiara Mastroianni (Jeanne), Clotilde Hesme (Alice), Grégoire Leprince-Ringuet (Erwann), Brigitte Roüan (Julie's mother), Alice Butaud (Jasmine, Julie's sister), Jean-Marie Winling (Julie's father), Yannick Renier (Gwendal), Annabelle Hettmann, Esteban Carvajal Alegria, Sylvain Tempier, Guillaume Clérice
France, 2007, 35mm, color, 100 mins.
Distributed by Bac Films

LA BELLE PERSONNE (*THE BEAUTIFUL PERSON*, 2008)

Directed by Christophe Honoré
Written by Christophe Honoré and Gilles Taurand
From the novel *La Princesse de Clèves* by Madame de Lafayette
Produced by Scarlett Production (Paris), Arte France Cinéma
Producers: Florence Dormoy and Joëy Faré
Assistant director: Sylvie Peyre
Director of photography: Laurent Brunet
Sound: Guillaume Le Braz, Thierry Delor
Composer of original music: Alex Beaupain
Composer of preexisting music: Nick Drake
Editor: Chantal Hymans
Production designer: Samuel Deshors
Costume designer: Pierre Canitrot
Cast: Louis Garrel (Jacques Nemours), Léa Seydoux (Junie de Chartres), Grégoire Leprince-Ringuet (Otto Clèves), Esteban Carvajal Alegria (Matthias de Chartres), Simon Truxillo (Henri), Agathe Bonitzer (Marie Vlois), Anaïs Demoustier (Catherine), Jacob Lyon (Jacob),

Tanel Derard (Tanel), Martin Siméon (Martin), Jeanne Audiard (Jeanne), Esther Garrel (Esther), Valérie Lang (Florence Perrin), Chantal Neuwirth (Nicole, la owner of the café Sully), Jean-Michel Portal (Estouteville), Dominic Gould (English teacher), Alice Butaud (Russian teacher), Clotilde Hesme (Mme. de Tournon, the librarian), Chiara Mastroianni (young woman at café), Mathilde Incerti (French teacher), Candice Zaccagnino (replacement Italian teacher), Julien Honoré

France, 2008, 35mm, color, 90 mins.
Distributed by Le Pacte

HÔTEL KUNTZ (2008)

Directed by Christophe Honoré
Written by Christophe Honoré
Producer: Agathe Berman
Coproducer: Béatrice Horn
Director of photography: David Chizallet
Production manager: Katya Laraison
Editor: Chantal Hymans
Sound: Guillaume Le Braz, Valérie Deloof, Thierry Delor
Costume designer: Pierre Canitrot
Cast: Olivier Dubois, Tanel Derard, Jacob Lyon, Lucas Ruffié, Simon Truxillo

France, 2008, 35mm, black and white, 15 mins.

NON MA FILLE, TU N'IRAS PAS DANSER (MAKING PLANS FOR LENA, 2009)

Directed by Christophe Honoré
Written by Christophe Honoré and Geneviève Brisac
Produced by Why Not Productions (Paris), France 3 Cinéma, Le Pacte (Paris)
Producer: Pascal Caucheteux
Executive producer: Béatrice Mauduit
Director of production: Isabelle Tillou
Assistant director: Sylvie Peyre
Unit director: Thibault Mattei
Director of photography: Laurent Brunet
Editor: Chantal Hymans
Sound: Guillaume Le Braz, Valerie de Loof, Thierry Delor

Production designer: Samuel Deshors
Costume designer: Pierre Canitrot
Casting: Richard Rousseau
Cast: Chiara Mastroianni (Léna), Marina Foïs (Frédérique), Marie-Christine Barrault (Annie), Jean-Marc Barr (Nigel), Marcial Di Fonzo Bo (Thibault), Fred Ulysse (Michel), Julien Honoré (Gulven), Alice Butaud (Elise), Louis Garrel (Simon), Caroline Sihol (florist), Donatien Suner (Anton), Lou Pasquerault (Augustine), Jean-Baptiste Fonck (José)
France, 2009, 35mm, color, 105 mins.
Distributed by Le Pacte

HOMME AU BAIN (*MAN AT BATH*, 2010)

Directed by Christophe Honoré
Written by Christophe Honoré
Produced by Les Films du Bélier
Producer: Justin Taurand
Assistant director: Franck Morand
Director of photography: Stéphane Vallée
Sound: Nicolas Waschkowski, Thierry Delor
Editor: Chantal Hymans
Set designer: Samuel Deshors
Makeup: Thomas Majorosi
Casting: Sébastien Levy
Cast: François Sagat (Emmanuel), Chiara Mastroianni (actress), Omar Ben Sellem (Omar), Rabah Zahi (Rabah), Kate Moran (Kate), Lahcen El Mazouzi (Hicham), Andreas Leflamand (Andréas), Ronald Piwele (Ronald), Sebastian D'Azeglio (man with a moustache), Sébastien Pouderoux (Kate's fiancé), Dennis Cooper (Robin), Dustin Segura-Suarez (Dustin)
France, 2010, 35mm, color, 72 mins.
Distributed by Le Pacte

LES BIEN-AIMÉS (*BELOVED*, 2010)

Directed by Christophe Honoré
Written by Christophe Honoré
Produced by Why Not Productions (Paris), France 2 Cinéma, Sixteen Films, Negativ (Praha)

Director of photography: Rémy Chevrin
Sound: Guillaume Le Braz
Editor: Chantal Hymans
Composer: Alex Beaupain
Production designers: Samuel Deshors, Pascaline Chavanne
Costume designer: Pascaline Chavanne
Cast: Chiara Mastroianni (Vera), Catherine Deneuve (Madeleine), Ludivine Sagnier (young Madeleine), Louis Garrel (Clément), Milos Forman (Jaromil), Paul Schneider (Henderson), Rasha Bukvic (young Jaromil), Michel Delpech (François Gouriot), Omar Ben Sellen (Omar), Dustin Segura-Suarez (Mathieu), Guillaume Denaiffe (young François Gouriot), Clara Couste (adolescent Vera)
France, Great Britain, Czech Republic, 35mm, color, 135 mins.
Distributed by Le Pacte

MÉTAMORPHOSES (2014)

Directed by Christophe Honoré
Written by Christophe Honoré
Based on Ovid's poem *The Metamorphoses*
Produced by Les Films Pelléas, France 3 Cinéma, Le Pacte
Director of photography: André Chemetoff
Sound: Guillaume Le Braz, Valérie Deloof, Cyril Holtz
Editor: Chantal Hymans
Production designer: Nicolas Leclère
Costume designer: Pascaline Chavanne
Cast: Amira Akili (Europe), Sébastien Hirel (Jupiter), Mélodie Richard (Junon), Damien Chapelle (Bacchus), George Babluani (Orphée), Matthis Lebrun (Actéon), Samantha Avrillaud (Diane), Coralie Rouet (Io), Nadir Sönmez (Mercure), Vincent Massimino (Argus), Olivier Müller (Pan), Myriam Guizani (Syrinx), Gabrielle Chuiton (Baucis), Jean Courte (Philémon), Rachid O. (Tirésias), Arthur Jacquin (Narcisse), Anna Camplan (a sister of Mynias), Eléonor Vergez (a sister of Mynias), Margot Guitton (a sister of Mynias), Julien Antonini (Hermaphrodite), Marlène Saldana (Salmacis), Yannick Guyomard (Penthée), Jimmy Lenoir (Cadmus), Vimala Pons (Atalante), Erwan Larcher (Hippomène), Keti Bicolli (Vénus)
France, 35mm, color, 102 mins.
Distributed by Sophie Dulac Distribution

APPENDIX B

Authored Books

Our thanks to Cécile Boulaire at the University François-Rabelais at Tours for helping to compile this bibliography.

NOVELS

L'infamille. Paris: Éditions de l'Olivier, 1997.
La douceur. Paris: Éditions de l'Olivier, 1999.
Le pire du troupeau. Paris: Éditions de l'Olivier, 2001.
Scarborough. Paris: Éditions de l'Olivier, 2002.
Le livre pour enfants. Paris: Éditions de l'Olivier, 2005.
La faculté suivie de Un jeune se tue. Arles, France: Actes Sud, 2012.

CHILDREN'S BOOKS AND SHORT STORIES

Tout contre Léo. Paris: L'École des Loisirs, 1996.
C'est plus fort que moi. Paris: L'École des loisirs, 1996.
Je joue très bien tout seul. Illustrated by Nathalie Baetens. Paris: L'École des loisirs, 1997.
Je ne suis pas une fille à papa. Illustrated by Antoine Guilloppé. Paris: Éditions Thierry Magnier, 1998.
L'affaire P'tit Marcel. Paris: L'École des loisirs, 1998.
Les débutantes. Paris: L'École des loisirs, 1998.
Une toute petite histoire d'amour. Paris: L'École des loisirs, 1998.
Zéro de lecture. Paris: L'École des loisirs, 1998.

Bretonneries. Illustrated by Gwen Le Gac. Paris: Éditions Thierry Magnier, 1999.

Mon coeur bouleversé. Paris: L'École des loisirs, 1999.

Les nuits ou personne ne dort. Paris: L'École des loisirs, 1999.

M'aimer. Illustrated by Alan Mets. Paris: L'École des Loisirs, 2004.

Noël, c'est couic ! Illustrated by Gwen Le Gac. Paris: L'École des Loisirs, 2005.

Torse nu. Illustrated by Gwen Le Gac. Paris: L'École des Loisirs, 2005.

Viens. Coauthored with Kéthévane Davrichewy. Paris: L'École des Loisirs, 2006.

Juke-box. Coauthored with Kéthévane Davrichewy, Marie Desplechin, Nathalie Kuperman, Mary Chloé, and Martin Page. Paris: L'École des loisirs, 2007.

Le terrible six heures du soir. Illustrated by Gwen Le Gac. Arles, France: Actes Sud, 2008.

J'élève ma poupée. Illustrated by Stephanie Blake. Paris: L'École des Loisirs, 2010.

La règle d'or du cache-cache. Illustrated by Gwen Le Gac. Arles, France: Actes Sud Junior, 2010.

L'une belle, l'autre pas. Illustrated by Gwen Le Gac. Arles: Actes Sud Junior, 2013.

APPENDIX C

Other Media Productions Directed by Christophe Honoré

TELEVISION

Tout contre Léo (2002, M6 Productions). See appendix A for complete details.

SCREENWRITER

Les deux amis (2015). Directed by Louis Garrel.
Let My People Go (2011). Directed by Mikael Buch.
Le bruit des gens autour (2008). Directed by Diastème.
Après lui (2007). Directed by Gaël Morel.
Le clan (*Three Dancing Slaves*, 2004). Directed by Gaël Morel.
Novo (2002). Directed by Jean-Pierre Limosin.
Les filles ne savent nager (*Girls Can't Swim*, 2000). Directed by Anne-Sophie Birot.

THEATER

Fin de l'Histoire (2015). Paris, Théâtre national de la Colline.
Violent femmes (2015). Nanterre-Amandiers, centre dramatique national.
La faculté (2012). Festival d'Avignon, Théâtre national de la Colline.
Nouveau roman (2012). Festival d'Avignon, Théâtre national de la Colline.
Angelo, tyran de Padoue (2009). Avignon, Opéra-Théâtre.
Faune(s) (2008, cochoreographer and original idea with Olivier Dubois). Avignon, Cloître des Célestins.
Dionysos impuissant (2005). Festival d'Avignon, Théâtre national de la Colline.

Beautiful Guys (2004). Festival d'Avignon, Théâtre national de la Colline.
Le pire du troupeau (2001). Montreuil, Centre dramatique national de Montreuil.
Les débutantes (1998). Festival "Off" d'Avignon.

OPERA

Dialogues des carmélites (2013). Opéra de Lyon.

NOTES

PREFACE

1. See, in a positive register, Noémie Luciani's review in *Le Monde*, "*Métamorphoses*: Bavardages de bacchantes en baskets," September 2, 2014, www.lemonde.fr/culture/article/2014/09/02/metamorphoses-bavardages-de-bacchantes-en-baskets_4480169_3246.html?xtmc=christophe_honore&xtcr=7; and, in a less positive light, "Christophe Honoré perd son latin dans la première bande-annonce de *Métamorphoses*," *Premiere*, June 23, 2014, www.premiere.fr/Cinema/News-Cinema/Video/VIDEO-Christophe-Honore-perd-son-latin-dans-la-premiere-bande-annonce-de-Metamorphoses-4009100. Honoré's adaptation of la comtesse de Ségur's novel *Les malheurs de Sophie* (1858) is set for release in 2016. From Ovid to Ségur, Honoré's expansive cinematic aesthetic reaches across a wide generic landscape.
2. Led by Valérie Vignaux and Catherine Douzou, French film and theater scholars participated in a rewarding dialogue about Honoré's multimedia accomplishments. Vignaux, Stéphane Bouquet, and Rémi Lecompte delivered especially relevant papers that continue to open new analytical possibilities for Honoré's cinema. As part of the conversation, Gerstner presented his paper "La caméra-stylo et l'histoire de l'art dans *La belle personne*," a work derived from part 3 of this volume.
3. See, for instance, pages 197, 202, 208, and 214 in Fox et al., eds., *A Companion to Contemporary French Cinema*.
4. One of the authors of this book (Gerstner) served on a dissertation committee in 2014 at New York University in which Honoré's representation of women and mothers was discussed. See Iris Brey's "Monstrous Mothers in French Contemporary Cinema."
5. Julien Nahmias interview with Christophe Honoré, this volume (171–202). Throughout our study, we refer to the interviews that Nahmias conducted in Paris on two separate occasions in 2012. Further references in the text are cited as "JNCH."

INTRODUCTION

1. Although *Les chansons* pivots on death and raises the specter of AIDS, the significance of the epidemic as a narrative focus is more centrally positioned in the other films' narratives, particularly *Tout contre Léo* and *Les bien-aimés*. In our discussion about *Les chansons*, however, we explain Honoré's personal story with friendship and AIDS and its personal rendering.

2. Of the three films, *Les chansons d'amour* is Honoré's best-known and most internationally recognized film. It is also, to date, his most financially successful film. *Dans Paris* is not far behind in terms of the numbers, but perhaps because of its more esoteric narrative structure, it is less recognized beyond art-house audiences. According to *JP's Box-Office* (the French-based company that began organizing this information in 1998), *Les chansons* accrued $2,451,677 in international ticket sales (including the United States). Since this source only calculates cinema attendance ("Entrées") in France and not overseas' ticket-sale receipts by city, for example, New York, it is difficult to compare the appeal of *Les chansons* in, say, Paris and New York. Nevertheless, in France, *Les chansons* seated 302,423 people, while 130,883 viewed the film in Paris (www.jpbox-office.com/fichfilm.php?id=79, accessed June 15, 2014). *Dans Paris* generated $1,809,834 internationally with just under 300,000 spectators attending the film in France (www.jpbox-office.com/fichfilm.php?id=451, accessed June 15, 2014).

Since, in this introduction, we concentrate our discussion of twenty-first-century French queers around François Ozon and Honoré, it is interesting to look at the reception of an Ozon film from around the same period. For instance, Ozon's star-driven comedy about labor, family, and the role of woman-as-wife is representative of the director's appeal on the world stage. With Catherine Deneuve at the helm, *Potiche* (2010) made $23,175,043 at the international box office. Slightly less than three million people attended the film in France (www.jpbox-office.com/fichfilm.php?id=11624, accessed June 15, 2014). In 2002, Ozon's most successful film, which starred Deneuve (among other signature French actresses), *8 femmes*, garnered $42,403,014 in international receipts with nearly four million people seeing the mixed-genre spectacle in France (www.jpbox-office.com/fichfilm.php?id=1748, accessed June 15, 2014). And while Honoré's film *Les bien-aimés*, carried significant star power—similarly led by Deneuve—it returned $1,662,013 internationally with 250,000 French in attendance at the cinema (www.jpbox-office.com/fichfilm.php?id=12208, accessed June 15, 2014).

It is important to note, however, that more thoughtful and art-house-manufactured Ozon films, such as *Le temps qui reste* (2005), made $2,883,058 with only 287,480 patrons at French cinemas (www.jpbox-office.com/fichfilm.php?id=831, accessed June 15, 2014); *Sous le sable* (2000) drew in $6,531,687.00 with 682,777 attendees in France (www.jpbox-office.com/fichfilm.php?id=2137, accessed June 15, 2014). Three years later, Honoré's final contribution to the trilogy, *La belle personne,* apparently did not even register on the international "Recettes" scale; only 80,257 people viewed the film in France (www.jpbox-office.com/fichfilm.php?id=10478, accessed June 15, 2014).

3. Jordan Mintzer makes the connection to *Les chansons* in his *Variety* review for *La belle personne*, "Review: 'The Beautiful Person,'" September 17, 2008, http://variety.com/2008/film/reviews/the-beautiful-person-1200470465/. See, further, A. O. Scott's "New Girl Comes to Town: Cue Adolescent Dramatics," *New York Times*, March 5, 2009, www.nytimes.com/2009/03/06/movies/06bell.html. On *Dans Paris*, see Manohla Dargis's "Two Brothers, One Down and One Out" in the *New York Times*, August 8, 2007, www.nytimes.com/2007/08/08/movies/08dans.html, as well as Julia Wallace's "Not without My Brother" in the *Village Voice*, in which J. D. Salinger is not inaccurately evoked in comparison with Honoré's narrative and film style. We will shortly cite quite a few more reviews about *Les*

chansons. For now, see A. O. Scott, "Parisians Singing from Bed to Bed," *New York Times*, March 19, 2008, www.nytimes.com/2008/03/19/movies/19love.html?r=0.

4. For a list of Honoré's multimedia endeavors, see appendix C.

5. Nick Dawson, "Christophe Honoré, *Love Songs*," *Filmmaker Magazine*, March 21, 2008, www.filmmakermagazine.com/news/2008/03/christophe-honore-love-songs/.

6. Elsaesser, *Fassbinder's Germany*, 52. Further references to this work are cited parenthetically in the text.

7. Elizabeth Vincentelli, "Outtakes with Christopher [*sic*] Honoré and Louis Garrel," *Time Out London*, n.d., www.timeout.com/london/film/outtakes-with-christopher-honora-and-louis-garrel (accessed June 2, 2014). Christopher Pullen sees things differently when looking at Ducastel and Martineau. For him, the "groundbreaking" directors "possess a unique talent in examining the 'possibilities' for gay identity" ("The Films of Ducastel and Martineau," 59). On scholarship that critiques Honoré's cinema as something less than queer, see, for instance, Nick Rees-Roberts's short book, *French Queer Cinema*. Darren Waldron in his book *Queering Contemporary French Popular Cinema*, although concentrated on French-audience reception, is more nuanced in his reading of Honoré's cinema: "What is clear, though, is that a strong distinction emerges in the types of pleasure offered to the spectator by this film and those furnished by the other corpus texts" (72). For a rigorous approach to queer cinema's formal and historical dimensions, see Daniel Humphrey's *Queer Bergman*. Through close film analysis, Humphrey rethinks just what a queer auteur might be. In other disciplinary areas, Lee Edelman's precise film criticism connects film form with queer modes of thinking; see, especially, his study of Hitchcock's *North by Northwest* (1959) in his book *No Future*. His reading of Otto Preminger's *Laura* (1944) in *Homographesis* provocatively complements Kristin Thompson's formalist study of the same film in her book *Breaking the Glass Armor*.

8. Gaudreault, "Narration and Monstration in the Cinema," 34.

9. Truffaut, introduction to *Hitchcock*, 17 (emphasis in original). Simon Daniellou draws on cinematic connections between Hitchcock and Honoré (see "La cinéphilie comme contémporanéité," 38).

10. In "The 'Beautiful People' of Christophe Honoré," Isabelle Vanderschelden brings into sharp relief the New Wave "legacy" in which Honoré is located. On the occasion of the New Wave's fiftieth anniversary, Vanderschelden looks at the trilogy and points to Honoré's auteurist impulses in order to frame his place within the tradition of the French auteur.

11. The familial metaphor may come across as glib, but it is not unwarranted for two reasons: First, and as we explore in this book, the cinematic family is a conceptual centerpiece as portrayed in Honoré's films. Second, gossipy malaise over France's "cinematic family" has emerged as its cinematic royalty appears to lock in family members into the French film industry. See Fergus's 2013 report from Cannes ("Cinéma: L'effarante invasion des 'fils et filles de,'" Agora Vox, May 16, 2013, http://mobile.agoravox.fr/culture-loisirs/culture/article/cinema-l-effarante-invasion-des-135878. Our later discussion more rigorously takes up this issue.

12. Marie, *The French New Wave*, 127. Further references to this work are cited parenthetically in the text.

13. Cavitch, "Sex after Death," 323–24.

14. Handyside, "The Possibilities of a Beach," 54.
15. Schilt, *François Ozon*, 9. Further references to this work are cited parenthetically in the text. Throughout our biographical account of Ozon, Schilt's study of the director has been invaluable.
16. Kate Ince, "Queering the Family?," 91. On France and the debates about French "universalism" and its import for the nation's outlook on queer culture, families, and the child, see Enda McCaffrey's *The Gay Republic*; Naomi Schor's "The Crisis of French Universalism"; and Gerstner's "Choreographing Homosexual Desire in Philippe Vallois's *Johan*," 130.
17. Scott, *Parité*, 111. Bruno Perreau's *The Politics of Adoption* is one of the first English-language texts to present the complex legalities and histories that shape the debates about "*homoparentalité*" in France. Perreau draws on a number of important books written in French. Éric Fassin's contributions are many, including *L'inversion de la question homosexuelle* and the essay "Entre famille et nation: La filiation naturalisée." This is an important essay for the way Fassin demonstrates the legal and cultural matrices that link *homoparentalité* and immigration in France. See, further, Camille Robcis's *The Law of Kinship*.
18. See further thoughts on Ozon's child and heterosexual "futurity" in Handyside, "The Possibilities of a Beach," 67; Michelle Chilcoat also considers Ozon's emphasis of reconfigured and queer kinship in "Queering the Family in François Ozon's *Sitcom*," 30.
19. Ozon's comments here about women's relationship to children and men and its depiction in, for instance, *8 femmes* flags the misogyny that often occurs in his films.
20. Not separating from one's child, or from the idea of the child, leads to violent consequences against the mother in Ozon's *Regard la mer* (*See the Sea*, 1997). It is Ozon's most troubling film about motherhood, the child, and desire. In this film, two women share space in a seaside hamlet. Sasha (Sasha Hails) is waiting for her husband with their ten-month-old child, Sioffra, at their summer house when Tatiana (Marina de Van) appears and asks if she may camp on the family's property. As the narrative unfolds, we discover that Tatiana has worked as a nanny, has aborted a pregnancy, and wanders aimlessly because she is bored with her present circumstances. While the women's relationship anticipates an erotic encounter, it is later revealed that Tatiana's desire is focused on the child, not Sasha.
21. It is interesting to compare *Ricky* with Ozon's *Le refuge* (*Hideaway*, 2009). This film "doesn't speak about the relationship with child, because we virtually don't see the child" (Schilt, *Ozon*, 158). In both *Ricky* and *Le refuge*, the father is pushed out of the scene either by death or romantic separation because the mother problematically (if not biologically) merges with the child. In *Le refuge*, once the child is born, the mother departs and deposits her baby girl with her deceased lover's gay (and adopted) brother. The gestation period that covers the film's narrative arc allegorically therefore serves as the transformation period for the mother (getting off heroin, mourning her dead lover, and so forth). Her literal merging with the child and subsequent break from it establishes her freedom. As in *Ricky*, the image of the child redirects mothers, in these instances, toward a better-equipped existence. On the basis of *Ricky* and Ozon's interview about the film, we may surmise that the redirection toward a fuller self involves proper roles for women and mothers.
22. Christophe Honoré, *Le livre pour enfants*, 23. Further references to this work are cited parenthetically in the text.

23. Honoré, *Le livre pour enfants*, 24–25. "Parce que je suis un narrateur homosexuel. Ce qui n'aura pas échappé à mon lecteur confident. Parce que j'ai dans l'idée que mon lecteur—si tant est que j'admettre être lu, et que donc ce livre, et les romans qui ont précédé et les films sont bien des lettres adressées à ce confident—est convaincu des préférence de mon sexe. J'ai lutté contre cette idée, et aussi contre celle d'écrire pour quelqu'un, je me suis répandu sans craindre le ridicule sur mon obstination à n'écrire pour personne, à juste écrire, par discipline, comme on va à l'église, une gymnastique pour mon âme abîmée, une si minuscule transe, une fragile expérience, mais non, j'écris bien pour, et parce que j'écris pour, je suis un narrateur homosexuel. Je ne pensais qu'à moi, je doutais du lecteur, mais c'est fini. La preuve, je ne crains pas de vous inviter dans ce texte. Le courage revient. J'écris pour, la preuve: j'ai écrit des livres pour enfants. Et là aussi, j'étais un narrateur homosexuel." Translation by the authors. We are grateful to Maud Ceuterick for her assistance during the translation.
24. For revealing commentary by Honoré about his clear articulation of his homosexuality, being a father, and organizing a French family, see Doan Bui's article "Christophe Honoré: 'Je ne crois pas au modèle familiale unique,'" *L'Obs*, January 27, 2013, http://tempsreel.nouvelobs.com/politique/mariage-gay/20130124.OBS6566/christophe-honore-je-ne-crois-pas-au-modele-familiale-unique.html.
25. Scott, *Parité*, 110.
26. For Honoré's listing as an alumnus, see "University of Rennes 2—Upper Brittany," *Wikipedia*, http://en.wikipedia.org/wiki/University_of_Rennes_2_-_Upper_Brittany (accessed June 8, 2014).
27. "Christophe Honoré Discusses His New Film, *Beloved*, Starring Catherine Deneuve," *Huffington Post*, August 18, 2012, www.huffingtonpost.com/2012/08/18/christophe-honore-discuss_n_1797093.html?view=print&comm_ref=false.
28. "Christophe Honoré Discusses His New Film"; see, further, JNCH, 192.
29. "Le cinéma français qui va bien m'emmerde." Translation by the authors. Honoré, "La triste moralité du cinéma français," 4. Further references to this article are cited parenthetically in the text.
30. "Alors oui, *L'Anguille, Goodbye South, Goodbye, Happy Together, La Rivière, Lost Highway, En chair et en os* [*Live Flesh*], mais aussi, *Le Destin, Nowhere, Basquiat, Le Goût de la cerise, Scream* sont trente mille fois plus intéressants que le meilleur des meilleurs films français de l'année." Translation by the authors.
31. "Christophe Honoré Discusses His New Film."
32. Derrida, *Specters of Marx*, 91–92. Further references to this work are cited parenthetically in the text.
33. Palmer's short but invaluable overview of La Fémis in *Brutal Intimacy* provides a glimpse into France's institutionalization of film culture. He is correct to suggest that more research from English-language scholars is needed. Further references to this work are cited parenthetically in the text.
34. Short films such as *Victor* (1993) and *Scènes de lit* (*Bed Scenes*, 1998), along with a handful of feature films, such as *Sitcom* (1998) and *Potiche* (2010), confirm Honoré's thoughts about Ozon's talents with the dark-comedy genre.
35. On this event, see Marja Warehime's *French Film Directors: Maurice Pialat*, 2–3.

36. Quoted and translated by Warehime, *French Film Directors*, 2. Further references to this work are cited parenthetically in the text.
37. Warehime goes on to explain Pialat's contradictory interest in Carné's grand cinematic studio spectacle *Les enfants du paradis* (1945) and the just-as-grand yet financially pared-down production of Renoir's *La règle du jeu* (1939) as a concept of cinema that would ideally look like "a Renoir film done by Carné" (28).
38. Honoré is not *un*touched by Pialat. Before making his first film he was "on a Pialat kick" (JNCH, 195). Honoré's film *La belle personne*, for instance, mirrors Pialat's cinematic "moments" of youth and their encounters with the vicissitudes of sexual desire and love as seen in *L'enfance nue* (*Naked Childhood*, 1968) as well as *À nos amours* (1983).
39. Quoted in Warehime, *French Film Directors*, 23 (emphasis in original). For all Pialat's huff and puff, characters in his films often reference his New Wave comrades.
40. Projansky and Ono, "Making Films Asian American," 264.
41. Kate Ince does a fine job situating Ozon as France's "first mainstream queer filmmaker" ("François Ozon's Cinema of Desire," 134).
42. Bingham, "The Relentless Vision of Maurice Pialat."
43. Pialat's award-winning short film *L'amour existe* (1960) highlights the generic force that underlines his work.
44. Wollen, "Godard and Counter-Cinema," 123.
45. Derrida, *Of Grammatology*, 9.
46. Edelman, *Homographesis*, 14. Further references to this work are cited parenthetically in the text (emphasis added).
47. Steven Jenkins, "Christophe Honoré: New Wave Love Songs," *Keyframe*, August 19, 2012, www.fandor.com/keyframe/christophe-honore-new-wave-love-songs.
48. In *French Cinema in the 1970s*, Alison Smith argues that the generation of French filmmakers from the 1990s turned their critical and aesthetic eye to filmmakers from the 1970s. Organized in 1997 under the "appel des 59," young filmmakers (along with Bertrand Tavernier and Patrice Chéreau) announced the group's "political identity," which called for direct political action against such issues as "harsh new immigration laws." Those who signed the 1997 manifesto include Olivier Assayas, Pascal Bonitzer, Catherine Breillat, and Mathieu Kassovitz. The list ultimately grew to sixty-six signatories. Smith sees the original "appel des 59" as "an unambiguous declaration which certainly owed more to the ideals of the early 1970s than to the strictly cinematic rebellion of the Nouvelle Vague, to which their films are often compared" (105). Honoré obviously returns to the New Wave with a very different "political" spin, one aligned with neither his cinematic grandparents *or* parents. See further, "'L'appel des 66 cinéastes,' contre les lois Debré," Fabrique de sens, www.fabriquedesens.net/L-appel-des-66-cineastes-contre (accessed January 24, 2014).
49. Peter Bradshaw, "*Les chansons d'amour*," *Guardian*, December 13, 2007, www.theguardian.com/film/2007/dec/14/worldcinema.musical; Thomas Dawson, "*Love Songs (Les chansons d'amour)*," BBC News, December 7, 2007, www.bbc.co.uk/films/2007/12/10/love_songs_2007_review.shtml.
50. Lee Hill, "The Third Mind of Christophe Honoré," *Vertigo* 14 (December 2007), www.closeupfilmcentre.com/vertigo_magazine/issue-14-december-2007/the-third-mind-of-christophe-honore/.

51. A. O. Scott, "Parisians Singing from Bed to Bed," *New York Times*, March 19, 2008, www.nytimes.com/2008/03/19/movies/19love.html?_r=0; Kevin Thomas, "In Paris, Love Sings—*naturellement*," *Los Angeles Times*, April 4, 2008, http://articles.latimes.com/2008/apr/04/entertainment/et-lovesongs4.
52. Scott Foundas, "Bed-Hopping *Love Songs* Wilts in the Shadow of Godard," *Village Voice*, March 18, 2008, www.villagevoice.com/2008-03-18/film/bed-hopping-love-songs-wilts-in-the-shadow-of-godard/.
53. "Les chansons d'amour—La critique," avoir-alire.com, May 23, 2007, www.avoir-alire.com/les-chansons-d-amour-la-critique. Translations for French reviews by Gerstner.
54. Jérôme Momcilovic, "*Les chansons d'amour*," *Chronic'art*, May 25, 2007, www.chronicart.com/cinema/les-chansons-d-amour/.
55. Thomas Sontinel, "*Les chansons d'amour*: Petit arrangement musical avec la mort," *Le Monde*, May 19, 2007, www.lemonde.fr/cinema/article/2007/05/19/les-chansons-d-amour-petit-arrangement-musical-avec-la-mort_912302_3476.html. "Comme tous les films musicaux, *Les Chansons d'amour* demande beaucoup au spectateur et aux acteurs. Il faut surmonter ce moment incertain où les personnages arrêtent de parler et se mettent à chanter. D'autant que l'écoute des lyrics (comme on disait temps de l'opérette) d'Alex Beaupain est indispensable à la compréhension des personnages. Passé ce seuil, on entre dans un film où les chansons d'amour se confondent avec l'amour lui-même." Translation by Gerstner.
56. Douglas Morrey provides a useful list that culls Honoré's references to Godard and the New Wave in *Dans Paris*. Additionally, Morrey stresses Honoré's turn to "real emotion" as an indication of his revision of Godard's more ironic and less-than-"credible characters." Morrey, "Jean-Luc Godard, Christophe Honoré, and the Legacy of the New Wave in French Cinema," 10.
57. Vincendeau, "*Dans Paris*," 59.
58. Vincendeau, "*Dans Paris*," 55.
59. Rees-Roberts, *French Queer Cinema*, 111. Further references to this work are cited parenthetically in the text.
60. David Calhoun, "Cannes Latest: Reviews of *Control*, *The Banishment*, and *Les Chansons d'amour*," *Time Out London*, May 18, 2007, http://w02.timeout.com/film/news/1889/cannes-latest-reviews-of-control-the-banishment-and-les-chansons-damour.html# (accessed January 15, 2014; as of March 7, 2015, however, the link was not available).
61. For remarks on Sarkozy, see Nick Dawson's interview with Honoré, "Christophe Honoré, *Love Songs*"; and JNCH, 199.
62. A short overview on films outside the trilogy is noteworthy for highlighting the pattern of response to Honoré's work. Tina Kendall, for instance, succinctly rounds up the reviews for *Ma mère* by pointing out that critics, less focused on "troublingly explicit portrayals of sex and violence," were annoyed by "Honoré's transposition of Bataille's philosophical musings to the Canary Islands setting, [and] on its soaring pretentiousness, or both" ("Reframing Bataille," 46); Stephen Murray on the Epinions website sums up his response to *Tout contre Léo* this way: "In many ways very good, but disturbing and offputting" ("They All Loved Each Other So Much—Which Was Not Enough," Epinions, July 28, 2008, www.epinions.com/review/close_to_leo_dvd_2004/content_438982184580?sb=1); and, finally, Jay Weissberg in *Variety* finds "an unprettified

matte quality characterizes much of [*Homme au bain*]," while Honoré misses the opportunity to provocatively deal with his casting of the porn star François Sagat: "while it is apt to cast a porn star when dealing with concepts of viewing and being viewed, Honoré barely explores the idea" ("Review: *Man at Bath*," *Variety*, August 15, 2010, http://variety.com/2010/film/reviews/man-at-bath-1117943335/).
63. Hill, "The New Wave Meets the Tradition of Quality."
64. Duggan, *Queer Enchantments*, 3-4.
65. Duggan notes the rather large gap in biographical accounts—including those by his wife, Agnès Varda—about Demy's sexuality and his death by AIDS (*Queer Enchantment*, 6-7).
66. Much has been written about the New Wave's masculinism and homophobia. As early as 1980, Laura Mulvey critiqued Godard's patriarchal display of women, even if at the same time the filmmaker's cinematic form interrogated the apparatus in which this representation takes place. Mulvey was one of the first to point to Godardian cinema (a filmmaker "out of synch") and, on the one hand, the exploitation of women's images that his films encouraged while, on the other, their more general critique of the capitalist system. Mulvey, "Images of Women, Images of Sexuality," 52. In 2008, Duke University Press translated Geneviève Sellier's *Nouvelle vague: Un cinéma au masculine singulier* (*Masculine Singular: French New Wave Cinema*), a work that articulates the strong androcentric ideologies that saturate the New Wave filmmakers, their work, and their champions. More recently (2010), Vanessa Schwartz reconfirmed Sellier's tracing of misogyny and masculinism that underscores French New Wave culture ("Who Killed Brigitte Bardot?"). In 2006, Deleuzian theorists revisited Mulvey's critique and argued that a more malleable, or "rhizomatic," representation of Godard's women could be gleaned. See Vegari, "Calling the Shots."
67. On the notion of "Right Bank" and "Left Bank" New Wave filmmakers and culture, see Catherine Lupton's *Chris Marker*, 42. Duggan, following Richard Neupert's (*A History of the French New Wave Cinema*) and Geneviève Sellier's work, notes that Demy's outsiderness relates to his love for the musical, while his colleagues were drawn to the western, film noir, and science fiction. Even though Godard's *Une femme est une femme* stands out, Duggan argues that Godard's impulse for directing the musical had more to do with "abstraction" and experimentation on the genre, whereas Demy "gives very concrete form—with a focus on costume, music, and color—to his singular conception of what a musical is and can do" (4-5).
68. In 1983, Godard's strongest champion, Alain Badiou ("Mention Godard First!"), takes Demy to task for what he views as the dubious "[crossing] between the political as such and formal excess (or arbitrariness)" in *Une chambre en ville* (*A Room in Town*, 1982). For Badiou, "Demy would have us believe that there is no crisis, either of the people or of cinema." Indeed, "the conjunction of a realism and a formalism, that of musical comedy" is "a problem of the times." Demy's operatic queering of the political did not sit comfortably during this particular period, when Badiou, along with his colleagues at *La feuille foudre*, were set up as a "tribunal" that "issued judgments" on politics and cinema. It is quite possible Badiou has since rethought his comments about Demy's film ("The Demy Affair," 65; further references to this work are cited parenthetically in the text). On Badiou's assertion "Mention Godard First!" see "Reference Points for Cinema's Second Modernity."

69. Elsaesser, *Fassbinder's Germany*, 52. Further references to this work are cited parenthetically in the text.
70. Greene, *Pier Paolo Pasolini*, 112. Further references to this work are cited parenthetically in the text.
71. Greene, *Pasolini*, 168; Elsaesser, *Fassbinder*, 54.
72. Drawing comparison between Pasolini and Honoré takes on more currency with the recent release of *Métamorphoses*. The review on the TLC website makes a direct connection between filmmakers. See "*Les métamorphoses*, Christophe Honoré adapte et exalte la liberté d'Ovide," Toute La Culture, August 20, 2014, http://toutelaculture.com/cinema/a-laffiche/critiquue-les-metamorphoses-christophe-honore-adapte-et-exalte-la-liberte-dovide/.
73. Thomsen, "Conversations with Rainer Werner Fassbinder," 89.
74. Stack, *Pasolini on Pasolini*, 121; see further on Pasolini's *Oedipus Rex*, Naomi Greene's *Pier Paolo Pasolini*, 153; and Pasolini's book *Teorema* (*Theorem*) and his poem that bridges parts 1 and 2, "Identification of Incest with Reality" (*Theorem*, 83).
75. Stilwell, "Le Demy-monde," 123.
76. "And if you are intrigued by the idea of a fairy tale with an incest theme, you won't want to miss *Donkey Skin*." Martin Knelman drops this suggestive but enthusiastic appraisal of Demy's film in his overview of the director's films in preparation for the retrospective in Toronto. Martin Knelman, "Jacques Demy's Fairy-Tale Films at TIFF Bell Lightbox until July 20," *Star*, July 3, 2013, www.thestar.com/entertainment/movies/2013/07/03/jacques_demys_fairytale_films_at_tiff_bell_lightbox_until_july_20.html. Demy's less known musical *Trois places pour le 26* (1988) receives nary a mention with regard to its incestuous story line. Anne E. Duggan, even in her introduction to *Queer Enchantments*, states in her preliminary notes for her analysis of *Peau d'âne* that she explores the film "from the particular angle of gay aesthetics. Drawing on the cinema of Jean Cocteau in particular and camp poetics in general, Demy uses the tale to explore alternative forms of sexuality and to denaturalize conceptions of gender" (11). Duggan does not mention incest.
77. Mitry, *The Aesthetics and Psychology of the Cinema*, 334. Mitry's concept suggestively recalls Erwin Panofsky's theory that the cinema's "unique and specific possibilities can be defined as *dynamization of space* and, accordingly, the *spatialization of time*." Panofsky, "Style and Medium in the Motion Pictures," 249. On early French film theory and its preoccupation with the cinematic apparatus and space, see Richard Abel's "*Photogénie* and Company," 107.
78. Sedgwick, *Touching Feeling*, 9.
79. Tyler, "Ode to Hollywood," 222.
80. Mitry, *The Aesthetics and Psychology of the Cinema*, 334 (emphasis added).
81. Sontag, "Notes on 'Camp,'" 280.
82. Babuscio, "Camp and the Gay Sensibility," 20.
83. Dyer, "It's Being So Camp as Keeps Us Going," 138.
84. Chris Darke refers to homage in this way when discussing Michelangelo Antonioni's *Beyond the Clouds* (1995) and Wim Wenders's involvement in the production—a film according to Darke that presses homage further into redundancy: "One can't help wondering if all this genuflecting to elderly, dying, and dead directors is healthy, if it is a case of Wenders the vampire in the guise of the ever-respectful amanuensis to the great

filmmakers." Darke, *Light Readings*, 45. The evocation of a religious gesture is intriguing when taking up queer cinematic homage (consider Kenneth Anger's *Scorpio Rising*, 1963).
85. The terms are Mikhail Bakhtin's. See Gerstner, "The Practices of Authorship," 12.
86. Durgnat, *Jean Renoir*, 25.
87. With great aplomb, classical film theory is making a return to film studies. See, for instance, "Roundtable on the Return to Classical Film Theory" in *October*; and the edition of "Dossier" in *Screen*: "What's New in Classical Film Theory?"
88. Keller, Wall-Romana, and Morgan are indebted to their mentors, whose work in film theory cannot be underestimated. See, further, Tom Gunning's preface to Keller's collection *Jean Epstein*; Dudley Andrew's work on Bazin (*Opening Bazin*); as well as Morgan's "Rethinking Bazin"; and David N. Rodowick's recent contributions to film theory (*Elegy for Theory*; *The Virtual Life of Film*).
89. Wall-Romana, "Epstein's *Photogénie* as Corporeal Vision." Further references to this work are cited parenthetically in the text. The link between Epstein and Honoré is highly noteworthy when one considers their queer orientation and their relationship to Brittany and Breton culture. Films by Epstein, such as *Finis terrae* (1929), *Chansons d'armor* (1934), *La Bretagne* (1936), and *Le tempestaire* (1947) deserve mention in this regard and promise a rewarding future study on Honoré's films set in Brittany.
90. Several very good essays have developed the necessarily nuanced approach to studying queer French cinema. For example, see the writings by James S. Williams ("His Life to Film") and Claude Evans ("Fantasies and Ambiguous Sexuality in Patrice Leconte's *Le Mari de la coiffeuse* and *La Fille sur le pont*").
91. Perec, *An Attempt at Exhausting a Place in Paris*, 3.
92. For a politically astute and moving account of a queer boy's journey from the provinces to Paris, see Didier Eribon's *Returning to Reims*.

PART I

1. For an excellent overview of Godard's cinematic fonts, see the Walker Art Center's exhibition notes: Andrea Hyde, "Godard's Intertitles," *The Gradient* (blog), Walker Art Center, November 10, 2009, http://blogs.walkerart.org/design/2009/11/10/godards-intertitles2/.
2. Paul Branco is a well-known producer of European cinema. His IMDb profile indicates his wide support for important independent film production in Europe. Along with Honoré's films, Branco has produced films for David Cronenberg, Wim Wenders, Chantal Akerman, Philippe Garrel, Cédric Kahn, and André Téchiné. See "Paulo Branco," IMDb, www.imdb.com/name/nm0104418/ (accessed June 16, 2014).
3. Recall our earlier discussion about Pialat, Ozon, and Honoré in which the idea of documentary is instrumental to their cinematic aesthetic. Whereas Pialat's films are noted for his research prior to making narrative films for the purposes of bringing documentary to fiction, Honoré's concept of documentary is perceived as an always already condition of his cinema. Pialat's documentary mode thus exists a priori; Honoré's occurs at the instant the camera rolls.
4. Honoré views his performers as family, sort of. The relationship is certainly queer. He queries the relationship this way: "Who I am for them? Their grandfather, their father? Their

mother? It's always a little strange, because it's not really a family. That's not true. I've known Louis since he was very, very young, and I speak to him basically every week on the phone. And right now, I'm writing a screenplay with him that he's going to film. It's true that when it comes to Ludivine or Chiara, they'll talk to me about their projects, they'll say, 'Hey, I just got a script from this director, what do you think?' etc., so it ends up being a group. A team, but not quite a family. Even if I sometimes have some somewhat negative thoughts, for instance, if I see them in somebody else's movie, I feel jealous and possessive. But the relationship of an actor and a director, it's not an untouchable entity. That's good. You want it to stay a little bit shaky, because if you offer a role to an actor, you want them to feel that you're offering the role because you really want them to play it, not out of some kind of habit." Interview with Colleen Kelsey, "Christophe Honoré's Lost (and Found) Loves," *Interview*, May 2012, www.interviewmagazine.com/film/christophe-honore-the-beloved/#_.

5. Honoré referred to his interest in the "literariness" of film during a Q&A session following a screening of *Les bien-aimés* at the Brooklyn Academy of Music (August 13, 2012). Gerstner attended this screening.

6. J. Williams, "His Life to Film," 181.

7. Garrel makes clear the connection between his and Léaud's acting style. See Kristen Hohenadel, "Louis Garrel: France's All-Purpose Heartthrob," *New York Times*, March 18, 2008, www.nytimes.com/2008/03/18/arts/18iht-16hohe.11222377.html?pagewanted=all&_r=0.

8. Peter Bradshaw, "*Les chansons d'amour*," *Guardian*, December 13, 2007, www.theguardian.com/film/2007/dec/14/worldcinema.musical.

9. Manohla Dargis, "Two Brothers, One Down and Out," *New York Times*, August 8, 2007, www.nytimes.com/2007/08/08/movies/08dans.html?ref=movies&_r=1&.

10. On Honoré's concept for directing actors, see his comments on his work with Catherine Deneuve, in which he asserts that he, unlike the film director François Ozon, does not treat the iconic actor as a "porcelain doll." Jerry Portwood, "Christophe Honoré Does Not Treat Deneuve Like a 'Porcelain Doll,'" *Out*, August 22, 2012, www.out.com/entertainment/movies/2012/08/22/christophe-honore-beloved-catherine-deneuve.

11. Pasolini noted this problem when working with Anna Magnani in *Mamma Roma* (1962). Pasolini reflects on his casting: "Although Anna Magnani made a moving effort to do what I asked of her, the character simply did not emerge. I wanted to bring out the ambiguity of subproletarian life with a petit bourgeois superstructure. This didn't come out, because Anna Magnani is a woman who was born and has lived as a petite bourgeoise and then as an actress and so hasn't got those characteristics." Quoted in Stack, *Pasolini on Pasolini*, 49.

12. Faulkner, interactive map essay.

13. By including Joana Preiss's son in the film, Honoré keeps true to his word insofar as making his films involves and creates a family.

14. Barthes, *A Lover's Discourse*, 55.

15. The flashback sequence also appears to include flashforwards from Paul's perspective, within Jonathan's framing. The linearity of events thus remains ambiguous as it plays out in Jonathan's cinematic imaginary.

16. Drobnick, "Inhaling Passions," 38.

17. Gilbert, *What the Nose Knows*, 147-49.
18. Bersani, *The Freudian Body*, 17. Further references to this work are cited parenthetically in the text.
19. On "apparatus theory," see especially Jean-Louis Baudry's seminal essays "Ideological Effects of the Basic Cinematographic Apparatus" and "The Apparatus: Metapsychological Approaches to the Impression of Reality in Cinema." Both essays are included in Philip Rosen's edited collection *Narrative, Apparatus, Ideology*. "Suture" is, of course, the critical term that conveys the ideological stitching that occurs with "classical Hollywood" narration and its reliance on shot/reverse-shot sequences to establish a realist point of view for the spectator. See Daniel Dayan's essay "The Tutor Code of Classical Cinema."
20. We have come to learn, of course, that the "shit" that the young people eat is actually chocolate. The trivia is not unimportant since it begs the question of why it is we still "smell" the chocolate as if it were shit. See Christopher Sharrett's "*Salò, or the 120 Days of Sodom*."
21. Althusser describes the life events during his youth that buttressed his intellectual thinking, giving a detailed account of the tactile world and, most especially, smells that enabled him to "'think' with [his] body": "It was no longer a question of thinking distantly and passively by merely looking, but 'thinking' actively with my hands, through the unbounded interplay of all my muscles and bodily sensations." Althusser, *The Future Lasts Forever*, 214.
22. Later, when the boys share the bathtub, Paul directs the showerhead's forceful flow of water into his mouth, blocking any possibility for speech.
23. Describing Melanie Klein's use of the "split imago," Élisabeth Roudinesco states, "Whether it is a part object, as in the case of the breast, the excreta, or the penis, or a whole object, when it is concerned with a person, the object is always an *imago*—the image of a real object that the subject absorbs by introjection into his or her ego and endows with the status of a fantasy." Roudinesco, *Jacques Lacan*, 109.
24. On the intersection between the erotic and the sentimental in the Christ figure, see Eve Kosofsky Sedgwick's *The Epistemology of the Closet*, 179-80.
25. Julius, *Transgressions*, 76.
26. Barthes, *A Lover's Discourse*, 154 (emphasis in original).
27. Honoré shares another distinguishing feature with Pasolini: cinematic mothers. Pasolini's *Mamma Roma* arguably plays a significant part in Honoré's depiction of mothers, particularly as they walk. Consider Deneuve in *Les bien-aimés* and Huppert in *Ma mère* in comparison with Anna Magnani's stroll along the Roman avenues.
28. See our discussion about family and (homo)sexuality in the introduction. While Honoré's film *Ma mère* deals directly with incest, Honoré's other films saliently brush up against it in unexpected ways. His familial bed raises a series of questions about the production of affective memory that provocatively serves as a cinematic site in which the very concept of the historical French family is broadened and transformed.
29. One cannot help but further link *Loulou* with the character of the same name in Pialat's film *Loulou* (1980), in which the protagonist (Gérard Depardieu) consistently, yet wolfishly, defends family, friends, and lovers.
30. While much is made of Honoré's visual homage, Rémi Lecompte demonstrates Honoré's *cinematic ear*, reminding us of the importance of music and sound in the director's films ("La représentation de l'écoute").

PART II

1. Rees-Roberts, *French Queer Cinema*, 112.
2. "Jean-Claude Guiguet: Biographie," *L'Express*, n.d., http://fiches.lexpress.fr/personnalite/jean-claude-guiguet_208545/biographie (accessed June 12, 2014; as of March 4, 2015, access to this source was no longer available). The biographical information sketched here may be found in the *L'Express* obituary and the following sources: Julien Dokhan, "Décès du cinéaste Jean-Claude Guiguet," Allocine, September 19, 2005, www.allocine.fr/article/fichearticle_gen_carticle=18376525.html; "Mediathèque: DVDs of Jean-Claude Guiguet," Objectif Cinéma, n.d., www.objectif-cinema.com/mediatheque/0282b.php (accessed June 12, 2014); and "Jean-Claude Guiguet," IMDb, www.imdb.com/name/nm0346837/ (accessed June 12, 2014)
3. *Le livre pour enfants* briefly explores this relationship (143).
4. Sylvain Zimmerman, "Alex Beaupain: 'J'ai été attire par les garçons sur le tard,'" Têtu, May 23, 2011, www.tetu.com/2011/05/23/news/culture/alex-beaupain-jai-ete-attire-par-les-garcons-sur-le-tard/.
5. Marie-Laure Delorme, "Kéthévane Davrichewy et Alex Beaupain, la vie en chantant," *Le Journal du Dimanche*, February 24, 2014, www.lejdd.fr/Culture/Livres/Kethevane-Davrichewy-et-Alex-Beaupain-la-vie-en-chantant-654527.
6. Quoted in Tom Dawson's "Les Chansons d'Amour—Profile of Christophe Honoré," The List, December 13, 2007, http://film.list.co.uk/article/5858-les-chansons-damour-profile-of-christophe-honore/.
7. Aloysius J. Gleek, "Interview with Christophe Honoré," BetterMost, n.d., www.bettermost.net/forum/index.php?topic=18293.15;wap2 (accessed June 14, 2014; emphasis added).
8. For the citation of Monnin's work, see "Aude Monnin," Pratiques De L'Interdisciplinarité, n.d.,www.master-pdi.ens.fr/hopmasters.php?action=ficheperso&id=216&id_rub=(accessed June 14, 2014). We are indebted to Éric Fassin and Wilfried Rault for assisting us in confirming the work cited here as that belonging to Aude Monnin, to whom *Les chansons* is dedicated. Rault also clarified dates of Honoré's relationship with Monnin.
9. *Les chansons* was banned from screening on Russian television in 2013 because it brushed up against Putin's law that media could not serve as "propaganda for nontraditional sexual relations." See Lucas Armati, "'Les chansons d'amour' interdit de télé russe," Télérama, September 19, 2013, www.telerama.fr/cinema/les-chansons-d-amour-interdit-de-tele-russe,102506.php.
10. Gleek, "Interview with Christophe Honoré."
11. HADOPI is an acronym for *Haute autorite pour la diffusion des œuvres et la protection des droits d'auteur sur Internet*, which is roughly translated as the "Creation and Internet Law." Ben Woods provides the clearest presentation on the law and its myriad transformations and debates: "France U-Turns on Controversial 'Three-Strikes' Hadopi Internet Disconnection Law," The Next Web, July 9, 2013, http://thenextweb.com/eu/2013/07/09/france-performs-u-turn-on-three-strikes-hadopi-disconnection-law/.
12. See *Le Monde*'s coverage at "Inquiet de son avenir, le Salon du livre jenuesse de Montreuil lance une pétition," April 1, 2010, www.lemonde.fr/livres/article/2010/04/01/inquiet-de-son-avenir-le-salon-du-livre-jeunesse-de-montreuil-lance-une-petition_1327673_3260.html.

13. Charles Dantzig, Dominique Fernandez, Christophe Honoré, and Olivier Poivre d'Arvor, "Mariage gay: Non à la collusion de la haine," *Le Monde,* November 17, 2012, www.lemonde.fr/idees/article/2012/11/17/mariage-gay-non-a-la-collusion-de-la-haine_1792087_3232.html.
14. The video may be seen here: https://www.findspire.com/fr/profile/christophe.honore/videos/all/?viewer=wc0j0368ze81n6h4esf3jchvqeptktuw (accessed June 14, 2014).
15. Rees-Roberts, *French Queer Cinema,* 112. Ducastel, born in 1962, studied film in Paris and worked as an assistant with Demy. Martineau, born in 1963, did not study film institutionally when he moved to Paris. The cinematic output of the personal and professional partners has been dedicated to French queer culture, especially with a focus on AIDS and gay men. See Christopher Pullen's essay "The Films of Ducastel and Martineau: Gay Identity, the Family, and the Autobiographical Self."
16. Gleek, "Interview with Christophe Honoré." *Les bien-aimés* deals directly with the topic of AIDS.
17. Gleek, "Interview with Christophe Honoré."
18. Dawson, "Les Chansons d'Amour—Profile of Christophe Honoré."
19. For more on Honoré's concept "film with song," see Michelle Orange's interview "Talking with Christopher [*sic*] Honoré and Louis Garrel" in the *Village Voice,* March 18, 2008, www.villagevoice.com/2008-03-18/film/talking-with-christopher-honore-and-louis-garrel/full/.
20. Feuer, "Hollywood Musicals." For Dyer, the Hollywood musical [here, *On the Town*] "shows people making utopia rather than just showing them from time to time finding themselves in it." Dyer, "Entertainment and Utopia," 33. Honoré is quite clear about his concept for and historical placement of "song in film." See Steven Jenkins, "Christophe Honoré: New Wave Love Songs," *Keyframe* (blog), Fandor, August 19, 2012, www.fandor.com/blog/christophe-honore-new-wave-love-songs.
21. Conway, *Chanteuse in the City,* 88. We can add Raymond Durgnat's elegant and useful description of cinematic "atmosphere." As he sees it in Renoir's *La nuit du carrefour* (1932), cinematic atmosphere is often "assumed to be merely superficial but it arises from an amalgam of sensuous and poetic reminiscence; a balance of feelings, not an absence of them. And balance implies structure. [Renoir's film] is impregnated with air, light, liquid, stone, fabric and flesh." Durgnat, *Jean Renoir,* 77.
22. Conway, *Chanteuse in the City,* 86. On "poetic realism," see further Andrew's *Mists of Regret,* 11–16.
23. Although no prostitutes, per se, are present in the trilogy, the line between mother and whore is a delicate preoccupation with Honoré. Recall that the mother in *Dans Paris* is referred to by her sons as the "Saint-of-a-Whore." In Honoré's other films, the line between prostitute and mother is blurred (*Ma mère*), while at other times it is directly linked (*Les bien-aimés*). The moral baggage assigned to the prostitute, historically rendered, is not dissimilar to that placed on the homosexual. The prostitute is equally queer.
24. Powrie, "The Disintegration of Community," 98.
25. "This would be," Powrie writes, "in the logic of the developments charted in this chapter, from an imagined French community brought together in epiphanic *chanson,* to the slow infiltration of American music which has occurred at the same time as French community has deteriorated (broadly since the early 1950s)" ("The Disintegration of Community," 115).

26. Powrie, "The Disintegration of Community," 99 (emphasis in original).
27. Conway, *Chanteuse in the City*, 83 (emphasis in original).
28. Resnais's other musical, *Pas sur la bouche* (2003), similarly contains characters within a world immersed in song. Less experimental in form than *On connaît la chanson*, the film, as an adaption of an operetta of the same name, arguably draws on Demy's signature-style films such as *Les parapluies de Cherbourg* and *Une chambre en ville*.
29. For an excellent account on France's nineteenth-century government initiative that placed a national "seal of originality" on *chansons populaires*, see Jane Alden's "Excavating Chansonniers."
30. Conway, *Chanteuse in the City*, 35.
31. On the Godardian-like contradictions around politics and consumer culture in Honoré's cinema, see Daniellou, "La cinéphilie comme contémporanéité," 33–34.
32. "Alex Beaupain est son [Hollande] chanteur préféré." Delorme, "Kéthévane Davrichewy et Alex Beaupain, la vie en chantant."
33. See Aloysius J. Gleek, "Interview with Alex Beaupain," BetterMost, n.d., www.bettermost.net/forum/index.php?topic=18293.15;wap2 (accessed June 14, 2014; emphasis added).
34. Alistair Horne prefaces his conservative history of Paris with the rather remarkable line, "Whereas London, through the ages, has always betrayed clearly male orientations, and New York has a certain ambivalence, has any sensible person ever doubted that Paris is fundamentally a woman?" Horne, *Seven Ages of Paris*, xiii.
35. According to the INSEE (National Institute of Statistics and Economic Studies, France), the immigrant population in Paris has increased between 1999 and 2007, whereas it was stable in the rest of France. Of the 20 percent of immigrants to Paris, 6 percent are from the European Union and 14 percent from the rest of the world (mostly Asia and sub-Saharan Africa). The new Maghreb immigrants live mostly in the tenth, eleventh, eighteenth, nineteenth, and twentieth arrondissements; the sub-Saharans live in the thirteenth, fourteenth, eighteenth, nineteenth, and twentieth. Most Asians immigrants dwell in the second, third, tenth, thirteenth, sixteenth, and nineteenth. INSEE, "Davantage d'immigrés dans le centre de l'agglomération, notamment en Seine-Saint-Denis," n.d., www.insee.fr/fr/themes/document.asp?reg_id=20&ref_id=18086&page=alapage/alap376/alap376_encadr.htm (accessed July 22, 2013).
36. "En rupture avec la tradition artistique, la liberté est symbolisée par une figure masculine." Valérie Montalbetti, "*Le Génie de la Liberté*," The Louvre website, www.louvre.fr/oeuvre-notices/le-genie-de-la-liberte (accessed June 26, 2013).
37. "Svelte, les bras étendus, les ailes déployées, en appui sur la pointe du pied gauche, le génie s'élance dans les airs" (Montalbetti, "*Le Génie de la Liberté*").
38. Compared with, say, Ducastel and Martineau's *Jeanne et le garçon formidable*, in which the movements in public and private spaces recall Demy's theatricalized choreography in *Les demoiselles de Rochefort*, Honoré's choreography—in the public and private realms—is less Hollywood-musical style and relies on less dramatized everyday movements. In "Le sens du décor dans l'oeuvre de Christophe Honoré," Stéphane Bouquet describes the complex urban scene in "le décor chez Honoré = géographie idéale du désir."
39. Freud, "A Note upon the 'Mystic Writing-Pad.'"

40. Surrealists have long played with the point at which dreaming and being awake converge. Alistair Charles Rolls in *The Flight of the Angels* points to Boris Vian's "concept of dreams, and of dream journeys" (104). He follows Bruno Maillé's note that "Via nest Surrealiste dans le rêve et le réveil" (quoted in Rolls, *The Flight of the Angels*, 104). See further, Jacques-B. Brunius's *En marge du cinéma français*: "Il n'est en effet possible de noter la description d'un rêve qu'au réveil. Il n'est pas plus question de fixer directement le rêve sur la pellicule que de l'écrire au fur et à mesure, ou de le peindre automatiquement sure une toile" (69).
41. Gerstner has taken this up elsewhere in "Christophe Honoré's *Les Chansons d'amour* and the Musical's Queer-abilities."
42. *Fragments sur la grâce* is a film directed by Vincent Dieutre that, according to *Cahiers du Cinéma*, follows "the same [aesthetic] plan" as Honoré's *Les chansons*. "Journal de Cannes," *Cahiers du Cinéma*, May 27, 2007, www.cahiersducinema.com/May-27th.html. Translation by Anna Harrison.
43. Alice reads James Salter's *Un bonheur parfait* (Perfect Happiness), Julie reads *Volupté singulière* (Voluptuous Pleasures) by A. L. Kennedy, and Ismaël reads Adam Thirlwell's *Politique*.
44. Rees-Roberts, *French Queer Cinema*, 111.
45. Castle, *The Literature of Lesbianism*, 26 (emphasis in original). Further references to this work are cited parenthetically in the text. Along with *The Apparitional Lesbian*, Castle's research on lesbian literature and representation is remarkable for its breadth and comprehensiveness. I thank Rebecca Martin for drawing our attention to Castle's work.

    It is interesting to consider Castle's remarks and the widely divergent critical responses to Abdellatif Kechiche's *La vie d'Adèle* (*Blue Is the Warmest Color*, 2013). It is also worth noting that Honoré is dismissive of Kechiche's cinema as too beholden to a message (JNCH, 199).
46. Chow, *Sentimental Fabulations*, 182. Further references to this work are cited parenthetically in the text.
47. Vincendeau, "Daddy's Girls," 72.
48. Conway, *Chanteuse in the City*, 14 (emphasis added).
49. As Valérie Vignaux points out in "Christophe Honoré et le cinéma ou l'invention d'une écriture," Honoré's fixed-tracking shot resonates not only with Demy but with Cocteau's provocative floating "Beauty" in *La belle et la bête* (1946). Indeed, the device has a varied history that may be seen most readily in Spike Lee's films.
50. Deathbeds play significant roles in Honoré's films, here and in films such as *Ma mère*.
51. The closest to "Delta Charlie Delta" in English is "DOA," or "dead on arrival."
52. Translation from IFC-distributed DVD of the film (2008). In the film, Honoré cuts to a close-up of the passage in the book. It reads, "Quantité de personnes ont ainsi une âme qui adore nager. On les appelle vulgairement des paresseux. Quand l'âme quitte le corps par le ventre pour nager, il se produit une telle libération de je ne sais quoi, c'est un abandon, une jouissance, un relâchement si intime."
53. Consider the calligraphy on the wall in the tennis stadium toward the end of *Strangers on a Train*: "And Treat Those Two Impostors Just the Same."
54. Gleek, "Interview with Christophe Honoré."
55. "Il faut se taire," lyrics by Alex Beaupain. Translation by Gerstner.

56. Gleek, "Interview with Christophe Honoré."
57. The comfort that the two boys offer each other in this scene evokes the homoerotic and brotherly tenderness we see in Jean Epstein's Breton tale *Finis terrae* (1929).
58. Wilson, *The Romantic Dream*, 25.
59. Elizabeth Vincentelli, "Outtakes with Christopher [*sic*] Honoré and Louis Garrel," *Time Out London*, n.d., www.timeout.com/london/film/outtakes-with-christopher-honora-and-louis-garrel (accessed June 2, 2014).
60. As we have discussed, incest and its erotic exchange is central to Honoré's cinema. The domestic sphere is presented with a range of familial emotions underscored by a familial erotic.
61. A similar painting hangs in *Dans Paris* during a discussion between Mirko and Paul.
62. It is important to note that Ismaël's outsiderness is further confirmed since he is Jewish, which the film highlights when we see him enter a synagogue to pray following Julie's death.

PART III

1. Nick Dawson, "Christophe Honoré, *Love Songs*," *Filmmaker Magazine*, March 21, 2008, www.filmmakermagazine.com/news/2008/03/christophe-honore-love-songs/.
2. Arnheim, "A New Laocoön," 213. Further references to this work are cited parenthetically in the text.
3. See, for example, John MacKay's translations of Rudolf Arnheim's essay "Chaplin's Early Films" and Walter Benjamin's essay "A Look at Chaplin" in "Walter Benjamin and Rudolf Arnheim on Charlie Chaplin."
4. Cooper, conversation with Gerstner, Paris, January 13, 2012.
5. Buss, introduction to Lafayette's *The Princesse de Clèves*, 2. Further references to this work, both the introduction and the novel itself, are cited parenthetically in the text.
6. See, for instance, David's *Self-Portrait* (1794) and *Portrait of a Young Woman in a Turban* (c. 1797) and Gustave Courbet's *Self-Portrait (The Desperate Man)* (c. 1843) and *Portrait of Jo, the Beautiful Irish Girl* (c. 1865).
7. See Régis Sauder's 2012 film *The Children of the Princesse of Clèves*, as another recent example of the way Lafayette's *roman historique* is embraced and reimagined.
8. Interview with Pasolini in Stack, *Pasolini on Pasolini*, 83.
9. On the history of the courtyard in Florentine and Tuscan architecture, see Grazia Gobbi Sica's *The Florentine Villa*, 44-48, and Richard A. Goldthwaite's *The Building of Renaissance Florence*, 13-16.
10. On this, see Cecil Jenkins's *A Brief History of France*, 50-51.
11. The name Otto is also freighted by Franco-German history dating back to 1214, when Philippe Auguste ruled and battled it out with the Holy Roman Emperor, Otto IV. And, as if the Franco-German connection cannot be twisted further, the French Tomi Ungerer's consistent theme in his children's books is built on strengthening Franco-German ties. On Philippe Auguste and Otto, see Alistair Horne's *Seven Ages of Paris*, 24-26.
12. It is interesting to draw out the ways a French-Italian lingua franca developed through French history. Along with, for instance, François I's France being besotted with Italian culture and language via Cellini and Da Vinci, while setting the stage for the

Bibliothèque Nationale, Du Bellay (during the same period) penned *Défense et illustration de la langue française* (*La deffence et illustration de la langue françoyse*). And even though nearly a century later (1635), Cardinal Richelieu solidified the French language with a dictionary and the Académie Française, the romance with Italian culture—from architecture to painting to the Roman Empire—saturated France's very claims to its "unique" identity. See Jenkins's *A Brief History of France*, 53, 81.

13. Nemours's Italian connections further include organizing a (failed) field trip to Italy and conducting an affair with a colleague named, appropriately, Florence. Together—the canceled field trip to Italy, Nemours's cut-short affair with Florence, and Junie's necessitated avoidance of Italian class once she realizes the dangerous love that Nemours's presence creates—the narrative threads that hinge on Italy and Italian culture function in historical parallelism and symbolic seepage. Although Henri II, for example, captured several Italian cities in his bid to dominate Europe, he was ultimately held back from securing Tuscany in 1553.

14. Jenkins, *A Brief History of France*, 80-81.

15. Few French films portray France's regional accents. Important exceptions include Renoir's *Toni* (1935) and Marcel Pagnol's "Mareilles Trilogy": *Marius* (1931), *Fanny* (1932), and *César* (1936).

16. Just as Sauder's film opens *La princesse Clèves* to a French multicultural translation (against the remarks of then-president Sarkozy), others in France fret endlessly about the failure of cultural assimilation. See Alain Finkielkraut's comments in Dan Bilefsky and Aurelien Breeden's article "2 Nobels Fail to Quiet Talk of France's Malaise," *New York Times*, October 14, 2014, A4. Recent events around the attacks on *Charlie Hebdo* and the kosher supermarket in Paris have tightened the political and cultural focus on France's definition of national identity.

17. Taurand, "Le scénario." Taurand cowrote the screenplay with Honoré: "*La Princesse de Clèves* est aussi une histoire de silences et de jeux de regards.... Le film de Christophe, à l'arrivée, fait la part belle à ces jeux de regards qui sont au bout du compte, plus brûlants que les mots puisqu'il y a derrière le désir retenu" (233). Translation by the authors.

18. On the movement, see Lauren Elkin and Scott Esposito's *The End of Oulipo?*, Harry Mathews and Alastair Brotchie's *Oulipo Compendium*, and Warren F. Motte's edited volume *Oulipo: A Primer of Potential Literature*.

19. Yet another Hitchcockian echo occurs here. Consider the drunken professor who shares a train car with Guy (Farley Granger) in *Strangers on a Train* while Bruno commits a murder in Guy's name. The drunk professor rattles on about "integration" and how the "differentiated is obtained."

20. Lyotard, *The Postmodern Condition*, 58-59.

21. Mallarmé, *Collected Poems*, 67.

22. For a comprehensive review of *Yaaba* and the filmmaker, as well as criticisms of the film, see Josef Gugler's *African Film*, 30-36.

23. This scene from *Yaaba* anticipates Honoré's traditional Breton wedding celebration in *Non ma fille*. While *Yaaba* deserves a longer discussion, it is decidedly an important film for Honoré and suggests his interest in connecting the similarities and distinctions between cultural rituals.

24. Foucault, "Truth and Power," 61.
25. The letter appears this way in the film: "Je t'aime trop pour te laisser croire que je pouvais me passer de toi. Que tu me trompes, je m'en fous. Tant que tu as la sincérité de me le dire. Que tu me caches, je m'en fous. Tant que tu viens me retrouver même pour une minute, même pour une seconde. La patience me va, et en t'attendant, c'est tout ton corps que je récite par coeur, tes bras si doux, tes lèvres, l'odeur de tes cheveux. Et tes genoux. Dire que même de tes genoux, je suis amoureux." Translation by the authors.
26. Quoted in Nietzsche, *Human, All Too Human*, 61. Further references to this source are cited parenthetically in the text.
27. "The Romantics were enamored of death," Allan H. Pasco writes. But by "the mid-1830s," Pasco continues, "literary death and especially literary suicide had become a tired cliché.... As a means of closure it was a bore." Pasco, *Sick Heroes*, 134.
28. On this, see our discussion about *Dans Paris*. See, further, Sedgwick's *Epistemology of the Closet*, 179-80.
29. Vincendeau, "*Dans Paris*," 60.
30. On this, see Riedel's "Scientific Theory or Practical Doctrine?"
31. Nietzsche, *The Gay Science*, 91–92.
32. Consider Alice's lyrics in *Les chansons* while she drinks Ismaël's "sweet venom"; his poison may be romantically sacrificial for him, but for Alice it is, for but a moment, sensually rewarding.
33. Riedel, "Scientific Theory or Practical Doctrine?," 188.
34. François Le Lionnais asserts in his "Second Manifesto," "Most writers and readers feel (or pretend to feel) that extremely constraining structures such as the acrostic, spoonerisms, the lipogram, the palindrome, or the holorhyme (to cite only these five) are mere examples of acrobatics and deserve nothing more than a wry grin, since they could never help to engender truly valid works of art. Never? Indeed. People are a little too quick to sneer at acrobatics. Breaking a record in one of those extremely constraining structures can in itself serve to justify the work; the emotion that derives from its semantic aspect constitutes a value which should certainly not be overlooked, but which remains nonetheless secondary." Le Lionnais, "Second Manifesto," 30.
35. Bénabou, "Rule and Constraint," 41.
36. Although another chapter could be dedicated to Honoré's biblical references of the allegorical trees and the so-called expulsion narrative in which the trees are rooted (that is, the Adam and Eve narrative that sees the young couple evicted from the Garden of Eden), time and space preclude such a digression.
37. Lanfer, *Remembering Eden*, 33, 64 (see chapter 2).
38. Nietzsche, *Human, All Too Human*, 302.
39. Gayatri Chakravorty Spivak raises a similar point regarding the "double bind": "To some," Spivak writes, "the double bind ... may seem a dangerous idea. And yet, to deny its pervasiveness leads to failed revolution. Paradoxically, to acknowledge its pervasiveness does not lead to unqualified success. This is its danger.... This paradox by no means exhausts the power and danger of the double bind. The one thing we can propose is that the fiction and reality comparativism in extremis often makes visible the double bind between ethics and politics." Spivak, "Rethinking Comparativism," 476.

40. Godard, *Godard on Godard*, 217.
41. Louis Lumière's favored camera setup "as well as a means of structuring an image is a way of suggesting depth. Often the diagonal component will be an axis of motion. . . . Sometimes it is merely a decorative element in an essentially flat composition." A. Williams, *Republic of Images*, 28.
42. See Thomas Elsaesser's "Tales of Sound and Fury."
43. *Metamorphoses* expands on the complex arrangement between choice and existence, between nature and consumer culture. Although drawn from Ovid, the film fully resonates with contemporary culture.
44. Hough, *Nietzsche's Noontide Friend*, 55. Further references to this work will be cited parenthetically in the text.
45. It is tempting to pair *La belle personne*'s final image with Maurice Pialat's opening title sequence in *À nos amours*. The similarity is most likely a conscious decision on Honoré's part. The distinction, however, lies in Honoré's framing of Junie's self-determination rather than Pialat's treatment of the character Suzanne (Sandrine Bonnaire), whose position on the boat suggests a complex and uncertain self-identity.

INTERVIEW

1. References to years in the French school system have been translated into the American school system. Here Honoré says "la cinquième," which corresponds to the seventh grade in the United States. Subsequent references are translated in similar fashion.—Trans.
2. Annual rock-music festival held in Rennes.
3. Honoré uses the term "cinéaste" for a concept that is translated alternatively as "director" or "filmmaker," depending on the context.—Trans.
4. *Astérix* and *Tintin* are well-known comic books. *Astérix* has been published in France since the 1960s and chronicles the resistance of the Gauls against the invasion of the Romans. *Tintin* is a Belgian comic-book series that has been published since the 1950s; it relates the tales of a young Belgian reporter, Tintin, and his faithful dog, Milou (later called Snowy).—Trans.
5. *Le nouveau roman*, or the New Novel, was a style of novelistic writing in the mid- to late 1950s, claiming to personalize the author's observations of the physical world by focusing more on objects than on plot and characters. Some proponents of the New Novel were Alain Robbe-Grillet, Michel Butor, Georges Perec, Nathalie Sarraute, and Marguerite Duras.—Trans.
6. *J'élève ma poupée* is a short, humoristic book about how to raise a doll. It is written in a camp style, making fun of the "how to raise a girl" books that were popular during the 1950s and 1960s.
7. Autofiction is a literary term coined by Serge Doubrovsky in his novel *Fils* (1977) to designate the mixture of autobiography and fiction.—Trans.
8. Transformism is the notion that everything and everyone progresses, meaning that everything will always get better. For example, because the twenty-first century comes after the twelfth century, de facto things and people are better. In the queer world, it suggests that things are getting better and it's unnecessary to make a fuss about things because everything will all work out. Honoré is clearly criticizing this concept here.—Trans.

9. The address of *Cahiers du Cinéma*.
10. "La triste moralité du cinéma français." We discuss Honoré's article on p. 16.
11. "Cinema of power" is Honoré's term in which he refers to filmmakers who use their directorial position to manipulate the spectator. Later, the director Kechiche serves as an example.
12. The tale of Katell Gollet is about a young and beautiful girl from Brittany. Her great beauty, however, is not as great as her perverse spirit. Her father, the count of La Roche Maurice, believes she needs to be married so as to redeem her soul. Nevertheless, she prefers to dance at typical Breton parties than to think about marriage. Finally, she makes a commitment to her father that she will marry the man who can dance with her for twelve hours. This is a disaster. Many men of the county who are drawn to her beauty are killed during their dance with Katell because of the alcohol they imbibe and because Katell is inexhaustible. She survives them all until the Devil comes to earth in the guise of a male suitor. He dances with her, but it is her final dance, since he brings her to hell. See, further, "Katell Gollet dans la gueule de l'enfer," Bretagne.com, last updated March 15, 2015, www.bretagne.com/fr/culture_bretonne/contes_et_legendes/katell_gollet.
13. Honoré uses "lyrisme" twice in this sentence. The French term has a complex constellation of connotations, which includes "lyricism" or "musicality," as well as "enthusiasm" and "sensitivity."—Trans.
14. La Rochelle Film Festival in 2003.
15. "Être au cadre" is to be the camera operator. Honoré is thus commenting on Ozon's control of the shooting process that often involves him directly behind the camera.
16. Garrel's new film, cowritten with Honoré, is *Les deux amis* (2015).
17. "Les gérard du cinema" is a satiric award ceremony for the worst film and actors in French cinema, sort of like the Razzi Awards.
18. Honoré refers to Morel's film *Le clan* (*Three Dancing Slaves*, 2004).
19. A monthly French magazine, launched in 1991, that looks at cultural events and society.
20. The play opened in the summer of 2012.
21. Julien can also be seen in the role of Sancerre in *La belle personne*.
22. Bel is a French choreographer and modern dancer who has partnered with the dancer Andrieux on several projects. They met in 2007 at the Opéra de Lyon.
23. Haute autorité pour la diffusion des oeuvres et la protection des droits d'auteur sur Internet. This was a law adopted in 2009 ostensibly to protect artists and others from copyright infringement on the Internet. The law was revoked in 2013 when it was decided that the penalties on copyright infringers were too punitive. See note 11 to part 2.
24. In both 2006 and 2009, Sarkozy claimed that reading such historical French novels was not valuable, especially for French citizens training to work as civil servants. Simon Daniellou directs our attention to Honoré's savvy critique of Sarkozy in "La cinéphilie comme contemporanéité" (35).
25. Honoré is referring here to the years before Sarkozy became president (2007-12), when he moved rather quickly from the Ministry of the Interior to the Ministry of Finance and then again to the Ministry of the Interior. His trajectory demonstrated a clear plan to vie for the presidency.—Trans.
26. Films by the Tunisian director include *La faute à Voltaire* (*Poetical Refugee*, 2000) and *La vie d'Adèle* (*Blue Is the Warmest Color*, 2013).

27. "Liberté, Égalité, Fraternité" (liberty, equality, brotherhood), the motto of the French Republic, one of many used during the 1789 Revolution, which only in the Third Republic (1870–1940) became the national motto.—Trans.
28. "Défense et illustration [de la langue française]." This phrase refers to the document written by Joachim DuBellay in 1549 as manifesto of the Pleiade poets, claiming the right to use French, instead of Greek or Latin, as a legitimately expressive and beautiful language for poetry. The interviewer questions here whether Honoré considers his film *Homme au bain* as an aesthetic manifesto that problematizes the concept of French Revolution universalism dressed in "blue, white, and red." Here, the white, black, and "beur" would parallel and substitute the "blue, white, and red" of the republican flag of modern France.—Trans.
29. "Beur" is a term used to designate French-born people of North African, or Maghrebin, origin. The term is an example of *verlan*, a linguistic slang that reverses syllables commonly used by high school and college students; here "arabe" (where the final "e" is pronounced) becomes "beu-ra-a" and then "beur" by contraction. The term is used only in familiar registers of language. ("Rebeu," a doubly *verlan*-ized term, is now also used.)—Trans.
30. Gennevilliers is a town in the northern suburbs ("banlieue") of Paris. The term "banlieue" often conjures ideas of crime and delinquency for some French people (consider Mathieu Kassovitz's 1995 *La haine*), whereas "suburbs" usually makes Americans think of upper-middle-class people who have escaped the inner cities. The realities of the American and French suburb are, of course, more complex. Nonetheless, François Sagat comes from Royan in the Vendée, an area in the south of Brittany on the Atlantic coast; he has nothing of the Paris "banlieue" about him.—Trans.
31. "Positive discrimination," as Honoré uses the expression, indicates a situation in which people are profiled for positive reasons. He sees this as a common practice in the United States, possibly because of affirmative action, but it seems he's also considering the multiplicity of ethnicities in America in contrast with the more limited differences, according to him, in the French population.—Trans.
32. Honoré directed Francis Poulenc's 1957 opera at the Opéra de Lyon in 2013.

BIBLIOGRAPHY

Abel, Richard. "*Photogénie* and Company." In *French Film Theory and Criticism, 1907–1939*, vol. 1, *1907–1929*, 95–124. Princeton, NJ: Princeton University Press, 1988.

Alden, Jane. "Excavating Chansonniers: Musical Archaeology and the Search for Popular Song." *Journal of Musicology* 25, no. 1 (2008): 46–87.

Althusser, Louis. *The Future Lasts Forever: A Memoir*. Edited by Olivier Corpet and Yann Moulier Boutang. Translated by Richard Vesey. New York: New Press, 1992.

Andrew, Dudley. *Mists of Regret: Culture and Sensibility in Classic French Film*. Princeton, NJ: Princeton University Press, 1995.

Andrew, Dudley, with Hervé Joubert-Laurencin. *Opening Bazin: Postwar Film Theory and Its Afterlife*. New York: Oxford University Press, 2011.

Armes, Roy. *French Cinema since 1946*. London: Tantivy, 1976.

Arnheim, Rudolf. "A New Laocoön: Artistic Composites and the Talking Film." In *Film as Art*, 199–230. Berkeley: University of California, 1957.

Babuscio, Jack. "Camp and the Gay Sensibility." In *Camp Grounds: Style and Homosexuality*, edited by David Bergman, 19–38. Amherst: University of Massachusetts Press, 1993.

Badiou, Alain. "The Demy Affair." In *Cinema*, translated by Susan Spitzer, 64–66. Cambridge, UK: Polity, 2013.

———. "Reference Points for Cinema's Second Modernity." In *Cinema*, translated by Susan Spitzer, 58–63. Cambridge, UK: Polity, 2013.

Barthes, Roland. *A Lover's Discourse: Fragments*. New York: Hill and Wang, 1978.

Baudry, Jean-Louis. "The Apparatus: Metapsychological Approaches to the Impression of Reality in Cinema." In *Narrative, Apparatus, Ideology: A Film Theory Reader*, edited by Philip Rosen, 299–318. New York: Columbia University Press, 1986.

———. "Ideological Effects of the Basic Cinematographic Apparatus." In *Narrative, Apparatus, Ideology: A Film Theory Reader*, edited by Philip Rosen, 286–98. New York: Columbia University Press, 1986.

Bazin, André. *Qu'est-ce que le cinéma?* Paris: Éditions Du Cerf, 1958.

———. *Jean Renoir*. Edited by François Truffaut. New York: Simon and Schuster, 1973.

Bénabou, Marcel. "Rule and Constraint." In *Oulipo: A Primer of Potential Literature*, edited by Warren F. Motte, 40–46. Normal, IL: Dalkey Archive, 1998.

Bergson, Henri. *Matter and Memory*. Translated by Nancy Margaret Paul and W. Scott Palmer. New York: Macmillan, 1913.

Bersani, Leo. *The Freudian Body: Psychoanalysis and Art.* New York: Columbia University Press, 1986.
Bingham, Adam. "The Relentless Vision of Maurice Pialat." *Cineaste* 35, no. 1 (2009). www.cineaste.com/articles/the-relentless-vision-of-maurice-pialat-web-exclusive.
Bouquet, Stéphane. "Le sens du décor dans l'oeuvre de Christophe Honoré." Paper presented at the "Journée d'études doctorale: Christophe Honoré ou l'invention d'une écriture" symposium, Tours, France, February 20, 2015.
Bourcier, Marie-Hélène. *Queer Zones.* Paris: La Fabrique, 2005.
Brey, Iris. "Monstrous Mothers in French Contemporary Cinema." Ph.D. diss., Department of French, New York University, 2014.
Brunius, Jacques-B. *En marge du cinéma français.* Lausanne, France: Editions L'Age d'Homme, 1987.
Buss, Robin. Introduction to *The Princesse de Clèves,* by Madame de Lafayette, 1–18. London: Penguin, 2004.
Castle, Terry. *The Apparitional Lesbian: Female Homosexuality and Modern Culture.* New York: Columbia University Press, 1993.
———. *The Literature of Lesbianism: A Historical Anthology from Ariosto to Stonewall.* New York: Columbia University Press, 2003.
Cavitch, Max. "Sex after Death: François Ozon's Libidinal Invasions." *Screen* 48, no. 3 (2007): 313–26.
Chilcoat, Michelle. "Queering the Family in François Ozon's *Sitcom.*" In *Queer Cinema in Europe,* edited by Robin Griffiths, 23–33. Chicago: Intellect Books, University of Chicago Press, 2008.
Chow, Rey. *Sentimental Fabulations, Contemporary Chinese Films: Attachment in the Age of Global Visibility.* New York: Columbia University Press, 2007.
Cléder, Jean, and Timothée Picard, eds. *Christophe Honoré: Le cinéma nous inachève.* Lormont, France: Éditions le Bord d'Leau, 2014.
Cleto, Fabio. "Introduction: Queering the Camp." In *Camp: Queer Aesthetics and the Performing Subject: A Reader,* ed. Cleto, 1–42. Ann Arbor: University of Michigan Press, 1999.
Conway, Kelley. *Chanteuse in the City: The Realist Singer in French Film.* Berkeley: University of California Press, 2004.
Daniellou, Simon. "La cinéphilie comme contémporanéité dans le cinéma de Christophe Honoré." In *Christophe Honoré: Le cinéma nous inachève,* edited by Jean Cléder and Timothée Picard, 33–47. Lormont, France: Éditions le Bord d'Leau, 2014.
Darke, Chris. *Light Readings: Film Criticism and Screen Arts.* London: Wallflower, 2000.
Dayan, Daniel. "The Tutor Code of Classical Cinema." *Film Quarterly* 28, no. 1 (1974): 22–31.
Derrida, Jacques. *Of Grammatology.* Translated by Gayatri Chakravorty Spivak. Baltimore: Johns Hopkins University Press, 1997.
———. *Specters of Marx: The State of the Debt, the Work of Mourning, and the New International.* Translated by Peggy Kamuf. New York: Routledge, 1994.
Drobnick, Jim. "Inhaling Passions: Art, Sex, and Scent." *Sexuality and Culture* 4, no. 3 (2000): 37–56.
Du Bellay, Joachim. *La deffence et illustration de la langue françoyse.* 1549. Edited by Francis Goyet and Oliver Millet. Paris: Champion, 2003.

Duggan, Anne E. *Queer Enchantments: Gender, Sexuality, and Class in the Fairy-Tale Cinema of Jacques Demy.* Detroit: Wayne State University Press, 2013.
Durgnat, Raymond. *Jean Renoir.* Berkeley: University of California Press, 1974.
Dyer, Richard. "Entertainment and Utopia." In *Only Entertainment,* 19–35. London: Routledge, 1992.
———. "It's Being So Camp as Keeps Us Going." In *Only Entertainment,* 135–47. London: Routledge, 1992.
Dyer, Richard, and Julianne Pidduck. *Now You See It: Studies in Lesbian and Gay Film.* London: Routledge, 2003.
Edelman, Lee. *Homographesis: Essays in Gay Literary and Cultural Theory.* New York: Routledge, 1994.
———. *No Future: Queer Theory and the Death Drive.* Durham, NC: Duke University Press, 2004.
Elkin, Lauren, and Scott Esposito. *The End of Oulipo? An Attempt to Exhaust a Movement.* Winchester, UK: Zero, 2013.
Elsaesser, Thomas. *Fassbinder's Germany: History, Identity, Subject.* Amsterdam: Amsterdam University Press, 1996.
———. "Tales of Sound and Fury: Observations on the Family Melodrama." In *Film Genre Reader III,* edited by Barry Keith Grant, 366–97. Austin: University of Texas Press, 2003.
Eribon, Didier. *Returning to Reims.* Translated by Michael Lucey. Los Angeles: Semiotext(e), 2013.
Evans, Claude. "Fantasies and Ambiguous Sexuality in Patrice Leconte's *Le Mari de la coiffeuse* and *La Fille sur le pont.*" *Studies in French Cinema* 4, no. 2 (2004): 135–46.
Fassin, Éric. "Entre famille et nation: La filiation naturalisée." *Droit et Société* 72, no. 2 (2009): 373–82.
———. *L'inversion de la question homosexuelle.* Paris: Éditions Amsterdam, 2005.
Faulkner, Christopher. Interactive map essay. *Boudu Saved from Drowning / Boudu Sauvé Des Eaux.* Dir. Jean Renoir. Criterion Collection, 2005. Film originally released 1931, Pathé.
Feuer, Jane. "Hollywood Musicals: Mass Art as Folk Art." *Jump Cut* 23 (1980): 23–25.
Foucault, Michel. "Truth and Power." In *The Foucault Reader,* edited by Paul Rabinow, 51–75. New York: Pantheon, 1984.
Fox, Alistair, Michel Marie, Raphaëlle Moine, and Hilary Radner, eds. *A Companion to Contemporary French Cinema.* Malden, MA: Wiley-Blackwell, 2015.
Freud, Sigmund. "A Note upon the 'Mystic Writing-Pad' (1925)." In *General Psychological Theory: Papers on Metapsychology,* 211–16. New York: Collier, 1963.
Gaudreault, André. "Narration and Monstration in the Cinema." *Journal of Film and Video* 39, no. 2 (1987): 29–36.
Gerstner, David A. "Choreographing Homosexual Desire in Philippe Vallois's *Johan.*" *Camera Obscura 84* 28, no. 3 (2013): 125–56.
———. "Christophe Honoré's *Les Chansons d'amour* and the Musical's Queer-abilities." In *The Sound of Musicals,* edited by Steven Cohan, 188–99. London: BFI, 2010.
———. "The Practices of Authorship." In *Authorship and Film,* edited by David A. Gerstner and Janet Staiger, 3–25. New York: Routledge, 2003.

Gilbert, Avery. *What the Nose Knows: The Science of Scent in Everyday Life*. New York: Crown Books, 2008.

Gobbi Sica, Grazia. *The Florentine Villa: Architecture, History, Society*. New York: Routledge, 2007.

Godard, Jean-Luc. *Godard on Godard: Critical Writings by Jean-Luc Godard*. Edited by Jean Narboni and Tom Milne. Translated by Tom Milne. New York: Da Capo, 1972.

Goldthwaite, Richard A. *The Building of Renaissance Florence: An Economic and Social History*. Baltimore: Johns Hopkins University Press, 1982.

Greene, Naomi. *Pier Paolo Pasolini: Cinema as Heresy*. Princeton, NJ: Princeton University Press, 1990.

Gugler, Josef. *African Film: Re-imagining a Continent*. Bloomington: Indiana University Press, 2003.

Gunning, Tom. Preface to *Jean Epstein: Critical Essays and New Translations*, edited by Sarah Keller and Jason N. Paul, 13–21. Amsterdam: Amsterdam University Press, 2012.

Handyside, Fiona. "The Possibilities of a Beach: Queerness and François Ozon's Beaches." *Screen* 53, no. 1 (2012): 54–71.

Hayward, Susan, and Ginette Vincendeau, eds. *French Film: Texts and Contexts*. London: Routledge, 2000.

Hill, Rodney, "The New Wave Meets the Tradition of Quality: Jacques Demy's *The Umbrellas of Cherbourg*." *Cinema Journal* 48, no. 1 (2008): 27–50.

Honoré, Christophe. "La triste moralité du cinéma français." *Cahiers du Cinéma* 521 (1998): 4–5.

———. *Le livre pour enfants*. Paris: Éditions de l'Olivier, 2005.

———. "Peep-Show Troopers." *Cahiers du Cinéma* 523 (1998): 8.

Horne, Alistair. *Seven Ages of Paris*. New York: Vintage, 2004.

Hough, Sheridan. *Nietzsche's Noontide Friend: The Self as Metaphoric Double*. University Park: Pennsylvania State University Press, 1997.

Humphrey, Daniel. *Queer Bergman: Sexuality, Gender, and the European Art Cinema*. Austin: University of Texas Press, 2013.

Ince, Kate. "François Ozon's Cinema of Desire." In *Five Directors: Auteurism from Assayas to Ozon*, edited by Ince, 112–34. Manchester: University of Manchester Press, 2011.

———. "Queering the Family? Fantasy and the Performance of Sexuality and Gay Relations in French Cinema, 1995–2000." *Studies in French Cinema* 2, no. 2 (2002): 90–97.

Jenkins, Cecil. *A Brief History of France*. Philadelphia: Running Press, 2011.

Julius, Anthony. *Transgressions: The Offences of Art*. Chicago: University of Chicago Press, 2002.

Keller, Sarah, and Jason N. Paul, eds. *Jean Epstein: Critical Essays and New Translations*. Amsterdam: Amsterdam University Press, 2012.

Kendall, Tina. "Reframing Bataille: On Tacky Spectatorship in the New European Extremism." In *The New Extremism in Cinema: From France to Europe*, edited by Tanya Horeck and Tina Kendall, 43–54. Edinburgh: Edinburgh University Press, 2013.

Kracauer, Siegfried. *Theory of Film: The Redemption of Physical Reality*. New York: Oxford University Press, 1960.

Kuntzel, Thierry. "Film Works 2." *Camera Obscura* 5 (1980): 7–68.

Lafayette, Madame de. *The Princesse de Clèves.* 1678. Translated by Robin Buss. London: Penguin, 2004.

Lanfer, Peter Thacher. *Remembering Eden: The Reception History of Genesis 3: 22–24.* New York: Oxford University Press, 2012.

Lecompte, Rémi. "La représentation de l'écoute dans le cinéma de Christophe Honoré." Paper presented at the "Journée d'études doctorale: Christophe Honoré ou l'invention d'une écriture" symposium, Tours, France February 20, 2015.

Le Lionnais, François. "Second Manifesto." In *Oulipo: A Primer of Potential Literature,* edited by Warren F. Motte, 29–31. Normal, IL: Dalkey Archive, 1998.

Leutrat, Jean-Louis. "The Declension." In *Jean-Luc Godard: Son + Image, 1974–1991,* edited by Raymond Bellour, Mary Lea Bandy, Laurence Kardish, Barbara London, and Colin MacCabe, 23–42. New York: Museum of Modern Art, 1992.

Lupton, Catherine. *Chris Marker: Memories of the Future.* London: Reaktion Books, 2005.

Lyotard, Jean-François. *The Postmodern Condition: A Report on Knowledge.* Minneapolis: University of Minnesota Press, 1984.

MacKay, John, trans. "Walter Benjamin and Rudolf Arnheim on Charlie Chaplin." *Yale Journal of Criticism* 9 (Fall 1996): 309–14.

Mallarmé, Stéphane. *Collected Poems: A Bilingual Edition.* Translated and edited by Henry Weinfeld. Berkeley: University of California Press, 1994.

Marie, Michel. *The French New Wave: An Artistic School.* Translated by Richard John Neupert. Malden, MA: Blackwell, 2003.

Mathews, Harry, and Alastair Brotchie. *Oulipo Compendium.* London: Atlas, 2005.

McCaffrey, Enda. *The Gay Republic: Sexuality, Citizenship and Subversion in France.* Aldershot, UK: Ashgate, 2005.

Milner, Sally. "Documenting the Motherland: Nation and Mothers in *Tarnation, Mamma Roma,* and *Heavenly Creatures.*" Master's thesis, College of Staten Island, 2007.

Mitry, Jean. *The Aesthetics and Psychology of the Cinema.* 1963. Translated by Christopher King. Bloomington: Indiana University Press, 1997.

Morgan, Daniel. "Rethinking Bazin: Ontology and Realist Aesthetics." *Critical Inquiry* 32 (2006): 443–81.

Morrey, Douglas. "Jean-Luc Godard, Christophe Honoré, and the Legacy of the New Wave in French Cinema." In *The Legacies of Jean-Luc Godard,* edited by Douglas Morrey, Christina Stojanova, and Nicole Côté, 3–14. Waterloo, ON: Wilfrid Laurier University Press, 2014.

Motte, Warren F., ed. *Oulipo: A Primer of Potential Literature.* Normal, IL: Dalkey Archive, 1998.

Mulvey, Laura. "Images of Women, Images of Sexuality: Some Films by Godard." In *Visual and Other Pleasures,* 2nd ed., 51–65. Basingstoke, UK: Palgrave Macmillan, 2009.

Nesbitt, Molly. "History without Object." In *Art and Film since 1945: Hall of Mirrors (Museum of Contemporary Art, Los Angeles, 17 March 1996–28 July 1996),* edited by Russell Fergusson. Los Angeles: Museum of Contemporary Art, 1996.

Neupert, Richard John. *A History of the French New Wave Cinema.* Madison: University of Wisconsin Press, 2007.

Nietzsche, Friedrich Wilhelm. *The Gay Science: With a Prelude in Rhymes and an Appendix of Songs*. Translated by Walter Arnold Kaufmann. New York: Vintage, 1974.

———. *Human, All Too Human: A Book for Free Spirits*. Translated by R. J. Hollingdale. Cambridge: Cambridge University Press, 2004.

———. *The Portable Nietzsche*. Edited and translated by Walter Kaufmann. New York: Penguin, 1976.

Palmer, Tim. *Brutal Intimacy: Analyzing Contemporary French Cinema*. Middletown, CT: Wesleyan University Press, 2011.

Panofsky, Erwin. "Style and Medium in the Motion Pictures." In *Film Theory and Criticism*, 7th ed., edited by Leo Braudy and Marshall Cohen, 247–61. New York: Oxford University Press, 2009.

Pasco, Allan H. *Sick Heroes: French Society and Literature in the Romantic Age, 1750–1850*. Exeter, UK: University of Exeter Press, 1997.

Pasolini, Pier Paolo. *Theorem*. 1968. Translated by Stuart Hood. London: Quartet Books, 1992.

Pearl, Monica. "AIDS and New Queer Cinema." *New Queer Cinema: A Critical Reader*, edited by Michele Aaron, 23–38. New Brunswick, NJ: Rutgers University Press, 2004.

Perec, Georges. *An Attempt at Exhausting a Place in Paris*. Translated by Marc Lowenthal. Cambridge, MA: Wakefield, 2010.

Perreau, Bruno. *The Politics of Adoption: Gender and the Making of French Citizenship*. Cambridge, MA: MIT Press, 2014.

Powrie, Phil. "The Disintegration of Community: Popular Music in French Cinema, 1945–Present." In *Popular Music in France from Chanson to Techno: Culture, Identity, and Society*, edited by Steve Cannon and Hugh Dauncey, 97–115. Aldershot, UK: Ashgate, 2003.

Projansky, Sarah, and Kent A. Ono. "Making Films Asian American: *Shopping for Fangs* and the Discursive Auteur." In *Authorship and Film*, edited by David A. Gerstner and Janet Staiger, 263–80. New York: Routledge, 2003.

Pullen, Christopher. "The Films of Ducastel and Martineau: Gay Identity, the Family, and the Autobiographical Self." In *Queer Cinema in Europe*, edited by Robin Griffiths, 49–62. Bristol, UK: Intellect Books, 2008.

Rees-Roberts, Nick. *French Queer Cinema*. Edinburgh: Edinburgh University Press, 2008.

Riedel, Manfred. "Scientific Theory or Practical Doctrine?" In *Nietzsche, Theories of Knowledge, and Critical Theory*, edited by Babette Babich and Robert S. Cohen, 187–208. Dordrecht, Netherlands: Kluwer Academic, 1999.

Robcis, Camille. *The Law of Kinship: Anthropology, Psychoanalysis, and the Family in France*. Ithaca, NY: Cornell University Press, 2013.

Rodowick, D. N. *Elegy for Theory*. Cambridge, MA: Harvard University Press, 2014.

———. *The Virtual Life of Film*. Cambridge, MA: Harvard University Press, 2007.

Rolls, Alistair Charles. *The Flight of the Angels: Intertextuality in Four Novels of Boris Vian*. Amsterdam: Rodopi, 1999.

Rosen, Philip, ed. *Narrative, Apparatus, Ideology: A Film Theory Reader*. New York: Columbia University Press, 1986.

Roudinesco, Élisabeth. *Jacques Lacan*. Translated by Barbara Bray. New York: Columbia University Press, 1997.

"Roundtable on the Return to Classical Film Theory." *October* 148 (Spring 2014): 5–26.

Russell, Lee (Peter Wollen). "Jean Renoir." *New Left Review* 1, no. 12 (1964): 57–60.

Schilt, Thibaut. *François Ozon*. Urbana: University of Illinois Press, 2011.

Schor, Naomi. "The Crisis of French Universalism." *Yale French Studies* 100 (2001): 43–64.

Schwartz, Vanessa. "Who Killed Brigitte Bardot? Perspectives on the New Wave at Fifty." *Cinema Journal* 49, no. 4 (2010): 145–52.

Scott, Joan Wallach. *Parité: Sexual Equality and the Crisis of French Universalism*. Chicago: University of Chicago Press, 2005.

Sedgwick, Eve Kosofsky. *The Epistemology of the Closet*. Berkeley: University of California Press, 1990.

———. *Touching Feeling: Affect, Pedagogy, Performativity*. Durham, NC: Duke University Press, 2004.

Sellier, Geneviève. *Masculine Singular: French New Wave Cinema*. Durham, NC: Duke University Press, 2008.

Sharrett, Christopher. "*Salò, or the 120 Days of Sodom*." *Senses of Cinema* (Cinémathèque Annotations on Film) 70 (March 2014). http://sensesofcinema.com/2013/cteq/salo-or-the-120-days-of-sodom/.

Smith, Alison. *French Cinema in the 1970s: The Echoes of May*. Manchester: Manchester University Press, 2005.

Sontag, Susan. "Notes on 'Camp.'" In *Against Interpretation and Other Essays*, 275–92. New York: Picador, 2001.

Spivak, Gayatri Chakravorty. "Rethinking Comparativism." In *An Aesthetic Education in the Era of Globalization*, 467–83. Cambridge, MA: Harvard University Press, 2012.

Stack, Oswald. *Pasolini on Pasolini: Interviews with Oswald Stack*. Bloomington: Indiana University Press, 1969.

Stilwell, Robynn J. "Le Demy-monde: The Bewitched, Betwixt, and Between French Musical." In *Popular Music in France from Chanson to Techno: Culture, Identity, and Society*, edited by Hugh Dauncey and Steve Cannon, 123–38. Aldershot, UK: Ashgate, 2003.

Taurand, Gilles. "Le scénario: Un objet malléable, forcément inachevé." Interview with Jean Cléder and Aurélie Julien. In *Christophe Honoré: Le cinéma nous inachève*, edited by Jean Cléder and Timothée Picard, 229–42. Lormont, France: Éditions le Bord d'L'eau, 2014.

Thompson, Kristin. *Breaking the Glass Armor: Neoformalist Film Analysis*. Princeton, NJ: Princeton University Press, 1988.

Thomsen, Christian Braad. "Conversations with Rainer Werner Fassbinder." In *Rainer Werner Fassbinder*, edited by Laurence Kardish and Juliane Lorenz, 85–89. New York: Museum of Modern Art, 1997.

Truffaut, François. *Hitchcock*. Rev ed. New York: Simon and Schuster, 1983.

Tyler, Parker. "Ode to Hollywood." In *Masquerade: Queer Poetry in America to the End of World War II*, edited by Jim Elledge, 222. Bloomington: Indiana University Press, 2004.

Ungerer, Tomi. *Otto: The Autobiography of a Teddy Bear*. London: Phaidon, 2010.

Vanderschelden, Isabelle. "The 'Beautiful People' of Christophe Honoré: New Wave Legacies and New Directions in French Auteur Cinema." *Studies in European Cinema* 7, no. 2 (2010): 135–48.

Vasse, David. *Le nouvel âge du cinéma d'auteur français*. Paris: Klincksieck, 2008.

Vegari, Amy. "Calling the Shots: Women as Deleuzian Material in the Cinema of Godard." *Michigan Feminist Studies* 19 (Fall 2005–Spring 2006). http://hdl.handle.net/2027/spo.ark5583.0019.005.

Vignaux, Valérie. "Christophe Honoré et le cinéma ou l'invention d'une écriture." Paper presented at the "Journée d'études doctorale: Christophe Honoré ou l'invention d'une écriture" symposium, Tours, France, February 20, 2015.

Vincendeau, Ginette. "Daddy's Girls: Oedipal Narratives in 1930s French Films." *Iris* 8 (1988): 70–81.

———. "Dans Paris." *Sight and Sound* 17, no. 5 (2007): 59–60.

Waldron, Darren. *Queering Contemporary French Popular Cinema: Images and Their Reception.* New York: Peter Lang, 2009.

Wall-Romana, Christophe. "Epstein's *Photogénie* as Corporeal Vision: Inner Sensation, Queer Embodiment, and Ethics." In *Jean Epstein: Critical Essays and New Translations,* edited by Sarah Keller and Jason N. Paul, 51–71. Amsterdam: Amsterdam University Press, 2012.

Warehime, Marja. *French Film Directors: Maurice Pialat.* Manchester: University of Manchester Press, 2011.

Weber, Samuel. *Benjamin's -abilities.* Cambridge, MA: Harvard University Press, 2008.

"What's New in Classical Film Theory?" *Screen* 5, no. 3 (2014): 396–420.

Williams, Alan. *Republic of Images: A History of French Filmmaking.* Cambridge, MA: Harvard University Press, 1992.

Williams, James S. "His Life to Film: The Extreme Art of Jacques Nolot." *Studies in French Cinema* 9, no. 2 (2009): 177–90.

Wilson, Douglas B. *The Romantic Dream: Wordsworth and the Poetics of the Unconscious.* Lincoln: University of Nebraska Press, 1993.

Wollen, Peter. "Godard and Counter-Cinema: *Vent d'Est.*" In *Narrative, Apparatus, Ideology,* edited by Philip Rosen, 120–29. New York: Columbia University Press, 1986.

———. *Raiding the Icebox: Reflections on Twentieth-Century Culture.* Bloomington: Indiana University Press, 1993.

———. "Rules of the Game." In *Paris Hollywood: Writings on Film,* 149–63. London: Verso, 2002.

———. *Signs and Meaning in the Cinema.* Bloomington: Indiana University Press, 1972.

———. *Singin' in the Rain.* London: BFI, 1992.

INDEX

3 Dancing Slaves (2004), 235n18
8 Women (2002), 23, 185, 218n19
17 fois Cécile Cassard (2002), 93, 94, 187, 188, 194
400 Blows, The (1959), 13, 23, 24, 25

Adventures of Felix, The (2000), 4, 8, 88
After Him (2006), 99, 185
All That Heaven Allows (1955), 23
Allemagne année zéro (1948), 8, 202
Almodóvar, Pedro, 176, 180
Althusser, Louis, 68, 103, 226n21
amants criminels, Les (1999), 184
"Amoureux solitaires" (song), 196
Anatomy of Hell (2004), 193
À nos amours (1983), 24, 220n38, 234n45
Andrews, Dudley, 90
Andrieux, Cédric, 196–97, 235n22
Anger, Kenneth, 224n84
Angot, Christine, 175
Antonioni, Michelangelo, 223n84
Après lui (2006), 99, 185
Arnheim, Rudolf, xii, 128, 130, 137, 231n3
"AromaRama", 66
Artist, The (2011), 179
Ascenseur pur l'échafaud (1958), 111
Asterix (comics), 173, 234n4
"Au départ" (song), 93
"Au parc" (song), 115
Audiard, Jacques, 188, 194
"Avant la haine" (song), 76, 195
Aviator's Wife, The (1981), 182
Avignon Festival, 186, 187

Babuscio, Jack, 43, 44
Bad and the Beautiful, The (1952), 94
Badiou, Alain, 33, 222n68
Bagouet, Dominique, 192, 196
Balzac, Honoré de, 24, 201
Bardot, Brigitte, 58
Barrault, Marie-Christine, 189
Barry, Roukietou, 148
Barthes, Roland, 50, 62, 63, 77, 191
"Bastille, La" (song), 98
Bataille, Georges, 174, 190
Bazin, André, 44, 45
Beaupain, Alex: and "Avant la haine," 76, 195; and "Brooklyn Bridge," 111; and *Les chansons d'amour*, 30, 86–87, 89, 91–93, 111, 114; as collaborator, 91, 187; and *Dan Paris*, 103, 111; and "De bonnes raisons," 103; relationship with Christophe Honoré, 86, 89, 93, 187; and "Inventaire," 103; as lyricist, 30, 114, 118, 164
Beautiful Person, The (2008). See *La belle personne*
Beauty and the Beast (1946), 230n49
Bel, Jérôme, 186, 235n22
belle et la bête, La (1946), 230n49
belle personne, La (2008): use of actors, 188; as adaptation, 127, 131, 133–39, 142–43, 145–46, 152, 165, 198–99; and bodies, 151–52; and children's books, 136, 165–66; as cinema of monstration, 127, 128, 138, 147; cinema as trope, 143, 145–152; critical reception

of, 31, 180; theme of death, 137, 148, 157, 160–161, 164, 166; and double-bind politics, 161; Eros/Thanatos tension, 162; theme of incest, 39; use of the look, 127–128, 132, 138–41, 154; Lycée Molière as backdrop, 135–36, 146, 160, 198; and mathematics, 142–43, 145, 159; and media technology, 127, 129–30, 132; narrative arc, 127; opening sequence, 130–32; Paris setting, 128, 130–31, 135; place in Paris Trilogy, ix, 2, 128, 130, 133, 146, 155, 158–59, 161, 168–69, 202; and poetry, 143–44; and the Romantics, 155–60; 167–69; and song, 157, 161, 164, 168; trees as symbol, 155–56, 158, 160–67; and *Yaaba*, 146–52
Belmondo, Jean-Paul, 58, 194
Beloved (2010). See *Les bien-aimés*
Bénabou, Marcel, 159
Bersani, Leo, xii, 66–68
Bertolucci, Bernardo, 58
Beware of a Holy Whore (1971), 37
bien-aimés, Les (2010): 1, 191, 198; use of actors, 54, 59, 187, 188, 190, 216n2; and AIDS, 192, 215n1; choreography, 196, 197; cinematic mothers, 77, 226n27; critical reception of, 185, 186, 216n2; Eros/Thanatos tension, 41; female characters, 77, 135, 167, 226n27; and male bodies, 56; and music, 92, 93, 194, 195
Bingham, Adam, 23–24
Blanchot, Maurice, 174
Bonello, Bertrand, 179
Born in '68 (2008), 4
Boyfriends and Girlfriends (1987), 182
Bradshaw, Peter, 30, 58
Branco, Paulo, 51, 52, 53, 224n2
Breillat, Catherine, 20, 193
Brel, Jacques, 76
Bretagne, La (1936), 224n89
Britannicus (play), 133, 136
"Brooklyn Bridge" (song), 111

Buch, Mikael, 17, 18, 185
Buss, Robin, 131–32, 133, 139
Butaud, Alice, 52, 54
Butler, Judith, 39
Byron, George Gordon, 155, 156–57

café des Jules, Le (1989), 183
Cahiers du Cinéma: 6, 20, 86, 178, 181; Christophe Honoré as author, 16, 106, 174, 179; Christophe Honoré as subject, x, 176, 230n42
Calhoun, David, 31
Callas, Maria, 137, 146, 154, 165
Calvin, John, 139, 140
Carné, Marcel, 21, 220n37
Carvajal-Alegria, Esteban, 145
Castle, Terry, 105–6, 107
Catinchi, Philippe-Jean, xi
Cavalier, Alain, 182
Cavitch, Max, 8, 10
Ceux qui m'aiment prendront le train (1998), 184
Chabrol, Claude, 6, 7, 19, 28, 33
chambre en ville, Une (1982), 33, 229n28
Change pas de main (1975), 86
chansons d'amour, Les (2007): use of actors, 188–90; and AIDS, 88–89; bed as trope, 103–5, 108, 112, 116, 118, 125; and bodies, 94, 108–9, 113–15; use of bridges and passageways, 110–15; choreography and movement, 94, 112, 118, 121, 197; critical reception of, 30–33, 176–77, 180; theme of death, 86, 94, 101–2, 112–13, 119, 191; as homage to Jacques Demy, 89, 92, 99–100, 109, 115, 123, 125; theme of Ephipany, 121–25; Eros/Thanatos tension, 1, 111, 114; theme of family, 85–87, 92, 98, 104, 106–7, 120–25; as homage to Jean-Luc Godard, 93, 98–100, 105, 107, 114; theme of incest, 39, 105–7, 123–24; theme of loss, 85–87, 94, 113, 118; theme of love, 85–86, 94, 99, 109, 125–26; narrative

INDEX

arc, 85, and odors, 109, 125; opening sequence, 95–99, Paris setting, 90, 94–95, 98–99, 101, 120; place in Paris Trilogy, ix, 2, 110, 128, 130, 133, 146, 155, 158, 168, 169, 202; and prayer, 103; and song, 85–86, 90–94, 103–4, 109–13, 115, 117, 120, 194, 195; and technology, 102; as homage to François Truffaut, 105

Chaplin, Charlie, 130

Chéreau, Patrice: as gay, 6, 29; influence on Christophe Honoré, 176, 184, 186, 193, 220n48

Children of the Princess of Clèves, The (2013), 231n7

Chinese Roulette (1976), 94

chinoise, La (1967), 58, 201

Chow, Rey, xii, 106, 107

Chronic'art, 30

Christ mort et les anges, Le (painting), 70, 71–72

Civeyrac, Jaen-Paul, 179

clan, Le (2004), 235n18

Claire's Knee (1970), 182

Cléder, Jean, x1

Cléo de 5 a 7 (1962), 90

Clerc, Julien, 93

Cocteau, Jean, 125, 230n49

Cœur di lilas (1932), 90

"Comme la pluie" (song), 164

Conway, Kelley, 45, 90, 91, 107

Cooper, Dennis, 130, 192

Courbet, Gustave, 132

Craven, Wes, 16

Criminal Lovers (1999), 184

Cronenberg, David, 83

Cunningham, Merce, 196

Curtain Raiser, A (2006), 28

"cygne, Le" (poem), 133, 144

Cukor, George, 23

Daney, Serge, 16, 192

Daniellou, Simon, 217n9, 235n24

Dans Paris (2006): use of actors, 50, 51–54, 56, 58–59, 80, 187, 190; bed as trope, 54, 56–57, 61, 63, 65, 68, 75, 78–81, 191; and bodies, 56, 65–66, 68, 72–73, 75, 79; choreography, 61; as cinema of monstration, 66, 68, 78; cinematic mothers 55, 77–79; critical reception of, 30, 31, 45, 180; theme of death, 49, 76, 77, 82, 83; and double-bind politics, 58, 67; theme of family, 54–55, 61–62, 65, 68, 70, 73, 75–76, 78–80, 83, 177, 178; as homage to Jean-Luc Godard, 51, 55; theme of incest, 39; theme of love, 62–64, 75, 82; narrative arc, 49; and New Wave, 50–51, 55, 58, 80, 180; and odors, 61, 63, 65–69, 73, 75; opening sequence, 49–55, 59, 75; Paris setting, 55, 59–62, 64–65, 75; place in Paris Trilogy, ix, 2, 50–51, 59–60, 62, 71, 76, 128, 130, 133, 146, 155, 158, 168, 169, 202; and prayer, 69, 70–74; and song, 76

Dargis, Manohla, 58

Darke, Chris, 223n84

David, Jacques-Louis, 132

Davis, Miles, 111

Dawson, Thomas, 30

"Day Is Done" (song), 168

Dead Christ and the Angels, The (painting), 70, 71–72

"De bonnes raisons" (song), 103

Delaive, François, 10

Delon, Alain, 194

Delorme, Marie-Laure, 86

"Delta Charllie Delta" (song), 112–13, 230n51

demoiselles de Rochefort, Les (1967), 181, 229n38

Demy, Jacques: and AIDS, 16, 33, 88, 192, 222n65; and Balzac, 201; critical reception of, 7, 35, 36, 222n68; theme of fairy tale, 37, 223n76; as cinematic godfather, 6, 89, 123; as source of homage, ix, 4, 23, 30, 32, 89, 92; as "Left Bank" auteur; musical style, 23,

247

33, 195, 222n67, 229n28; and New Wave, 1, 3, 6, 7, 32; as queer director, 32, 33, 92, 115, 176, 181

Deneuve, Catherine: 123, 125, 185, 190, 225n10; as cinematic mother, 79, 189, 226n27; as signature French star, 33, 46, 54, 56, 216n2

Denis, Claire, 20, 194

Depardieu, Gerard, 194, 226n29

Derrida, Jacques, 18, 28

Desplechin, Arnaud, 20, 21

deux amis, Les (2015), 235n16

Diaghilev, Sergei, 196

Dialogues des carmélites (opera), 201

Dieutre, Vincent, 230n42

"distance, La" (song), 117

Dix-sept fois Cécile Cassard (2002), 93, 94, 187, 188, 194

Doane, Mary Ann, 117

doigts dans le vestre, Les (1988), 17

Domicile conjugal (1970), 39, 105

Donizetti, Gaetano, 133, 137, 151

Donkey Skin (1970), 33, 37, 123, 125, 181, 223n76

Doubrovsky, Serge, 234n7

Drake, Nick, 168

Dreamers, The (2003), 58

Dreyer, Carl, 12

Drobnick, Jim, 66–67

Drôle de Félix (2000), 4, 8, 88

Dubois, Olivier, 196

Ducastel, Olivier: 28, 228n15; and AIDS, 88; gay identity of, 4, 8, 217n7; films as pastiche, 46, 89, 229n38

Duggan, Ann, 32, 223n76

Dumont, Auguste, 95

Durgnat, Raymond, xii, 44, 228n21

Duris, Roman: as actor of choice, 187, 188, 195; in *Dan Paris,* 51–55; male body of, 56, 193

Dustan, Guillaume, 185

Dyer, Richard, 43, 44, 90. 228n20

Eastwood, Clint, 184

École Nationale Supérieure des Métiers de l'Image et du Son. *See* La Fémis

Edelman, Lee, 28, 29, 44, 139, 217n7

égarés, Les (2003), 116

Eiffel Tower, 98

Eight Women (2002), 23, 185, 218n19

Elsaesser, Thomas, 3, 4, 34, 161

Encore (1988), 183

L'enfance neu (1968), 23, 24, 220n38

enfants du paradis, Les (1945), 220n37

Epstein, Jean, 44, 45, 224n89, 231n57

Eustache, Jean: bed as trope, 38, 46; as heterocentric, 35; and New Wave, 1, 30, 58, 181

faculté, La (play), 187

Fassbinder, Rainer Werner: as auteur, xi; and double-bind politics, 4, 31–32, 34–36; choreography, 94; theme of incest, 37; as influence, 176, 186; as queer, 3, 5

Fassin, Éric, 218n17

Faulkner, Christopher, 60

Faustrecht der Freiheit (1975), 4

Fémis, La, 17–19, 24, 28, 219n33

femme de l'aviateur, La (1981), 182

femme est une femme, Une (1961), 90, 98, 105

Femmes femmes (1974), 183

Feuer, Jane, 90

Fils (novel), 234n7

Finis terrae (1929), 224n89, 231n57

Flesh (1968), 183

Fontaine, Anne, 16

Fosse, Bob, 194

Four Hundred Blows, The (1959), 13, 23, 24, 25

Fox and His Friends (1965), 4

Fragments sur la grâce (2006), 99, 102, 103, 230n42

French Cancan (1954), 90

Freud, Sigmund, 35, 36, 98, 116

Gabin, Jean, 194

Gainsbourg, Serge, 93

INDEX

Garrel, Louis: as actor of choice, 46, 182, 190; in *Les chansons d'amour*, 36, 37, 41, 57; as collaborator, 59, 185, 187, 188, 235n16; in *Dans Paris*, 51–55, 83, 101; opinion of Christophe Honoré, 186; male body of, 56, 58, 194

Garrel, Maurice, 56

Garrel, Philippe, 56

Gaudreault, André, 5, 26, 67

Gavras, Romain, 196

Gay Science, The (book), 159

Genet, Jean, 116, 176, 186

Génie de la liberté, La (statue), 95, 98, 101, 108–9, 120

genou de Claire, Le (1970), 182

Gentlemen Prefer Blondes (1953), 104

Germania anno zero (1948), 8, 202

Germany Year Zero (1948), 8, 202

Gilbert, Avery, 66

Gilles, Guy, 183

Godard, Jean-Luc: use of actors, 58; bed as trope, 38, 105; as critic, 44, 178; and critical concepts, 6–7; and cinematic fonts, 51, 95, 99–100; as cinematic grandfather, 6; as source of homage, ix, 43, 46, 89, 95, 99–100, 221n56; as influence, 19–23, 30, 32, 50, 54, 93, 98, 107, 181–82, 201; and New Wave, xi, 1, 3, 6–7, 28, 33, 180, 201, 222n66; Christophe Honoré's opinion of, 181–82, 201; and Paris Trilogy, 95, 98, 105, 107, 221n56; as "Right Bank" auteur, 33

Gouttes d'eau sur pierres brûlantes (2000), 23, 184

Gospel According to Saint Matthew, The (1964), 133

Grahame, Gloria, 94

Greene, Naomi, 34–35

Griffith, David Wark, 183

Guédiguian, Robert, 16, 179

Guibert, Hervé, 16, 176, 177, 192

Guignuet, Jean-Claude, 86, 87

Handyside, Fiona, 8

Hansen-Løve, Mia, 179

Happy Together (1997), 16

Hardy, Françoise, 76, 93

Hawks, Howard, 104

He liu (1997), 16, 106, 107

Hesme, Clotilde, 36, 101, 142

Hill, Lee, 30

Hill, Rodney, 32

History of Violence, A (2005), 83

Hitchcock, Alfred: influence of, 72, 113, 152, 217n9, 232n19; as stylist, 5, 72, 183, 217n7

Hocquenghem, Guy, 186

Hollande, François, 93

Homme au bain (2010): ix, 185, 186, 198; Eros/Thanatos tension, 41, 191; and male bodies, 56, 94, 183, 193–94, 200; as manifesto, 199, 236n28

Honoré, Christophe: use of actors, 33, 46, 5-51, 54, 56, 59, 80, 89, 182, 185–90; and AIDS, xii, 1, 4, 7, 16, 32–33, 86, 88–89, 173, 174, 183, 192, 215n1; bed as trope, 38–42, 48, 54, 56–57, 61, 63, 75, 78–81, 103–5, 108, 112, 116, 118, 125, 190–91; and bodies, 56, 58, 65–66, 68, 72–73, 75, 79, 94, 108–9, 113–15, 151–52, 183, 193–94, 200; as Breton, 47–48, 55, 171–72, 175–76, 181, 191, 232n23; use of bridges and passageways, 110–15; and *Cahiers du Cinéma*, x, 16, 106, 174, 176, 179, 230n42; and children's books, 1, 2, 14, 15, 56, 136, 165–66, 173–74, 201; choreography and movement, 61, 94, 112, 118, 121, 192, 196, 197; cinema as trope, 143, 145–52; and cinema of monstration, 5, 23, 28–29, 66, 68, 78, 127–28, 138; and cinematic mothers, 55, 65, 77–79, 189, 226n27, 228n23; critical reception of, ix–xii, 29–33, 36, 45–46. 105, 176–77, 179–80, 185, 186–87, 216n2, 217n7; theme of death, 1, 7, 30, 49, 76–77, 82–83, 86, 94, 101–2,

112–13, 119, 137, 148, 157, 160, 164, 166, 176, 191, 192; and double-bind politics, 3, 6, 31, 32–36, 58, 67, 161; Eros/Thanatos tension, x, 1, 12, 17, 41, 111, 114, 162, 191; theme of family, x, 1, 7, 8, 36, 54–55, 61–62, 65, 68, 70, 73, 75–76, 78–80, 83, 86–87, 92, 98, 104, 106–7, 120–25, 177–78, 181, 189–90, 226n28; use of homage, ix, 4, 23, 30, 32, 43–47, 51, 89, 92–93, 95, 98–100, 105, 107, 109, 114–15, 123, 125, 189, 221n56; as homosexual narrator, 13, 14–15, 26–27, 176; theme of incest, 39, 105–7, 123–24; and the look, 127, 128, 132, 138–41, 154; theme of loss, 85–87, 94, 113, 118, 191; theme of love, 62–64, 75, 82, 85–86, 94, 99, 109, 125–26; music and song, 85–86, 90–94, 103–4, 109–13, 115, 117, 120, 157, 161, 164, 168, 194, 195–96; and New Wave, 1–3, 6–7, 16, 21–22, 29–30, 32–33, 50–51, 55, 58, 80, 176, 178–83, 192, 200–202; and odors, 61, 63, 65–69, 73, 75, 109, 125, 193; and François Ozon, xiii, 3, 5–7, 9, 12, 16–17, 26–27, 29, 184–85, 193, 225n10, 235n15; and Paris, 47–48, 55, 59–60, 62, 64–65, 75, 90, 94–95, 98–99, 101, 120, 128, 130–31, 135, 173–75, 178, 197, 199; as queer auteur, x–xii, 2, 4, 5, 22, 23, 28, 32–33, 43–48, 177, 185, 187–89; representation of sex, 192–93, 221n62; and sexual politics, 31, 175, 185; trees as symbol, 155–56, 158, 160–67

Honoré, Julien, 189

Horne, Alistair, 229n34

Hôtel Kuntz (2008), 1, 196

Hough, Sheridan, 167, 168, 169

Huffington Post, 16, 17

Huit femmes (2002), 23, 185, 218n19

Human, All Too Human (book), 155–57

Humphrey, Daniel, 217n7

Huppert, Isabelle, 31, 46, 54, 79, 226n27

"Il dolce suono, mi colpi di sua voce" (aria), 137

Imitation of Life (1959), 23

Ince, Kate, 8, 220n41

Inside Paris (2006). See *Dan Paris*

Intimacy (2001), 184

Intimité (2001), 184

"Inventaire" (song), 103, 104

James, Henry, 67

Jarmusch, Jim, 180

J'élève ma poupée (book), 175, 234n6

"Je n'aime que toi" (song), 109

Jeanne and the Perfect Guy (1998), 4, 88, 89, 229n38

Jeanne et le garçon formidable (1998), 4, 88, 89, 229n38

Jenkins, Carl, 138

Johan, mon été 75 (1976), 183

Johan, One Summer 1975 (1976), 183

Jordana, Camélia, 196

jour se lève, Le (1939), 90

Jules et Jim (1962), 90

Kahn, Cédric, 20–21

Kechiche, Abdellatif, 199, 230n45, 235n11

Keep Your Right Up (1987), 182

Keller, Sarah, 45

Kendall, Tina, 221n62

Klein, Melanie, 226n23

Kluge, Alexander, 37

Knelman, Martin, 223n76

Koltès, Bernard-Marie, 192

Kuntzel, Thierry, 49, 50, 155

Lafayette, Madame de: as author, 127, 131, 139, 145; characterizations, 134, 136, 142, 145, 146; and history, 133, 135, 137, 138, 231n7; and *Yaaba*, 151, 152

Lafont, Bernadette, 38

L'ami de mon amie (1987), 182

Lamy, Alexandra, 11

L'amour existe (1960), 220n43

Lanfer, Peter Thacher, 160

Lang, Valérie, 139

Lange, Rémi, 183–84
L'après-midi d'un faune (ballet), 196
Last Days (2005), 83
L'Atalante (1934), 90
Léaud, Jean-Pierre, 24, 38, 58, 105, 225n7
Lebrun, Françoise, 38
Lecompte, Rémi, 226n30
Lee, Spike, 230n49
Legrand, Michel, 89, 195
Lelouch, Claude, 172
L'enfance nue (1968), 23–26, 220n38
Leprince-Ringuet, Grégoire, 116, 136, 176, 193
Let My People Go (2011), 17, 185
Letourneur, Sophie, 179
lever de rideau, Un (2006), 28
Lionnais, François, Le, 142, 159, 233n34
livre pour enfants, Le (book), 12–15, 56, 116, 175, 219n23
Lola (1961), 16, 98, 181
"Lola" (song), 195
López, Sergi, 11
Lost Highway (1997), 16
Loulou (book), 82–83, 226n29
Loulou (1980), 226n29
Love Songs (2007). See *Les chansons d'amour*
Luchini, Fabrice, 26
Lucia de Lammermoor (opera), 133, 137
Lumière, Louis, 165, 234n41
Luther, Martin, 139, 151
Lvovsky, Noémie, 20–21
Lycée Molière, 135–36, 146, 160, 198
Lynch, David, 16
Lyon, Jacob, 142
Lyotard, Jean-François, 143

"Ma biche" (song), 196
MacOrlan, Pierre, 90
Made in USA (1966), 201
Ma Mère (2004): use of actors, 54, 187–88; cinematic mothers, 77, 226n27, 228n23; critical reception of, ix; Eros/Thanatos tension, 1, 41; theme of family, 177–78, 190, 226n28; female characters, 167; making of, 12; and odors, 193; representation of sex, 193, 221n62; and sexual politics, 31, 185
Magnani, Anna, 58, 225n11, 226n27
Making Plans for Lena (2009). See *Non ma fille tu n'iras pas danser*
Malle, Louis, 111, 142
Mamma Roma (1962), 58, 225n11, 226n27
maman et la putain, La (1973), 35, 38, 58
Man at Bath (2010). See *Homme au bain*
Manet, Édouard, 70, 71, 72, 157
"Manfred: A Dramatic Poem" (poem), 155
Marais, Jean, 123, 125
Marchand, Guy, 53, 54, 61, 79, 188
Marie, Michel, 6–7, 18, 32
Marius et Jeannette (1997), 16
Martineau, Jacques: 28, 228n15; and AIDS, 88; and gay identity, 4, 8, 217n7; films as pastiche, 46, 89, 229n38
Marx, Karl, 18, 35
Marxism, 33
Masculin féminin (1966), 39, 58, 105
Massin, Robert, 55
Mastroianni, Chiara: as actor of choice, 33, 46, 56, 186; in *Les bien-aimés*, 191, 196–97, 198; in *Les chansons d'amour*, 92, 113; as collaborator, 187, 225n4; as cinematic mother, 79, 189; as cinematic royalty, 33, 56, 125, 189
Mastroianni, Marcello, 56, 125
Mayance, Mélusine, 11
Mekas, Jonas, 183, 198
mépris, Le (1963), 58
Mes parents (book), 177
Métamorphoses (2014), x, 171, 192, 223n72, 234n43
Ming-liang, Tsai, 16, 106, 107
Minnelli, Vincente, 94, 165
mirage, Le (1992), 86
Mississippi Mermaid (1969), 201
Mitry, Jean, xii, 39, 40, 41, 44
Modern Times (1936), 129, 130
Monde, Le, 87–88, 185
Monnin, Aude, 86, 87, 102

Monroe, Marilyn, 104
Montalbetti, Valérie, 95
Morel, Gaël: 99, 148, 179, 235n18; as queer filmmaker, 46, 184, 185, 193
Moretti, Nanni, 180
Morgan, Daniel, 45
Morrey, Douglas, 221n56
Mulvey, Laura, 45, 222n66
Mýa, 196

Naked Childhood (1968), 23–26, 220n38
Nés en '68 (2008), 4
Nettoyage à sec (1997), 16
Newton, Esther, 39, 40
Nietzsche, Friedrich, 50, 83, 155–60, 167–69
Nolot, Jacques, 6, 184
Non ma fille tu n'iras pas danser (2009): use of actors, 56, 59, 188–89; and AIDS, 192; and bodies, 94; as Breton folk tale, 171, 181, 191, 232n23; choreography, 94; cinematic mothers, 77; Eros/Thanatos tension, 191; theme of family, 177, 181; female characters, 135, 167; making of, 198
North by Northwest (1959), 217n7
Nous ne vieillirons pas ensemble (1972), 24
Nouveau Roman (play), 186
nuit du carrefour, La (1932), 228n21
nuit ordinaire, Une (1996), 86
Nun, The (1966), 182

Oedipus Rex (1967), 37
Omelette (1998), 184
On connait la chanson (1997), 92, 229n28
Once More (1988), 183
Ono, Kent A., 22
Ophüls, Max, 145
Otto: The Autobiography of a Teddy Bear (book), 136, 166
Ouedraogo, Assita, 149
Ouedraogo, Idrissa, 146, 148, 151
Ouedraogo, Noufou, 147
Oulipo (literary group), 142–43, 145, 151, 159, 166

Ouvroir de littérature potentielle. *See* Oulipo
Ovid, 192, 215n1, 234n43
Ozon, François: figure of the child, 10–12, 15, 28, 218n18–21; and cinema of monstration, 23; and cinema of narration, 6, 23, 26; critical reception of, 216n2; Eros/thanatos tension, 12, 17; theme of family, 17–18; film studies of, 16–19, 24; compared with Christophe Honoré, xlll, 3, 5–7, 9, 12, 16–17, 26–27, 29, 225n10; Honoré's opinion of, 184–85, 193, 225n10, 235n15; and New Wave, 7, 20, 22, 25, 28; and Pier Paolo Pasolini, 67–68; and Maurice Pialat, 7, 21–22, 24–26, 28; and queer cinema, 3, 6, 8, 10–12, 23, 220n41

Pagnol, Marcel, 232n15
Palmer, Tim, 18, 19, 219n33
Panofsky, Erwin, 223n77
parapluies de Cherbourg, Les (1964): 16, 89, 181, 229n28; as source of homage, 99, 109, 123, 125, 189
Parking (1985), 33
Pas sur la bouche (2003), 229n28
Pasco, Allan H., 233n27
Pasolini, Pier Paolo: as auteur, xi; and double-bind politics, 4, 31–32, 34–36, 58, 67–68; theme of incest, 3; as influence, 5, 27, 133, 186, 223n72, 226n27; and Anna Magnani, 58, 225n11, 226n27; and François Ozon, 67–68; as queer, 3, 4, 67
passagers, Les (1999), 86
Peau d'âne (1970), 33, 37, 123, 125, 181, 223n76
Perec, Georges, 47, 142
Perreau, Bruno, 218n17
petite mort, La (1995), 10
Pialat, Maurice: Christophe Honoré's opinion of, 182, 195, 220n38; as influence, 12, 21, 24, 220n38, 226n29, 234n45; and New Wave, 7, 19–23, 25, 220n39; research of, 26, 28, 224n3

INDEX

Picard, Timothée, xi
Pinget, Robert, 186
Pisier, Marie France: as cinematic mother, 55, 65, 79, 189; as signature French star, 46, 53, 54, 58
Polisse (2011), 179
Portal, Jean-Michel, 142
Potiche (2010), 23, 28, 185, 216n2, 219n34
Poupaud, Melvil, 9
Powell, Dick, 94
Powrie, Phil, 91, 93, 228n25
Preiss, Joana, 31, 52, 54, 61, 225n13
princesse de Clèves, La (novel): adaptation of, 127, 131–33, 139, 145, 165, 199; as canonical text, 127, 131, 139; and *Yaaba*, 152
Projansky, Sarah, 22
Proust, Marcel, 183
Providence (1977), 8
Pullen, Christopher, 217n7

quatre cents coups, Les (1959), 13, 23, 24, 25
Queen (rock band), 116
Queneau, Raymond, 142

Racine, Jean Baptiste, 133, 136, 151
Ray, Satyajit, 200
Rear Window (1954), 26
Rebecca (1940), 72
Rees-Roberts, Nick: and AIDS, 86, 88; critique of Jean Eustache, 35; critique of Christophe Honoré, 31, 46, 105, 217n7
refuge, Le (2009), 218n21
règle du jeu, La (1939), 220n37
religieuse, La (1966), 182
Renier, Yannick, 115
Renoir, Jean: influence of, 44, 130, 220n37, 228n21, 232n15; and New Wave, 18, 21, 183
Resnais, Alain: 7, 8, 92, 229n28; as "Left Bank" auteur, 33
Ricky (2009), 11, 23, 28, 218n21
Riedel, Manfred, 159

River, The (1997), 16, 106, 107
Rivette, Jacques: influence of, 30, 181–82, 189; and New Wave, 1, 18, 28, 30
Rohmer, Eric: influence of, 19, 28, 182, 189; and New Wave, 1, 18, 183, 201
roseaux sauvages, Les (1994), 184
Rossellini, Roberto, 8, 9, 12, 179, 202
Rothafel, Samuel "Roxy," 66
Roüan, Brigitte, 117, 183
Roudinesco, Élisabeth, 226n23
Russell, Jane, 104

Sagat, François: as actor of choice, 185, 193; in *Homme au bain*, 191, 193, 200, 222n62, 236n30; male body of, 194, 200
Sagnier, Ludivine, 36, 92, 101, 186, 225n4
Salinger, J. D., 216n3
Salò o le 120 giornate di Sodoma (1975), 67, 68, 226n20
Salo, or the 120 Days of Sodom (1975), 67, 68, 226n20
Same Old Songs (1997), 92, 229n28
Sanga, Fatimata, 147
Sarkozy, Nicholas, 31, 87, 199, 202, 235n24, n25
Sartre, Jean-Paul, 199
Sauder, Régis, 231n7
Sautet, Claude, 182
Scènes de lit (1998), 28, 219n34
Schiffer, Claudia, 193
Schilt, Thibaut, 8–9, 11–12, 17, 19, 20, 24, 28
Schwartz, Vanessa, 222n66
Scorpio Rising (1963), 224n84
Scott, A. O., 30
Scott, Joan Wallach, 8–9, 14
Scream (1996), 16
Sedgwick, Eve Kosofsky, xii, 39, 40, 44
Segura-Suarez, Dustin, 194
Self as Metaphoric Double, The (book), 167
Sellem, Omar Ben, 194
Sellier, Geneviève, 45, 201, 222n66, n67
Seventeen Times Cécile Cassard (2002), 93, 94, 187, 188, 194

Seydoux, Léa, 42, 136
Siffredi, Rocco, 193
Sirène du Mississippi (1969), 201
Sirk, Douglas, 23, 165
Sitcom (1998), 219n34
"Smell-O-Vision," 66
Smith, Alison, 220n48
Smith, Jack, 43
Snow White and the Seven Dwarfs (1937), 172
Soigne to droite (1987), 182
Solotareff, Grégoire, 82
Sontag, Susan, 43, 44
Sontinel, Thomas, 30, 221n55
Soukaz, Lionel, 4–5, 183
Sous le sable (2000), 24, 25, 216n2
Spivak, Gayatri, 223n39
Strangers on a Train (1951), 72, 230n53, 232n19
Strayed (2003), 116
"Swan, The" (poem), 133, 144
Swimming Pool (2003), 23, 24, 25, 28
Sy, Brigitte, 56

Tarantino, Quentin, 189
Taurand, Gilles, 139, 232n17
Tavernier, Bertrand, 220n48
Téchiné, André, 6, 29, 116, 176, 184, 186
tempestaire, Le (1947), 224n89
temps que reste, Le (2005), 9, 10, 216n2
Teorema (1968), 4, 27
Terrazon, Michel, 24
That's Dancing (television show), 116
Thérèse (1986), 182
Thirlwell, Adam, 192
Thom, René, 143
Thomas, Kevin, 30
Thomas, Kristin Scott, 26
Those Who Love Me Can Take the Train (1998), 184
Three Dancing Slaves (2004), 235n18
Thus Spake Zarathustra (book), 167–68
Time to Leave (2005), 9, 10, 216n2
Tintin (comic book series), 173, 234

Todd, Michael, 66
Toure, Amadé, 149
Toute contre Léo (2002), 1, 88, 215n1, 221n62
Toute contre Léo (book), 173, 174
Trois places pour le 26 (1988), 33, 181, 223n76
Trophy Wife (2010), 23, 28, 185, 216n2, 219n34
Truffaut, François: use of actors, 58, 185, 189; bed as trope, 38, 39, 46, 105; as critic, 5, 6, 16, 17, 44–45, 178, 181; as cinematic grandfather, 6; on Alfred Hitchcock, 72; as influence, 5, 13, 16–17, 19–21, 24–25, 28, 105, 178, 181; and New Wave, xi, 1, 3, 6, 18, 23, 25, 28, 30, 58, 180; as "Right Bank" auteur, 33; and sexual politics, 185, 201
Truxillo, Simon, 137
"Two Little Girls from Little Rock" (song), 104
Two or Three Things I Know About Her (1967), 201
Tyler, Parker, 36, 40, 41

Ughetto, Bastien, 26
Umbrellas of Cherbourg, The (1964). See *les parapluies de Cherbourg*
Umhauer, Ernst, 25
Under the Sand (2000), 24, 25, 216n2
Ungerer, Tomi, 136, 166

Vallois, Philippe, 183
Vanderschelden, Isabelle, 217n10
Van Sant, Gus, 83
Varda, Agnès, 33, 222n65
Vecchiali, Paul, 86, 183, 193
Vertigo (1958), 72
Victor (1993), 219n34
Vignaux, Valérie, 230n49
Vignier, Éric, 187
Village Voice, 30
Vincendeau, Ginette, 30–31, 45–46, 107, 158

Visconti, Luchino, 86, 176

Wai, Wong Kar, 16
Waldron, Darren, 217n7
Wall-Romana, Christophe, 45
Warehime, Marja, 20, 21, 23, 25, 220n37
Warhol, Andy, 112, 183
Water Drops on Burning Rocks (2000), 23, 184
Waters, John, 66
We Won't Grow Old Together (1972), 24
Wenders, Wim, 223n84
White, Edmund, 116, 176
Wild Reeds (1994), 184
Wilde, Oscar, 43
Williams, Alan, 165
Williams, James S., 45, 56
Wilson, Douglas B., 116
Winling, Jean-Marie, 117
Wollen, Peter, 28, 44
Women, The (1939), 23
Workshop of Potential Literature.
    See Oulipo

X2000 (1998), 28

Yaaba (1989): and *La belle personne*, 146, 148–52; as cinema of monstration, 147; narrative structure, 146–48; and *Non ma fille tu n'iras pas danser*, 232n23
Young Girls of Rochefort, The (1967), 181, 229n38

Zazie dans le metro (1960), 142
Zazie dans le metro (novel), 142

Index prepared by Catherine Burke.